Frontiers in Re
and Rural Economics

Human-Nature, Rural-Urban
Interdependencies

EDITED BY

JunJie Wu
Paul W. Barkley
Bruce A. Weber

RESOURCES FOR THE FUTURE
Washington, DC, USA

Printed in the United States of America.

An RFF Press book
Published by Resources for the Future
1616 P Street NW
Washington, DC 20036–1400
USA
www.rffpress.org

Library of Congress Cataloging-in-Publication Data

Frontiers in resource and rural economics : human-nature, rural-urban interdependencies.
Edited By JunJie Wu, Paul W. Barkley, Bruce A. Weber.
    p. cm.
  Includes bibliographical references and index.
  ISBN 978-1-933115-64-1 (hbk. : alk. paper) — ISBN 978-1-933115-65-8 (pbk. : alk.
paper) 1. Natural resources—Management. 2. Rural development. I. Wu, JunJie. II. Barkley,
Paul W. III. Weber, Bruce A.
HC85.F77 2007
333.7—dc22   2007041451

The paper in this book meets the guidelines for permanence and durability of the Committee
on Production Guidelines for Book Longevity of the Council on Library Resources. This
book was typeset by Andrea Reider. It was copyedited by Sally Atwater. The cover was
designed by Henry Rosenbohm.

ISBN 978-1-933115-64-1 (cloth)   ISBN 978-1-933115-65-8 (paper)

About Resources for the Future *and* RFF Press

Resources for the Future (RFF) improves environmental and natural resource policymaking worldwide through independent social science research of the highest caliber. Founded in 1952, RFF pioneered the application of economics as a tool for developing more effective policy about the use and conservation of natural resources. Its scholars continue to employ social science methods to analyze critical issues concerning pollution control, energy policy, land and water use, hazardous waste, climate change, biodiversity, and the environmental challenges of developing countries.

RFF Press supports the mission of RFF by publishing book-length works that present a broad range of approaches to the study of natural resources and the environment. Its authors and editors include RFF staff, researchers from the larger academic and policy communities, and journalists. Audiences for publications by RFF Press include all of the participants in the policymaking process—scholars, the media, advocacy groups, NGOs, professionals in business and government, and the public.

Resources for the Future

Contents

Preface . . . . *vii*

Contributors . . . . *xi*

1. Frontiers in Resource and Rural Economics: A Synthesis 1
   Emery N. Castle and David E. Ervin

Part I. THE PAST 50 YEARS

2. The Emergence and Evolution of Environmental and Natural
   Resource Economics 11
   Daniel W. Bromley

3. Rural Economics: People, Land, and Capital 29
   Paul W. Barkley

Part II. HUMAN-NATURE AND RURAL-URBAN INTERDEPENDENCE

4. Environmental Economics and the "Curse" of the Circular Flow 43
   V. Kerry Smith and Jared C. Carbone

5. The New Rural Economics 63
   Maureen Kilkenny

6. Exploring the Prospects for Amenity-Driven Growth
   in Rural Areas 82
   Elena G. Irwin, Alan Randall, and Yong Chen

7. Natural Amenities, Human Capital, and Economic Growth:
   An Empirical Analysis 94
   JunJie Wu and Sanjiv Mishra

Part III. POLICIES AND PROGRAMS FOR PEOPLE AND PLACES

8. People and Places at the Ragged Edge: Place–Based Policy
   for Reducing Rural Poverty 111
   Bruce A. Weber

9. Rural Human Capital Development 132
   Maureen Kilkenny and Monica Haddad

10. Property Taxation and the Redistribution of Rural
    Resource Rents 150
    Mitch Kunce and Jason F. Shogren

11. The Politics of Place: Linking Rural and Environmental
    Governance 169
    Ronald J. Oakerson

12. Frontiers in Resource and Rural Economics:
    A Methodological Perspective 192
    Emery N. Castle

Part IV. THE NEXT 25 YEARS

13. Resources and Rural Communities: Looking Ahead 211
    Kathleen Segerson

14. The Future of Rural America Through a
    Social–Demographic Lens 229
    David L. Brown

Index 249

Preface

DRAMATIC SOCIOECONOMIC CHANGES have occurred in rural America during the past 25 years. Shifting population, job loss, declining education and health services, and weakening community structures have caused the quality of life to deteriorate in many rural communities. In some areas, dwindling rural economies have turned once-viable communities into ghost towns. In others, urban sprawl and suburbanization have encroached to such an extent that the community itself has been lost. Global competition, changes in market structure, and increasing demands for recreational and environmental services from rural places have also changed the environment within which rural economies operate. These changes will likely continue for the next few decades. Their geographic scope and the ramifications for nature-human interdependence and rural-urban interaction pose a serious challenge for resource and rural economics research. Critical thinking about future research directions and innovative research approaches is essential.

This volume attempts to push back the frontiers of our knowledge about resource and rural economics by exploring the interdependencies between natural resource management and rural development as well as between rural and urban communities. Economic development in rural places affects the natural environment, and this in turn affects economic growth—both rural and urban. Interdependencies that bring urban and rural people and problems together also exist within economic systems. The people in rural places who make direct use of natural resources see nature quite differently than do many urban dwellers: those involved with the extraction of natural resources use the natural world as a source of economic survival; urban dwellers seek to enhance their lives by using natural resource products and the amenities associated with rural areas. More than 95 percent of the land area of the United States is rural, most of the water we use arises in rural places, and most of the atmosphere exists above rural space. Urbanites and institutions have legitimate concerns about the use and condition of rural natural resources, just as rural populations have legitimate concerns about urban-based pressures on the natural world. These shared interests in the natural environment are increasingly recognized as an economic, social, and political issue in the U.S. economy and will assume growing importance in the future.

This volume brings together leading scholars in resource economics, rural sociology, and political science to address these interdependencies. Some of the essays in this volume, although extensively revised, trace their origins to a symposium held at Oregon State University (OSU) in October 2005, titled "Research Frontiers in Resource and Rural Economics: Rural-Urban Interplay and Human-Ecosystems Interactions." Here, 21 internationally recognized scholars—economists, sociologists, and political scientists—and policymakers from across the nation convened to discuss the progress and prospects of research and policies in resource economics and rural studies and address the past, present, and future of their fields. Important future research directions and cutting-edge research methods were presented.

Many people contributed to the success of the symposium. We thank Bill Boggess for his leadership: he was instrumental in all stages of the operation, from the program design and fund raising to hosting the symposium. We also thank the organizing committee of the symposium, whose members included, along with the book's editors, Richard Adams, Walter Armbruster, Sandra Batie, Bill Boggess, John Miranowski, Alan Randall, Herb Stoevener, and David Zilberman. The symposium was sponsored by Resources for the Future (RFF), the National Research Initiative Rural Development Program, the Economic Research Service, the Department of Agricultural and Resource Economics at the Oregon State University, and the Oregon State University Rural Studies Program.

The symposium was conceived both as a celebration of Emery N. Castle's contributions to theoretical and applied developments in natural resource, environmental, and community economics during his six decades as an active and internationally respected scholar, and as an opportunity to advance social science research and policy design on these issues. This book follows in his honor.

Emery Castle was born in 1923 in Greenwood County, Kansas. He received a B.S. (1948) and M.S. (1950) in agricultural economics from Kansas State University, and a Ph.D. in agricultural economics from Iowa State University in 1952. Before joining Oregon State University's Department of Agricultural and Resource Economics in 1954, Castle served as an instructor in the Department of Economics at Kansas State University (1948–1952) and held the position of agricultural economist at the Federal Reserve Bank of Kansas City (1952–1954). At OSU, Castle was promoted to associate professor in 1957 and to professor in 1959. Castle also held a number of administrative posts at Oregon State, including dean of faculty (1965–1966), head of agricultural economics (1966–1972), director of the Water Resources Institute (1966–1969), and dean of the graduate school (1972–1976). In 1976, Castle became vice president and senior research fellow at Resources for the Future; he then served as president of RFF from 1979 to 1986. In 1986 Castle returned to Oregon State as chair of the University Graduate Faculty of Economics, a position he held until 1992, when he was awarded professor emeritus status. Castle has written or edited 7 books, 2 monographs, 17 book chapters, 48 refereed journal articles, and numerous other documents. He holds honorary Doctor of Humane Letters degrees from Iowa State University and Oregon

State University. He is a fellow of the American Academy of Arts and Sciences, the American Academy for the Advancement of Science, and the American Agricultural Economics Association. Without his inspiration, encouragement, and help, this volume would not have been possible.

Finally, we would like to thank Don Reisman of RFF Press for his thoughtful guidance on the book's substance, his careful editing of many of the chapters, and his encouragement throughout the process of preparing this manuscript. We also thank Sally Atwater for copyediting the manuscript. Her professional touch has improved the readability of this volume.

JUNJIE WU
PAUL W. BARKLEY
BRUCE A. WEBER

Contributors

PAUL W. BARKLEY is professor emeritus in the School of Economic Sciences at Washington State University and courtesy professor in agricultural economics at Oregon State University. His recent research focuses on farmland retention issues and public finance problems in rural areas. His books include *Economic Growth and Environmental Decay*. He is listed in *Who's Who in Economics* and is a fellow of the American Agricultural Economics Association.

DANIEL W. BROMLEY is Anderson-Bascom Professor of Applied Economics at the University of Wisconsin. His current interests relate to natural resource and environmental economics, institutional economics, and economic development. He currently serves as chair of the U.S. Federal Advisory Committee on Marine Protected Areas. His recent books include *Sufficient Reason: Volitional Pragmatism and the Meaning of Economic Institutions* and *Economics, Ethics, and Environmental Policy* (coauthored). He is a fellow of the American Agricultural Economics Association.

DAVID L. BROWN is professor of development sociology at Cornell University. Prior to joining the Cornell faculty, he conducted demographic research for the U.S. Department of Agriculture Economic Research Service. His research focuses on population dynamics and local social organization. Earlier work focused on the measurement of urbanization and on rural-urban migration and population redistribution. His most recent books include *Challenges for Rural America in the 21st Century* (coedited) and *Population Change and Rural Society* (coedited).

JARED C. CARBONE is assistant professor in the Department of Economics at Williams College. His work focuses on the economic impacts of large-scale environmental and health regulations and the influence of international trade on regional greenhouse gas abatement strategies.

EMERY N. CASTLE is professor emeritus, Oregon State University, and president and senior fellow emeritus, Resources for the Future. He is a fellow of the

American Academy of Arts and Sciences, the American Academy for the Advancement of Science, and the American Agricultural Economics Association. His books include *The Changing American Countryside* and *Economics and Public Water Policy in the West* (coedited).

YONG CHEN is a graduate student in the Department of Agricultural, Environmental, and Development Economics at The Ohio State University, where he is also a member of the team working on the Biocomplexity Project. His latest paper, "A Dynamic Model of Household Location, Regional Growth, and Endogenous Natural Amenities with Cross-Scale Interactions," was selected for presentation at a February 2007 RFF conference titled "The Frontiers of Environmental Economics."

DAVID E. ERVIN is professor of environmental studies and coordinator of academic sustainability programs at Portland State University. His current research includes studies of voluntary business environmental managements, the environmental effects of agriculture, and university–industry biotechnology relationships. He is coauthor of *Does Environmental Policy Work?* and coeditor of *Public Concerns, Environmental Standards, and Agricultural Trade.*

MONICA HADDAD is assistant professor in the Department of Community and Regional Planning and an extension specialist in geographic information systems (GIS) at Iowa State University. Her research activities center on the allocation of scarce public resources and examinations of distributions of populations and how they are related to employment centers, quality of education, and human development. Through her extension appointment, Haddad helps urban and regional planners across Iowa use GIS technology for functions beyond simple mapping.

ELENA G. IRWIN is associate professor in the Department of Agricultural, Environmental, and Development Economics at The Ohio State University. Her primary research interests focus on the causes and consequences of growth in local and regional areas. She also studies settlement patterns and other factors and how they affect households' residential location decisions, as well as open space preservation policies and environmental amenities.

MAUREEN KILKENNY is professor in the Department of Resource Economics at the University of Nevada. Her specialty is economic geography. Her research deals with rural banking markets and agroindustrial location. Her publications include articles, book chapters, and *Keystone Sector Identification: A Graph Theory-Social Network Analysis Approach* (coauthored). She has chaired the Community Economics Network as well as the North American Regional Science Council.

MITCH KUNCE is currently the head brewmaster of Big Nose Brewing in Laramie, Wyoming, and is adjunct professor in the Department of Economics and Finance at the University of Wyoming. His academic research interests include resource economics, public finance, public choice, and regional economics.

SANJIV MISHRA received his M.S. degree from the Department of Agriculture and Resource Economics at Oregon State University in 2005. His research focused on the interdependencies between migration and economic growth in the Pacific Northwest. He works as an economist in the Quality Planning Corporation in San Francisco.

RONALD J. OAKERSON is professor of political science at Houghton College. He served for 10 years as a member of the National Rural Studies Committee. He is the author of *Governing Local Public Economies: Creating the Civic Metropolis*, as well as numerous articles and book chapters on metropolitan governance, rural problems, and international development. His research interests focus on the governance of the Adirondack Park in New York.

ALAN RANDALL is professor and chair of the Department of Agricultural, Environmental, and Development Economics at The Ohio State University. His books include *Making the Environment Count: Selected Essays* and *Resource Economics: An Economic Approach to Natural Resource and Environmental Policy*. He is a fellow of the American Agricultural Economics Association and holds honorary doctorates from the University of Sydney and the Agricultural University of Norway.

KATHLEEN SEGERSON is professor in the Department of Economics at the University of Connecticut. Her research focuses on the incentive effects of alternative environmental policy instruments, with particular emphasis on the application of legal principles to environmental problems. She serves on three committees for the Environmental Protection Agency's Science Advisory Board. Her books include *Economics and Liability for Environmental Problems* (editor) and *Compensation for Regulatory Taking* (coauthored).

JASON F. SHOGREN is Stroock Distinguished Professor of Natural Resource Conservation and Management, and professor of economics at the University of Wyoming. His research focuses on the private motives of public policy, especially for environmental and natural resources. He serves on several national environmental committees, including the Science Advisory Board of the Environmental Protection Agency. His books include *Environmental Economics in Theory and Practice* (coauthored) and *Integrating Economic and Ecological Indicators*.

V. KERRY SMITH is a university distinguished professor in the Department of Agricultural and Resource Economics, North Carolina State University. He has also been a senior fellow at Resources for the Future and is a university fellow for the quality of the environment division at RFF. His research focuses on linking public and private mitigation policies for environmental and security risks. Smith's books include *Valuing Natural Assets: The Economics of Natural Damage Assessments* (coedited) and *Valuing Economic Values for Nature: Methods for Non-Market Valuation*.

BRUCE A. WEBER is professor of agricultural and resource economics and extension economist in the Department of Agricultural and Resource Economics at Oregon State University. His extension programs deal with Oregon tax policy, and his research focuses on the causes of poverty and hunger in rural areas. He is the coeditor of *Rural Dimensions of Welfare Reform* and is a fellow of the American Agricultural Economics Association.

JUNJIE WU is professor in the Department of Agricultural and Resource Economics at Oregon State University. He also holds the Emery N. Castle Professorship in Resource and Rural Economics at Oregon State University. He has studied a variety of economic and policy issues related to agricultural production, resource conservation, and environmental management. His projects have focused on optimal targeting of conservation efforts in the presence of threshold effects and ecosystem linkages, interactions between agricultural production and water quality, contract design for the purchase of ecosystem services, and spatial disparities in economic development.

CHAPTER I

Frontiers in Resource and Rural Economics

A Synthesis

Emery N. Castle and David E. Ervin

A N INEVITABLE TENSION exists between those who make use of natural resources to produce food, fiber, timber, energy, and minerals, and those who look to the natural environment for ecosystem services, such as natural amenities and recreational experiences. Tensions also arise on the rural–urban interface. Few deny that goods, people, and services need to move freely between rural and urban places, yet conflicts abound. Expansion of cities and suburbs may require conversion of farmland. Public programs intended for everyone may not work well for some unless explicit attention is given to human population density. Studies about resource-based economies or rural economies and rural people that make no reference to environmental effects or urban affairs clearly are doomed to irrelevance.

Resource economics and rural economics, as fields of study, have different intellectual traditions. Resource economics, a recognized specialization within economics, rose to prominence after the first Earth Day in 1970. Its literature reflects rigorous economic theory and sophisticated quantitative techniques. Rural economics generally is viewed as a part of the multidisciplinary field of rural studies, involving such disciplines as regional science, sociology, and political science. Within economics, rural economics is grouped with, and parallel to, regional and urban economics.

Despite those differences, there is substantial overlap in substance between the two. More than 95 percent of the land area of the United States is classified as rural. Most of the nation's natural resources and environmental amenities are found in rural areas, with their agricultural and forested lands, water resources, flora and fauna, open space and skies, minerals, and natural beauty. The rural environment provides the bulk of ecosystem services of value to both urban and rural populations. Obviously, both urban and rural people have an interest in the management of, and access to, rural natural resources. Global and domestic economic progress

I

places stress on both natural and human resources. The young migrate in great numbers to urban places as the relative income of rural people continues to decline. Urban development and suburbanization often encroach on and sometimes swallow rural communities. Such processes—and others treated elsewhere in this book—make clear that the study of rural economic welfare in isolation from urban affairs makes little sense.

The identification of tensions is not difficult. Nor does it require great originality to describe interdependencies that give rise to such tensions. It is a different matter to suggest solutions to the economic and social problems that stem from these conditions. The objective of this book is to identify specific areas for study within resource and rural economics and describe analytical approaches that will address the complex social and economic paradoxes inherent in these fields of study.

Part I. The Past 50 Years

We start by considering the insights afforded by past scholars—and the limitations of existing research. The built environment, enhanced human capital, and intellectual contributions constitute endowments as people and communities move from one time period to another. Path dependence often results because of the understandable human desire to use what is available, rather than begin anew. Yet in some circumstances, starting fresh is best. The editors asked Daniel Bromley and Paul Barkley to review resource and rural economic literature and appraise the intellectual legacy of each field. What parts should be used, and what supplemented? And if modification is attempted, can past mistakes be avoided?

Much of the literature in resource economics addresses the shortcomings of markets for some natural resources situations. In capitalist economies that rely heavily on markets, many natural resource problems often are considered exceptions and equated with market "failures." Under such circumstances, attempts are often made to estimate market outcomes if such failures did not exist. Benefit–cost analysis was invented to discover a simulated market solution when decentralized markets do not work well. Welfare economics, quantitative techniques, and the ability to process large amounts of data have made it possible to estimate alternative possible outcomes for many troublesome natural resource issues. It is not surprising that some such "solutions" would be advanced as a basis for public policy decisions.

Bromley, in Chapter 2, has provided a comprehensive review of resource and environmental economics literature from 1950 to 2000. He refers to attempts in resource economics to simulate market solutions when market failures occur as the "commodification" of nature. He expresses concern about reliance on normative analytical frameworks, such as benefit–cost analysis, for policy purposes. He notes the increasing popularity of the journal *Ecological Economics,* which emphasizes human system and ecosystem interactions. In contrast to *Ecological Economics,* Bromley states, the traditional resource economics approach to human and natural system interactions depends on motivations of self-interest, utility maximization, and rationality. He urges resource economists to reflect empirical conditions in their models to more accurately capture nature-human interdependencies. Readers are encouraged to keep Bromley's concerns in mind when they turn to Chapter 4, which describes the shift in emphasis in resource economics since this field of study first emerged a half-century ago. Whereas early effort directed attention to market failures in particular locations or specific situations, today awareness is emerging about relations between large systems. As a result, analytical problems of a different sort are coming to the fore.

In his review of rural economics literature in Chapter 3, Paul Barkley observes that both economists and sociologists have created a vast literature that provides empirical information about rural people and their problems. Some of that literature has been concerned with rural-urban economic interactions. Even so, many highly competent researchers have failed to create analytical frameworks that can be used for policy prescriptions to resolve rural-urban stresses that arise as economic development occurs. Although he does not use the term, readers may conclude that "a vast wasteland" would be an apt description of this field. Barkley identifies intermediate decisionmaking, natural amenities, migration, and the use of geographic space as worthy subjects for investigation—topics taken up in Chapters 5, 6, 7, 11, and 12.

The intellectual endowments of resource and rural economics are a study in contrasts. Resource economics is cited for a too-close adherence to the basic axioms of economics and neglect of actual environmental conditions. The rural economics literature is criticized because economic theory has not worked well and a conceptual framework is lacking. These contrasting characteristics receive serious attention in subsequent chapters.

Part II. Human-Nature and Rural-Urban Interdependence

V. Kerry Smith and Jared C. Carbone provide a fundamental examination of economic and ecosystem relations in Chapter 4. They consider the familiar subject of externalities (effects that are not properly valued by decentralized markets) in an unconventional way. The conventional wisdom holds that all goods are substitutes, and that the source and incidence of all environmental insults can be known. The conventional wisdom also holds that all polluting activities can be remedied by government action, perhaps with taxes or subsidies. Much environmental economics is concerned with partial equilibrium models that isolate individual producers and consumers from the remainder of the economy or ecosystem, with damage functions flowing only in one direction. Under such assumptions it may be logical to attempt some form of aggregation of partial equilibrium results to predict economy-wide effects.

Yet ecologists direct attention to the cumulative effects of incremental decisions on nature. Further, economists know that all goods are not substitutes—some are complements. Economists know a great deal about general equilibrium modeling, but they know less about modeling the cumulative ecological consequences of incremental economic decisions. What if the actions of producers affect one another, and producer and consumer actions have reciprocal effects? In the words of Smith and Carbone,

> We don't know the details of how people's choices are affecting the ability of these assets to provide services. Moreover, there is no information to allow analysts to select among the alternative descriptions linking activities that

damage ecosystem services to the objects of choice that people use and care about. ... Measures of the general equilibrium implications of policy choices are likely to be dramatically affected by the decisions about how to characterize nonmarket environmental services.

Daniel Bromley (Chapter 2) and Kathleen Segerson (Chapter 13) also direct attention to this view of nature–human interdependence, a central feature of resource economics.

The policy implications of the Smith and Carbone paper are profound. Their nontraditional view of environmental externalities suggests that the quest for benefit–cost solutions to important environmental questions may be misdirected. Their contribution promises to stimulate alternative approaches to this set of fundamental problems.

Maureen Kilkenny's Chapter 5, "The New Rural Economics," sets forth an economic disciplinary focus for rural economic research. She dissects the "old" and "new" economic geography models to show their strengths and limitations and extends that literature to reflect recent theoretical developments. She describes a conundrum, first identified by Edwin Mills, that neither the old nor the new economic geography readily resolves: how to achieve stability, over time, in the rural share of nonfarm employment despite the massive exodus of labor from agriculture, especially during the 20th century. She concludes that the new rural economics must place more emphasis on spatial microfoundations, demand-side ideas, and empirically tested models. This will provide opportunities for greater collaboration between rural and environmental economists and advance understanding of both nature–human and urban–rural interdependence. Her chapter sketches out an agenda for the necessary research.

In Chapter 6, Elena G. Irwin, Alan Randall, and Yong Chen are concerned with the extent to which natural amenities can affect the location of economic activity, both in central places and on the periphery. Traditional modeling efforts have neglected the location effects of qualitative, typically nonpriced features of the environment. These scholars recommend that attention be given to how the passage of time affects amenities, as well as to investments that enhance natural amenities and create social amenities.

JunJie Wu and Sanjiv Mishra, in Chapter 7, report empirical findings from their investigation of natural amenities, human capital investment, human migration, and economic growth in the Pacific Northwest. Locations with better natural amenities, larger expenditures on education, and higher rates of homeownership have attracted migration. They conclude that natural amenities and human capital are major drivers of economic growth and recommend that future research focus on the interaction between firms and households as location decisions are made, as well as between private and public policy decisions. These results direct attention to the relation of rural environmental quality to urban development patterns.

Part III. Policies and Programs for People and Places

The United States cannot be said to have a comprehensive, place-based public policy. In the 19th century, the nation sought to settle its vast undeveloped areas, and many policies were designed to serve that end. Remnants of those policies remain but with little relevance to contemporary issues. Even so, policies for universal application, administered uniformly, often have differing consequences when population density varies. Policies intended for everyone, then, often serve rural people and places imperfectly. The five chapters that constitute this section give explicit attention to how public policies reflect nature-human and urban-rural interdependence—a generally neglected subject. The subjects addressed—poverty, education, and taxation and redistribution—are very different, but the problems are common in rural places, and important to urban people as well.

Bruce Weber, in Chapter 8, writes one of the more comprehensive statements about rural poverty available. He relates poverty to location and identifies characteristics of places where poverty is most prevalent. Although poverty is not randomly distributed, national poverty programs are location blind, raising the question as to whether poverty programs should focus on people or places. Weber reviews the arguments and concludes that both should be taken into account. His chapter includes observations about social capital, natural resources, and intermediate decisionmaking.

Chapter 9 presents research results that pertain to rural education. Because rural young people migrate in great numbers to urban places, the quality of the education they receive is important to both urban and rural people. Professional educators have written and spoken a great deal about the minimum school size necessary for quality education. Maureen Kilkenny and Monica Haddad, taking a fresh look at this issue, agree that size does matter: the larger the group, the more likely a student will have peers who set a standard higher than the student has been able to attain—a "horizon" effect. However, standard-setting peers need not be of the same age or class. The one-room country school may not have been so bad after all. School consolidation may not always be necessary to attain quality education. Kilkenny's and Haddad's imaginative use of an extensive data set brings fresh insight to a long-standing issue in rural public policy.

Mitch Kunce and Jason F. Shogren, in Chapter 10, report the results of their investigation of property taxation and the distribution of rural resource rents. Their sophisticated analysis reveals that tax incentives are poor instruments both for increasing coal production and for fixing the location of coal extraction activities. The economic rent from coal extraction made possible by tax incentives tends to accrue to coal extraction firms rather than elsewhere in the private sector. However, the new growth theory discussed by Kilkenny (Chapter 5) explains why additional economic activity is so attractive to many rural places. Extractive resource management clearly affects nature-human interactions in rural places and provides another dimension of how the relative uniqueness or comparative advantage of particular places may be managed. This subject clearly is central in much rural economics, as discussed in Chapters 5, 8, and 12.

In Chapter 11, Ronald Oakerson describes how political systems reflect interdependence between rural and urban resource users and between rural and urban economies. Instead of the micro-macro distinctions familiar in economic theory, we see a continuous range of decisions at different levels of aggregation, always involving both individuals and groups. Oakerson collapses the values of a geographic place inhabited by humans to two: community and the environment. He notes that social capital creates and sustains good will among community members as they address problems. A multiplicity of objectives requires "multiple agency" involvement at all levels of government as well as by nongovernmental organizations and private citizens. The policy arena is the place where community and environmental values are harmonized at various levels of decisionmaking. And this is the setting within which resource and rural economists must collaborate if they wish to deal with the tensions that shape public policies. Oakerson's chapter provides a backdrop for the research results on intermediate decisionmaking reported in Chapter 12.

Emery N. Castle, in Chapter 12, adopts a methodological view of resource and rural economics, facilitating generalizations about the frontiers of resource and rural economics. Both resource and rural economics historically have been receptive to fundamental discoveries in their parent discipline of economics, and effort should be made to maintain this relationship. Both fields, he argues, will benefit from maintaining economics as a separate science, even as both will also be enhanced by collaboration with other disciplines, and additional integration of rural and resource economics is likely to occur. Neoclassical economic theory has traditionally neglected intermediate political decisionmaking, limiting its usefulness in rural economics. This chapter identifies conceptually, and illustrates empirically, the necessary and sufficient conditions required if intermediate decisionmaking is to be incorporated in neoclassical economic decision theory.

Part IV. The Next 25 Years

In Chapter 13, Kathleen Segerson provides a truly in-depth view of potential contributions of resource and environmental economics. The research agenda she advances focuses on nature-human interdependence (in common with Bromley, Chapter 2, as well as with Smith and Carbone, Chapter 4), land use conflicts, and opportunities for greater cooperation between private parties and regulators. She recommends an agenda that requires a fresh view of externalities, a decreased emphasis on efficiency per se, and greater emphasis on better understanding of incentives and sustainability. Throughout the chapter she calls attention to the great uncertainties that surround the choices to be made. She underlines the need for interdisciplinary research between economists and ecologists in order to better understand nature-human interactions. In addition, she recommends that urban and rural people's preferences for ecosystem services be investigated to provide better information for policy processes.

In Chapter 14, David Brown views the future of rural America through a social-demographic lens. His observations point to the intellectual activity likely to receive the greatest public attention and deliver the greatest value. Unfortunately, the two will not always be the same. He foresees a continuing decline in the percentage of the nonmetropolitan U.S. population, with a continuing increase in the Hispanic population. As a result, rural economic problems are likely to be severe, but there may not be a corresponding public concern about them. Amenity-related industries will become relatively more important in rural places, in Brown's view, suggesting that amenity-related research efforts are indeed appropriate. Brown believes that rural areas will become more residential in less concentrated development patterns. This will be associated with continued but gradual conversion of rural land to urban uses—an argument in support of Segerson's recommendation for more investigation of land use conflicts. Brown foresees both the growing economic dominance of urban places and their increasing need for access to the natural resources, environmental amenities, and ecosystem services of rural places.

Five Subjects on the Frontiers of Resource and Rural Economics

The chapters of this volume permit us to identify five high-priority frontier subjects. These subjects involve important social problems and provide evidence that policy decisions will be improved by the analytic approaches set forth.

1. Nature-human interaction and interdependence. Fundamental issues associated with this interdependence have been neglected. Our first priority frontier subject requires improved understanding of how two large, dynamic structures—ecological and economic systems—can interact and coexist. Techniques for conducting such investigations are not yet readily apparent and need to be developed. At some point dialogue among economists, biological scientists, and physical scientists will be required. A brief discussion of economics as a separate science can be found in Chapter 12. The major objective—to find ways to relate and integrate two large, complex systems—must not become obscured in futile efforts to address questions that cannot be answered as this subject area is explored. It is indeed significant that Bromley, Segerson, and Smith and Carbone independently identified this as a high-priority frontier.

2. Urban and rural social, political, and economic systems. The integration of complex systems is also the focus of a second high-priority frontier subject. Kilkenny, in Chapter 5, directs attention to economic phenomena pertaining to urban and rural economic relationships that cannot be explained or rationalized by existing economic theory. This deserves the attention of competent and curious scholars. Traditional economic theory suggests migration between urban and rural places is the principal way to reduce income and wealth disparities. Yet the ability to benefit from migration is not equal among all rural people. The old, the infirm, and the less well educated migrate less readily. Nonmarket social support systems become relatively more important to such people. How such support systems are best established and maintained is a fundamental public policy issue that affects both urban and rural places. Chapters 8 and 12 direct attention to this subject. Public policies that are designed for all citizens may not work equally well when applied in areas of different population density, and the disparities must be addressed if both urban and rural people are to be served. Here again, the principal objective—the integration of urban and rural economic, social, and political systems—must be kept in mind, and investigations need to be coordinated with those in item 1, above.

3. Intermediate decisionmaking. A more realistic conceptual location for decisionmaking in resource and rural economics constitutes a third priority frontier subject. This arena, intermediate to the micro and macro decisions assumed in traditional economic theory, is where many individual and group objectives with respect to communities and the environment must be reconciled. Local and regional uniqueness as well as comparative advantage affect potential outcomes, and differences in rural versus urban people's aspirations affect the way outcomes are valued. Only if such variations and differences are recognized can there be increased cooperation between regulators and the private sector. This frontier arena will require collaboration among workers in political science, public administration, regional science, and sociology and is consistent with the findings of Chapters 3, 8, 11, 12, and 13.

4. Land use conflicts. A fourth priority frontier, advanced by Segerson in Chapter 13 and underlined by other authors, pertains to the growing importance of land use conflicts in a changing society. As economic development occurs and societies change, land serves different purposes, and its use provides the nexus for resource use and ecosystem conflicts, urban and rural tensions, and community and environmental values. Given the structure of government in the United States, the results of many experiments in the resolution of land use conflict can be observed.

Segerson's fundamental discussion of economic efficiency and sustainability is relevant to land use issues as well as more generally. She cites research demonstrating that efficiency and sustainability choice indicators do not lead to identical evaluations of past economic performance. There is little doubt this will be a frontier subject in resource and rural economics for some time.

5. Maintenance of ecosystem services and resource use under uncertainty and irreversibility. Segerson, as well as other authors, identifies the great uncertainties that underlie the discussions in this book. This condition deserves special attention. Theory about decisionmaking under uncertainty has been developed largely under small group or individual assumptions but is not easily integrated into public policies and programs. Uncertainty may be taken into consideration when economic studies are conducted but typically is not reflected fully in public policy formation. Uncertainty, and the possibility of irreversible consequences, places a premium on adaptability and flexibility—decision characteristics that are difficult to incorporate in public policies. Bureaucracies tend to neglect uncertainty and to eschew adaptability and flexibility as well. Both the level of decisionmaking and the assignment of responsibility between public and private actors are affected by uncertainties and possible irreversibility. This frontier subject should be addressed within the context of the other frontier categories identified above, as well as separately.

Part I
THE PAST 50 YEARS

CHAPTER 2

The Emergence and Evolution of Environmental and Natural Resource Economics

Daniel W. Bromley

*T*HIS SURVEY OF THE FIELD of natural resource economics is concerned with three broad themes. First, the emergence and full development of this specialized field is explored, and a few comments on that emergence are offered (some of this section draws on Bromley 1997). Then several broad issues that challenge the continued coherence of environmental and natural resource economics are discussed. Finally, challenges to the practitioners of the field are offered in the hope that they will reinvigorate the practical relevance of our field for informing public policy discussions.

The Emergence and Development of the Field

The emergence of natural resource economics can be captured by reference to four general historical themes: (1) the development of the field through the merging of natural resource economics and its newer cousin, environmental economics; (2) the evolved practice of bringing nature into our economic models rather than the taking of economic insights to the natural world; (3) the coincident development of the field of welfare economics (and its applied cousin, benefit–cost analysis) as the guiding basis for rational public policy; and (4) the gradual emergence of a new and parallel field, ecological economics.

The field of environmental and natural resource economics as we know it today is most easily understood as the result of the gradual convergence of two quite distinct intellectual traditions—one concerned with the management of natural resources, and the other concerning pollution (externalities) and the problems of environmental quality. In the realm of natural resource management, the early focus was land—this work being influenced by David Ricardo, Johann Heinrich von

Thünen, Henry George, Richard T. Ely, and George Wehrwein. Early activity explored differential land quality, the geographical scope and spatial dispersion of economic activity, and the role of land in social and economic affairs. It is encouraging to see a resurgence of interest in land use matters. We have returned to the early realization that urban areas are surrounded by a great deal of "nature," and we once again realize that there are important research questions concerning the relationship between this natural environment and an increasingly urbanized population. The new interest in urban growth boundaries, urban green spaces, and subdivisions with dedicated common parkland are reflections of this.

This formative land economics tributary merged with another historically important line of work, that concerning the conservation and management of natural resources. Here the intellectual ancestors would seem to be John Muir, Aldo Leopold, Hugh Hammond Bennett, Martin Faustmann, and Gifford Pinchot. It is here that we also spot three small rivulets. The first, water resources, involves the work of Otto Eckstein, Arthur Maass, and Robert Dorfman of the Harvard Water Program. The second rivulet, concerning fishery economics, drew on the American biophysicist Alfred Lotka, the Italian mathematician Vito Volterra, and the fisheries biologist Milner B. Schaefer. Colin Clark and Vernon Smith used their biological models to craft a plausible bioeconomic vision. The third rivulet, drawing on the work of Harold Hotelling, concerned the management of nonrenewable resources, such as mined minerals, petroleum, and groundwater aquifers. More recent interest in species preservation and biodiversity fits well into this general mosaic. This early work across a spectrum of natural resources evolved through close collaboration among scholars from economics, forestry, fisheries, mining, wildlife ecology, agriculture, hydrology, engineering, and soil science.

The second major tributary is more recent in origin, and it emerged almost entirely from within economics—in particular, from public finance. Economists in public finance regard government as consisting of the efficiency branch, the distribution branch, and the stabilization branch. These economists tend to see the economy as something that is—and should remain—separate and distinct from the processes of governance. This idea has been central to the predominance of concern for optimal (or efficient) regulations. The influence from public finance brought into our field the general idea that there is something called "nature," there is the "economy," and then there is "politics." Within this branch of our now-combined field of environmental *and* natural resource economics, there is a general perception that nature serves us (and the economy), and it is essential that politics not be allowed to unduly (inefficiently) interfere with the economy in its use of nature. Indeed, the vast literature on the economics of environmental regulations can be read with two ideas in mind. The first is that if we must have environmental regulations, then it is in everyone's interest that the regulations be as minimally burdensome on the economy as possible. That is, we want regulations to be "efficient." The other reading of this literature is that unless regulations can be shown to be efficient, the economy is better off (will run more "efficiently") without them. These two readings will sometimes merge to suggest that environmental regulations in the absence of evidence of their efficiency are bad for the economy—something that all economists should resist. On this interpretation, it is the obligation of environmental and natural economists to make sure that society does not undertake uneconomical (irrational) environmental regulations. This issue will be discussed further below.

The Commoditization of Nature

The gradual convergence of a variety of specialized disciplines and fields of study brought with it an approach that I characterize as the commoditization of nature. In many respects, we seem to have pursued a research strategy of carving the natural environment, in all of its complexities, at the joints so that we could deal with each part as the need arose (Vatn and Bromley 1994). The natural environment seems to have become a constellation of near-commodities that yield value in production or consumption (we call these "environmental resources"), and nature seems to have become a sink into which wastes might be discarded (we call these "environmental services"). On the commodity side of the account, the Paley Commission—and later work (Barnett and Morse 1963)—was concerned with physical objects such as bauxite, copper, nickel, and magnesium. Although some of that still goes on, there is now an equal tendency to study visitor days on the water, visitor days looking at sunsets, and visitor days hanging from rock cliffs. On the services side of the account, nature processes oxygen-demanding material, the atmosphere absorbs certain industrial pollutants, and forest vegetation sequesters greenhouse gasses. Nature nurtures us.

This approach has allowed us to address nature as we address other economic inputs into production processes or individual consumption—through the lens of prices and quantities. Is nature usefully commoditized? Is it conceptually plausible to see nature as nothing but artfully carved out commodities? Of course, this approach has paid dividends in many respects. But it may also have served us badly if others, perhaps somewhat innocent of the intricate webs of interactions in nature, come to regard the natural environment as nothing but a warehouse of resources and services available for our selective use and enjoyment. Such beliefs might lead to the dangerous notion that we need to monitor and exploit only the pieces of that complex web as it suits us, and we can safely disregard the rest. An understanding of ecology suggests that this partial view is flawed.

Indeed, the overwhelming social trend over the period under discussion has been a continual evolution in the perceived purposes of nature. Until the 1950s, forests were "for" the production of timber, rivers were "for" hydroelectric power and irrigation water, public rangeland was "for" grazing sheep and cattle, the atmosphere was "for" free waste-processing services, and wetlands were "for" draining to control mosquitoes. In some respects, "nature" was the vast wilderness in parts of Africa or in remote North America, while the rest of it, closer to home, was there for our immediate use and degradation—just another object for humans to colonize and subjugate. Since the emergence of a comprehensive environmental consciousness in the early 1970s, it cannot be assumed that this is the case today. Forests are now "for" recreation and carbon sequestration, rivers are "for" boating and fishing, public rangeland is "for" wildlife and all-terrain vehicles, and wetlands are "for" nutrient filtering and animal habitat. More profoundly, much of nature is now understood to be valuable in its own right—quite irrespective of what it will do for us in direct production or consumption. Notice that the purpose—the social meaning—of the environment has profoundly changed during the period under discussion.

At times there is reason to doubt that our commodity-based models have quite captured this profound shift in thinking about nature and how to treat it in discussions about environmental policy. When many environmental economists still seem to insist that the value of a wetland is properly measured by how much people are willing to pay to keep it from being destroyed, one cannot but conclude that our discipline has yet to incorporate profound shifts in social attitudes about nature. Missing in our instrumental approach to the value of wetlands is any recognition that a wetland can actually mean something to many people without their having to commit to pay some amount so that it will not be destroyed (Bromley 1995). Notice that the popular idea of "existence value" may not capture the full extent of this broader idea of value.

How might our work differ if we were to take economic insights to nature, rather than forcing nature into our models? Perhaps we would take notice of the work of Matthew Rabin (1998) and others who are exploring the psychological aspects of our wants and our preferences. Perhaps we would focus on the work of Sam Bowles (1998) and others on the abundant evidence that preference formation is endogenous. We would take seriously Herbert Simon's work (1987, 1991) on rationality and markets. We would make an effort to understand the work of philosophers such as Mark Sagoff (2004) and Bryan Norton (Norton and Ruse 2003). Richard Howarth (2005) reminds us that to ignore this broader literature will lead to defective models of collective action. The essential point here is that the social meaning of nature has been undergoing profound shifts for much of the period covered by this survey, and it does not seem as if those broad shifts in the idea of nature have been adequately incorporated into economic work.

The Rise of Welfare Economics

Just as economics in general is usually defined as the application of rational choice models to individual action, environmental and natural resource economics is usually regarded as the application of welfare economics to collective action—public policy—about nature. In economics, rational choice theory is thought to reveal optimal choices for the individual, while welfare economics is thought to reveal optimal choices for society. Since most environmental and natural resources are not amenable to standard market exchange, much of the work in our field has been to develop various ways to bring marketlike processes to bear on those decisions. And when that is impossible, we have focused on ways to reveal "optimal" choices in an arena of choice over collective-consumption goods and services. But it seems that our first choice has always been to bring natural resources (as commodities) under the alleged discipline of the market and perceived notions of rational choice.

A parallel development in the political arena saw the emergence, at the end of the 19th century, of the Progressive Movement, which lasted until the 1930s. In our field, the first Flood Control Act (1928), prompted by the great floods on the Mississippi River in April 1927, and the Flood Control Act of 1936 brought us the legislative inspiration for benefit–cost analysis. Following World War II, Americans came to accept the idea that government could help secure and underwrite human progress here at home. Soon there were professional schools of government and public administration. It became useful to have expert opinion to help sort out the "best" ways for government to act. Welfare economics provided the conceptual underpinning of the new art of benefit–cost analysis. At last it appeared that economists had a tool that could bring rational choice to collective action, thereby putting public spending on a par with what took place at the individual level. Don't individuals weigh the benefits and costs of their possible actions? Evidence of market failure would now provide the necessary conditions for government action, and allegedly objective analysis could reveal whether the alleged market failure was or was not Pareto relevant. If it was, good analysis could also reveal the optimal arrangements for correcting the problem. This is the intellectual and political climate within which our field emerged, evolved, and matured.

To most environmental and natural resource economists, this seems so natural that it scarcely requires an explanation. But an explanation is necessary. In 1951 Kenneth Arrow published his famous book suggesting, in the very first sentence, that there are two ways to make social choices—markets and the political process (Arrow 1951). Unfortunately, Arrow made a category mistake. Markets do not and cannot make *social* choices—nor are markets a process for *making* social choices. Markets are arenas wherein millions of individual choices lead to social outcomes— be they good or bad. The only arena in which social choices are actually made is that of politics. But most economists are suspicious of choices made in the political arena because they regard politics as a realm of irrational behavior. It is true that politics is about trade-offs, and so one might assume that this is a market by other means. But such trades are suspect to economists because politicians are spending our money, not theirs. And so Arrow's dichotomy was readily embraced and has generally served to reinforce the idea that markets could do what politics cannot. Specifically, since Arrow "proved" that voting could not be relied upon to generate consistent social choices, the obvious alternative—the market—stood ready to do what elections could not.

Somewhat earlier, Lionel Robbins (1932) had singlehandedly redefined the subject matter of economics by offering an epistemological manifesto that has hampered economics to this day (McCloskey 1983). Robbins introduced economists to logical positivism—at that time an innovation emanating from Rudolf Carnap in Vienna. Milton Friedman popularized the idea of positive economics in his quasi-methodological tract *Essays in Positive Economics* (1953).[1] From this, many economists acquired the curious idea that good economics was positive economics (though there is confusion about what "positive" actually means), and bad economics was normative (or value laden). The association between positive and objective became firmly fixed in our collective mind. However, both Robbins and Friedman failed to offer a logical understanding of the idea of objectivity because they did not recognize that the notion of objectivity is meaningless unless one acknowledges the normative base on which the concept of objectivity rests. That is, objectivity has meaning only with reference to some prior standard. That standard, not revealed by a priori reason, must be chosen by the scientist; that is the normative base of science.[2]

Ironically, Robbins taught economists the tenets of logical positivism just as it was being abandoned by philosophers of science as a seriously flawed epistemology. Robbins was clear about what economics needed to be "scientific"; it needed a demarcation rule that would accomplish two things: (1) tell economists what they should study; and (2) tell them how they should study it.[3] It is from Robbins that contemporary economics received its epistemological program:"Economics is the science which studies human behaviour as a relationship between ends and scarce means which have alternative uses" (Robbins 1932, *16*). Unfortunately, this sharp distinction between ends and means is untenable (Shackle 1961).

And so today economics stands as one of the very few disciplines to be defined not by its subject matter (the economy) but by its epistemology (scarcity-driven rational choice). Although most of us insist that we do not make value judgments, an explicit preference for market solutions, or for solutions that seem to offer marketlike signals (such as willingness-to-pay studies), is nothing but a value judgment about how resource allocation decisions ought to be made in society.[4] That this value judgment is shared by most economists does not render it less value laden; it simply embeds the ideology of markets in the belief system into which aspiring economists are socialized (Bromley 1990, 2004).

The research program advanced by Robbins did not permit economists to say anything about public policy, since those declarations would require the introduction of something unobservable—interpersonal comparisons of utility. Some economists mounted forceful renunciations of Robbins—with the potential compensation test emerging to satisfy Robbins's stricture against interpersonal comparisons of utility, yet salvage a role for policy analysis under the pretense of scientific objectivity. Shortly thereafter, Abram Bergson (1938) would provide the theoretical underpinnings of modern welfare economics.

Indeed, the period up until the World War II saw the full development of optimism about judging welfare changes. Following the war, the optimism just as quickly dissipated under the assaults of Graaff (1957), Little (1950), and Samuelson (1950). Ironically, this realization of the intellectual incoherence of welfare economics coincided with the full flowering of the idea that government action—and public policy—could be a source of social improvement. Our growing disciplinary dependence on welfare economics was buttressed not so much by its theoretical coherence as by the newfound opportunity to provide an allegedly "scientific" (that is, objective) decision protocol to pass judgment on collective action. It was difficult for us, as applied economists, to admit that our only analytical tool was theoretically flawed just as public decisionmakers were clamoring for some way to bring "science" to the challenge of public choice. We were trapped by our desire to help rescue social choice from the alleged perils of politics—and Kenneth Arrow's "proof" that voting could be inconsistent.

The Emergence of Ecological Economics

The final strand of work pertinent to the emergence of our field is that of ecological economics. Despite a slow and uncertain beginning, this formerly small tributary now shows increasing signs of vigor and robustness. The journal *Ecological Economics* is widely read and cited. The International Society of Ecological Economics now stands as a plausible intellectual community with the capacity to engage scholars who do economics and those who do other things related to nature. *Ecological Economics* contains thoughtful, interesting, and pertinent work. For the most part, ecological economists are less committed to the sanctity of markets and economic efficiency as the best answer to environmental problems. This does not mean that many of them are not economists. It merely means that they approach economics and economic issues pertaining to nature from a different methodological commitment.

The ecological economists seem less committed to the received axiomatic truths that tend to define other environmental and natural resource economists. They tend to be somewhat more circumspect toward markets and the certitude of economic efficiency as a truth rule for guiding public policy. They seem open to acknowledging the legitimacy of environmental problems as articulated by citizens and politicians, quite apart from a finding that such problems constitute evidence of market failure. That may be why their journal is widely read and cited. Their more inclusive epistemology offers the ecological economists a broader perspective from which to undertake empirical research and to work out innovative conceptual advancements. I will return to this point below.

Future Challenges to the Discipline

My comments so far have concerned the conceptual evolution of our field and the general constituent parts that now give it shape and focus. It is now time to reflect and ask whether our specialized field is well positioned to be relevant in the future. By relevant, I mean, do we have a theoretical apparatus that will allow us to advance plausible empirical claims about important issues that concern the relation between nature and the economy? I would like to raise this question with two ideas in mind. First, do we have internal processes and incentives to detect and quickly contribute to emerging social problems in the realm of nature and the economy? Second, does our conceptual approach promise to bring warranted and valuable insights to pressing economy-nature problems?

Our Agility in the Face of Emerging Problems

It would be easy to believe that applied economists set the intellectual agenda for public policy in the area of environment and natural resources. But what if it is the sudden urgency of particular public policy issues—not our disciplinary research and its insights—that drives our intellectual agenda forward? Were our colleagues working on the extraordinary vulnerability of New Orleans and other low-lying metropolitan areas to severe weather events? Did we lead the intellectual agenda pertaining to research on spatial patterns of land use, location of cities, channeling of rivers, occupation of floodplains, and a host of other research areas? Were we working on "smart growth," or did that emerge from planners and politicians? Have we done plausible work on the implications of the recent energy boom in Wyoming—with particular reference to the environmental destruction that now seems widespread? Have we done much work in fisheries economics other than extolling the alleged virtues of individual fishing quotas as the necessary and sufficient instrument to preserve fish stocks and bring "efficiency" to ocean policy?

Indeed, the attraction of an applied discipline is that we presumably take our research ideas from new problems in the public sphere. But doing so requires that we be alert to new problems and pay attention to what is transpiring in the political realm. This dimension has, from time to time, been important in motivating work. I have already mentioned the Flood Control Act of 1936. The language in that act concerning the tallying up of benefits and costs of water projects inspired an extensive research program on benefit–cost analysis that lasted into the Carter presidency, 1977 to 1981. The act motivated a wide-ranging research program—much of it initiated at Oregon State University by Emery Castle and Herb Stoevener. Indeed, the period between 1960 and 1980 was one in which benefit–cost analysis was the defining activity of many natural resource economists.

But the landscape changed profoundly in the 1970s, and it is not clear that we were in the forefront of those changes. By the early 1970s, as the era of water resource development was drawing to a close, the National Environmental Policy Act (1970), the Clean Air Act (1970), the Clean Water Act (1972), the Coastal Zone Management Act (1972), the Endangered Species Act (1973), and then the National Forest Management Act (1976) signaled a new era in natural resource management. How many of us saw these developments coming, helped shape their nature and content, and were ready with useful and applicable analytical tools? These public commitments to enhanced environmental quality supplanted earlier concerns over the shortage of material resources (including water resources and river navigation) that had prevailed in the 1950s and 1960s (Barnett and Morse 1963). With the first Earth Day in April 1972, we entered an era of public concern for—and federal legislation concerning—environmental quality. Many states followed the lead of the federal government. This was an exciting time in the general area of nature and the economy.

It was not long, however, before these new initiatives of the 1970s were under serious attack. First, in 1979 with Margaret Thatcher in Britain, and then in 1981 with Ronald Reagan in the United States, we saw an aggressive backlash against much of what governments did and had been doing since the Great Depression of the 1930s. In an odd display of Hobbesian pessimism, Thatcher captured the emerging worldview by asserting that there was "no such thing as society—there was only the individual." Reagan followed her in a widespread assault on a range of collective actions (from unionized air traffic controllers to regulations that were said to be bad for the economy). Indeed, just three weeks after his inauguration, Reagan issued Executive Order 12291, which was generally seen as the "regulatory relief" act. The order stated,

> (b) Regulatory action shall not be undertaken unless the potential benefits to society for the regulation outweigh the potential costs to society; (c) Regulatory objectives shall be chosen to maximize the net benefits to society; (d) Among alternative approaches to any given regulatory objective, the alternative involving the least net cost to society shall be chosen; and (e) Agencies shall set regulatory priorities with the aim of maximizing the aggregate net benefits to society, taking into account the condition of the particular industries affected by regulations, the condition of the national economy, and other regulatory actions contemplated for the future.

Implicit in this utopian prose is the fanciful notion that it is possible to know what must be done to "maximize the net benefits to society." Then, during the presidency of George H.W. Bush, 1989 to 1993, Vice President Dan Quayle was put in charge of a "Competitiveness Council." The motivation here was to make public policy less menacing than it already was for what some are pleased to call "free markets." Indeed, the dominant *zeitgeist* since 1980 seems to concern getting government "off our backs and out of our lives." Did environmental and natural resource economists play a useful role in this period? The answer to that question hinges on what one means by "useful."

What is not in doubt is that the language of Executive Order 12291 continues to define how many economists regard environmental policy. This idea was clearly played out in the debate over the Porter Hypothesis in the fall 1995 issue of the *Journal of Economic Perspectives* (Palmer et al. 1995; Porter and van der Linde 1995). Many environmental economists were astonished at the Porter Hypothesis—and the debate seemed to reinforce the idea that the field was united behind the idea that one could not possibly know "how much" environmental quality was rational (optimal) unless strict benefit–cost analysis was brought to bear on that question. However, if those surprised by the Porter Hypothesis had considered two quite plausible assumptions, they might have been inspired to build quite intuitive and simple models demonstrating the possibility—not the certainty, but the possibility—of there being solid grounds for accepting the Porter Hypothesis. Specifically, if technical change had been treated as endogenous (which it assuredly is), and if the first-mover advantage in a world of thoroughgoing competition had been considered (and there is an extensive literature on the many advantages to being the first mover in a dynamic industry), it would have been rather easy to see that the Porter Hypothesis is not at all surprising.

Instead of an open-minded—might we say "intellectually curious"?—consideration of a proposition from Michael Porter (no slouch in academic circles), a number of environmental economists fought back with two curious claims: the Porter Hypothesis was impossible, and besides, environmental policy would be in dangerous hands indeed if such ideas were allowed to spread. In fact, recent work has undermined the naïve models of those who were shocked by the Porter Hypothesis (Alpay et al. 2002; Altman 2001; Gabel and Sinclair-Desgagné 1998; Mohr 2002). Why, one wonders, were so many environmental economists threatened by Porter's ideas?

We see, I fear, the durable residue of how aspiring members of a discipline become socialized into a particular and quite dominant belief system. That is, whereas the 1960s and 1970s was a period in which benefit–cost analysis became the method of choice for analyzing government investments in water resource projects, the 1980s and 1990s was a time in which many of our colleagues came to believe that the main, legitimate intellectual pursuit concerned assessing the benefits and costs of environmental regulations. Indeed, the enormous growth in contingent valuation methods can be seen in this light.[5]

Although environmental and resource economists have, at times, taken the broad themes of our work from actions in the public arena—citizen outcries, legislative initiatives, administrative rulings, judicial decrees—we have adhered rather too closely for my tastes to perceived disciplinary truths (beliefs) and protocols and persisted in our commitments to those beliefs long past the time that they serve us, or the general public, well. The danger, it seems, is that we continue to work on disciplinary problems—models and methods—long past the point of diminishing marginal returns in such work.

In other words, I worry that we lack reliable signals *internal to our field* that can help us spot promising new economy-nature problems. In the absence of such signals, there is a tendency for us to continue doing what we have been doing—and fervently believing in its legitimacy—long past the time that useful insights might thereby result. Our commitment to the axiomatic origins of knowledge often render us tentative and without apparent grounds to identify new problems. If new problems are not thrust upon us by external events, it is too easy to keep tinkering around the edges of our solutions to earlier problems.

It is my view that our specialized field would be profoundly invigorated by internal discussions and debates about when a particular line of research—or a particular worldview—is no longer yielding net marginal benefits.

Our Conceptual Grounding

My second concern is related to the above, but it goes to the pervasive and deeply insinuated value judgments and justifications that undermine our intellectual currency in the economics profession. Some will be surprised to be told that environmental and natural resource economics is contaminated by values and normative prescriptions. But the discussion immediately above concerned precisely this problem. If we are to offer coherent policy advice to the general public—and that includes the catchall category of public decisionmakers—then it is necessary that our prescriptions stand on solid economic footing. If that conceptual footing is problematic, then our policy prescriptions are tendentious.

To grasp the nature of the problem, we might start with the recent work in complexity theory. The work emanating from the Sante Fe Institute on complexity inspired William A. Brock and David Colander to write,

> ... complexity ... takes away the reference point for theory's defense of the market. In the complexity vision there is no proof that the market solves problems. There is no unambiguous way of stating what is and what is not an externality, and there is no guarantee that the market leads to the most desirable equilibrium. Thus deductive theory cannot provide a basis for the defense of laissez faire (Brock and Colander 2000, *82*).

In other words, complexity denies to us the essential tractability and predictability we need to advance our purposefully normative Paretian prescriptions about what is efficient or rational or optimal in the realm of human action concerning the environment. Brock and Colander continue:

> As an example, consider the question: Do free markets and well defined property rights make society a better place? In the complexity approach, the answer to this question becomes ... [an] empirical, not a deductive theoretical, question as it is in conventional theory. It [the complexity approach] does not approach the issue: Given assumptions X, Y, Z can we prove that competitive equilibrium is "Pareto optimal?" Instead, it approaches it as an empirical issue whose answer may lie in areas totally untouched by simplified general equilibrium theory. As another example of how this does not change

sophisticated economists' worldview, consider Frank Hahn's ... favorite challenge ... "How can you tell if the economy is in a Pareto optimal state or not?" Such a challenge demonstrates an understanding of the limits of a deductive approach, and the existence of a more sophisticated worldview ... (Brock and Colander 2000, 78–79).

These writers reinforce the criticism of Frank Hahn—and they make the essential point that Pareto optimality, a concept of unrivaled importance to welfare economists, is incoherent. Therefore, it is now impossible to regard prescriptive assertions predicated on welfarism as comprising warranted truth claims from within our parent discipline of economics (Bromley 1990, 2004, 2006).

Some may seek to retain the benefit–cost side of the bargain while jettisoning the connection to claims about policies that are socially preferred, Pareto optimal, welfare enhancing, or contributing to the public interest. This was the advice first offered by Mishan some 25 years ago (1969, 1980). That advice has been ignored. But even a de minimus adherence to benefit–cost analysis, without the flawed association with social welfare, is less secure than even Mishan hoped. Important doubts continue to be raised about the role of benefit–cost analysis in public choice settings (Adler and Posner 2001). In a review of that volume we read,

> This is a magnificent collection of essays on cost–benefit analysis (CBA) written by economists, and by law professors and philosophers with some knowledge of economics ... Many will be surprised ... that the overall tone of a series of essays on this topic coming out of a law school very much influenced by economics, and by "Chicago-school" economics at that, is more questioning about CBA's use for regulatory policymaking for health, safety and the environment than would be mainstream discussions coming out of the prescriptive literature in economics or policy analysis. . . . It is fair to characterize their modal conclusions as follows: (1) policymakers should examine costs and benefits ... but the decision rule "maximize net benefits" is frequently problematic; (2) some of the most problematic issues CBA raises as a decision rule involve the use of existing private preferences as the sole raw material for public choices; (3) we should pay more attention than typically has been done to political considerations involving CBA (Kelman, 2002, *1241*).

I have advanced this position before (Bromley 1990, 2004, 2006) and will not repeat the full case against prescriptive consequentialism. But notice the concerns in the above quote: (1) the concept of net benefits is seriously problematic; (2) it is incoherent to regard public choices as but the simple monetized aggregate of private preferences; and (3) political considerations must be reincorporated into discussions of public policy. This is unwelcome news for many environmental and resource economists. Just how unwelcome it is can be surmised by the fact that these points have been well known for at least three decades and they are still ignored (Tribe 1972).

Few economists take welfare economics seriously. Why have we been so captivated by this utopian ideology? The ideology is utopian precisely because there is no solid theoretical ground beneath it. It is fiction, and adherence to it precludes us from recognizing many environmental problems until there is clear evidence of some putative market failure. As suggested above, we tend to wait until environmental problems have been brought to public attention by citizens who are tired of fish they dare not eat, water not fit for swimming, air that conceals rather than reveals the sky, and groundwater aquifers that are being diminished by the month. These environmental problems will soon result in demands by the citizenry—and a few politicians—for some resolution. Many environmental economists will be suspicious of such demands made on the political process (Palmer et al. 1995). It will be said that those who demand a cleaner environment are seeking to free-ride on the political process by getting something through the legislature (new institutional arrangements leading to an improved environment) so that they can benefit without having to pay polluters to stop destroying parts of nature. It will be asserted that society might actually end up with "too much" environmental quality—the air and water will be too clean, the fish will have too few chemical residues in their edible flesh, and there will be too many hectares devoted to wildlife and waterfowl habitat.

Left unaddressed in this complaint is precisely why those seeking to be free of pollutants should have to pay polluters to change their unwanted and harmful behavior. Why should payment not flow the other way? That is, why are polluters not made to pay victims of pollution for the ability to keep fouling the air or the water? The standard answer will be that the status quo—privileged by being called the market—must be consulted to see whether it is socially preferable (or welfare enhancing) to correct these nontrivial problems with the status quo institutional setup. If we cannot show efficiency gains from corrective action, then it is necessary for us to announce that although pollution is perhaps, a serious problem, we regret to report that the many complaints of the citizens are best ignored on the grounds that they are Pareto-Irrelevant Externalities. This revelation will be unlikely to satisfy anyone. And then, as a last resort, that marvelous conversation stopper—the Coase Theorem—will be deployed to "prove" that marketlike solutions maximize social welfare.[6]

Many of our colleagues seem to fret that we might solve environmental problems without subjecting the policy solution to benefit–cost analysis (Arrow et al. 1996; Cropper 2000; Palmer et al. 1995). And it will often be asserted that since the efficiency conditions were not met, the institutional change cannot possibly be *socially* preferred. And then many environmental economists, unaware that positive net benefits of institutional change are neither necessary nor sufficient for a social improvement (and conversely), will lament the meddling of politicians in the economy (Bromley 1990, 2004; Mishan 1980; Samuels 1971, 1974, 1989; Vatn 2005; Vatn and Bromley 1994, 1997). One gets the impression that in the absence of benefit–cost analysis, politicians will be quite unable to make up their mind what to do. And so economists will conduct benefit–cost studies to light the way.

In one recent study of New Delhi, we are assured that the research sought to estimate the social benefits of cleaning the Ganges River—apparently on the belief that no action can be rationally taken unless it is found that the social benefits exceed the costs of cleaning up this foul open sewer (Markandya and Murty 2004). In estimating the "social benefits" of cleaner water in the river, both market and nonmarket valuation of environmental goods is used. Even without including benefits to the fishing industry, the program of cleaning the Ganges is reported to have "positive net present social benefits at a 10 percent social rate of discount and an internal rate of return as high as 15 percent" (Markandya and Murty 2004, *61*). The basis of much of the "benefits" from this cleaning program is the lost wages from workers being sick and unable to work for part of the year from their necessary reliance on drinking water from this highly polluted river.

One might suppose that if the lost wages of New Delhi's poor are sufficient to justify (to rationalize) an investment in cleaning a river that now makes most of them sick enough to stay away from much-needed wage employment, politicians might be able to find plausible reasons for a cleanup without the necessity of ascertaining what the poor say they would be willing to pay not to be poisoned. There are, after all, ample data on the debilitating implications of morbidity. And what would we conclude about social welfare if the only persons victimized by the foul river happened to be the many in Delhi without a job of any kind? In other words, what might we conclude if the harms ("damages") from this open sewer fell on those without wages to be forgone because they cannot find employment? If this were the case, there could be very few social "benefits" (the elimination of lost wages due to sickness) from cleaning the Ganges. And thus it would seem—at least to the Paretian economist—that it is socially optimal for the Ganges to remain polluted. I doubt if the authors are unaware of this problem, but notice how such studies proceed as if it were not an issue worth serious reflection.

As a second example, one very recent study noted the number of fatal and non-fatal cancer incidents in Bangladesh from the slow arsenic poisoning arising from new wells (Maddison et al. 2005). This study reveals that poor Bangladeshis' willingness to pay to avoid these tragic health problems is approximately $2.7 billion annually—this in a country where the per capita income is just above $400 per year. Studies such as this seem no longer to surprise us, but would we be surprised to read a study of American urban residents' annual willingness to pay to avoid being shot by handguns? Would we be surprised to read an article estimating the willingness of the poor in New Orleans—the vast majority of whom do not own cars—to pay to avoid being stranded in their flooded homes for a week without food and water? Perhaps the researchers might then advance a "policy implication" that the costs of providing escape transportation cannot be justified (that is, would not be efficient) since the net benefits appear to be negative. Why then are we not surprised to hear that a study has been conducted to determine what the 10 million to 15 million poverty-stricken citizens of Bangladesh would be willing to pay to avoid drinking poison?

The point in these studies—as with much of what is written in environmental economics these days—is to discover whether environmental resources are being used "efficiently." Or, such studies seek to discover whether it would be "efficient" to clean up some serious environmental problem. In other words, our colleagues seek to discover whether "social welfare" would be enhanced or diminished by steps to reduce the extent to which the residents of New Delhi or Bangladesh are being poisoned by their only source of drinking water. If it is found that the costs of avoiding this situation of widespread illness and morbidity somehow exceed the very low level of lost wages in an urban economy where there is not much in the way of wages to be lost (forgone), or if their willingness to pay to spare being poisoned is not large enough, then it would seem that the "logic of efficiency" reveals to us that it is not worth it to prevent a public health problem that would seem—on mature reflection—to be rather serious. Can it really be that environmental economists find this logic compelling?

Confident assertions concerning efficient and socially beneficial environmental policies entail empirical claims—by which I mean claims with empirical content and empirical implications. Empirical claims require plausible evidence of their coherence and their truth content. Unfortunately, empirical claims about the social welfare implications of various policies are never subjected to testing. Worse, these empirical claims about social welfare cannot possibly be tested, and so their confident and regular assertion constitutes intellectual fraud. I eagerly await a plausible test of the empirical claim about the social benefits of cleaning or not cleaning the open sewer we know as the Ganges River—or of addressing Bangladesh's carcinogenic drinking water. And by the idea of a plausible test, I do not mean another study to replicate what was done in the first study. A second study would check the validity of the first, but it would not in any way address the truth content of one or both sets of estimates. There is no plausible empirical study of the "social value" of clean, nonpoisonous water. There is no coherent test of these empirical claims, and thus they constitute, in the vernacular of the contingent valuation literature, mere cheap talk. They are an elaborate bluff.

Until environmental and natural resource economists are able to devise coherent tests of our empirical claims about efficiency, socially preferred policies, Pareto-improving policies, welfare-enhancing policies, hypothetical values of nature, and most other empirical assertions of this sort, the analysis and policy advice we advance with such confidence are scientific deceits. These empirical claims arise from—and are therefore quarantined by—the self-referential models within which they are embedded.

I believe the problem springs from the fact that we are too ready to declare that our field is a policy science and therefore we are under some obligation to offer up policy prescriptions. Such claims are not wrong—they are simply incomplete. Economics is an empirical science, and any subfield within economics that persists in offering up untestable empirical claims cannot possibly be taken seriously. We have ample evidence from the economic theorists that they regard our frequent welfaristic empirical claims to be indefensible (Brock and Colander 2000; Chipman and Moore 1978; Diamond and Hausman 1994; Gillroy 1992; Gorman 1955; Hahn 1970).

Choosing Our Future

The period under review, 1950 to 2000, coincides almost precisely with the emergence and maturation of the field of environmental and natural resource economics. The breadth of work carried out under that general label is impressive in its scope and in its quantitative methods. Unfortunately, our theoretical and methodological grounding remain seriously flawed. In his article "Natural Resource and Environmental Economics: A Retrospective View" (1999), Emery Castle raised many of the troubling issues I have discussed here. I have every confidence that Emery, while he may disagree with a few of the specifics, stands with me when it comes to making sure that our theoretical and empirical house rests on a solid foundation. Indeed, his singular contribution as mentor and teacher was to push us hard on the logical validity, the theoretical legitimacy, and the fundamental coherence of our empirical claims. Honest scholarship demands nothing less. I lament the decline of real Emery Castle-like scholarship in our field. I fear that we have become mechanics and technicians, struggling to keep a deeply flawed machine running long past its useful life while ignoring the incoherence at the core of that machine. No wonder so few policymakers bother to seek our advice. And when they do ask us what we think, they are usually confident that we will provide them with answers they dare not attempt to explain or justify to a large audience of sapient adults. Our answers may mollify minions in the U.S. Office of Management and Budget whose blessing is now required for all manner of public actions. But our answers do not fool the general public.

Economics gives us the theoretical grounding to offer descriptions, prescriptions, and predictions. Description is the act of writing sentences that seem to fit the world out there. Prescription is the act of getting the world out there to fit the sentences we write about it. Prediction is the act of writing hopeful and promising sentences about the prescriptions we offer. Notice that every policy prescription is necessarily a policy prediction. To assert that "problem Y can be rectified by policy X" is to prescribe policy X. But this assertion is also a prediction of the form: "policy X will fix problem Y." Another prediction of dubious provenance is of the form, "policy Z will enhance social welfare." How often are such predictions held to account? Our field is mired in justificationism—the act of explaining why, exactly, the world out there *ought* to coincide with our prescriptions for it.

Let me be very clear—the flaws I am discussing have nothing to do with the discipline of economics. Our parent discipline is rich in ideas and approaches. It is we, the more applied practitioners, who have ignored the profound theoretical rigor—and who have abandoned the deep insights—of our parent discipline. In our rush to appear useful we have become bad economists and flawed policy advisers. As Isaac Newton put the matter: "it is not the art but the artificers" that are the more serious problem.

It is time for environmental and natural resource economists to start the long-overdue quest for new conceptual ground on which to build our specialty. The old metaphors and models—market failure, potential Pareto improvements, positive versus normative, efficiency versus equity, Pareto-irrelevant externalities, made-up values for contrived pieces of nature wrung out of bemused citizens by eager graduate students—have failed to serve us in a manner that the political process finds useful or edifying. And our pretensions have brought us scorn from the general economists and theorists who serve the essential role of keeping incestuous cells of applied economists intellectually honest. We appear quite happy to ignore what other economists think of our models and empirical claims, and we belittle politicians as shortsighted and perverse. We still act as if we wish for a world of policy without politics. We still dream of a world in which policymakers wait for us to pronounce, with abundant but misplaced confidence, which environmental policy will deliver efficient levels of pollution, maximum welfare, and optimum social bliss.

Socrates warned that the unexamined life is not worth living. I say that unexamined science is not worth doing. Our specialized field is now large enough, and self-assured enough, that reflection and self-criticism are both long overdue and of great potential value. We spend far too little time reflecting on what we do, and why we do it that way. Those who do reflect, who ask inconvenient questions, are regarded as disloyal. The single most pernicious flaw in applied fields is the lack of interest in reflective thought. It is too easy to keep busy on routine tasks (Kuhn's "normal science") and thus ignore necessary self-criticism (Kuhn 1962). We have, it seems, a conspiracy of silence. Work that does not accord with perceived truths is not debated because it is rejected by reviewers, or it is simply ignored.

The health of a discipline must not be associated with the sounds of silence within it. Indeed, the healthiest disciplines are the ones in which spirited debates rage. We make a serious mistake when we confuse contrived silence for accepted truth. Silence is a symptom of sterility, stasis, and a lack of intellectual vigor.

After a reasonable start, it is my hope that environmental and natural resource economists will finally turn our attention to a much-needed critical inquiry into our assumptions, our methods, our empirical claims, and our value-laden justifications. If we fail to address these matters, we will fail to attract the brightest young students to our discipline. And then some day we will simply disappear. There is a brighter future. It is a future driven by debates, by contending truth claims, by contending epistemologies, and by contending beliefs about how to bring economics to nature. That is an exciting future. Let us grasp *that* future.

References

Adler, M.D., and E.A. Posner. 2001. *Cost-Benefit Analysis: Legal, Economic and Philosophical Perspectives*. Chicago: University of Chicago Press.

Alpay, E., S. Buccola, and J. Kerkvliet. 2002. Productivity Growth and Environmental Regulation in Mexican and U.S. Food Manufacturing. *American Journal of Agricultural Economics* 84(4): 887–901.

Altman, M. 2001. When Green Isn't Mean: Economic Theory and the Heuristics of the Impacts of Environmental Regulations on Competitiveness and Opportunity Cost. *Ecological Economics* 36(1): 31–44.

Arrow, K.J. 1951. *Social Choice and Individual Values*. New Haven, CT: Yale University Press.

Arrow, K.J., M.J. Cropper, G.C. Eads, R.W. Hahn, L.B. Lave, R.G. Noll, P.R. Portney, M. Russell, R. Schmalensee, V.K. Smith, and R.N. Stavins. 1996. Is There a Role for Benefit-Cost Analysis in Environmental, Health, and Safety Regulation? *Science* 272: 221–22.

Barnett, H.J., and C. Morse. 1963. *Scarcity and Growth: The Economics of Natural Resource Availability*. Baltimore: Johns Hopkins University Press.

Bergson, A. 1938. A Reformulation of Certain Aspects of Welfare Economics. *Quarterly Journal of Economics* 52: 310–34.

Bowles, S. 1998. Endogenous Preferences: The Cultural Consequences of Markets and other Economic Institutions. *Journal of Economic Literature* 36 (March): 75–111.

Brock, W.A., and D. Colander. 2000. Complexity and Policy. In *The Complexity Vision and the Teaching of Economics*, edited by D. Colander. Cheltenham, UK: Edward Elgar.

Bromley, D.W. 1990. The Ideology of Efficiency: Searching for a Theory of Policy Analysis. *Journal of Environmental Economics and Management* 19(1): 86–107.

———. 1995. Property Rights and Natural Resource Damage Assessment. *Ecological Economics* 14: 129–35.

———. 1997. Rethinking Markets. *American Journal of Agricultural Economics* 79(5): 1383–93.

———. 2004. Reconsidering Environmental Policy: Prescriptive Consequentialism and Volitional Pragmatism. *Environmental and Resource Economics* 28(1): 73–99.

————. 2006. *Sufficient Reason: Volitional Pragmatism and the Meaning of Economic Institutions.* Princeton, NJ: Princeton University Press.

Castle, E.N. 1999. Natural Resource and Environmental Economics: A Retrospective View. *Review of Agricultural Economics* 21(2): 288–304.

Chipman, J.S., and J.C. Moore. 1978. The New Welfare Economics: 1939–1974. *International Economic Review* 19(3): 547–84.

Coase, R. 1937. The Nature of the Firm. *Economica* 4: 386–405.

Cropper, M.L. 2000. Has Economic Research Answered the Needs of Environmental Policy? *Journal of Environmental Economics and Management* 39(3): 328–50.

Diamond, P.A., and J.A. Hausman. 1994. Contingent Valuation: Is Some Number Better Than No Number? *The Journal of Economic Perspectives* 8(Autumn): 45–64.

Fraser, L. M. 1937. *Economic Thought and Language.* London: Black Ltd.

Friedman, M. 1953. *Essays in Positive Economics.* Chicago: University of Chicago Press.

Gabel, H., and B. Sinclair-Desgagné. 1998. The Firm, Its Routines and the Environment. In *The International Yearbook of Environmental Economics: 1998–1999*, edited by T. Tietenberg and H. Folmer. Cheltenham, UK: Edward Elgar.

Gillroy, J.M. 1992. The Ethical Poverty of Cost-Benefit Methods: Autonomy, Efficiency, and Public Policy Choice. *Policy Science* 25: 83–102.

Gorman, W.M. 1955. The Intransitivity of Certain Criteria Used in Welfare Economics. *Oxford Economic Papers* 7(1): 25–35.

Graaff, J. De V. 1957. *Theoretical Welfare Economics.* Cambridge: Cambridge University Press.

Hahn, F.H. 1970. Some Adjustment Problems. *Econometrica* 38 (January): 1–17.

Howarth, R.B. 2005. Review of Mark Sagoff, *Price, Principle, and the Environment.* Cambridge: Cambridge University Press. 2004. In *Land Economics* 81(4): 587–91.

Kelman, S. 2002. Review of M.D. Adler and E.A. Posner (eds.). 2001. *Cost-Benefit Analysis: Legal, Economic and Philosophical Perspectives.* Chicago: University of Chicago Press. In *Journal of Economic Literature* 60 (December): 1241–42.

Kuhn, T. 1962. *The Structure of Scientific Revolutions.* Chicago: University of Chicago Press.

Little, I.M.D. 1950. *A Critique of Welfare Economics.* London: Oxford University Press.

Mccloskey, D. 1983. The Rhetoric of Economics. *Journal of Economic Literature* 21: 481–517.

Maddison, D., R. Catala-Luque, and D. Pearce. 2005. Valuing the Arsenic Contamination of Groundwater in Bangladesh. *Environmental and Resource Economics* 31: 459–76.

Markandya, A., and M.N. Murty. 2004. Cost-Benefit Analysis of Cleaning the Ganges: Some Emerging Environmental and Development Issues. *Environment and Development Economics* 9: 61–81.

Mishan, E.J. 1969. *Welfare Economics: An Assessment.* Amsterdam: North-Holland.

————. 1980. How Valid Are Economic Evaluations of Allocative Changes? *Journal of Economic Issues* 14 (March): 143–61.

Mohr, R.D. 2002. Technical Change, External Economies, and the Porter Hypothesis. *Journal of Environmental Economics and Management* 43(1): 158–68.

Norton, B.G., and M. Ruse. 2003. *Searching for Sustainability: Interdisciplinary Essays in the Philosophy of Conservation Biology.* Cambridge: Cambridge University Press.

Palmer, K., W. Oates, and P.R. Portney. 1995. Tightening Environmental Standards: The Benefit-Cost or the No-Cost Paradigm? *Journal of Economic Perspectives* 9(4): 119–132.

Porter, M.E., and C. van der Linde. 1995. Toward a New Conception of the Environment-Competitiveness Relationship. *Journal of Economic Perspectives* 9(4): 97–118.

Rabin, M. 1998. Psychology and Economics. *Journal of Economic Literature* 36 (March): 11–46.

Robbins, L. 1932. *An Essay on the Nature and Significance of Economic Science.* London: Macmillan.

Sagoff, M. 2004. *Price, Principle, and the Environment.* Cambridge: Cambridge University Press.

Samuels, W.J. 1971. The Interrelations between Legal and Economic Processes. *Journal of Law and Economics* 14 (October): 435–50.

————. 1974. The Coase Theorem and the Study of Law and Economics. *Natural Resources Journal* 14 (January): 1–33.

————. 1989. The Legal-Economic Nexus. *George Washington Law Review* 57:(6): 1556–78.

Samuelson, P.A. 1950. Evaluation of Real National Income. *Oxford Economic Papers* 2(1): 1–29.

Shackle, G.L.S. 1961. *Decision, Order, and Time in Human Affairs.* Cambridge: Cambridge University Press.

Simon, H. 1987. Rationality in Psychology and Economics. In *Rational Choice*, edited by Hogarth, Robin and Reder. Chicago: University of Chicago Press.

———. 1991. Organizations and Markets. *Journal of Economic Perspectives* 5(2): 25–44.

Tribe, L.H. 1972. Policy Science: Analysis or Ideology? *Philosophy and Public Affairs* 2(1): 66–110.

Vatn, A. 2005. *Institutions and the Environment*. Cheltenham, UK: Edward Elgar.

Vatn, A., and D.W. Bromley. 1994. Choices without Prices without Apologies. *Journal of Environmental Economics and Management* 26(2): 129–48.

———. 1997. Externalities: A Market Model Failure. *Environmental and Resource Economics* 9: 135–51.

Acknowledgments

I am grateful to Glen D. Anderson and the editors for helpful comments on an earlier draft.

Notes

1. Friedman is not a positivist but a methodological instrumentalist: theory is merely an instrument to allow predictions.

2. Emery Castle was very helpful in clarifying this fundamental point for me.

3. It is interesting to see Robbins be dismissive of the economics of the day as being simply "classificatory" and then offer up his own classificatory scheme. Equally surprising is that Robbins failed to notice that his manifesto regarding the necessary conditions for science (consisting exclusively of either analytic or synthetic propositions) violated his own demarcation rule (since his rule fails to satisfy either of his two conditions for being a scientific proposition). So much for "science" in the service of defining the proper domain of science. This point was noticed as far back as 1937 by Fraser.

4. The work of Coase (1937) and Simon (1991) reminds us that in fact the vast majority of allocative decisions in a modern economy are not made in markets *guided* by prices, but are made in organizations *compelled* by command and obedience. Simon insists that ours should be called an organizational economy rather than a market economy.

5. In 1990, 24 percent of the papers in *Land Economics* and the *Journal of Environmental Economics and Management* concerned environmental valuation. In 1991 that proportion had increased to 28 percent, and by 1992 it was up to 42 percent (Vatn and Bromley 1994). By 2004 that proportion for both journals had fallen to approximately 17 percent.

6. Notice that the Coase Theorem is simply a restatement of the first (direct) and second (indirect) theorems of welfare economics.

CHAPTER 3

Rural Economics
People, Land, and Capital

Paul W. Barkley

*E*VEN THOUGH THE FUNDAMENTAL percepts of economics trace to antiquity, the discipline and its recommendations were not systematic and generally available in the western world until about 150 to 200 years ago. Agricultural economics, a prominent subdiscipline of economics, developed along a path parallel to that of the parent discipline and began to take on a character of its own somewhat later, about 1900 (U.S. Country Life Commission 1910).[1] Rural economics (or community economics or area development) came still later, and although some general economists and some agriculturalists have studied and continue to study the nonfarm economic problems of rural areas, this spin-off from economics and agricultural economics did not emerge until at least the Progressive Era—some will say not until the Great Depression, some will say not until after World War II (Bailey 1897, 1911).[2] Even then, it lay off to the side, never taking on either disciplinary or organizational structure. This is unfortunate because rural areas, farm and nonfarm, have serious economic problems that beg for consideration, research, and policy.

Sociology has its roots in human interactions. Like economics, the discipline took shape in the late 1800s. The parent discipline quickly spun off a cadre of professionals, the "rural sociologists," who were interested in rural themes. These individuals became a cohesive group in the 1930s.

For some decades, primarily before the two subdisciplines had organized on their own, economists and sociologists looked at the same rural problems, published in the same journals, and brought to bear the strengths of their separate disciplines in an effort to understand what was happening in the countryside. Although the two groups have a history of talking to each other, their efforts at working with each other have not always yielded critical insights.

Investments, Land, and People

During its first 100 years, the United States's westward movement stemmed from an implicit policy to establish sovereignty over the lands in the West. The federal government made modest investments in the unsettled areas that increased accessibility for settlers, but its policies did not necessarily result in the forms of public capital that would provide increases in the welfare of early settlers. Thus, surveying crews established boundaries, military outposts provided a modicum of protection, and rudimentary transportation corridors were developed between the interior and the eastern seaboard. The stream of settlers was rather constant, and at each stopping place, Frederick Jackson Turner's thesis regarding the frontier played out one more time (Turner 1893).

Immediately after the Civil War, President Andrew Johnson tapped Oliver Hudson Kelley, a government clerk in Washington, D.C., to head a team of observers charged with inquiring into the extent of poverty and devastation in the postwar rural South. Conditions in the South were so appalling that Kelley decided to act on his own and do what he could to help alleviate some of the suffering in the South's rural areas. His main thrust centered on creating a rural-based nongovernmental organization. He spent the remainder of his active life organizing and leading the Patrons of Husbandry, or as we know it today, the National Grange.[3]

The Grange was a private, voluntary, farm-based, semi-secret society designed to foster education, reestablish agricultural production, provide social organization, and set up buying and selling cooperatives in the South. The result was a self-help effort to improve the economic and social environments in which rural families lived.[4]

Kelley's work touched off and then amplified a half-century of activism among farmers and rural residents. His work expanded to other parts of the nation and eventually led to several agrarian-oriented organizations. In the 1890s, these organizations combined with organized labor to form the People's Party (the Populists). With this, rural America began to have a voice in, yet little effect on, national affairs and politics.

In 1880, the U.S. Census Bureau defined a rural place as any place with a population of fewer than 2,500. Although everything else in our world has changed demonstrably, this designation has proved durable. Even now, 125 years later, an area with 2,500 or fewer people is considered rural in the United States. The 2,500 definition makes little difference for research. However, the researchers working with urban-rural problems find the fixed definition to be very useful.[5]

In the early 1900s, President Theodore Roosevelt could not ignore the rural problems articulated by the Populists and the rural-based organizations. A city-raised patrician, Roosevelt was nevertheless sympathetic to conditions in rural America and to the growing and multifaceted divide between rural areas and urban areas. Under Roosevelt's guidance, the national political leadership reasoned that it was worth an attempt to close the gap. This closure would require vast sums of money as well as effort from politicians, scientists, and local people themselves. Despite the complexity of the issue, the stage was set for action.

In August 1908, near the end of his presidency, Roosevelt asked Liberty Hyde Bailey, a prominent agricultural scientist from Cornell University, to serve as the leader of the Commission on Country Life. The commission was a group of seven accomplished and well-placed individuals who were asked to inquire into the problems of rural America.[6] Although the primary focus was on farms and farming, the recommendations had much broader application.[7] The commission submitted its report in late January 1909[8] and listed the following as the "Main Special Deficiencies in Country Life":

- disregard for the inherent rights of land-workers;
- highways;
- soil depletion;
- agricultural labor;
- health; and
- woman's work on the farm.

These deficiencies provided the starting point for possible actions to help alleviate the problems. The "General Corrective Forces That Should Be Set in Motion" were listed as follows:

- a need for agricultural or country life surveys;
- a need for redirected education;
- the necessity of working together;
- the country church; and
- personal ideals and local leadership.[9]

Political parties, rural organizations, and the White House all showed interest in rural life and living. Rural communities and rural people quickly became legitimate themes for careful study by the social scientists and policymakers of the era. And the social scientists responded. Other commentators might specify other dates and themes, but the following are capsule versions of how social scientists responded during the time that has elapsed since Oliver Hudson Kelley established the Patrons of Husbandry:

- Before 1900, economists concerned with rural issues examined land and land settlement, availability of credit, transportation, taxation, and international trade (with special interest in the tariff) (Bailey 1897, *52–67*; Bemis 1893, *193–213*).

- 1900–1920 was a period of definitions and problem identification. By 1955, Hillery could look back and count 94 definitions of "rural community."

- 1920–1930 saw a move to themes related to the distribution and redistribution of the population. The frontier filled and disappeared, so settlement and resettlement became a critically important issue. The divide between rural and urban began to appear in terms of education and poverty (Meriam 1946).

- 1930–1950 was, for understandable reasons, devoted to poverty, the government's obligations, and the effects of institutional change. The Resettlement Administration (1935–1937) and the Farm Security Administration (1937–1942) played important roles in structuring rural areas. Their influences escaped careful consideration by the social scientists who contributed to the literature of that time (Tugwell 1937; Goldschmidt 1978).

- 1950–1960 was a period of relative calm in the literature. It was a time to catch up after two decades of disruption. Location theory, which had first appeared in the literature in the 1890s or before, began to make an important impact on the understanding of people and place (Jansma and Goode 1976).

- 1960–1970 saw the interest in rural areas soar, mainly because rural places were resuming their old trend of falling behind the remainder of the economy. Economic base studies merged into input-output studies, the forerunner of today's very popular work with IMPLAN (Kasal and Magelby 1988; Fox 1962).[10]

- The 1970s brought the hope and the probable failure of the Rural Development Act of 1972. It also brought the interest in "growth points," a specific recognition that not all places can grow at the same time. The highly touted population turnaround, much discussed in the literature, failed to sustain itself.[11] Conditions in the U.S. economy drew attention to landownership and tenure, credit, and foreign involvement in real property in the United States (Fuguitt 1985).

- The 1980–1990 period saw the comparison of grinding poverty in rural areas to the grinding poverty in urban America. Equal access to public services was important as a research theme and policy recommendation. Efforts aimed at self-help and community organization became popular, as did the broad issue of infrastructure (Tweeten and Brinkman 1986, Chapter 6; Beale, 1993).

- The 1990s saw the literature respond to the complete restructuring of rural areas at the hands of corporate and industrial utilization of rural resources. This decade also saw the development and maturing of a subliterature dealing with the desires and attitudes of rural people. Much research effort was reported dealing with the health and stability of communities and the ability of communities to organize and sustain themselves in the light of what was seen to be urban encroachment or development. The rural–urban fringe, present for decades, became a specific research and policy issue (Loveredge and Schmid 1993).

- In large measure, the work being done in this new century is a broad-gauge continuation that picks up bits and pieces from each previous time period and each previous topic. Population movement, urban encroachment, the importance of boundaries, and environmental themes seem close to the top of the research agenda.

No one pervasive thread appears to run through the literature. Discussions of migration—in either direction—are nearly always present, as are discussions of poverty, but these are most often just enumerations measured with respect to other variables. Typically, such counts fail to address or even find basic causes. The literature also includes the interminable homilies that describe bucolic living and happiness in the countryside. Just as often, the homilies comment on the serious disadvantages associated with the isolation that comes with rurality. It is surprising how many of the early leaders of the discipline took up either or both of these country living themes (among them, Kenyon Butterfield, T.N. Carver, M.L. Wilson, E.G. Nourse, Charles Galpin, H.C. Taylor, and Benjamin Waugh).

Land, People, and Capital

People and capital continually move into and out of any given rural area. They arrive to take advantage of the opportunities offered by the area and leave when the opportunities are exhausted. At the beginning of settlement, people enter and face a vast collection of natural resources. Other people also arrive to provide goods and services needed or desired by the primary labor force. At some point, after the area has absorbed as many people as it effectively can, productivity per person begins to drop and the population begins to exit. When this occurs, two options are available if the region is to maintain its viability as a community and as a definable economy: either labor must continue to exit, or infusions of capital must substitute for the now-depleted land and its associated natural resources.

Capital becomes extremely important to a community or an area. The relationships among land and capital and income form the basis for hypotheses regarding the health of rural areas. At some point, the availability and use of capital become limiting factors in the development and maintenance of rural areas. Even allowing for this degree of importance, land and especially capital enter discussions in sometimes broad or even ambiguous ways that may not lend themselves to either enhanced understanding or community policy. Most of the U.S. frontier began as unpopulated or under populated areas, but early settlement policies soon allowed population to overwhelm the carrying capacity of the local resource endowment, and no arrangements were made for a followup using capital instead of land-based resources.

The problem turned out to be more severe than simply too many people trying to exploit a limited natural resource base. The early influx of farmers, miners, and loggers, taken together, frequently provided an income base sufficiently large to induce entrepreneurs to make capital investments in buildings and inventories and to establish an identifiable trading center. In later years, when technology, transportation, and economics conspired to force the farmers, miners, and forest workers to leave the area, the entrepreneurs were trapped by the fixity of their capital—assets that could not be moved or sold. The town thus developed overcapacity and the value of the fixed and immobile physical capital dropped, perhaps to zero.

Circumstances of these kinds reveal the unstable relationships that exist between resources, population, and capital. The population that is dependent on extractive activities is large enough to attract capital, but the high returns to capital are short lived and the population overwhelms the resource base. Thus, both the extractors and the entrepreneurs find themselves in uncomfortable economic positions.

A sequence similar to this occurred, and is continuing to occur, in the Ohio River valley, the northern Plains, and the Great Basin in the United States. These areas—and others as well—are dotted with communities that at one time provided opportunity for labor (population) and capital but now sit, mainly idle, while population and new forms of capital investment either exit or pass them by.

Too Many People

At about the turn of the 20th century, economists and other social scientists began to note that too many people had taken advantage of the homestead laws, low-cost land grants, and other efforts to distribute the public domain. In 1914, Thomas Nixon Carver, then of Harvard University, reasoned that the continual migration to rural areas would reduce the average productivity of rural residents to the point that they would have to pursue alternative forms of employment or sources of income. There were three ways to stop this reduction in the productivity of labor: halt immigration into an area, pump additional capital into the area (allowing capital to substitute for land), or encourage people to leave (Carver 1914).[12]

The third option was quite clearly the easiest because it required no obvious intervention into local economic activity and it fit with the dominant value set of the population. It suggested that markets could make appropriate adjustments when misallocations occurred. However, encouraging people to leave would appeal mainly to those with high opportunity costs, including the educated and the skilled members of the local population. Carver reasoned that this would leave a residual population of individuals who were less productive and who would require additional infusions of capital if they were to reach national standards of economic or social norms. Any choice other than further capital infusions would result in continued disequilibrium between rural and urban areas.[13] Alleviating the disequilibrium would require continual and likely massive infusions of capital—industrial capital to provide jobs, commercial capital to revive or to buy out the lost business opportunities, and human capital to help provide a basis for future development or additional emigration.

Land as Capital

Even though Carver recommended letting the market do its work to send people away from an area, many jurisdictions, from very local to national, chose to invite more people in by providing easy access to additional land and natural resources.[14] Policies of this kind frequently pushed settlement onto submarginal land, and in so doing, they may have intensified the problems of poverty: family incomes were surely reduced by this move. Writing in 1929, Eke looked into solving the problem of settlement on submarginal land in West Virginia and found that in the state's poor agricultural areas, the tax loadings were not sufficient to support schools and roads. After some very straightforward calculations (his major assumption was a 4.5 percent return to capital), Eke concluded that the rural counties in West Virginia could sell bonds, buy the farms outright, idle the land, and pocket a huge surplus as a result of avoiding future expenditures on such public capital as roads and schools. Since there was very little industrial activity in the region, buying out the farms would effectively close the communities as well. Eke does not discuss the problems associated with driving the return to immobile, nonfarm capital to very low levels (Eke 1929).

Wehrwein and Baker, writing in 1937, drew the difference between urban areas and rural areas in Wisconsin by noting that each new rural settler required "start-up" capital costing $1,600 in public funds for the construction or improvement of public infrastructure, such as schools and roads. Although clearly unreasonable, the authors estimated that there was zero marginal cost associated with each new urban resident, so encouraging the rural population to move would result in a net gain of $1,600 for each person who relocated to the city. At the time Wehrwein and Baker were writing, Wisconsin was implementing a policy to withdraw and idle five million acres from settlement because of the expense of developing and maintaining roads and schools and other forms of public capital (Wehrwein and Baker 1937).

Also in 1937, Wehrwein noted that the proposed Columbia Basin Irrigation Project in central Washington was scheduled to irrigate 1.2 million acres, most of it to be homesteaded by irrigation farmers. Wehrwein noted that the previous waves of homesteaders had been forced into dire circumstances because they had settled on submarginal land. He reasoned that the Columbia Basin project offered the opportunity to right some wrongs, so he suggested that the federal government buy back and idle 10 marginal acres for every 1 acre brought into production in the newly irrigated lands—a trade of 12 million marginal acres for 1.2 million irrigated acres. Wehrwein did not specify how, when, or where the buybacks should take place. Nor was he concerned with the capital losses suffered by owners of fixed nonfarm capital.

In each of these cases—West Virginia, Wisconsin, and the Columbia Basin—the policy suggestion was to alter the relationship between population and resources in such a way as to improve the status of rural residents, through either increased income or increased availability of public services.

Other scholars of the pre-WWII era noted that rural residents themselves were contributing to the loss of capital whenever they decided to leave a rural area. In 1927, R.M. Rutledge examined emigration patterns from Cache County, Utah, and found that emigrants from the farms took with them notes or mortgages valued at an average of $2,000 per farm when they left. The reduction in local bank deposits coupled with the enhancement of deposits elsewhere left a $4,000 gap in capital availability between the rural and urban areas. Rutledge (1930) reasoned that the gap was not likely to close.

In 1937, Yoder provided additional detail in a similar study of Whitman County, Washington. Yoder isolated 246 former owners of agricultural land who had left their Whitman County farms. When these people left, 25 percent went to other farms and 75 percent moved to urban areas. Those who went to the cities took an average of $17,058 with them. Additionally, 115 individuals inherited money from Whitman County farm sales. Eighty percent of these were in urban locations and received an average of $5,068 each. In both cases—Cache County and Whitman County—leaving the farm represented a transfer of capital that further intensified the disequilibrium between rural and urban areas (Yoder 1937).

In 1947, Johnson, Timmons, and Howenstein produced a complex but overarching study in which they showed that, for the nation, huge expenditures would be required to bring rural areas up to a standard comparable to urban areas in the availability of services. They based their estimates on 1940 needs and costs and listed the recommended expenditures by function:

- Roads: $12 billion for improving 300,000 miles.

- Schools: $5 billion to bring rural schools up to urban standards.

- Hospitals: $420 million to make services in rural counties (1.5 beds/1,000 population) comparable to those in urban areas (4.5 beds/per 1,000).

- Health centers: $100 million.

- Water and sewer systems: $250 million.

- Agricultural education facilities: $150 million.

- Soil and forest improvements: $8 million to $10 million.

- Residential housing improvements: no estimate.

They calculated the total need to be nearly $18 billion (1940 dollars or, using the consumer price index to adjust for changes in purchasing power, about $180 billion in 2005 dollars). The authors also estimated that bringing these rural services and facilities up to urban standards would require 18 million to 25 million man-years of effort.[15] The authors did not specify which level of government should or even might undertake each of the tasks.

Continuing Migration

Out-migration is likely the most persistent theme in the contemporary literature of rural economies and rural communities. Many officials and policymakers continue to advocate policies that purposefully or incidentally result in this out-migration—advice that forces social scientists into a policy-related trap. Sociologists and economists advocate policies that provide incentives for people to move away from the limited resources of rural areas. At the same time, they recommend policies that provide the impoverished rural areas with the technological advantages normally associated with urbanity. The appropriate question is: will it cost more to keep the rural population in place or to move the people to the cities? And to this question must be added another: Will the cost associated with attracting new immigrants to rurality be higher than the rewards associated with their departure from urban areas? These questions do not have answers.

Today, the United States is dotted with rural areas that are unable to provide their residents with acceptable access to modern collections of opportunity. Moreover, it is slow and expensive to raise the residents' opportunity costs to levels that allow them to leave. At the same time, another population is seeking access to the collections of natural and capital resources (amenities) currently found in rural areas. Some economists suggest that a "hands-off" market can help people on either side of this issue realize their aspirations. However, that would likely require more time than our sense of justice allows, and it would be a very selective policy allowing only those who can afford it to move in the direction that is calling them.

Economists must be very careful in applying the interests and skills of their discipline to the problems of rural areas and rural communities. The body of theory is huge and sometimes complex. In addition, very little of the theory fits the problems found in today's rural areas. The theory that we have inherited divides into micro theory and macro theory—themes that appear in several chapters of this book. In an ideal world, many problems of resource allocation found in communities are suited to study using some of the aspects of micro theory. Micro theory works best when decisionmakers are trying to allocate resources so that the local cadre of taxpayers will get the greatest possible collection of benefits from the expenditures decided upon by those whose job it is to buy more of one thing and less of another. However, these same decisionmakers seldom have enough information to optimize in ways consistent with economists' use of the term. Local decisionmakers "make do" by compromising, and no suitable theory or even a suitable guiding principle is available for either compromising or making do.

The other great division of economics is macroeconomics. It calls attention to problems and possibilities in the economy as a whole. Macro theories or concepts are inappropriate for a small locality because they rest on the ability of decisionmakers to take actions that will nudge the level of regional unemployment or moderate the rate of growth of the entire economy. Control of the money supply is likely the most powerful tool used by macroeconomists. These kinds of decisions are generally beyond the purview of local decisionmakers in all but the largest of the nation's local jurisdictions. So where does that leave the economists who specialize in rural problems? Even though many rural and community problems lie outside their expertise, training and experience make them particularly suited for certain contributions. The short list includes the following:

1. An economist's training provides a framework that allows concentration on the appropriate allocation of available resources among possible tasks or jobs. Although economists are not able to determine how much education is needed to make the marginal expenditures on education equal to the marginal returns from education, data and research will tell whether adding to the existing education package will increase the opportunities open to those who absorb it. Similarly, economists are not able to apply the law of equimarginal returns to determine whether limited public monies should purchase a new fire truck or a new opera house, but experience and careful observation of the market at work should allow them to help individuals, families, and businesses know when the opportunity cost of their labor or capital is high enough to act on.

2. A simple tracking of the values and the changes in values of various forms of capital in local areas could lead to identification of serious problems and causes of a local disequilibrium. Observers of single communities or isolated economies can take a page from economists who track international trade. International transactions are rationalized by balancing a capital account. The same kind of balance should be highly interesting and highly useful to economists and policymakers who work with rural areas. Disequilibrium defined by persistent imbalances may provide early warnings regarding the future of the local economy.

3. The degree of access to amenities often lies at the center of conflicts between rural and urban areas. Economists can help estimate the demand for and virtual price of these. The estimated value becomes a vital part of the policies that define an appropriate boundary for development. Such values are also necessary to assist in establishing standards for the availability of certain amenity-related public services.

4. All social scientists need to visit and revisit the notion of space when that term denotes territory rather than a heavenly frontier. People are continually passing

across the boundary—however defined—that separates rural from urban. More-over, this passage goes both ways, with people being pushed and pulled from either direction. Knowledge of activity near the divide is critical to the provision of appropriate collections of public capital, private capital, and amenity capital on either side of the divide.

5. Perhaps most of all, economists and other observers need assistance in coming to grips with the limits of their discipline. Economics inquires into a very narrow dimension of the problems that seem to be forever plaguing people in rural communities or areas. Cooperation with sociologists and psychologists may be of great help as economists try to link with the future. This is especially true if we want policymakers to listen—and that should be one of the main reasons for our existence.

The century of concern that economists and sociologists have exhibited toward the relationship between city and country should convince others that this is a difficult topic with no easy answers. The literature of the field—which should be a barometer of knowledge, interests, and activity—is vast, repetitious, and sometimes naïve. Counting pages and titles tells how vast it is. The repetition of certain words—migration, poverty, housing, education—attests to the study and repetition of particular themes. There is no "proof" of naïveté, but one suspects that we may be guilty as charged, based on a literature that does not take the discipline forward at a very rapid pace. The discipline counts and multiplies, and adds and compares, but its findings very seldom inform policy. And this is a great disappointment that we hope the future corrects.

References

Bailey, L.H. 1897. Is There a Distinct Agricultural Question? *Economic Studies* 2(1).

———. 1911. The Country-Life Movement in the United States. New York: Macmillan.

Beale, C.L. 1993. Persistent Poverty in Rural Areas and Small Towns. Economic Research Service. Washington, DC: U.S. Department of Agriculture.

Bemis, E.W. 1893. The Discontent of the Farmer. *Journal of Political Economy* 1 (March): 193–213.

Carver, T.N. 1914. The Work of Rural Organization. *The Journal of Political Economy* 22 (November): 821–844.

Eke, P.A. 1929. The Community as a Factor in Classifying Land for Agricultural and Forestry Utilization in the West Virginia Appalachians. *Journal of Farm Economics* 11: 412–421.

Fox, K. 1962. The Study of Interactions between Agriculture and Non-Farm Economy: Local, Regional, and National. *Journal of Farm Economics* 44 (February): 1–34.

Fuguitt, G.V. 1985. The Nonmetropolitan Population Turnaround. *Annual Review of Sociology* 11:259–80.

Gilman, R., and P. Smith. 2000. Oliver Hudson Kelley, Minnesota Pioneer, 1848–1869. http://www.mnhs.org/places/sites/ohkf/ohkf-doc.html.

Goldschmidt, W.R. 1978. *As You Sow: Three Studies in the Social Consequences of Agribusiness.* Montclair, N.J.: Allanheld, Osmun.

Hillery, G.A. Jr. 1955. Definitions of Community: Areas of Agreement. *Rural Sociology* 20 (June): 111–123.

Jansma, J.D., and F.M. Goode. 1976. Rural Development Research: Conceptualizing and Measuring Key Concepts. *American Journal of Agricultural Economics* 58 (December): 922–927.

Johnson, V.W., J.F. Timmons, and E.J. Howenstein. 1947. Rural Public Works Part I: Needed Improvements and Useful Jobs. *Journal of Land and Public Utility Economics* 23 (February): 12–21.

Kasal, J., and R.S. Magelby. 1988. *Economic Impact Evaluation Using IMPLAN: A Case Study of the Nebraska Panhandle Project.* Economic Research Service, Resources and Technology Division. Washington, DC: U.S. Department of Agriculture.

Loveredge, S., and A.A. Schmid. 1993. Strategic Planning and Population Settlement. *American Journal of Agricultural Economics* 75 (December): 1160–63.

Meriam, L. 1946. *Relief and Social Security.* Washington, DC: Brookings Institution.

Peters, S.J., and P.A. Morgan. 2004. The Country Life Commission: Reconsidering a Milestone in American Agricultural History. *Agricultural History* 78 (Summer): 289–316.

Rutledge, R.M. 1930. The Relation of the Flow of Population to the Problem of Rural and Urban Inequality. *Journal of Farm Economics* 12 (July): 427–39.

Tugwell, R. 1937. Resettlement Administration Program. Senate Document 213, 74th Congress, 2nd session, 1936.

Turner, F.J. 1920 (1893). The Significance of the Frontier in American History. *Proceedings of the State Historical Society of Wisconsin,* December 14. New York: H. Holt.

Tweeten, L.G., and G.L. Brinkman. 1986. *Micropolitan Development: Theory and Practice of Greater-Rural Economic Development.* Ames: Iowa State University Press.

U.S. Country Life Commission. 1910. *Report of the Commission on Country Life.* New York: Sturgis and Walton.

U.S. Senate. 1909. *Report of the Country Life Commission.* Senate Document 705, 60th Congress, 2nd session. Washington, DC: Government Printing Office.

Walton, G.M., and H. Rockoff. 2004. *History of the American Economy.* New York: Harcourt, Brace, Jovanovich.

Wehrwein, G.S., and J.A. Baker. 1937. The Cost of Isolated Settlement in Northern Wisconsin. *Rural Sociology* 2 (September): 253–67.

Woods, T.A. 1991. *Knights of the Plow: Oliver H. Kelley and the Origins of the Grange in Republican Ideology.* Ames: Iowa State University Press.

Yoder, F.R. 1937. Migration of Population and the Flow of Farm Wealth. *Journal of Farm Economics* 19 (February): 358–359.

Notes

1. Some scholars argue that the early economists in the modern period—Quesnay, Ricardo, and Malthus, for example—studied agriculture. While this is true, it is also true that these scholars and others like them examined agriculture as an object of their studies of major aspects of economic theory. Agriculture was a vehicle for larger observations.

2. A major and undeniable starting place for public concern over rural issues came with Roosevelt's Country Life Commission which was appointed in 1909. See notes 7, 8, and 9 below.

3. The life and contributions made by Kelley are difficult to track and more difficult to verify. His role in establishing the Grange is generally accepted and fits with the "goals" stated above. In some respects, he was a reformer. He allowed women into the Grange on an equal footing with men. However, there was no specific place for former slaves. For additional information see Woods (1991). An excellent biography of Kelley was written by Gilman and Smith (2000).

4. Interestingly, Kelley and his associates made explicit their desire to keep the Grange out of politics. There would be no political agenda. Even so, the 1870s and 1880s brought a number of "Granger Laws" to statehouses in the mid-west and upper mid-west. Most of these laws sought relief from confiscatory railroad freight rates or usurious interest rates. The Grange was essentially ineffective in its lobbying for change at the national level.

5. The 2,500 figure has enormous ramifications in the world of policy. It frequently becomes the deciding limit between an area that does and an area that does not receive assistance and benefits from a particular program.

6. The seven commissioners were professor Liberty Hyde Bailey, editor Henry C. Wallace, professor Kenyon L. Butterfield, forester Gifford Pinchot, editor Walter H. Page, president Charles S. Bennett of the National Farmers' Union, and William A. Beard, a farmer/capitalist from Sacramento, California. Not all observers agreed with the efforts and conclusions of the Commission's conclusions; see Peters and Morgan (2004).

7. The Commission's report (U.S. Senate 1909) has been an object of mild controversy. This Senate document was not widely circulated. In July 1910, the Spokane (Washington) Chamber of Commerce published the report as the U.S. Country Life Commission (1910).

8. The text of the report breaks each of these into several more detailed problems. Education and social interaction themes are prominent across nearly all of the problems and recommendations.

9. In 1962, Karl Fox contributed a major article on the relationship between agriculture and the non-agricultural economy. It offers suggestions on how aggregation within the agricultural sector and between the agricultural and the non-agricultural sectors should proceed. His observations are still pertinent. See Fox (1962).

10. The literature, both technical and popular, on this point is vast. Calvin Beale and David Brown have also made significant contributions to the literature on this point.

11. Carver proposed that reducing the birth rate would solve the problems posed by the influx of people. While this may be "a good idea," it does not seem a reasonable policy choice at the present time.

12. Even in Carver's era, the possibility of shifting population from rural to urban places caused alarm. Carver himself characterized it using an analogy, "If we were distressed to find that water was flowing from one lake to another, we should not think it a very wise plan to try to pump some of it back into the upper lake." *Op.cit.* page 822.

13. Subnational jurisdictions had another reason for moving land resources into private hands: once in private ownership, the land could be taxed and thus make a contribution to the local treasury.

14. These figures are as suspect as any aggregate estimates of national costs of local improvements. Find details in Johnson et al. (1947). These authors made no effort to rank the problems in order of importance. The article is especially useful because of its inclusion of data sources and methods of calculation.

Part II

HUMAN-NATURE AND RURAL-URBAN INTERDEPENDENCE

Environmental Economics and the "Curse" of the Circular Flow

V. Kerry Smith and Jared C. Carbone

*M*ORE THAN FORTY YEARS AGO Emery Castle (1965) challenged agricultural (and would-be resource) economists to rethink the methods used to evaluate land management policies. He highlighted the importance of the physical interdependencies underlying externalities in economic analyses of land use (see box). Emery's insights have broad relevance today. Once these interdependencies are recognized as a major source for externalities, it is a short step to acknowledge a multiplicity of interactions that stem from the interdependencies among producers and consumers outside markets.[1] Indeed, within a general equilibrium model, the physical world implies that all external effects are reciprocal. The importance of this reciprocity is determined by the activities involved and the media providing the links between economic agents.[2]

Castle's Treatment of Externalities

... The distinguishing characteristic of the diseconomies being treated here is that they are non-pecuniary; they do not enter the decisionmaking framework through the stimuli provided by a decentralized pricing system. Externalities, of course can go both ways. A's production may also be a variable in B's production function. By the same token this type of interdependence may be reflected between production and functions as well as between consumption functions. These relationships may be illustrated by the following diagram. Assume four decision units—two producers, Pa and Pb, and two consumers, Ca and Cb.

Interdependencies between producers may exist as follows.

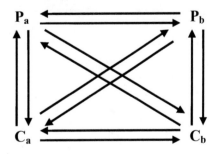

> With the four decision units, the possibility of 12 external relations exists. (Possible externalities are $n^2 - n$ where n is the number of decision units.)
>
> Physical interdependence is the main reason for the importance of externalities in the economics of land. Society has long been aware of externalities as they affect land management; the wide variety of institutional arrangements that have evolved to deal with them are testimony to this fact. As economic development proceeds, externalities become important in different contexts than was previously the case (Castle 1965, *547–48*).

Economic analyses of the interactions between agents have focused on those taking place in markets. Moreover, until recently there was general acceptance that under ideal conditions, market outcomes reveal to us *everything* that is important about the interactions that constitute exchange. Experimental economics has awakened renewed interest in the details of how learning arises through exchange and in the implications of agent heterogeneity for the process. There are many reasons for this reconsideration: few markets meet the ideal conditions; information is imperfect; and so forth. Unfortunately, most of the interest among mainstream economists seems to stop with efforts to understand market-based interaction. Emery Castle's argument suggests this is an important mistake. Our paper confirms his reasoning.

Numerical computations are used to establish the relevance of Castle's recommendations for the evaluation of policies affecting environmental resources. We use a stylized example to make a more general argument. That is, our results are based on a model developed to gauge the importance of environmental amenities for measuring the efficiency costs arising from tax interactions (see Carbone and Smith 2007). To illustrate how much the linkage between emissions of pollutants and the measure we use for each "unit of environmental quality" influences general equilibrium outcomes, we consider several modifications to the basic model. One of the factors differentiating these modifications is the relationship between amenities and leisure. A second considers the linkage between pollution and amenities as they contribute to preferences. In this second dimension, we consider two alternatives. Each represents a different strategy to describe how air pollution arising from the emissions of particulate matter might be introduced into a simple general equilibrium model. Both select measures for the benefits attributed to environmental amenities that are grounded in the empirical literature. One uses estimates of the marginal willingness to pay from the range of values found in its hedonic literature (see Smith and Huang 1995). For this case, air quality is hypothesized to be defined as the reciprocal of emissions. In the second, the Environmental Protection Agency (EPA) concentration-response model for the mortality effects of particulate matter is treated as the measure of air quality.[3] Both formulations are calibrated so that air quality is about the same small share of the benchmark virtual income.

Three results follow from these computations. First, the treatment of the emissions-to-amenity link is found to be central to the judgments made about the efficiency costs of any policy that seeks to raise revenue, regulate activity, or alter private incentives through tax or fee systems. The differential in outcomes for these two linkages between emissions and amenities reinforces Castle's early argument. Physical interdependencies are at the heart of how externalities influence the outcomes relevant to the design of environmental policy.

Second, these effects are not limited to Hicksian measures of consumer surplus.[4] Even if our efficiency costs consider only the price effects of a new policy (in our examples we use an energy tax), the physical connection between emissions and amenities as well as the structure of preferences influence the size of the losses. As expected, these effects are modest when preferences imply amenities and market goods are separable. However, they are not zero. For example, when the energy tax is 5 percent with preferences consistent with separability, the efficiency loss is 2 percent larger when pollution's influence is through the mortality concentration response function as compared with the inverse of emissions. The discrepancy increases to 75 percent when preferences are such that air quality and leisure are substitutes. In this case, the inverse relationship implies a larger efficiency loss than the concentration response. This finding is the opposite of what was implied in the separable case.

Finally, conventional benefit approximations (i.e. marginal willingness to pay times the estimated change in amenities due to the policy) are quite sensitive to the assumptions about physical interdependence. Estimates using the concentration-response calibration are more than seven times larger than the reciprocal formulation. However, they are largely unaffected by the general equilibrium effects on marginal willingness to pay used in these approximations. This finding does not mean that simple benefit approximations are accurate. Although they generally do improve the performance of price-based measures of the inefficiency of distortions, the errors for these measures are also large.

Overall, nonseparabilities are important in measuring the efficiency costs of policies with indirect effects on environmental quality. The nature of the relationship between emissions and air quality is especially important. Our analysis illustrates a linkage that might be described as the health equivalent of the physical interdependency that Castle highlighted for land uses. It is difficult to generalize our conclusions. It is reasonable to expect that the importance of these linkages will vary with the environmental resource considered and the sources for externalities, but the specific details of how this happens seem likely to depend on each individual application. Nonetheless, the general point remains solidly true, even though it has had a difficult time penetrating the perspective of mainstream public economics. Economic interactions outside markets influence what takes place inside those markets. This conclusion seems like common sense and would no doubt be widely accepted by the lay public. There appears to be much less acceptance among mainstream economists.

To attempt to understand the sources for this discrepancy between the public and experts, we consider why economists have systematically overlooked these situations. The next section explains our answer. It suggests that the circular flow model for economic activity has been a "curse" to progress in integrating nonmarket effects in general equilibrium analysis. The section also provides some added reasons to reconsider Castle's suggestions. They arise from Allen Kneese's proposal to introduce energy and materials balances, along with the residuals they imply, into a Walrasian general equilibrium framework. The following section summarizes the logic underlying nonmarket interactions in general equilibrium, outlines our specific model, and discusses calibration of computable general equilibrium (CGE) models with market and nonmarket resources.[5] The final two sections summarize our results and discuss the challenges facing efforts to use general equilibrium analysis with other environmental resources.

The Curse of the Circular Flow

The circular flow is probably the first "model" of economic activity that economics students learn. It describes the parallel real and monetary flows that characterize all the "important" interactions that constitute economic activity. The flows are treated as taking place exclusively within markets. The flow of goods and services from firms to households arises from trades made in output markets. The payments for these commodities are household expenditures and revenues for firms. Comparable activities in factor markets give rise to the flows of inputs from households to firms. The firms' payments are the basis for measuring their costs. They are also the source of household incomes in this pure exchange economy.

The origin of the model has been ascribed to a number of sources. Mirowski (1989), for example, suggests that initial attempts to describe economic processes as rational mechanics offer one explanation. The most comprehensive historical evaluation of its origin appears to be Patinkin's (1973) analysis attributing the logic to Frank Knight. As Patinkin notes, the diagram was originally intended to illustrate a circular flow of money, but Knight's use was different. He used it

> ... to illustrate certain basic aspects of value theory: namely, the differentiated roles that families and businesses fulfill in the specialization and exchange that characterize a market economy; the ways in which the respective activities of these units are guided by the prices of productive services, on one hand, and the prices of final goods and services, on the other; ... these two sets of prices enables the economic system to fulfill its basic functions of determining what to produce, how to produce, and how to distribute the product. (Patinkin 1973, *1037–38*)

Thus, in the circular flow model, we describe economic activities such that all the important interactions between agents balance "incentives" at the margin. Other sources of interaction are not precluded, but they are usually ignored. Most are considered to be of secondary importance.

The model allows production but the focus is on valued added. Labor and capital transform "things" (i.e., the material inputs to production). Marshall apparently labeled materials as "incidental" expenses in neoclassical production models (see Christensen 1989, *24–25*). This characterization is important because it causes the physical dimensions of production activities to be left out.

As Patinkin observes (1973, footnote 14, *1044*) the circular flow model received an increasing share of the spotlight in Samuelson's classic introductory text, and by the fourth edition it was presented three times and was important to his explanation of the general equilibrium determination of prices. Today the prominence of the model has not diminished. Hulten (2006, *213*), for example, argues that the circular flow model (CFM) "provides a useful architecture for sorting out many accounting problems associated with 'capital'" and that "Moving current accounting practices forward, the CFM structure should be a central goal of the field of national income and wealth accounting."

We argue that this recommendation would be a serious mistake from the perspective of developing a framework that permits natural resources and environmental services to be included in the national accounts. This process must begin with an appreciation for nonmarket interactions and the physical dimensions of consumption and production activities.

Ayres and Kneese (1969) were the first to discuss the importance of materials and energy balances in modeling consumption and production activities. Kneese et al. (1970) expanded this initial argument to describe how these effects could be integrated within a Walrasian general equilibrium model. Two strategic assumptions are made in their discussion. The first arises from using a Leontief or fixed coefficient technology to describe all production activities. In this setting, substitution responses cannot have effects that influence the generation of residuals and, ultimately, pollution. Second, the analysis focuses on the role of pollution impacts *for other production activities.* Environmental media add sectors to the activity analysis that describes production. However, these services remain unpriced. The Ayres-Kneese framework implies that policies that limit the use of environmental services (or price them) will raise unit costs but will not alter the patterns of input usage.

In their closing discussion of the welfare effects of residual disposal, they do consider what would happen if residual flows were allowed to affect individual well-being. Kneese et al. (1970) suggest that final product prices need to be adjusted to include these marginal damages as incremental "costs" along with effects of residuals on production and factor input costs. This strategy fails to recognize that physical interdependences, along with nonseparability, imply that demands for market goods are altered as external effects change. This demand response changes the level of the external effects when production activities change to meet these demands. This is the feedback effect we are concerned with here. None of the summaries of the Ayres-Kneese paper and related research consider this issue. Instead, they focus on their efforts to accurately characterize the materials and energy balances as ways to estimate residuals. Behavioral responses to external effects, especially those of consumers, are not acknowledged. Thus, their analysis strategy caused the feedback effects underlying what we label as reciprocity to be overlooked.

By contrast, Castle's emphasis was on physical interdependence—not in the flows in and out of natural assets but rather the interdependence due to the nonmarket interaction between agents.[6] Thus, the Ayres-Kneese accounting system required neoclassical models of production and consumption to be revised to take account of the sources and receptacles for residuals. Castle's suggestions focus on the additions to the modeling structure that are necessary to complete the story. They are about using the accounting system as a key element in getting the reciprocal effects of economic agents' choices into a general equilibrium model.

One might ask: how was this reciprocal relationship missed? It was not entirely overlooked, but it appears to have been misinterpreted. Writing about the same time as Buchanan and Kafoglis (1963) described how reciprocal relationships influence the incentives to supply public goods privately. Their argument was intended to demonstrate that in the presence of significant externalities that a market fails to internalize, private behavior may not be Pareto-inefficient. Under these conditions, Diamond and Mirrlees (1973) later described this result as creating the potential for anomalous behavior. They labeled these cases this way because the slope (with respect to price) of the aggregate compensated demand function is not guaranteed to be negative. A primary objective of their influential paper was to derive the conditions required to "rule out" the demand responses that strong reciprocity can create.

Modern public economics follows Diamond and Mirrlees's lead and, as a result, the literature largely ignored the issues raised by Castle's paper. In their framework, the feedback effects arising from nonseparability and reciprocity are usually excluded in general equilibrium analyses of environmental policies.[7] One of two explanations is offered: (1) amenities are average substitutes for market commodities; or (2) the importance of feedbacks between nonmarket impacts and market responses is an empirical issue. If the intervention is "small," then the effects of the feedbacks are likely to be small as well. Unfortunately, as a practical matter, we usually don't know how the economic structure and the scale of the intervention interact to determine the definitions for what are small and large nonmarket impulses to a market economy.

Overall, then, it seems to us that the widespread use of the circular flow framework to introduce general equilibrium concepts, along with the Diamond-Mirrlees proposal to rule out anomalies, has caused economic models to overlook physical interdependencies. We suspect few economists would debate this conclusion. However, they would likely debate its empirical importance.

To consider the significance of physical interdependencies for policy analysis, we must reconcile the trade-offs people would make to increase amenities with a full accounting of expenditures and incomes used to describe and calibrate general equilibrium processes. A corrected circular flow requires some measures for these services in the benchmark solution, along with the assumed physical link between emissions and ambient concentrations of pollutants.

To address those limitations, it is also important to acknowledge that we do not know the "amount" of the service that is consumed in the benchmark. Instead we "know" a marginal or a total willingness to pay for a loss avoided or for an improvement gained through a policy. This limitation in our baseline information is one of the motivations for the alternative specifications we have used to describe how emissions link to measures of the amounts of services of environmental resources.

Incorporating the economic values associated with changes in the amounts of nonmarket environmental services (or in their qualities), along with the physical interdependencies that influence them, into a model that describes a general equilibrium system does not mean the external effects are internalized. Instead, it requires that the structure treat amenities as outside individual control but nonetheless influenced, in the aggregate, by the representative consumer's choices. In short, the patterns of market and nonmarket outcomes must be reconciled so that the market economy reproduces both outcomes. The general equilibrium in this expanded view includes the expenditure flows and incomes (i.e., the circular flow) plus the emissions, the realized levels of environmental quality, and the benchmark marginal values. In this setting the analysis expands the concept of income defined in the circular flow. For our analysis, we define a concept of virtual income. It is the sum of the market expenditures and the virtual expenditures consistent with "purchases" of the nonmarket environmental services at a set of values for each service's marginal willingness to pay that would be consistent with the representative agent's "purchase" of the amount delivered. To see how this process would work out, we review the definitions for general equilibrium welfare measures.

Nonseparable Amenities and Welfare Measurement

The distinction between general equilibrium (GE) and partial equilibrium (PE) measures for equivalent variation depends on whether a policy change is assumed to alter prices of all (or a large number of) the goods and services a representative consumer selects. In this context, the policy change can be anything—a change in a regulation, a tax, or a limit on behavior. For simplicity, assume the change is altering the amount of a nonmarket good, which we label as q. Later, for the numerical exercises, we use a new tax as the policy. This allows for direct effects on the incentives for allocating resources and indirect effects on environmental quality. These indirect consequences arise because changes in the consumption of market goods alter the emissions that are produced. Each set of market goods and services would be responsible for a different mix of emissions. Because the tax changes the relative prices of final goods and demands respond, we should anticipate change in emissions. When preferences are nonseparable, these emissions changes can feed back and affect the demands for market goods, and so forth until the process stabilizes.

To formalize this logic, assume there are k market goods. The definition for the partial equilibrium willingness to accept (WTA) for a policy changing q from q_0 to q_1 (with q a desirable service and $q_0 < q_1$) is given in equation (1).

$$WTA^{PE}(q_0, q_1) = e(p_1^0, p_2^0, ..., p_k^0, q_0, u^1) - e(p_1^0, p_2^0, ..., p_k^0, q_1, u^1) \qquad (1)$$

$e(.)$ designates the Hicksian expenditure function. p_i is the price of the ith marketed good. The superscripts refer to whether the prices are evaluated in the baseline case (i.e., 0 = without the policy and 1 = with the policy and general equilibrium market adjustment). u^1 designates the utility level, which is held at the new value for the improved level of q (q_1).

This expression can be written in two alternative forms. The first uses the compensated demands for market goods that include q. It is given in equation (2).

$$WTA^{PE}(q_0, q_1) = \sum p_j^0 \cdot x_j (p_1^0, ...p_k^0, q_0, u^1) - \sum p_j^0 \cdot x_j (p_1^0, ..., p_k^0, q_1, u^1) \quad (2)$$

To integrate nonmarket resources into a general equilibrium description of a market economy, we need to modify this definition. The goal is to develop an extension to the circular flow logic that recognizes there are trade-offs between nonmarket goods (or services) and market goods that don't get recognized in the conventional accounting schemes. This parallel logic exploits results from rationing (see Cornes 1992) and rewrites the definitions for Hicksian equivalent variation in terms of virtual prices. More specifically, suppose q was priced. We can define this virtual price to correspond to what would have induced a person to select the level of q that is provided. Thus, this set of virtual price functions for q, defined as $\pi(q)$, ensure that the observed levels of $q - q_0$ in the benchmark situation and q_1 in the case with the policy intervention would be selected.[8] This respecification allows an equivalent description for the willingness to accept. It describes the change using these virtual prices to measure WTA. The willingness to accept is defined for a given level of utility. When we alter the expenditures to represent a situation where an individual is assumed to "purchase" q *and* realize the same level of utility in the baseline condition and with the policy, we must adjust the income available. For nonmarket goods, the services are available to consumers outside the market, so all income is spent on marketed goods. An analytical abstraction that alters this situation, allowing the logic used in computing general equilibrium analysis to be applied, must ensure that the initial conditions are consistently represented. This is what the virtual income adjustment in equation (3) is representing. It is "correcting" for the changes in virtual income implied by the change from q_0 to q_1.

$$WTA^{PE}(q_0,q_1) = e(p_1^0, p_2^0,...p_k^0,\pi^0,u^1) - e(p_1^0, p_2^0...,p_k^0,\pi^1,u^1) -$$
$$(\pi(p_1^0,...p_k^0,q_0,u^1)\cdot q_0 - \pi(p_1^0,...p_k^0,q_1,u^1)\cdot q_1) \tag{3}$$

The income "correction" corresponds to the last set of terms in parentheses on the right side of the equation. As we noted, it ensures that u^1 is realized when all goods are "priced." With this income change, equations (1) through (3) are equivalent expressions for the Hicksian equivalent variation for the change in q. The sum of $e(p_1^0, p_2^0,..., p_k^0,q_0,u^1)$ and $\pi^0 \cdot q_0$, or the virtual expenditure $-e(p_1^0, p_2^0,..., p_k^0,\pi^0,u^1)$, is the income concept that we use to calibrate a computable general equilibrium model with nonseparable environmental services. This virtual income allows the market flows and nonmarket outcomes to be reproduced for a benchmark solution.

Removing the Curse: Calibrating CGE Models with Nonmarket Goods

A general equilibrium can be described in terms of complementary slackness conditions that involve two sets of relations: (1) market excess demands and prices, and (2) unit profits and production activity levels (see Mathiesen 1985). Most descriptions for CGE models follow this logic. They restructure the problem and use the first-order conditions for a constrained optimization problem for a representative agent to describe the equilibrium for a set of markets. This reformulation offers a simple way to calibrate numerical models when homogeneous, constant elasticity of substitution (CES), or nested CES functions are used to describe preferences and production (see Rutherford 2002). Basically, the process involves selecting the substitution elasticities for the preference function (as well as for the production functions) and then using the expenditure shares (cost shares) for the function's distribution parameters.[9]

Introducing nonmarket goods into this logic creates several problems. One arises with the concept of externality. That is, with a single agent one might ask what reciprocal effects can possibly mean. Externalities arise as consequences of choices of market consumption goods. In the aggregate they are outside the control of each individual member of the set of consumers that is being described by a representative agent.[10] To meet this condition with a single representative agent, we assume the commodity representing the contribution of the externality to preferences is a quasi-fixed good. That is, the agent cannot choose its level. However, if the same individual's consumption choices alter the amount of emissions, then the analysis does take account of the implied change to the level of q. To ensure that this characterization mimics an externality, the link between q and these consumption goods (i.e., through the emissions) is not recognized by the agent as a "cost" or a gain from the choices he makes.

The placement of q in the preference function, along with nesting assumptions for preferences (or production) and the relative sizes of the elasticities at each step in the preference tree, will determine what is assumed about substitution or complementarity with market goods. With nonseparability, the level of q will influence market demands for the other xs. Moreover, if these xs contribute to processes (i.e., through the physical media) that cause increases or decreases in q, these changes feed back to influence market demands. Although this amendment in the logic is reasonably straightforward to describe, the calibration of a CGE model to include it consistently is not so straightforward. Estimates of the incremental willingness to pay for q and the benchmark level of q must be reconciled with all the components of an equilibrium of marketed goods and services, including these nonmarket responses due to the feedback effects.

Carbone and Smith (2007) exploit an argument by Perroni (1992) to amend the Rutherford calibrated share form of the CES. When q is quasi-fixed, a CES or nested CES is no longer a homogeneous (of degree one) function, so the logic associated with Rutherford's calibrated share parameterization of homogeneous CES and nested CES functions does not apply. This is where the virtual price logic discussed in terms of defining welfare measures can be used. That is, there exists an income adjustment with the estimate of the marginal willingness to pay for a change in q that would lead the benchmark level of q, designated here as q_0, to be selected. The marginal willingness to pay is a Hicksian virtual price, labeled $\hat{\pi}^0$ for this example. This amendment treats preferences or production as if they arose from a homogeneous CES or nested CES and the same calibrated share logic were used. Once the benchmark conditions are reconciled with preference and production functions, the nonhomogeneous form of preferences, with q treated as quasi-fixed from the perspective of individual choice, can be used for subsequent numerical analysis. Thus, the circular flow of market goods is preserved *and* the outcomes arising from the implications of these exchanges outside the market for the services of environmental resources are maintained as well.

Although the conceptual logic seems straightforward, once the problem is recast as Perroni suggests, important "details" need to be resolved to ensure consistency.

One detail arises from an issue we noted at the outset. With environmental services, often we know a willingness to pay (marginal willingness to pay) for a discrete (small) change in some measure that is assumed to be related to the services of an environmental resource. We do not know how the actual amount of services changes. In fact, we may not have measures for the services themselves. This limitation doesn't affect benefit–cost analysis because if we assume some estimate, say $\hat{c}$, corresponds to the willingness to pay for a change from z_0 to z_1 where z is a proxy for q that is correlated with it, then this is often sufficient information for policy analysis. In these cases, all we need to know is that the $\hat{c}$ corresponds to what people would pay for the change from q_0 to q_1. If the only way to measure it is by describing how people react to z, this does not prevent an evaluation of the policy intervention.

However, in calibrating the role of q in the market economy, we want a measure for virtual expenditures at the benchmark level of q. Knowing the value of changes in z (or q) does not necessarily help if we do not know the value of the level z or q at the benchmark where we wish to calibrate the model.

This situation contrasts with market goods where the national income and product accounts keep track of what consumers spend, so we can normalize prices to unity, treat expenditures as our measure of economic quantities, and be confident we have the expenditure share correctly scaled in the benchmark solution. When we have measures only for incremental willingness to pay, selecting a value for q arbitrarily (to compute its share) will then assign a level of importance to q in the virtual budget. That is, if we simply scale an arbitrary measure of q by a marginal willingness to pay, it is possible to exaggerate or understate the importance of q in the calibrated share preference function.[11]

Here we will avoid the problem by holding this share constant, but the issue seems to be a part of a larger set of questions. A general equilibrium solution for an economy with market and nonmarket "sectors" needs to be consistent with the market behavior and choices that are observed. As we expand the accounting of nonmarket choices and attempt to include them as if they were "virtual expenditures," it is conceivable that the patterns might not be reconciled easily. That is, we might not find a set of expenditures, factor usage, *and* residuals plus environmental services that all appear to characterize the equilibrium.

This issue is not a matter related to what we observe. The patterns have been observed and in most cases recorded. The problem arises in selecting values for the elasticities to describe preferences. In many cases we do not know how to select substitution elasticities involving market and nonmarket goods. Any effort to address this issue is beyond our scope here. Instead, we have used several different values that span the range of substitution and complementarity relationships. Moreover, we deliberately selected values for the marginal willingness to pay for air quality and the form for air quality services such that the share of virtual income is small.

We do consider a related issue that arises in the hypothesized relationship between the emissions of a pollutant and the assumed level of environmental quality. In our earlier example, z might correspond to an observable pollution measure and q the environmental quality as it is perceived by consumers. This interrelationship may be important to the behavior we observe. To address this question, we consider two hypothesized relationships between what can be measured for z and the assumed q.

The Numerical Model[12]

Our model uses a modification to a numerical model developed in Goulder and Williams (2003) as part of their numerical assessment of the effects of preexisting taxes on the excess burden measures for new taxes. The policy we consider is the same as one of their cases: a new energy tax. To allow comparison with their results, we also assume the presence of a 40 percent income tax. We use the same 1995 social accounting matrix for the U.S. economy. Our example economy has five final consumption goods (food and alcohol, consumer services, consumer manufactures, transportation, and utilities), four intermediate sectors (energy, services, agriculture, and manufactures), and one primary factor (labor). Our labor supply elasticities match their specification. Production functions for primary and intermediate goods follow their specifications and parameterizations. The primary distinction in our model is a formulation that allows air quality to be influenced by particulate matter emissions from production activities. The emissions coefficients correspond to the Environmental Protection Agency's estimates for these sectors for emissions of particulate matter 10 microns or smaller (PM10) in 1995.[13]

The amenity effects of air pollution are introduced in a nonseparable, nested, two-level CES specification for preferences. The relationship is given here using Rutherford's (2002) calibrated share form by equation (4). l_0, q_0, x_{CSVO} and x_{JO} correspond to the benchmark values for leisure, air quality, consumer services, and the other remaining market goods.

$$u(l, x_1, ..., x_5, q) = [\alpha(\gamma(\frac{l}{l_0})^s + (1-\gamma)(\theta(\frac{q}{q_0})^r + (1-\theta)(\frac{x_{CSV}}{x_{CSVO}})^r)^{s/r})$$

$$+ (1-\alpha)(\sum_{j \neq CSV}^{s} \delta_j(\frac{x_j}{x_{j0}})^w)^{\rho/w}]^{1/\rho} \tag{4}$$

where l is leisure, x_j, $j \neq CSV$ denote other market goods, and x_{CSV} corresponds to consumption of consumer services (with $\sigma_c = \frac{1}{1-w}$ the elasticity of substitution among the remaining five consumption goods). We assume $r = s$, and thus the relationship between s ($\sigma_1 = \frac{1}{1-s}$) and ρ ($\sigma_1 = \frac{1}{1-p}$) determines whether air quality, leisure, and consumer services are complements ($\sigma_1 < \sigma$), separable ($\sigma_1 = \sigma$), or substitutes ($\sigma_1 > \sigma$). ρ is calibrated to match labor supply elasticities and σ_1 restricted to be a multiple of σ to describe these three alternative relationships.

The final component of the calibration relates to the measure of q and its virtual price in the benchmark solution. In the benchmark the prices for all market goods are set at unity. The quantities of these goods correspond to expenditures and match the benchmark social accounting matrix. This same process cannot be followed for nonmarket resources. We use two descriptions for the physical interdependence of air quality as our measure of amenities on consumption and production activities. The first represents q as the reciprocal of emissions. Higher emissions imply lower environmental quality. We approximate the marginal willingness to pay using an estimate at the high end of those summarized in Smith and Huang (1995), $18.08 in 1982–1984 dollars for a unit change in environmental quality. This is converted to 1995 dollars and to units consistent with our measure of particulate matter.

Our second linkage between emissions and a specified definition for q relies on the EPA prospective analysis. It uses the concentration-response function that provides the basis for this assessment's estimates of the mortality risk reductions due to reductions in emissions of particulate matter 2.5 microns or smaller (PM2.5; see Table D-18 in EPA 1999). This function describes the increments in mortality estimated from Pope et al. (1995) with changes in particulate matter. This model relies on a hazard function that yields the increment in nonaccidental deaths, ΔM, as a function of benchmark accidental deaths, M, and an exponential function of the change in particulate matter, measured as PM2.5, as given in equation (5).

$$\Delta M = M(\exp(\beta \cdot \Delta PM_{2.5}) - 1) \tag{5}$$

Mortality risk reductions are valued using the value of a statistical life (VSL, the estimated marginal rate of wage compensation required to accept increased fatality risk in the workplace). We use $5.597 million per statistical life (the value proposed by EPA and converted to 1995 dollars). The model is calibrated so that it reproduces a share of virtual income in the benchmark solution that closely matches the case where the link between emissions and air quality is assumed to be defined using the reciprocal of emissions. We use the emissions of particulate matter in 1995 and then solve for the initial value for PM2.5, using the assumed value for the VSL and the parameters of the model such that the implied "expenditure" for the health effects avoided (at the 1995 level of emissions) yields the same budget share as we derived using the inverse of emissions along with the hedonic-based estimate for the marginal willingness to pay (2.84 percent).

Let k be the virtual expenditures from the reciprocal emissions calibration, then equation (6) provides the required solution for $PM_{2.5}^{0}$

$$PM_{2.5}^{0} = PM_{2.5}^{b} + \frac{1}{\beta} \ln\left(\frac{k}{VSL} \middle/ M^{b} + 1\right) \tag{6}$$

where $PM_{2.5}^{0}$, the benchmark level of PM2.5, and M^{b} = benchmark number of nonaccidental fatalities.

Both specifications imply a nonlinear relationship between emissions and environmental quality. An important contrast between the two formulations stems from the definition of a reference point $PM_{2.5}^{0}$ for ambient quality in the absence of the controls implied by the 1990 Clean Air Act amendments. There is also a distinct difference in the adjustment pattern each specification implies for the relationship between air quality as it contributes to well-being and the emissions of air pollutants arising in production that reduce air quality. Figure 4-1 plots the air quality level on the vertical axis and the size of the reduction in particulate matter, starting from the initial baseline level of emissions on the horizontal axis. Larger

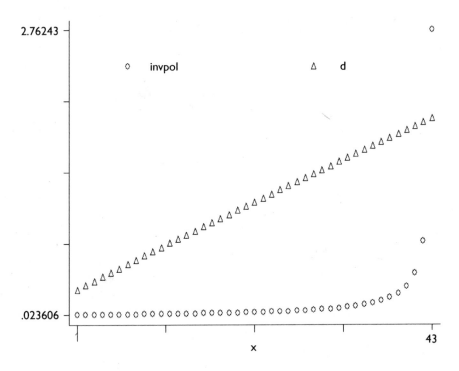

Figure 4-1. *Illustration of Reciprocal and Concentration-Response Models for Amenity Services*

Note: x = reduction in emissions from baseline emissions of 43; reduced x implies lower emissions and higher amenity services. invpol = quality of amenities determined by inverse of emissions in each period. d = quantity of amenity services determined by concentration-response function defined in terms of change in mortality rates as function of particulate matter.

decreases (in absolute magnitude) imply higher levels of air quality. As Figure 4-1 suggests, when air quality is defined as the inverse of emissions, there is a modest response to large reductions. As the size of the reduction approaches the baseline level of emissions such that the difference approaches zero, air quality increases dramatically. By contrast, the concentration response function implies consistently large responses to modest changes in emissions over the full range of values we considered. This difference no doubt accounts for the fairly dramatic difference in the findings implied with each model, as we discuss below.

Results

Our analysis considers three variations on the basic CGE model. They correspond to complementary ($\sigma_1 = \sigma/2$), separable ($\sigma_1 = \sigma$), and substitution ($\sigma_1 = 2\sigma$)

Table 4-1. *Comparison of Two Types of Physical Interdependency for Measures of the Effects of New Taxes*[a]

Policy energy tax rate (percentage)	Substitution pattern	q as reciprocal of E				q as concentration/response			
		EV	EB	PE	GE	EV	EB	PE	GE
2.5	Complements	1.079	1.507	-0.387	-0.387	-1.156	1.851	-2.933	-3.005
	Separable	0.775	1.181	-0.366	-0.366	-1.609	1.204	-2.738	-2.814
	Substitutes	0.495	0.883	-0.348	-0.349	-2.145	0.456	-2.525	-2.604
5	Complements	2.237	3.159	-0.759	-0.759	-2.671	3.822	-5.609	-5.878
	Separable	1.635	2.514	-0.717	-0.718	-2.954	2.558	-5.223	-5.507
	Substitutes	1.081	1.923	-0.680	-0.684	-3.997	1.102	-4.807	-5.103
10	Complements	4.744	6.850	-1.464	-1.463	-3.300	8.080	-10.325	-11.268
	Separable	3.565	5.579	-1.379	-1.384	-4.978	5.665	-9.572	-10.570
	Substitutes	2.482	4.419	-1.303	-1.318	-6.955	2.895	-8.771	-9.814

Note: The values are in billions of 1995 U.S. dollars.

[a] E = emissions of particulate matter.

relationships between amenities, consumer services, and leisure. For each model we evaluate the reciprocal and the concentration-response descriptions of the link between emissions and amenities. Finally, we follow Goulder and Williams (2003) by varying the energy tax from 2.5 to 10 percent. Table 4-1 reports our results.

To evaluate how physical interdependence, preference relationships, and the scale of the policy affect welfare measurement, four measures are considered. The first is the Hicksian equivalent variation (EV)—the income compensation required to be indifferent to the tax increase. It is the general equilibrium measure considering the changes in both relative prices and amenity levels. It corresponds to equation (4), where u^1 is now the new, lower utility level (i.e., with the tax). As a result, EV is the willingness to pay to avoid the change. The second measure is a Harberger (1964) approximation of the welfare consequences of the tax increases with the preexisting labor tax (EB). It ignores the amenity effects but does evaluate the response to the new tax along general equilibrium demand functions. The specific relationship is given in equation (7).

$$EB = -\frac{1}{2}t_k^2\frac{dx_k}{dt_k} - t_k \cdot t_L \frac{dl}{dt_k}$$

(7)

where k = taxed sector, t_k = new tax rate, t_L = pre-existing tax on labor, l = GE leisure demand, and x_k = GE demand for kth good (k = energy).

The last two measures correspond to Rosenberger and Loomis's (2003) unit value approach to benefit transfer as measures for benefits associated with improved amenities (in this case, air quality) that accompany as secondary effects of the new energy tax. This is a measure comparable to what is often used in regulatory analysis—a unit benefit for some change (derived as approximation from the literature) times the size of the change. In our case, this strategy is proposed as one basis for measuring the incremental benefits from the amenity changes due to the energy tax. The marginal willingness to pay for the amenity in the benchmark and the with-tax GE solutions are used as if they were the unit benefits per unit change in q. This estimate is then applied to the actual (GE) incremental change in q, as in equations (8a) and (8b).

$$PE = MWTP^0 \cdot \Delta q = \pi^0 \cdot \Delta q \qquad (8a)$$

$$GE = MWTP^1 \cdot \Delta q = \pi^1 \cdot \Delta q \qquad (8b)$$

Table 4-1 reports these results for six distinct versions of the basic model. The most striking aspect of our findings is the difference in the willingness to pay (EV) measures. The verdict on the tax would be reversed simply because of how the physical interdependency is treated. With q defined as the reciprocal of emissions, the price effects dominate the environmental quality effects. Incremental benefits as measured by our PE and GE approximations are 10 to 15 percent the size of what they are measured to be when we use concentration-response as the physical linkage between emissions and amenities. Looking a little closer at the findings in these scenarios, it is clear that when the amenity services are not separable from leisure and consumer services, the GE excess burden measure of pure price inefficiency is also quite different in the two cases. The concentration-response linkage implies *greater* efficiency losses because of distortions for the case where amenities are complements with (or separable from) leisure and consumer services and *smaller* losses for the case where they are substitutes than for the corresponding cases with the reciprocal linkage.

This relationship seems to be purely the result of the way the interdependence between emissions and quality is described. The equilibrium reductions in emissions are comparable for each preference assumption across the two models for the emissions-amenity linkage. It is the implied amenity change attributed to the policy that is responsible for these large differences. For the reciprocal relationship, the change in quality is modest for a change in emissions, as illustrated in Figure 4-1. With the concentration-response linkage, the same emissions changes translate into much larger increases in the amenity services. It is important to note that each of these cases corresponds to a different model for the economy. The scenarios are not reflecting "mistakes" in what is assumed about the emissions-to-amenity relationship. Each situation assumes the Δqs in equations (8a) and (8b) are correctly measured.

With each specification for the emissions-amenity relationship, the effects of preferences are what would be expected. For example, when amenities, consumer services, and leisure are complements, improvements in the amenity increase the demand for leisure and cause the new tax to have a larger effect than for the case where leisure and amenity services are separable or are assumed to be substitutes. We expect these effects would be larger when the incremental value of the amenity is greater. With the concentration-response formulation, the marginal willingness to pay for the amenity is substantially larger than with the reciprocal characterization. This pattern reverses for the case of substitution because the amenity does a "better job" in substituting, at the margin, for leisure. As a result, the price distortion effects of the new energy tax with the preexisting labor tax are smaller. Leisure can be replaced by amenities. This outcome is especially clear with the concentration response model because the reductions in emissions offer large increases in amenity services.

The general equilibrium effects on the unit benefit measures used in transfer appear to be negligible for the case of the reciprocal linkage. With the concentration-response function linking emissions and amenity services, the differences are larger. The magnitude of the difference between the PE and GE measures depends on the size of the tax and the nature of the substitution-versus-complementarity relationship among amenities, leisure, and consumer services.

With complementarity and small energy taxes (i.e., the case of 2.5 percent) the difference is about 2.5 percent. When the tax increases to 10 percent, the discrepancy between PE and GE measures is about 9 percent. For substitution relationships and lower energy taxes, the PE and GE estimates are more comparable. For larger tax increases, the differences become larger: 11 percent for the 10 percent tax rate. Finally, one might ask how the combination measures for EB-PE or EB-GE fare as a measure of the net benefits of policies that have market and nonmarket effects. The record here is that EB alone is a very poor gauge of the correct welfare measure for the concentration response case—more than twice as large as it should be. Adjusting for the effects of amenities provides a superior measure of the efficiency costs of the tax. The extent of the improvement depends on what we assume about substitution or complementarity of the environmental service with leisure and consumer services; nonetheless, the composite measure is always superior to ignoring this information.

In the situation where amenities are the reciprocal of emissions, EB is closer to the net welfare effects of the tax because the secondary benefits due to air quality improvements are smaller. Using the approximate benefit measure does improve the net effect measure, but the differences with EV are not as great as in the concentration-response scenarios.

Implications

The circular flow model provided the historical precedent that seems to have allowed modern general equilibrium models to ignore the physical world. Early research in environmental and resource economics identified the problems with this logic. Notable among these contributions were Castle's early writings (1965, 1966) and the work of Kneese and his collaborators. Today many economists seem willing to acknowledge the importance of these concerns as conceptual "details" but continue to maintain that they are not empirically important. We selected a stylized example that demonstrates why this view can no longer be supported. Using a small, transparent, general equilibrium model with the virtual expenditures on amenities related to air quality calibrated to less than 3 percent of virtual income, we demonstrate that the physical link between emissions and air quality can alter judgments about the net benefits of policies as well as the excess burden measure of the inefficiency costs of new taxes. In short, the physical world and how we assume it is perceived by people matters!

Certainly, this conclusion comes as no surprise to environmental economists. Nonmarket valuation, especially stated preference analysis, has established that estimates of willingness to pay for changes in amenities depend on how they are interpreted by respondents. Our point is different. These simple computations confirm that *market* outcomes and *market-based* measures of efficiency losses depend on how nonmarket effects are characterized. The physical linkages between emissions and ambient quality can alter excess burden measures as well as measures for the net benefits of a policy change. These effects are not due to misunderstandings of survey respondents. Rather, they arise from the nature and magnitude of general equilibrium interactions. These effects come in response to the descriptions used for physical interdependencies between the outcomes of economic agents' behaviors that contribute to preferences but do not trade on markets.

Our example selected the health effects of air pollution because they have been extensively studied. Despite this extensive research, it seems fair to suggest that we still do not have an acceptable characterization of health outcomes as economic commodities, comparable to other consumption goods and services. This observation may seem discouraging. After all, these cases, along with recreation trips, are very likely examples backed by a great deal of empirical research and compatible with the conventional nomenclature of general equilibrium modeling. As we move to consider open space or ecosystem services, the prospects for developing an empirical basis for integrating these services are not good. Thus, there is a clear challenge. The areas where there may well be the greatest need for a general equilibrium approach for benefit analysis (e.g., ecosystem services, where large changes are likely to affect multiple markets simultaneously) are most definitely vulnerable to manipulation. We do not know the details of how people's choices are affecting the ability of these assets to provide services. Moreover, there is no information to allow analysts to select among the alternative descriptions linking activities that damage ecosystem services to the objects of choice that people use and care about.

Incomplete information should not be used as an excuse. Measures of the general equilibrium implications of policy choices are likely to be dramatically affected by the decisions about how to characterize nonmarket environmental services. Learning what matters by considering alternative specifications is an important first step in this process. Bringing the nonmarket interactions that are inherent to the real world into the world of our models of economics activities is overdue.

Patinkin's historical account of the roots of the circular flow reproduces a diagram proposed by Fleeming Jenkin in 1887 that displays rudimentary people whose hands are connected with pen strokes to illustrate production and sale. It does something else implicitly. Agents are displayed as interacting with each other and interdependent. His text highlights exchange. As Castle suggests, this is only a subset of the mutually dependent interactions that can affect the market-based general equilibrium. Perhaps explicitly adding "rudimentary people" and ecological processes to the circular flow would be a better metaphor to help in understanding how to design and evaluate the sustainability of all interactions that affect well-being.

References

Ayres, R.V., and A.V. Kneese. 1969. Production, Consumption and Externalities. *American Economic Review* 59(3): 282–97.

Buchanan, J.M., and M.Z. Kafoglis. 1963. A Note of Public Goods Supply. *American Economic Review* 53 (June): 403–14.

Carbone, J. 2005. Calibrating Nonseparable General Equilibrium Models. Unpublished working paper, CEnREP, North Carolina State University, March.

Carbone, J.C., and V.K. Smith. 2007. Evaluating Policy Interventions with General Equilibrium Externalities. *Journal of Public Economics* (in press).

Castle, E.N. 1966. Multiple Use Relationship—Timber Production and Fishery Resources. Proceedings, *Society of American Foresters*, Seattle, 52–54.

———. 1965. The Market Mechanism, Externalities and Land Economics. *Journal of Farm Economics* 47 (August): 542–56.

Christensen, P.P. 1989. Historical Roots for Ecological Economics—Biophysical Versus Allocative Approaches. *Ecological Economics* 1: 17–36.

Cornes, R. 1992. *Duality and Modern Economics*. Cambridge: Cambridge University Press.

Diamond, P.A., and J. Mirrlees. 1973. Aggregate Production with Consumption Externalities. *Quarterly Journal of Economics* 87 (February): 1–24.

Dorfman, R. 1974. The Technical Basis for Decision Making. In *The Governance of Common Property Resources*, edited by E.J. Haefel. Baltimore: Johns Hopkins University Press for Resources for the Future.

Fullerton, D., Y.K. Henderson, and J.B. Shoven. 1984. A Comparison of Equilibrium Models of Taxation. In *Applied General Equilibrium Analysis,* edited by H.E. Scarf and J.B. Shoven. Cambridge: Cambridge University Press.

Goulder, L.H. and R.C. Williams III. 2003. The Substantial Bias from Ignoring General Equilibrium Effects in Estimating Excess Burden, and a Practical Solution. *Journal of Political Economy* 111(4): 898–927.

Goulder, L. H., I.W.H. Parry., R.C. Williams III, and D. Burtraw. 1997. Revenue-Raising versus Other Approaches to Environmental Protection: The Critical Significance of Preexisting Tax Distortions. *The RAND Journal of Economics*, 28(4): 708–731.

Harberger, A.C. 1964. The Measurement of Waste. *American Economic Review, Papers and Proceedings* 54: 58–76.

Hulten, C.R. 2006. The 'Architecture' of Capital Accounting: Basic Design Principles. In *Income and Wealth,* edited by D.W. Joregenson, J.S. Landefeld, and W.D. Nordhaus. Chicago: University of Chicago Press, 66.

Kneese, A.V., R.V. Ayres, and R.C. d'Arge. 1970. *Economics and the Environment: A Materials Balance Approach*. Baltimore: Johns Hopkins University Press for Resources for the Future.

Mathiesen, L. 1985. Computation of Economic Equilibrium by a Sequence of Linear Complementarity Problems. *Mathematical Programming Study* 23: 144–62.

Mirowski, P. 1989. *More Heat Than Light: Economics as Sound Physics: Physics as Nature's Economics.* Cambridge: Cambridge University Press.

Patinkin, D. 1973. In Search of the 'Wheel of Wealth': On the Origin of Frank Knight's Circular Flow Diagram. *American Economic Review* 63(5): 1037–46.

Perroni, C. 1992. Homothetic Representations of Regular Non-Homothetic Preferences. *Economics Letters* 40: 19–22.

Pope, C.A., M.J. Than, M.M. Nanboodire, D.W. Dockery, J.S. Evans, F.E. Spenzer, and C.W. Heath. 1995. Particulate Air Pollution as a Predictor of Mortality in a Prospective Study of U.S. Adults. *American Journal of Respiratory Critical Care Medicine* 151(3): 669–74.

Rosenberger, R., and J. Loomis. 2003. Benefit Transfer. In *A Primer on Non Market Valuation*, edited by P.A. Champ, K.J. Boyle, and T.C. Brown. Dordrecht: Kluwer Academic Publishers.

Rutherford, T. 2002. Lecture Notes on Constant Elasticity Forms. Unpublished paper. Boulder: University of Colorado, November.

Shogren, J.F., and T.D. Crocker. 1991. Risk, Self Protection, and Ex Ante Economic Value. *Journal of Environmental Economics and Management* 20 (January): 1–15.

————. 1999. Risk and Its Consequences. *Journal of Environmental Economics and Management* 37 (January): 44–51.

Smith, V.K., and H.S. Banzhaf. 2004. A Diagrammatic Exposition of Weak Complementarity and the Willig Condition. *American Journal of Agricultural Economics* 86 (May): 455–66.

Smith, V.K., and J.-C. Huang. 1995. Monte Carlo Benchmarks for Discrete Response Valuation Methods. Working Paper, Washington, DC: Resources for the Future.

U.S. Environmental Protection Agency. 1999. *The Benefits and Costs of the Clean Air Act 1990 to 2010*. EPA Report to Congress. Washington, DC: Office of Air and Radiation, November.

Acknowledgments

Thanks are due to H. Spencer Banzhaf and E. Roy Weintraub for suggestions in tracing the roots of the circular flow model; to Don Reisman, the editors of this volume, and an anonymous reviewer for helpful comments on an earlier draft; and to Kenny Pickle and Vicenta Ditto for carefully preparing several earlier drafts of this paper. Partial support for this research was provided by the U.S. Environmental Protection Agency Star Grant Program under grant number Rd83-092301 through RTI subcontract number 1-420.

Notes

1. Castle emphasized the extent of these interactions, using simple combinatorial relationships to suggest that even with four decisionmaking units, there was the possibility of 12 external relationships (see Castle 1965, *548*). In Castle (1966) the concepts are operationalized for the case of interactions between forestry and sport fishing.

2. This description adopts a structure suggested by Dorfman (1974) a year after the Diamond-Mirrlees paper was published. For him an externality was a situation where "… an action taken by some economic unit has a direct impact on the welfare or productivity of some other economic unit" (Dorfman 1974, *5*). His discussion acknowledges that these behavioral effects can occur in a vast number of ways, but he argues it is important to be aware of the physical media for some of them. The word "direct" is used to distinguish technological and pecuniary externalities. This is unfortunate because the essence of the distinction is the fact that the interaction is outside markets. There are physical and other media that provide the linkages that generate external effects. It is Dorfman's "myriad of connections" that lead to our suggestion to treat environmental externalities as reciprocal. Castle's sketch (see box, p. 43) also identifies interactions between producers and consumers and highlights the multiple possible interactions.

3. We do not use an expected utility framework with the concentration-response logic even though it underlies the strategy EPA uses to measure benefits in this case. An expected utility specification would imply separability. Ideally, a model that used the link to risk would also include the prospects for self-protection as discussed by Shogren and Crocker (1991, 1999). Under these circumstances, the commodities and services used for these activities would provide the sources for nonseparable relationships between the amenity and market goods and services. Our formulation can be interpreted as one way to approximate this more realistic but more complex description.

4. We use the equivalent variation measure of consumer surplus to gauge the net efficiency cost of intervention.

5. This paper uses the model developed in Carbone and Smith (2007). The details are not repeated here and are available in that paper's discussion and appendixes.

6. Dorfman (1974, *6*), writing nearly a decade later, makes a similar point, noting that "… externalities are technological relationships and not matters of law or institutional

arrangements." For him, common property resources were the physical media that allow the effects of one agent's activities to be transmitted to others.

7. One example where these types of arguments are developed is Goulder et al. (1997). There are many others. See Carbone and Smith (2007) for a more complete discussion.

8. This formulation parallels what would be found in the early literature on rationing (see Cornes 1992 for discussion). The virtual prices will be a function of all the parameters of the consumer's optimization problem, as illustrated in equation (3).

9. These distribution parameters are the coefficients weighting the goods in preference or the factor inputs in production functions. They are the $\cdot$, A, and ι parameters in equation (4). When a function is a nested CES, as is our specification for the current application, then the shares correspond to the share of expenditures on the good (or inputs) in the relevant nest.

10. This argument is developed in more detail in Carbone and Smith (2007).

11. A somewhat comparable issue arises with calibrating the role for leisure in preferences when it is not separable. We do not know the total available time for work. We know there are 168 hours in a week, but the bound for total feasible work is certainly less than this amount. The difference between it and actual hours worked defines leisure. Total available work hours also define full income. Conventional practice in calibrating the role for leisure has been to use the labor income and labor supply together with estimates of the Marshallian and Hicksian labor supply elasticities to determine the relevant share parameters (see Fullerton et al. 1984). See Carbone (2005) for a more detailed discussion of the general implications of these types of strategies for introducing nonseparability in a wide range of problems with general equilibrium responses.

12. See Carbone and Smith (2007) for a complete description of the model. This earlier paper uses the reciprocal linkage and a different set of benefit estimates for calibrating the contribution of amenities.

13. We adjust the PM10 estimates to correspond to PM2.5 using the EPA conversion factor of 0.56 to match the ambient concentrations with the benefit estimates based on reduced damages from changes in PM2.5.

CHAPTER 5

The New Rural Economics
Maureen Kilkenny

G ROWTH IN ECONOMIES is a consequence of numerous processes, including increased efficiency and expansions in productive resources. Populations
grow, employed labor expands, and output expands. By growth, we usually mean
increased material well-being per person, not just increased numbers of persons.
But with respect to rural development in high-income countries, the challenge is
often how to retain population alone. This is because the share of the population
that is urban has been steadily increasing at the expense of the share that is rural.
Later in this chapter we will revisit a chart originally presented by Mills in a book
edited by Emery Castle documenting that almost all of the growth in the urban
population share can be accounted for by the increase in nonfarm share of the labor
force. Nevertheless, there is a class of rural residents and shopkeepers whose material well-being is challenged by urbanization. What can be done to ensure that their
homes and businesses do not depreciate as a consequence of rural decline to the
extent that they become immobilized? What can be done to ensure that all young
people, regardless of where they are born or live, have access to quality educational
and income-generating opportunities?

In 1991 Emery Castle succinctly stated that rural areas are "remote, low density,
and dependent upon natural resource industry." He emphasized that the challenges
faced by rural areas are to harness the benefits of space as well as the costs of distance (Castle 1995). The hallmark of a great economist is the ability to focus on
essential abstractions. Also in 1991, Paul Krugman published a path-breaking paper
(1991a) and a short book (1991b) that formalized the economic development
trade-offs between places where the majority of residents are immobile and com-
petitively produce a commodity, and places where mobile residents produce varieties. Like Abdel-Rahman before him, Krugman assumed monopolistic
competition to close the model, and he labeled it "the new economic geography."

That new economic geography label echoed the label "the new trade theory" that Krugman gave to models of internationally trading countries, where there are also fixed costs of production, transport costs, and a monopolistically competitive market structure (Venables 1975; Krugman 1981).

The most famous demonstration that rural depopulation can arise because of transport cost reductions is arguably contained in the book summarizing the new economic geography by Fujita in collaboration with Krugman and Venables (1999). Drawing on the journal articles they published during the 1990s, they model urbanization relative to "agriculture" by formalizing the trade-off between increasing returns and the costs of serving a dispersed market of "farmers" tied to their land. Their conclusions might be summarized crudely by saying that urbanization is inevitable. There does not appear to be anything a government can do to promote a dispersed pattern of population or industry that does not entail a loss of economy-wide welfare (Krugman 1996).

Krugman-style new economic geography models provide only one vision—a vision that has nothing to say about rural development, only decline. Other models offer alternative visions. But traditional rural economic models are not that useful, either. Traditional rural economics has relied upon aspatial macroeconomics, supply-side ideas, and simulation models that have lost credibility by exaggerating the positive feedback opportunities in rural communities. Policies targeting a producing sector (agriculture) have been the main vehicle for rural development. Spatially moot input–output simulation models have been the main analytical tool. The point of this chapter is that the "new rural economics" rests on explicit spatial microfoundations, demand-side ideas, and empirically tested models.

The new rural economics is inspired by Paul Krugman's new economic geography, in which positive feedback and local growth are driven by consumers' preferences for variety. But it has many other progenitors, some much older, some very recent. The new rural economics is explicit that a critical mass of customers within a reasonable distance is important (Berry 1967) and, following Adam Smith, Marshall (1920), Stigler (1951), and Holmes (1999), that the division of labor is limited by the extent of the market. The new rural economics empirically scrutinizes the appropriateness of assumptions and implications of economies of agglomeration. Ideally, the new rural economics emphasizes models that have been tested on rural data over either untested theories or simulations using input–output, computable general equilibrium, or new economic geography models.

This chapter reviews old, new, and really new economic geography. It notes the strengths and weaknesses of the new economic geography with respect to modeling rural economies. It highlights empirical tests of both old and new economic geography ideas. It concludes with some suggestions for future rural economics research.

Economic Geography

In general, economic geography is not "new," as Samuelson (1983) elucidates in his article "Thünen at Two Hundred" about the father of marginal analysis. Broadly, economic geography is the study of what happens where. Why do firms and people tend to concentrate in a few locations (cities) rather than spread out evenly across the countryside? What explains the number and variety of economic activities in a region? What are the economic diversification prospects for rural places that are costly to get to or from and have low population densities? According to a long tradition in spatial economics, the answers to these questions depend on the trade-offs between scale (fixed costs and externalities) and the cost of distance (transport costs) and the fact that some crucial productive resources (fertile land or resources) are completely immobile and unevenly distributed across space.

Hoover (1948) identified three "foundation stones" half a century ago and summarized them more recently as follows:

> To sum up, an understanding of spatial and regional economic problems can be built on three facts of life: (1) natural-resource advantages, (2) economies of concentration, and (3) costs of transport and communication. In more technical language, these foundation stones can be identified as (1) imperfect factor mobility, (2) imperfect divisibility, and (3) imperfect mobility of goods and services." (Hoover and Giarratani, 1999, Chapter 1)

Imperfect divisibility and transportation costs currently preoccupy urban economists (and frighten rural economists). When a process is homogeneous of degree 1 (constant returns to scale), a doubling of inputs leads to doubled output. If a process is subject to increasing returns to scale (IRS), output more than doubles when inputs are doubled. By the same token, when a larger unit subject to IRS is halved, each half-unit produces less than half. This highlights that rural industry is not plagued by decreasing returns to scale (as some have erroneously argued) but subject to increasing returns to scale that rural firms are too small to enjoy. It underscores the critical importance of local demand. It also suggests why there is less product diversity or variety in the material goods available in rural areas. And this suggests why rural communities can be unattractive places to live. If a lack of product variety is not more than offset by other rural amenities, the quality of rural life suffers, and out-migration may be the consequence.

The most ubiquitous source of increasing returns to scale (imperfect divisibility) is fixed costs. And the most ubiquitous fixed costs are brick-and-mortar shops and shopkeeper labor. We tend to forget that a service sector establishment must have at least one person behind the service counter during every open hour, even if no customer ever appears. That means that a portion of labor is a fixed cost for that type of establishment. Our colleagues doing urban economics may be able to justify abstracting from that, but not new rural economists. Traditional rural economists often do, however, as when we use input-output impact analyses to investigate the local economic consequences of an expansion or contraction in one sector.

Average versus Marginal

A multiplier analysis relies on an assumption that the marginal effect of a change in one component of an economy can be measured by an average effect measured by the share of the total. The simplest example is the *economic base employment multiplier*. Total employment, E, comprises employment in export industry, often called "basic," E_B, and employment in service sectors, called nonbasic, E_N. Thus $E = E_B + E_N$. This accounting identity is a fact. The elaboration that follows, however, is suspect. Assuming that all nonbasic employment is dependent solely upon total employment, such that nonbasic employment equals an unchanging, constant, or average share, labeled β of total employment, manipulation of this identity gives an estimate of the change in total employment associated with a change in basic employment: $\partial E/\partial E_B = 1/(1-\beta)$. This "multiplier" derived from an accounting identity has no microfoundations and is thus unlikely to qualify for inclusion in the toolkit of the new rural economics.

The unrealistic implications of such multiplier models can be described as follows. When we assume that all service sector enterprises are operating at full capacity, this multiplier can be 4 or 5 or more, indicating that each new basic job filled in a small town ultimately induces 5 or 6 new total jobs. In fact, the identity indicates simply that 1 new basic job increases total employment by 1 job. The assumption that there would be nothing to do at all if there were no export markets (i.e., "we can't get rich taking in our own washing") is hard to justify. What else are all employees doing if not making a good or providing a service to meet human needs ("taking in our own washing")? Hoover and Giarratani (1999) provide a passionate critique of the "export" base assumption. The other two assumptions—that all activities display constant returns to scale and that all operate at full capacity—are also simply not appropriate for short-run ("impact") models of rural communities.

Rural service establishments rarely operate at full capacity. The rural businesses we are concerned about could happily serve many more clients per day without having to employ a single additional person. Table 5-1 and Figure 5-1 illustrate the implications for the rural multiplier of excess capacity in rural transport, retail, health, education, or administrative activities. The table shows the average non-

Table 5-1. *Rural Multipliers*

		Sector share of total employment	Nonbasic enterprises below capacity				
			0%	24%	51%	70%	100%
Farming, manufacturing, and construction	Basic	22%					
Wholesale and retail trade	Nonbasic	18%	24%				
Transportation and management	Nonbasic	22%	28%	28%			
Health and education	Nonbasic	15%	19%	19%	19%		
Administration and not-elsewhere-classified	Nonbasic	23%	30%	30%	30%	30%	
	Nonbasic enterprises at *full* capacity		100%	76%	49%	30%	0%
	Employment multiplier		4.6	2.5	1.6	1.3	1.0

Note: Rural multipliers are low because many nonbasic sectors operate below full capacity.
Source: 2003 county business pattern data on all nonmetro counties.

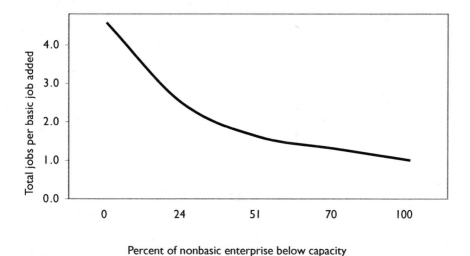

Percent of nonbasic enterprise below capacity

Figure 5-1. *Local Basic Employment Multipliers Are Inversely Related to Excess Capacity in Local Nonbasic Sectors*

metropolitan county's business pattern in 2003. Almost four-fifths of the people are employed in service sectors. If none of those establishments are operating at full capacity, an increment of 10 more basic sector jobs will net the town 10 more basic jobs. That is, the rural economic base multiplier is close to 1 in small towns where the service sectors are operating well below capacity.

Another important aspect of "average versus marginal" concerns pricing. Market prices are determined by local supply and demand. Local supply is determined by the number of establishments and their sizes. Even in the presence of internal or external scale economies, establishment size is determinant in general equilibrium. The accessible supply of factors of production and the effective demand for the product determine the size of establishments.

Local demand is determined by the number of local factors of production, the returns they capture, and their consumption preferences. But when we are explicit about increasing returns and fixed costs, which are central to open, stay-in-business, relocate, and shut-down decisions, market prices must cover more than marginal costs. Prices must also cover average costs, which are higher than marginal costs of production throughout the relevant range of output. This means that we have to be explicit about market structure. And finally, the relevant full or delivered price paid by customers is gross of transport costs, borne either by the producer who ships it or by the consumer who shops for it.

Transport Costs

The tyranny of imperfect divisibility looms larger for rural economies because of the imperfect mobility of goods, services, and resources: transport is costly. Hoover's "three foundation stones" always act in concert, never in isolation. Despite the ubiquity of increasing returns to scale, very few things are feasibly provided by single, very large firms. That is because the costs of transporting or collecting goods or services from a single location almost always outweigh the costs of opening other plants to serve customers who are farther away. Given dispersed resources and population, and technologies with nonzero minimum efficient scale (the level of output at which all economies of scale are exploited and average costs of production are lowest), there is a socially optimal number of firms dispersed across space that minimizes both fixed and transport costs paid by society. This can rationalize the dispersion of economic activity and population. But resources are not evenly dispersed. And clearly, neither is population.

Since the 1890s, overland transport costs have fallen 90 percent (Glaeser and Kohlhase 2004). And just since the 1950s, water-borne transport rates for bulk products have decreased up to 70 percent because of improved maritime technology (Lundgren 1996). Krantz (2000) argues that transportation remains a major determinant of location because relative spending on transport (6 to 8 percent of GDP across countries in the Organisation for Economic Co-operation and Development, OECD) has been relatively constant during the industrialization and modernization process. In contrast, Glaeser and Kohlhase (2004) argue that transport costs for goods have fallen enough to be negligible. We can reconcile their two positions by noting that while transport cost rates have fallen, our use of transport cost services has increased, and the mix of modes of transport has changed substantially. In particular, in the United States we buy more things that require high-cost truck transport (about 25 cents per ton-mile) and much less using cheap rail transport (3 cents).

Water-borne transport has always been 100 times cheaper than overland transport, and rail transport about 10 times cheaper than truck. The improvements in transport technology and infrastructure over the past century have meant that the relative costs of moving things *within* countries has fallen more than the cost of moving things *between* countries. What this has meant for rural development depends in part on how it has affected the size of markets and thus the optimal scale of enterprise. A region need not export to enjoy the benefits of returns to scale, specialization, and trade if its accessible local market is large enough. Markets can be larger when transport costs are lower.

Reductions in overland transport costs can make continental markets more accessible so that the benefits of trade can be captured just as well through *intra*regional specialization and *intra*regional trade. The economic history of the United States is one example of the efficacy of growth led by the domestic market. In developed economies where market areas are already all-inclusive, however, reductions in transport costs cannot make all market areas larger. As all transport cost rates fall, larger producers or establishments expand their market share at the expense of smaller ones. Thus, *intra*national transport cost reductions could be inimical to rural development. Good roads could be bad for rural development.

To demonstrate, consider two competing suppliers located in a linear space at A and B (Figure 5-2). Assume that the establishment at A is the lower-cost, larger supplier. Formally, $c_B = (1+\beta)c_A$, $\beta > 0$. In reality, average cost (c_i) is endogenous.

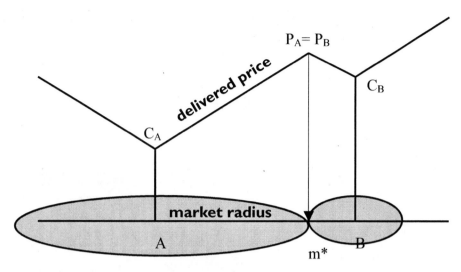

Figure 5-2. *Average Costs (fixed costs) and Transport Costs Determine the Size of an Establishment's Accessible Market and the Number of Establishments across Space*

The establishment at A may operate at lower cost simply because it serves a larger market and thus enjoys greater internal economies of scale, but we ignore that here to close the model.

Assume for simplicity that customer density is constant over space. Assume perfect competition. The delivered price charged by the large establishment at A just covers average costs plus transport: $P_A = c_A + t \cdot m_A$, where m_A is the distance to a customer from A. By the same logic, the delivered price of establishment B is $P_B = c_B + t \cdot m_B$. Normalizing the distance between A and B to 1, $m_B = (1 - m_A)$. The market radii of each firm thus measure market share of each on the interval AB. Under these abstractions, $P_B = (1 + \beta)c_A + t(1 - m_A)$.

The market share of the large establishment at A is determined by the $m^\star$ at which A's delivered price equates with B's: $m_A{}^\star = [\beta \cdot c_A + t]/2t$. By the quotient rule, $\frac{dm_A{}^\star}{dt} < 0$. This simple model highlights that as transport cost rates decline system-wide, the establishment with the larger initial market area will gain market area and market share at the expense of the smaller establishment (Figure 5-3). Furthermore, these pessimistic implications are strengthened if average costs (c_i) are endogenous. The foundation stones of "old" economic geography (transport costs, fixed costs, and the associated internal increasing returns to scale) suffice to explain the spatial concentration effect of transport cost reductions, without regard to assumptions about external localization economies of scale or noncompetitive market structures.

Another argument against transport cost reductions as a rural development strategy arises when some transport cost rates fall relative to others. In particular, using a general equilibrium model in the von Thünen tradition, Nerlove and Sadka (1991) showed that as the cost of transporting agricultural goods falls relative to

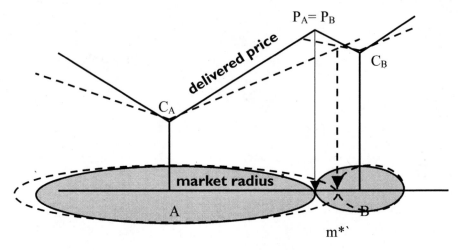

Figure 5-3. *A Reduction in Transport Cost Rates Supports the Expansion of Larger (big-city) Establishments at the Expense of Smaller (rural) Ones*

the cost of manufactures transport, it becomes economically feasible to cultivate land farther and farther from the city. The relative reduction in agricultural transport cost rates leads to (1) less farm labor per acre, (2) lower agricultural terms of trade, (3) a lower and more dispersed rural population, and (4) an increased proportion of the labor force that works in cities. In other words, according to their hypotheses, good roads are bad for rural development. Nerlove and Sadka's model, however, does not allow for the endogenous location of nonfarm activity. Thus, it cannot be used to explain why there are any nonfarm households outside the city, and it is not a model that should be used to analyze rural development in general.

The Demand-Side Basis of Localization Economies of Scale

"Old" economic geography has limitations. If internal returns to scale due to fixed costs were the only sources of increasing returns to size and resources were evenly distributed across space—to minimize the total costs of production and distribution— all economic activity would most efficiently locate at the best ports. Labor would concentrate at port cities. Those cities would continue to grow as new industries opened there to minimize transport costs to the markets. This rationalizes the preeminence of port cities like New York, Chicago, and Los Angeles, but it has nothing to say about Denver, Austin, or Reno, much less rural communities. It also offers no rationale for the observed co-location of competing establishments in the same place.

The widely observed clustering of similar industries in one location can be rationalized two ways. One is that the minimum efficient scale of an establishment in the industry is smaller than the size of the local market. Thus we expect to find more than one establishment supplying the same type of good or service. The other way to rationalize the clustering of competing establishments in the same place is that there are external increasing returns to scale, known as localization economies of scale.

There are a number of sources of localization economies of scale. With respect to service sector activity, known as "shopping goods" because the consumer bears the cost of transport, demand side externalities are paramount.

For example, clothing and shoe stores choose to aggregate in malls or districts, zoning regulations or not, because shoppers enjoy economies of scale in their transport activity by driving to one site where they can collect many things rather than to dispersed sites. Standalone shops see fewer customers, sell less, profit less. The static localization externality that supports the clustering of shopping goods establishments is called a "shopping goods externality." The empirical relevance of this for small towns has been ably demonstrated by Shonkwiler and Harris (1996), an excellent example of the new rural economics.

A different demand-side externality also supports the clustering of "shipping goods" establishments. Shipping goods are those for which the producer bears the cost of transport, so suppliers capture any returns to scale in transport. Farming, fisheries, forestry, and manufacturing are all shipping goods industries and all have rural location quotients significantly higher than average (Holmes and Stevens 2004). The relevant demand in this case is interindustry demand. Given transport and fixed costs and the associated minimum efficient scale and maximum extent of the market, there exists a minimum demand, threshold, or critical mass of customers necessary to support the existence of local input supply or output processing establishments at their minimum efficient scale. In particular, Adam Smith said, "the division of labor is limited by the extent of the market" (Stigler 1951). As an establishment's market increases, the opportunities to achieve economies of scale in intermediate input supply or output processing also increase.

These "Adam Smith" demand-side localization economies of scale are very relevant in rural farming communities, for example. They rationalize why fiercely competitive farmers spend significant resources promoting even fiercer competition on the supply side. Farmers do not support Future Farmers of America, 4-H, agricultural education, and beginning farmer clubs just because imitation is the sincerest form of flattery. Nor do they want demand for farmland to rise so that they can sell out. They want more farmers in their locality because of the benefits they all reap when they achieve critical mass as demanders of farm inputs, implements, and processing opportunities. Farmer cooperatives are a vertically integrated alternative to static Adam Smith localization economies of scale and specialization in demand.

A second type of static localization economy of scale that rationalizes the spatial clustering of shipping goods establishments was identified by Marshall (1920). He argued that the matching of firms and workers is more efficient (lower cost) where there is a larger labor pool. The empirical relevance of these types of externalities has been demonstrated by Holmes (1999) with respect to manufacturing in the United States (see also Barkley and Henry 1998). Note that the implications of Marshallian localization economies of scale for rural areas are pessimistic.

In sum, demand-side explanations have always been important, so it is surprising that traditional rural economics paid so little attention to them. In his seminal work in the 1930s, Chamberlin formalized a demand-side explanation for the observed multiplicity of similar firms in a single economy with his model of *monopolistic competition* (Chamberlin 1962). In his model, each firm in an industry produces one variety of the good (monopolistic). The market structure he formalized allows firms to price to just cover average costs, and there are no barriers to entry (competition). Because he assumed people prefer to consume as many varieties as possible, there is demand for each firm's product. Chamberlin was not trying to explain the clustering of similar firms in a single location, however, so he reasonably posited that the number of firms in the industry would be so large that the entry of a single firm would have a negligible effect on the residual demand, and thus the prices consumers would pay, for the products of all the other firms in the industry. This is an inframarginality assumption. In Chamberlin's world, competition between establishments in the same industry is *nonlocalized*.

In contrast to Chamberlin, Hotelling (1929) described the locational choices of firms in an industry in which all firms are rival, in the sense that each captures the market closest to it. Hotelling argued that firms would concentrate in the center of a market. With respect to establishments, this means that businesses choose to locate in a central place (see Mulligan 1984).

A third structure was posited by Kaldor (1935), who argued that competition was *localized*. Kaldor noted that the number of firms supported in any one location is too low for inframarginality to be a valid assumption. A new entrant can affect the sales of the other firms in the neighborhood, but it does not necessarily affect the sales of more remote firms. Not all firms are rivals, as in Hotelling, or inframarginal, as in Chamberlin. The analysis of establishment location in the context of Kaldor's market structure, however, begs the application of noncooperative game theory. At least, the local market price must be endogenous to the entrance of a new establishment, which means that the price-location problem does not have a closed-form solution and must be solved using computable general equilibrium (CGE) techniques (e.g., Kilkenny 1998).

The New Economic Geography

Unfortunately, neither game theory nor CGE techniques for solving fixed-point problems were well-developed until the 1980s. Thus, economists could not operationalize Kaldor's localized competition model. Rather, Chamberlin's theory of monopolistic competition was widely applied, as formalized by Dixit and Stiglitz to explain macroeconomic geography. Krugman applied it to close a model of trading regions, and the new economic geography was born. Fujita et al. (1999) provide a summary.

The prototypical new economic geography model has just two regions, two industries or goods ("food" and "manufactures"), and two primary factors of production ("farmers" and "workers"). Manufacturing is subject to internal increasing returns to scale. A monopolistically competitive market structure is assumed. Each firm produces a differentiated product, and each consumer demands a positive quantity of every variety. Firms do not need to disperse across space to serve the same markets profitably, but they do incur delivery costs to serve consumers in the other region. The degree of product differentiation is represented by the parametric elasticity of substitution ($\hat{U}$) characterizing consumer preferences.

Each household consumes some agricultural product, F, and a bundle of manufactures, M, to maximize satisfaction according to a Cobb-Douglas utility function:

$$U = M^\mu F^{1-\mu} \tag{1}$$

where μ also measures the budget share on manufactures. The manufactures are a constant elasticity of substitution (CES) aggregate of the varieties produced by n firms ($i = 1,...,n$):

$$M = [\Sigma_i \, m_i^\rho]^{1/\rho} \tag{2}$$

where the CES exponent $\rho = 1-(1/\sigma)$. All manufacturing firms have the same optimal scale, so (2) simplifies to

$$M = n^{1/\rho}m \tag{3}$$

The number of firms or varieties is an argument in consumer utility. Substituting (3) into (1) shows that utility is increasing in the number of varieties consumers have access to:

$$U = n^{\mu/\rho}m^\mu F^{1-\mu} \qquad \partial U/\partial n > 0 \tag{4}$$

Analysis of the consumer expenditure minimization problem concerning manufactures consumption reveals that σ is also the price elasticity of demand. The marginal cost is the local wage, W. Facing these costs and the elasticity of demand, industrial firms maximize profits by equating marginal revenue to marginal cost:

$$P \cdot [1-(1/\sigma)] = W \tag{5}$$

(variety and region subscripts dropped for ease of exposition) so that the profit-maximizing delivered (and mill) price to local markets is a parametric markup ($1/\rho$) over the local wage. Within each region each industrial firm charges the same delivered price to local residents. Equation (5) clarifies that the optimal delivered price would be lower the more substitutable products are (the larger is ρ, and σ). The optimal delivered price is higher if preferences for variety or the degree of differentiation is higher (lower ρ and σ), or the higher are local wages. To compete with another region's suppliers, therefore, one must either pay lower wages or differentiate one's product more.

The new economic geography models highlight that a preference for variety is a basis for increasing returns to scale. The higher the preference for variety, the higher the price premium and the larger the external economies of scale. The more producers in the region, the more workers, the wider the variety produced, the higher the real utility of the population there.

This insight is not new. Nearly 30 years ago, Lancaster (1979) pointed out that fewer different products (but possibly many plants) and smaller market areas are to be expected if localization scale economies are low. If preferences are such that no variety is desired in the consumption of commodities, but variety is desired for products (as in Dixit-Stiglitz), the opportunities to exploit localization economies will rise with local income or the number of consumers. This can happen over time simply because population accretes or capital is accumulated. This growth may support the positive feedback we saw above; as Lancaster (1979, 79) says:

> ... an increase in population will (1) increase the degree of product differentiation if the range of diversity is unchanged *and* the degree of economies of scale varies with output, but have no effect if it is constant, (2) increase the number of goods (and the degree of product differentiation in that sense) if the range of diversity is increased, and (3) lower the per capita resources required for a given level of welfare per capita, whether or not the degree of economies of scale varies with output.

Lancaster (1979) also showed that the economy of scale (θ) can be expressed as the inverse elasticity of cost (percentage change in cost with respect to percentage increase in quantity). It is an inverse function of the elasticity of substitution (σ) between differentiated goods. Taking the ratio of average cost ($AC=W\,6/1\text{-}6$) to marginal cost ($MC=W$),

$$\theta = AC/MC = W\sigma/W(\sigma\text{-}1) = \sigma/(\sigma\text{-}1) \tag{6}$$

In general, the production process is homogeneous of degree θ, which is inversely related to σ. All new economic geography models feature this demand-side engine of localization economies of scale.

The Dixit-Stiglitz market structure is, however, ill-suited for problems related to establishment size (Holmes 1999) or establishment size relative to the accessible market, which, we argued earlier, is critical for understanding rural competitiveness. In new economic geography models, the equilibrium firm size is essentially a fixed function of σ, a parameter of the model. All of the "action" in these models arises with respect to the number of firms in a place. Unfortunately, rural towns are often too small to host more than one firm. This is one of the least appealing features of new economic geography models with respect to rural economics.

Local competition is irrelevant, and local demand cannot affect prices or firm size. The Dixit-Stiglitz assumptions about pricing closes new economic geography models in the same way that a "small-country assumption" closes 2x2x2 trade models. The result is that general-equilibrium feedback is expressed only through local wages or utility (depending on worker mobility). Thus *"the size of the market affects neither the markup of price over marginal cost nor the scale at which individual goods are produced"* (Fujita et al. 1999, 52, italics in original). This is also at odds with empirical observation (Holmes 1999).

Another problem with new economic geography assumptions is that goods are not qualitatively differentiated according to their origin of production (an exception is Daniel and Kilkenny 2002). Most models abstract from the value of rural diversity (Castle 1993). Isserman (1996) criticizes new economic geography models for "oversimplifying both urban and rural places."

Rural areas, however, produce food, natural resources, and other goods and services that are tied to place-specific attributes. Many of these goods cannot be produced in cities. Leaving these goods out of the model becomes a problem when drawing conclusions about the effects of trade on urbanization . . . . (Isserman 1996, 39).

Furthermore, the inframarginality assumption is inappropriate for models of rural places. Alternatively, in my 1998 paper, I departed from the Dixit-Stiglitz tradition by assuming uniform delivered pricing and endogenized both market prices and firm size. Because I did not assume that firms perfectly price discriminate, my model has no closed-form solution and must be solved as a fixed-point problem (like a CGE model). Modeled firm profits depend explicitly on the spatial distribution of the population. Furthermore, my assumptions support stable equilibria in which all regions are occupied, at various population densities. In contrast, Krugman-style new economic geography models only have one stable equilibrium: full concentration in some region. The other equilibrium is equal population in both regions, but this is not stable. The smallest change in transport costs or endowments can induce full concentration in one region or the other.

There are many quasi-new economic geography analyses in the literature worth studying. Helpman (1998) shows that with the proper assumptions, concentration is not the only stable equilibrium; all regions are occupied when "housing" (the outside or homogeneous good) has the largest budget share, and people have sufficiently low preferences for variety. (In contrast, I found that all regions are occupied even if the share on the outside good is small). A highly stylized general equilibrium core-periphery model by Trionfetti (1997) was applied to investigate the types of policies that can support dispersed populations. Trionfetti showed that geographically targeted public expenditures can be a dispersive force. Charlot (2000) analyzed the impact of geographically targeted public expenditures that modify industrial productivity. She showed that public expenditures that reduce variable costs are more effective at encouraging a dispersal of activities than expenditures that reduce fixed costs. Alternatively, Martin and Rogers (1995), Walz (1996), and others have argued that tax-financed public expenditure on infrastructure that decreases the costs of interregional transport favors the agglomeration of activities.

Most recently, Baldwin, et al. (2003) presented a model that generates similar conclusions about the spatial effects of policies analytically. They show that when agglomeration generates not only positive externalities but also congestion costs (such as rising land rents) and there are positive intraregional spillovers, then policies that provide incentives to locate activities in poor regions can help the whole economy grow while improving both intra- and interregional income equality.

Empirical Evidence

The empirical evidence about trends in rural populations in high-income countries is not consistent with the implications of most new economic geography models. But it is consistent with the implications of old economic geography, such as the von Thünen model, as in the treatment by Nerlove and Sadka (1991).

Over the past 200 years, while the share of the U.S. population that is farmers has fallen from 70 percent to 2 percent, and the share that is rural has fallen from 90 percent to 24 percent (Figure 5-4), the share of the population that is rural but

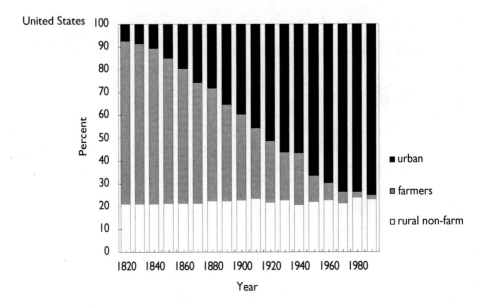

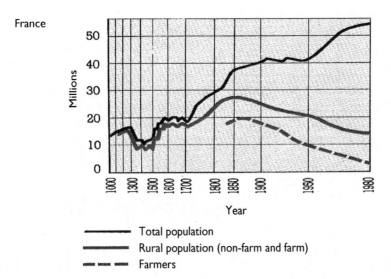

Figure 5-4. *Farm, Non-farm, and Rural Population Shares in the United States and France*

Note: The non-farm, rural shares of the populations of both the United States and France have been remarkably constant for two centuries.

not farmers, has stayed remarkably stable, at about 22 percent (Mills 1995). Similarly, in France, although the number of farmers has fallen dramatically, France's nonfarm rural population has remained at around eight million since 1850 (Ravignan and Roux 1990).

To date, those facts elude explanation. How could the nonfarm rural share of our country's population have stayed constant through colonization, homesteading, westward expansion, and the dramatic changes in the political geography of our own country? How could it have remained so constant in France through the transition from feudalism to capitalism, the Industrial Revolution, and international outmigration? The pattern is also observed in other OECD countries. The evidence contradicts any claim that agriculture is *the* long-run economic base of rural communities. The fact the shares and levels of nonfarm rural populations have not fallen with the farm population indicates that the former do not appear to depend, in the long run, on the number of farmers. It also contradicts Krugman-style new economic geography models, which find no economic rationale for the existence of any nonfarm, remote, low-density populations.

Contrary to the assumptions underlying most new economic geography models, an "immobile farm population" does not appear to be the main dispersive force supporting rural population in developed economies. Indeed, only a few new economic geographers have succeeded in rationalizing the stability of coexisting small and large concentrations of population and diverse economic activity in one competitive economy at all (Nakajima 1995; Calmette and Le Pottier 1995; Kilkenny 1998; Helpman 1998; Lanaspa and Sanz 2001; Daniel and Kilkenny 2002). To do so, they also had to formalize other dispersive forces.

For example, for my 1998 paper, I assumed that competition for workers and customers was localized. Second, I modeled the decision to invest in a locality as a function of latent or potential demand for local varieties. Third, people were modeled as choosing locations to maximize real rather than nominal income, where the *real* income of a rural resident was higher than that of a city resident who earned the same nominal wage if the rural cost of living was lower or the nonmarket amenity bundle supporting quality of life was higher.

Looking Forward

Since von Thünen, we have known that perfect labor mobility, costly goods transport, and land immobility together lead to two fundamental spatial consequences that are the flip sides of the same coin. One is that population and footloose productive activities tend to concentrate in cities to minimize transport costs. External agglomeration economies are additional reasons for concentration in urban areas. Thus, urban populations have grown and rural populations have declined as agricultural productivity and market accessibility rose over time. But the rate of rural population decline in advanced economies appears to have been no greater than the rate at which labor has been released from agriculture. The rural population that is not engaged in agriculture but in manufacturing and service sectors has remained stable over time. Rural areas are still, by definition, remote and low density; but new rural economists know that jobs in natural resource industries alone do not determine rural economies.

The second fundamental spatial consequence shown by von Thünen is that land values decline with distance from population concentrations or market centers, because transport is costly. Places can be so distant from markets that remote land use is not profitable. Because transport is costly, it is possible that people in remote places cannot enjoy a competitive advantage in land-intensive, natural resource–based industry even though they have the relative abundance of land. As transport costs fall, more land becomes valuable. However, the concurrent release of labor from farming and the attractions of cities have left some rural land idle and rural household income low. These reasons, all related to Hoover's three "foundation stones," underlie a market failure justification for rural development policy.

According to Eva Rabinowicz (1999, *269-70*),

> The future of rural areas depends on trends in the costs and benefits of urban compared to rural life. The picture is not clear and opposing forces are at work. . . . Scale economies are a major reason for clustering of economic activity. . . . The high cost of living and commuting is, on the other hand, an obvious disadvantage of urban life. . . . Could insights from agglomeration theories and New Economic Geography indicate how to design more efficient rural development policies?

Emery Castle could have been quoted saying something similar. External agglomeration economies of scale, costs of distance, and housing costs or land rent are indeed important determinants of the allocation of people and businesses across space. The models that present all those features, however, have yet to be developed and applied to analyze rural development policies.

To properly stylize the rural economy in advanced economies, new rural economists need to be explicit about at least three features that have received little attention in the past. One is the rural service sector. It is a competitive shopping goods sector subject to high transport costs, localization economies, a technology that includes fixed costs, and an efficient scale that is often no larger than the size of the local market (or smaller, for sectors that are relatively low in the central place hierarchy.) That stylization is important for two reasons: (1) even in rural areas, the majority of employment is in nonfarm service sectors (Table 5-1), and (2) service sectors are not linked directly to farming or agroindustry—they are indirectly related through household income, household expenditure, and workforce-residential location choices. Thus, the new rural economists will probably continue to employ general equilibrium approaches. The existence of a sector that is not directly tied to land provides an important degree-of-freedom that allows for the determination of land rent even though the land market does not clear. Which leads to the next issue.

Second, land is a location bundled with site-specific amenities, a factor of production, and an asset. Very few new economic geography models are explicit about land use and land values. Roback's (1982) seminal, empirically tested proposition that people migrate to places with higher amenities, all else equal, rescued the field of labor economics from decades of "wrong signs" on wages in migration functions. Attention to amenities has been rescuing both rural economies and rural development policy. Amenities are economically relevant and no new rural economist can forget that. It is important to specify the nonmarket attributes tied to land.

Third, the products of the natural resource industry are intermediate goods for industries that produce both vertically and horizontally differentiated outputs. It should be noted that interindustry linkages are at the heart of all input-output and computable general equilibrium (CGE) models. A return to land is also endogenous in CGE models. But unlike in those models, there are explicitly spatial aspects to the land rent and interindustry linkages. For example, food products are horizontally differentiated (Anderson et al. 1992). That is, products produced in different locations appeal to different subsets of consumers. In particular, the differentiation is tied to the geographic location of production of both the raw farm product and the manufacturing process. These are known as regional specialties—for example, Parma ham and Roquefort cheese. Many have become formally geolabeled products, with Protected Geographical Identification, Appelation d'Origine Contrôllée, or Denominazione di Origine Controllata e Garantita (see Sylvander et al. 2000).

A problem with some rural areas in the United States may be that communities do not differ one from the next. Rural places in the corn belt, for example, are not only small and remote, they are also homogeneous: soy and corn as far as the eye can see, no architectural variety, and all the towns have the same franchised fast food and gas stations. In the old days, high transport costs justified the proliferation of fixed costs and insulated one rural place from the next. Now that people can travel across a state in just a few hours, only a few rural places offering homogeneous services and amenities are needed. Rural places compete with each other for residents and rest-stop customers in the classic Hotelling sense.

One of the main points in this chapter is the importance of the demand side, and especially demand for services, in rural development. A preference for variety can motivate customers and residents to "go the extra mile." All new economic geography models highlight the fact that if consumers value diversity, those who supply it can capture supranormal profits. Thus, rural areas that offer desirable, unique, or distinctive products or lifestyles can capitalize on the premium prices they can charge for their fare. If all citizens and tourists, however, actually prefer crowded places and homogeneous products, consolidation is the only hope for the survival of a few, relatively accessible, rural towns. The workforce in such towns faces the prospect of competing with workers in other countries on the basis of lower wages. They can work in large factories to capture internal economies of scale, and they can merely mass-produce items in the final (domestic) stage of an American product's cycle. And they will cyclically face establishment closures as old products become obsolete.

All new economic geography papers also find that a place offering higher real wages, all else equal, can attract population. In general, a higher real rural wage can be obtained four ways: higher nominal rural wages, lower rural prices, subsidies, or more positive rural externalities. Unfortunately, high nominal rural wages and low rural prices would repel firms. Second, our models also show that government subsidies cannot substitute for the positive production externalities (external to firms but internal to an industry) of urban agglomeration in rural places (see also Goetz and Debertin 1996). As should be expected, subsidies ultimately go to the owners of the relatively fixed factor of production: urban land (Daniel and Kilkenny 2002). That leaves externalities. One way to raise real rural wages without repelling firms or raising urban land rents is to improve the quality of rural life. This would increase the demand for rural residences and may be a more effective strategy than attempting to alter private incentives facing farms or businesses.

This chapter reviewed some of the tools in the traditional rural economics toolkit and critiqued the new economic geography. It argued that the new rural economics needs to be more explicit about spatial microfoundations, demand-side ideas, and empirically tested models. We must be careful not to confound marginal with average. We should be explicit about market area issues and the division of labor supported in larger markets. Finally, if the new rural economics can explain why the nonfarm share of population has remained so stable over time, it will help us do a better job of figuring out which government programs more effectively promote rural and economy-wide growth.

References

Anderson, S.P., A. de Palma, and J.-F. Thisse. 1992. *Discrete Choice Theory of Product Differentiation.* Cambridge, MA: MIT Press.

Baldwin, R., R. Forslid, P. Martin, G. Ottaviano, and F. Robert-Nicoud. 2003. *Economic Geography and Public Policy.* Princeton, NJ: Princeton University Press.

Barkley, D., and M. Henry. 1998. Rural Industrial Development: To Cluster or Not to Cluster. *Review of Agricultural Economics* 19(2): 308–25.

Berry, B. 1967. *Geography of Market Centers and Retail Distribution.* Englewood Cliffs, NJ: Prentice-Hall.

Calmette, M.-F., and J. Le Pottier. 1995. Localisation des Activités: un modèle bi sectoriel avec couts de transports. *Revue Economique* 46(3).

Castle, E. 1991. The Benefits of Space and the Cost of Distance. In *The Future of Rural America: Anticipating Policies for Constructive Change,* edited by Kenneth Pigg. Boulder, CO: Westview Press.

———. 1993. Rural Diversity: An American Asset. *Annals AAPSS* 529: 12–21.

——— (ed.). 1995. *The Changing American Countryside.* Lawrence: University Press of Kansas.

Chamberlin, E. 1962. *The Theory of Monopolistic Competition: A Reorientation of the Theory of Value.* Cambridge, MA: Harvard University Press.

Charlot, S. 2000. Economie géographique et secteur public: des infrastructures de transport à la concurrence fiscale. *Revue d'Economie Régionale et Urbaine* 1: 5–16.

Daniel, K., and M. Kilkenny. 2002. Découplage des aides directes à l'agriculture et localisation des activités. *Economie Internationale* 91(3rd trimestre): 73–92.

Fujita, M., P. Krugman, and A. Venables, A. 1999. *The Spatial Economy: Cities, Regions, and International Trade.* Cambridge, MA: MIT Press.

Glaeser, E., and J. Kohlhase. 2004. Cities, Regions, and the Decline of Transport Costs. *Papers in Regional Science* 83(1): 197–228.

Goetz, S., and D. Debertin. 1996. Rural Population Decline in the 1980s: Impacts of Farm Structure and Federal Farm Programs. *American Journal of Agricultural Economics* 78(3): 517–29.

Helpman, E. 1998. The Size of Regions. In *Topics in Public Economics, Theoretical and Applied Analyses,* edited by D. Pines, E. Sadka, and I. Zilcha. Cambridge: Cambridge University Press, Chapter 2.

Holmes, T.J. 1999. Localization of Industry and Vertical Disintegration. *The Review of Economics and Statistics* 81(2): 314–25.

Holmes, T.J., and J.J. Stevens. 2004. Geographic Concentration and Establishment Size: Analysis in an Alternative Economic Geography Model. *Journal of Economic Geography* 4(3): 227–50.

Hoover, E. 1948. *The Location of Economic Activity.* New York: McGraw-Hill.

Hoover, E., and F. Giarratani. 1999. *An Introduction to Regional Economics.* In *The Web Book of Regional Science* (www.rri.wvu.edu/regscweb.htm), edited by S. Loveridge. Morgantown: Regional Research Institute, West Virginia University.

Hotelling, H. 1929. Stability in Competition. *Economic Journal* 39: 41–57.

Isserman, A. 1996. It's Obvious, It's Wrong, and Anyway They Said It Years Ago? Paul Krugman on Large Cities. *International Regional Science Review* 19(1-2): 37–48.

Kaldor, N. 1935. Market Imperfection and Excess Capacity. *Economica* 2: 35–50.

Kilkenny, M. 1998. Transport Costs and Rural Development. *Journal of Regional Science* 38(2): 293–312.

Krantz, O. 2000. The Transport and Communications Sector in Economic Development: Views from the Historical National Accounts. *Scandinavian Economic History Review* 48(2): 5–29.

Krugman, P. 1981. Intraindustry Specialization and the Gains from Trade. *Journal of Political Economy* 89(5): 959–73.

————. 1991a. Increasing Returns and Economic Geography. *Journal of Political Economy* 99: 483–99.

————. 1991b. *Geography and Trade.* Cambridge, MA: MIT Press.

————. 1996. Urban Concentration: The Role of Increasing Returns and Transport Costs. *International Regional Science Review* 19(1): 5–30.

Lanaspa, L.F., and F. Sanz. 2001. Multiple Equilibria, Stability, and Asymmetries in Krugman's Core-Periphery Model. *Papers in Regional Science.* 80(4): 425–38.

Lancaster, K. 1979. *Variety, Equity, and Efficiency.* New York: Columbia University Press.

Lundgren, N.G. 1996. Bulk Trade and Maritime Transport Costs: The Evolution of Global Markets. *Resources Policy* 22(1-2): 5–32.

Martin, P.J., and C.A. Rogers. 1995. Industrial Location and Public Infrastructure. *Journal of International Economics* 39(3-4): 335–51.

Marshall, A. 1920. *Principles of Economics*, 8th ed. London: Macmillan Press.

Mills, E.S. 1995. The Location of Economic Activity in Rural and Nonmetropolitan United States. In *The Changing American Countryside,* edited by E. Castle. Lawrence: University Press of Kansas, 103–33.

Mulligan, G. 1984. Agglomeration and Central Place Theory: A Review of the Literature. *International Regional Science Review* 9: 1–42.

Nakajima, T. 1995. Equilibrium with an Underpopulated Region and an Overpopulated Region. *Regional Science and Urban Economics* 25(1): 109–23.

Nerlove, M., and E. Sadka. 1991. Von Thünen's Model of the Dual Economy. *Journal of Economics* 54: 97–123.

Rabinowicz, E. 1999. EAAE Presidential Address: Redesigning the CAP to Meet the Challenges of EU Enlargement and the WTO: What Can Agricultural Economic Research Contribute? *European Review of Agricultural Economics* 26(3): 265–81.

Ravignan, F., and P. Roux. 1990. *L'Atlas de la France Verte.* INRA & SCEES, France: Editions Monza.

Roback, J. 1982. Wages, Rents and the Quality of Life. *Journal of Political Economy* 90(6): 1257–78.

Samuelson, P. 1983. Thünen at Two Hundred. *Journal of Economic Literature* 21(4): 1468–88.

Shonkwiler, J.S., and T.R. Harris. 1996. Rural Retail Business Thresholds and Interdependence. *Journal of Regional Science* 36: 617–30.

Stigler, G. 1951. The Division of Labor Is Limited by the Extent of the Market. *Journal of Political Economy* 59(3): 185–93.

Sylvander, B., D. Barjolle, and F. Arfini (eds.). 2000. *The Socio-Economics of Origin Labeled Products in Agri-Food Supply Chains: Spatial, Institutional and Co-ordination Aspects.* Paris: INRA.

Trionfetti, F. 1997. Public Expenditure and Economic Geography. *Annales d'Economie et de Statistiques* 47: 101–20.

Venables, A. 1975. Trade and Trade Policy with Imperfect Competition: The Case of Identical Products and Free Entry. *Journal of International Economics* 19: 1–20.

Walz, U. 1996. Long-run Effects of Regional Policy in an Economic Union. *The Annals of Regional Science* 30(2): 165–83.

CHAPTER 6

Exploring the Prospects
for Amenity-Driven Growth
in Rural Areas

Elena G. Irwin, Alan Randall, and Yong Chen

*H*IGH-AMENITY RURAL AREAS, particularly those in the Rocky Mountains, in parts of the inland West, and along coastlines, have experienced unprecedented population growth rates in recent decades. The mountain West, home to many amenity-rich and thriving communities, was the fastest-growing region in the United States in the 1990s, with a population growth rate of 25 percent. U.S. coastal counties, including those along the Great Lakes, account for 51 percent of the total U.S. population and 57 percent of total income (Rappaport and Sachs 2001).

Anecdotal and empirical evidence suggesting a strong role for environmental amenities in stimulating growth scarcely clinches the case. First, there are ambiguities in the empirical evidence. The prospering coastal counties may plausibly enjoy traditional kinds of economic advantages (in transportation and trade, for example) as well as superior amenities. Second, even if the empirical evidence were strong, economists would respond as we usually do: sure, it works in practice, but does it work in theory? That is, we demand sound reasons as well as empirical evidence to take a hypothesized relationship seriously.

For our purposes here, the issue of rurality also must be addressed: under what circumstances do environmental amenities countervail the agglomeration advantages of urban areas and drive rural growth? Some have hypothesized that the demand for high-amenity locations is substantially less than the supply of amenity-laden rural places, suggesting that only the places with the most valued amenities will prosper (Castle 1995). On the other hand, White and Hanink (2004) present empirical evidence from the U.S. Northeast suggesting that rural areas with more modest environmental amenities can experience amenity-based growth if they are within sufficient proximity of an urban area. On a smaller scale, Wu and Plantinga (2003) consider the attraction effect of open-space amenities within a metropolitan region and find that sufficiently strong effects can lead to a more dispersed urban form.

Clearly, the accessibility of rural places to urban populations, the quality of their environmental amenities, and the economic pull and quality of life of urban areas all influence the extent of population and economic growth in rural regions. We began to sort out the impacts of these various influences in a systematic way. We adapted a simple dynamic model of regional factor mobility and urban agglomeration (Fujita and Thisse 2002) to examine the role of environmental amenities and urban congestion in core-periphery patterns of regional development (Irwin et al. 2006). In what follows, we first explain the basic setup of the regional model and clarify the role of environmental amenities in the model. We then summarize the basic results of this model and draw implications regarding the prospects for amenity-driven growth in rural areas.

Our model reveals a number of interesting results. With growth in the urban core, urban disamenities (congestion, pollution) may eventually outweigh the production externalities and urban amenities that drove urban growth, dispersing population and economic activity to the periphery region. This outcome is not guaranteed; it depends on the relative amenity endowments of the two regions. For high-amenity periphery regions, the model predicts an irreversible change in population location such that growth concentrates not in the core but in the periphery. On the other hand, periphery regions with moderate amenity endowments may gain some population and production but will never develop into new core regions. Those regions with amenities below a certain value will fail to gain population, despite the core's degradation. Thus, rural regions may benefit from congestion and pollution in urban regions, but only if they have a sufficient "pull" of their own. Public policy can be used to promote rural growth. We find that local government investment in amenities in the periphery region can attract population and production to the periphery, but only if the initial amenity endowment is relatively high and the utility gain from augmenting amenities exceeds the utility loss from additional taxation.

Determinants of Growth: A Two-Region Model

To formalize these ideas, consider just two regions. What are the basic factors that will influence the distribution of people and economic activity across these two regions? Traditional models of regional economics emphasize the role of employment location in attracting people to a region, but as Krugman (1991) noted, the reverse linkage also occurs: people attract firms to a region because of availability of labor and demand for final goods. Firms may also attract additional firms because, for example, efficiencies in wholesale markets can arise from low transportation costs between input suppliers and manufacturers. Such positive interactions among firms and between firms and households can lead to clustering and agglomeration of population and economic activity. A simple means of representing these types of urbanization economies is via a positive production externality in which the benefits of clustering accrue to individual firms but are generated by scale effects that are external at the firm level. Here, we assume that these scale effects are a function of total population (i.e., labor), and therefore, firms become more productive as the population of the region increases.

Although the diversity of firms and differences across sectors can be important for regional growth, we simplify this aspect by assuming that all firms are the same within and across regions and produce a globally traded homogeneous output. In addition to labor, we assume that firms use natural resources as an input into the production of this good. Suppose these resources are spatially immobile and fixed, implying that increases in labor will decrease the marginal product of labor in the region. Without the production externality, the declining marginal product of labor leads to lower equilibrium wage rates for larger regions. However, the production externality increases the marginal productivity of labor and therefore wages could increase as regional population increases if the externality effect is sufficiently strong. Such a self-reinforcing effect can lead to concentration of population in one region (Fujita and Thisse 2002).

We assume that people are mobile between the two regions but must live where they work. So, their location decisions are influenced by the wages and amenity levels prevailing in each region. For simplification, we assume that total population across the two regions is fixed and that people have identical skills and preferences. In addition to the wage rate, we enrich the basic urban agglomeration model by considering three kinds of amenities: urban amenities and disamenities, both of which arise from the concentration of people in a single region, and environmental amenities. Urban amenities include the shopping, cultural, and recreational benefits that arise with more people in a region; urban disamenities include congestion, pollution, and other nonmarket costs associated with living in a more populated place. Both of these effects are determined by the distribution of population across the two regions and thus are endogenous. In contrast, environmental amenities, such as mountains, coastline, and water bodies, are determined by the fixed distribution of natural features across the two regions.

At the outset, utility differences may exist between the two regions, motivating people to migrate. Migration alters the regional wage and the pull and push of urban amenities and disamenities, which in turn influences migration. Ignoring relocation costs for the moment, people will move until utility differences are eliminated. At that point, people will be indifferent as to where they live: higher wages in one region will compensate exactly for superior amenities in the other.

Given this simple framework for modeling regional migration and growth, which builds on the basic model of Fujita and Thisse (2002), we are interested in exploring the role of environmental amenities in attracting people and economic growth to a region. In other words, what conditions lead to a core-periphery structure in which most people locate in the core, leaving the periphery sparsely populated? A second question, of particular relevance for our interests here, has to do with the reversal of this process: once a core-periphery structure is in place, what conditions weaken the core, leading to growth in the periphery region? Clearly, degradation of the urban area can make the rural area more attractive in a relative sense, but is this a sufficient condition for rural growth? Is rural growth limited, in the end, by the same sorts of factors that limit urban growth (i.e., increasing congestion and pollution)? How do migration costs and public policy influence this dynamic? For the remainder of this chapter, we consider these questions, first summarizing our modeling results and then indulging in some speculations beyond the model.

Emergence of a Core-Periphery Pattern

As Fujita and Thisse (2002) demonstrate, the production externality is a critical determinant of a core-periphery pattern in this simple framework. Intuitively, if there are sufficient benefits to firms and households from clustering together in one region, that region will emerge as the core. If the productivity benefits to firms from agglomeration are high enough to offset the declining marginal productivity of labor, wages will be higher in the region that has more people, and this will attract yet more workers. An increase in population lowers the average costs of production for individual firms, which stimulates more production in the region. These effects reinforce each other, and, eventually, most of the population and economic production become concentrated in a single region. Thus migration is driven by employment opportunities, and the benefits of agglomeration to firms outweigh the higher cost of labor in the larger region. Under such a regime, population concentrates in growing cities while rural regions continue to depopulate.

This story is driven by two key conditions, initial advantage and production externalities arising from concentration of population. It seems natural to think that the initial advantage arises from in situ resources or transportation advantages, and that urbanization is led by extractive, manufacturing, or processing industries. But initial advantage may also arise from superior environmental amenities. The rest of the story may follow the familiar pattern: production externalities and increasingly sophisticated urban amenities reinforce the initial advantage (production externalities arise not from proximity to traditional resources, but from concentration of population).

There is another possibility. Even in the absence of a strong production externality, agglomeration may occur if the consumption benefits associated with either urban or environmental amenities are sufficiently strong. In this case, high-quality amenities can induce growth, resulting in an economy that is very different from the production-driven agglomeration described by Fujita and Thisse (2002) and others. Rather than being driven primarily by higher wages, growth is driven by amenities that are sufficiently attractive to offset the declining wages that result in the absence of a strong production externality. One thinks of the regions and communities that attract retirees and workers in occupations that are not place-dependent. Over time, some such communities have built up an attractive array of urban amenities as a result of population growth.

In considering the specific role of environmental amenities in the formation of core-periphery patterns, we find that agglomeration is more likely to result when the distribution of amenities favors one region over another. However, in the absence of positive agglomeration economies, this benefit must be sufficiently large to offset the lower wage and congestion disamenities that are generated by a large population. In the presence of sufficiently strong production externalities or urban amenities or both, then any initial advantage of one region over another, including greater environmental amenities, will lead to agglomeration in that region.

Deconcentration of the Core Region

Our analysis is motivated by the question of whether and how the forces that led to an initial core-periphery regional structure may tend eventually to dampen or reverse that pattern. In particular, under what conditions will the "push" of urban congestion and pollution and the "pull" of rural environmental amenities lead to a more dispersed distribution of population or to a regime shift in which population concentrates not in the core but in the periphery?

Assuming that a core has already formed (that is, one of the regions has become urbanized), we consider how the initial amenity endowments of the two regions influence the core-periphery structure as the growth of congestion and pollution that accompanies population concentration in the core plays out. The outcome is found to depend on the level of initial environmental amenities in the core region and the magnitude of the decline in this amenity level. When the initial level of environmental amenities in the core region is high relative to the amenities in the periphery region, a small decline in the core's amenities will cause a small decline in the core's population as some households move out to the periphery. When the initial level of environmental amenities in the core is high, modest declines in the core's amenities will not cause a sudden or irreversible change in population migration. This implies that, in the real world beyond our model, the core may be able to stem a threatened decline by improving its environmental amenities or by enhancing urban amenities.

A different outcome is possible when the initial level of environmental amenities in the core region is only moderately better than that in the periphery region. In this case, a small increase in the core's congestion and pollution can cause an irreversible and nonmarginal change in the core-periphery structure. This "regime shift" is triggered when the level of environmental quality in the core region drops below a critical value. Then, the high concentration of population in the core is no longer stable and its population will leave. The critical value of the threshold is *not necessarily* equal to the level of amenities in the periphery region. Urban amenities and higher wages may allow the core region to sustain its advantage even as its environmental quality falls below that in the periphery region. However, if the difference grows too large, then the threshold is crossed and the core will disperse. Once this threshold has been crossed, the opportunity for offsetting growth in the core is past and the dispersal process is irreversible. Eventually, a new core may form in what had been the periphery, provided the benefits to agglomeration are sufficiently strong. Otherwise, the core-periphery structure will disappear and a dispersed structure in which population is more equally distributed across the two regions will emerge.

A Note on Time and History

Our model is dynamic, in that we trace the path of population in each region as the driving forces (production externalities, urban amenities, urban disamenities, and environmental amenities) play out. But it has no explicit concept of time and thus provides no insights about the time scales on which this panorama unfolds.

Furthermore, the model draws nothing from history. Initial advantage locates the core (if there is to be one), but it is not the force that drives agglomeration. We treat the source of initial advantage as uninteresting—it may arise from in situ resources, transportation advantages, or superior amenities—but our real interest is not in the happenstance of initial advantage but in the consequences of initial advantage for the subsequent concentration or dispersion of population and economic activity. Our driving forces—production externalities, urban amenities, urban disamenities, and environmental amenities—have recognizable historical counterparts, but they are seldom easy to separate from other historical forces that we do not consider explicitly, especially developments in technology and, in North America, the settlement of the frontier.

This modeling strategy has its advantages. Historical narrative is often unhelpful in the pursuit of cause and effect: typically, there are too many sufficient conditions for the observed historical outcome and few truly necessary conditions. But our modeling approach makes for storytelling that is much too austere.

Our story of the growth of great cities and depopulation of the countryside, and the possibilities for slowing or reversing that process, would be greatly enriched by some historical perspective. Pittsburgh had its historical moment of great advantage arising from a particular combination of in situ resources, location and technology—abundant coal resources, spiking demand for iron and steel, and access to ship and rail transportation for iron ore and finished products—all of which mattered more in the late 19th-century economy than they do today. For decades, Pittsburgh thrived despite pollution levels scarcely imaginable today. In more recent times, lower-cost competitors emerged, high-quality coal resources became scarcer, and steel simply mattered less in the new economy. Pittsburgh is doing everything it can to remake itself as a modern, high-amenity pillar of the new economy. But competition in that arena is tough.

Amenity-driven growth is much more common today and seems to be an important driver of urban growth in the Sunbelt of the United States. We might point to the Southwest (e.g., Phoenix), the South (e.g., Atlanta), and the West (e.g., Riverside–San Bernardino, California). The narrative starts with a technological development (refrigerated air-conditioning), but it depends also on the development of the postindustrial economy on a global scale: in situ resources matter less, value is provided less by bulky commodities and more by technologically sophisticated products and services, information substitutes in considerable degree for transportation, and workers and their employers face lower cost penalties for locating in high-amenity regions and places.

Closer to our concern with economic prospects for rural regions and communities, there are many examples of smaller cities that seem to be thriving because of environmental amenities (Coeur d'Alene, Idaho, and Sarasota, Florida), high levels of educational and cultural amenities (Charlottesville, Virginia), or both (Missoula, Montana). At this point, historical narrative can only point to possibilities. We hope our modeling exercise brings us a little closer to identifying a smaller set of sufficient conditions for growth in historically peripheral regions and places.

Moving Costs

Our results to this point have assumed that moving costs are zero and that location decisions respond only to the difference in utility across the two regions. The inclusion of a positive cost of relocating across regions implies that migration from one region to the other will occur only if the gain in utility from moving outweighs the costs. People will stay put when the utility difference between regions is less than the moving costs.

Moving costs can fundamentally change the regional structure, but whether they do or not depends on the starting point we choose. Suppose most people locate initially in the core region, but increasing congestion and pollution disamenities would (other things equal) eventually induce some to move to the periphery. Then, moving costs reduce the number of households that actually move, leaving the population as concentrated as before. A decrease in moving costs will induce additional households to move out of the core region, but a core-periphery pattern is maintained (even if moving costs go to zero) until urban congestion and pollution in the core rise above the critical level that reflects the combined effects of production externalities, urban amenities, and the difference in environmental amenity levels between the core and the periphery.[1]

In contrast to the above case, moving costs *do* fundamentally alter the regional structure when the initial population is equally dispersed across the two regions. In this case, a dispersed structure will be maintained until the utility gain from moving exceeds the moving cost. As moving costs decline, regional structure becomes more sensitive to ever-smaller differences in utility levels between the (potential) core and the periphery. The range of values for which an initial distribution of population leads to a dispersed equilibrium shrinks as moving costs approach zero. When moving costs are zero, a dispersed equilibrium is no longer stable in the face of agglomeration externalities, and concentration of population in one region or the other inevitably occurs.

Positive moving costs raise the issue of foresight. With zero moving costs, people relocate in response even to momentary utility gains, and thus foresight is not an issue. But when moving is costly, people who foresee that an ongoing wave of migration to the core will increase congestion and pollution there, eventually reversing the utility advantage, are reluctant to join that wave. Agglomeration is slowed not just by the costs of moving to the core, but also by the anticipated costs of moving back to the periphery when the core loses its advantage. With foresight, the dampening effect of moving costs on migration, agglomeration, and return migration is exacerbated, and the range of initial conditions that lead to a dispersed population is broadened.

Public Investment in Amenities

Finally, we consider the possibility that a peripheral region can stimulate its own growth by investing in enhanced environmental amenities, thereby attracting people from the core. Suppose the local government in the peripheral region taxes labor and uses these revenues to invest in the region's environmental amenities. We assume that the core does not implement such a tax, either on its own initiative or in response to the periphery's strategy.

The direct effect of such a tax is to reduce consumption and therefore utility in the peripheral region. However, investment of the tax revenues to augment environmental amenities will increase the quality of these amenities, which increases utility in the region. Whether the tax attracts or repels households depends on the net effect of the tax, which is determined in part by the government's productivity in converting tax revenues into amenity improvements. Suppose the government is efficient at converting tax dollars into amenity improvements. Then, the outcome is determined by the relative amenity endowments across the two regions and the strength of the production externalities, urban amenities, and urban congestion and pollution. If the benefits of agglomeration in the core are high, then any improvement in amenities in the periphery will lessen the initial utility difference between the two regions but are unlikely to alter its direction. The concentration of population in the core will dissipate slightly, but the basic core-periphery structure will be maintained. In this case, improved environmental amenities in the periphery cannot overcome the agglomeration advantages of the core, even though the absolute level of environmental amenities may be higher in the periphery.

On the other hand, if the advantages of the core are modest at the outset, public investment in amenities in the periphery may offset the benefits of agglomeration and switch the utility advantage of the core from positive to negative. If this occurs, people no longer have an incentive to concentrate in the historical core, and a nonmarginal and persistent change in the core-periphery structure occurs. Households migrate to the periphery, dispersing the core. Eventually a new core may form in the periphery region, if the advantage in environmental amenities is maintained and if the benefits of agglomeration (now working in favor of the periphery region) are sufficiently strong.

Of course, those results depend on the government's ability to effectively translate tax revenues into improvements in environmental amenities, such that the net effect of the local tax is indeed positive. They depend also on our assumption that the core does not invest to improve its own urban or environmental amenities, either independently for its own reasons or in a purposeful attempt to countervail the periphery's investment strategy. This is a nontrivial simplification: a bilateral game between the regions, each seeking comparative advantage from a tax-and-invest strategy, would likely change some of our results.

Implications for Rural Regions

We summarize the model results in terms of the implications for rural (periphery) regions and the conditions under which environmental amenities may offset urban agglomeration such that the periphery region benefits.

Good things may come to those who wait. Following the initial concentration of population and economic growth in a core region, the periphery eventually will attract economic growth at the expense of the core region if the environmental degradation due to the concentration of population in the core region is sufficiently large.

More good things come to more desirable places, and good things may never come to some places. Dispersion of growth from the core to the periphery region is more likely to happen the higher the environmental amenity level in the periphery region relative to the core. For highly desirable periphery regions (i.e., those with a relatively large endowment of environmental amenities), the model predicts a persistent and irreversible shift from agglomeration in the core to agglomeration in the periphery. For regions with more modest amenity levels, the model still predicts that the core region will lose population and production to the periphery, but full agglomeration will not occur in the periphery. For rural areas that are amenity poor, population and firms remain in the core area despite degradation of the core's amenity level.

Moving costs are a drag, particularly for remote regions. Costs of moving between regions create a drag on migration and reduce the willingness of individuals to move in response to utility differences. For an initial distribution of population that is dispersed across two regions, higher moving costs are more likely to prevent the evolution of a core-periphery pattern. Conversely, as moving costs decrease, agglomeration in either region (whichever is favored by endowments) is increasingly likely. However, if population is already highly concentrated in one region, then high moving costs to the periphery region will retard the exodus of core-region population that would otherwise be expected. Thus, a remote rural region is protected by its remoteness (and high moving costs) when population is more dispersed, as it was in earlier times. But today's pattern is much more agglomerated in and around urban areas. In the case where population is already agglomerated at the outset, the more remote the region (and the higher the moving cost), the emptier it is.

With positive moving costs, foresight moderates agglomeration and enhances retention of population in the periphery. If the negative effects of urban concentration on a region's environmental services are foreseen and moving costs are positive, then agglomeration will still occur, but to a lesser extent. Intuitively, some people will be deterred from moving to the core by anticipation of a future utility loss due to diminished environmental services there and a positive cost of return migration. Thus, if people "get it right," in terms of the extent to which agglomeration will reduce the environmental services in the core, then some will never move from the periphery, reducing the extent of agglomeration in the core.

If you build it, they may come. Periphery regions, recognizing the role of amenities as an engine of growth, may choose to invest in their own environmental amenities as an economic development strategy. However, this strategy is not a sure thing. Success depends on the relative distribution of amenity endowments between the core and periphery regions and the productivity of tax dollars in augmenting environmental amenities in the periphery. For periphery regions that are relatively amenity rich, such a strategy will pay off if the improved amenity level is sufficiently high to generate a regime shift away from the core region toward agglomeration in the periphery. However, if government is not particularly productive in converting tax revenues into tangible improvements, or if the periphery region has a relatively poor amenity endowment, then such a strategy will simply drive more people out of the periphery region because the tax reduces their effective wages. A final caveat: we have not considered the investment strategies available to the core region, to enhance its competitive advantage or to offset possible gains from investment in the periphery.

Remoteness is an outcome, not a given. From a static, or snapshot perspective, remoteness is a given—something predetermined that can be overcome only at substantial cost. The idea of remoteness is all about suffering the high cost of distance. But from a dynamic perspective, distance is literally endogenous. Distance is relative to some place thought central ("where the action is"), and as we have shown, regime shifts that make remote regions central (and vice versa) not only are conceivable but will happen under conditions that can be specified.

If the pull of the core weakens, if the cost of distance from the core decreases, if the location of the core changes, then the remoteness of any particular place may change along with the practical implications of that remoteness. What was once remote may become central or at least less remote; and remoteness itself may become less of an issue in the new economy. Seventy-five years ago, we conjecture, everyone would have agreed that Pittsburgh was central and Phoenix was remote. In the intervening years, it seems clear that the situation has been substantially reversed: Phoenix surely has become more central, and Pittsburgh struggles to avoid remoteness. If hope springs eternal for some remote rural communities, it must spring from the endogeneity of remoteness.

Extensions and Speculations

At this stage in our inquiries, our model is limited in several ways. Here, we consider possible extensions and speculate intuitively about what might be learned if extended analyses were completed.

The concept of time is not explicitly represented in our model. We unleash processes of various kinds—regional advantage, agglomeration externalities, relocation of workers, urban amenities and disamenities, and environmental amenities—and examine their effects, but we have no explicit treatment of the time it takes for these processes to work through the system. Yet, time obviously matters, especially for those considering proactive policy interventions. Along similar lines, although we discuss the role of expectations about the future in the relocation decisions when moving costs are positive, we do not fully endogenize expectations.

It is possible that we have overstated the pull of the core region because we have not modeled pollution as an explicit result of the production activities that drive agglomeration. We include pollution as a disamenity of urbanization, but it is driven by the concentration of population (which is plausible: consider automobile pollution) but not by the production of goods (also a plausible source of pollution) in urban places. If we were to consider pollution from production processes, we might well find that agglomeration based on resource-based economic growth is more readily reversed, with pollution externalities from production operating in concert with congestion externalities. If we allowed production of two kinds of goods, one resource-based and the other amenity-based, we would see regional specialization with perhaps improved prospects for amenity-based economic development in the periphery regime. Finally, in this vein, we could introduce two kinds of workers (perhaps distinguished by age) and examine the extent of regional stratification that emerges: for example, under what conditions do retired workers gravitate to the periphery?

Thus far, our examination of strategies that regions can use to improve their development prospects has been primitive. An ideal analysis would fully endogenize the taxes collected and the amenities augmented. Workers will be attracted to the periphery only if the utility gain from amenity augmentation exceeds the utility loss from the tax, and the amount of tax collected and hence the amount of amenity improvements provided depend on wages and employment (both endogenous) in both regions. Thus, the ideal analysis would make the "tax and invest" strategy available to both regions so that the core could also collect taxes and invest in amenities (urban or environmental or both) to improve its own prospects and counter the periphery's investment strategy. A model of this kind would open the door to formal consideration of various related issues: for example, the efficacy of the tax abatement strategy for regional economic development (it becomes ineffective when everybody does it, we hypothesize), and the "race to the bottom" hypothesis regarding environmental quality (the race to the bottom is self-limiting when people have to live with their own mess, we predict, but not when environmental degradation can be dispersed across regional boundaries).

Conclusion

Extending a simple model of regional factor mobility and urban agglomeration, we have clarified the role of amenities as an engine for economic growth. We show that congestion and pollution in the core region can disperse growth away from the core to the periphery, but only if the periphery has relatively high amenity levels. For high-amenity periphery regions, the model predicts a regime shift from the initial core-periphery pattern to agglomeration in the periphery. Relocation costs between regions create a drag on interregional migration and can dampen the degraded urban region's "push" of population and production to the rural region. Local government investment in amenities in the periphery region can attract population and production to the periphery, but only if the utility gain from augmenting amenities exceeds the utility loss from taxation, and the initial amenity base is relatively high. Finally, we sketch several potential extensions of the model that, if undertaken, would likely yield additional interesting results.

References

Castle, E. 1995. The Forgotten Hinterlands. In *The Contested Countryside*, edited by E. Castle. Lawrence: University of Kansas Press, 3–10.

Fujita, M., and J. Thisse. 2002. *Economics of Agglomeration: Cities, Industrial Location and Regional Growth*. Cambridge: Cambridge University Press.

Irwin, E., A. Randall, and Y. Chen. 2006. Environmental Amenities as a Driver of Regional Growth. Manuscript. http://www.sg.ohio-state.edu/biocomplexity/documents/irwinrandallchen06.pdf.

Krugman, P. 1991. Increasing Returns and Economic Geography. *Journal of Political Economy* 99: 483–99.

Rappaport, J., and J. Sachs. 2003. The United States as a Coastal Nation. *Journal of Economic Growth* 8: 5–46.

White, K., and D. Hanink. 2004. 'Moderate' Environmental Amenities and Economic Change: The Nonmetropolitan Northern Forest of the Northeast US, 1970–2000. *Growth and Change* 35(1): 42–60.

Wu, J., and A.J. Plantinga. 2003. The Influence of Public Open Space on Urban Spatial Structure. *Journal of Environmental Economics and Management* 46: 288–309.

Note

1. This result is in contrast to many of the new economic geography models (e.g., Krugman 1991) in which declining transportation costs cause *more* agglomeration. The difference arises because of the aspatial nature of the production and consumption externalities in our model: the benefits of agglomeration are a function of total population in the region and not a function of distance.

CHAPTER 7

Natural Amenities, Human Capital, and Economic Growth

An Empirical Analysis

JunJie Wu and Sanjiv Mishra

A MAJOR THEME OF THIS VOLUME is to explore the interdependencies between the natural environment and economic growth. Such interdependencies arise because economic development affects the state of the natural environment, which in turn affects the rate of economic growth. The previous chapter explored the role of natural amenities as an engine of economic growth in a theoretical framework. This chapter follows up with an empirical analysis. Specifically, we evaluate the effect of natural amenities, accumulated human and physical capital, and economic geography on several indicators of economic growth, including net migration rates, percentage changes in the number of jobs, and income growth.

Economic growth, as measured by changes in income, employment, and other economic indicators, is highly uneven across the United States. For example, from 1995 to 2001, the average median family income in the nonmetropolitan counties in the United States increased from \$36,881 to \$41,012 (in 2001 dollars), while the average median family income in the metropolitan counties increased from \$48,166 to \$54,657 (Economic Research Service 2006a). The increase in the metropolitan counties was 57 percent more than the increase in the nonmetropolitan counties. Other economic indicators also displayed large spatial variations across the United States. The unemployment and poverty rates in the nonmetropolitan counties were, respectively, 27 and 28 percent higher than in the metropolitan counties in 2001 (Economic Research Service 2006b).

In addition to the large spatial variations, there also existed large temporal variations in economic growth in the United States. Most counties, except some located along the east and west coasts, experienced negative growth during the 1970s and 1980s. However, during the 1990s, both the trend and the spatial pattern were reversed. Most counties, except some located along the east and west coasts, experienced positive growth during the 1990s.

Why do the spatial inequalities in economic growth exist? What drives economic growth? Understanding these issues is central to developing policies to promote economic growth in the distressed communities (Henderson et al. 2001). However, these issues cannot be addressed in isolation because economic growth is closely related to migration, employment, and many other factors. It is well known from the migration literature that higher wage rates attract immigration, which may in turn lead to increased economic activity in the region. However, the interdependence between the household and firm location choices raises the question of whether people follow jobs or jobs follow people.

Many studies in the economic literature have analyzed spatial variations in economic development (see the literature review in the next section) and identified four factors affecting economic growth: (1) social and economic institutions (e.g., types of governments, legal and property rights systems), (2) natural endowments (e.g., land quality, water availability), (3) accumulated human and physical capital (e.g., skilled laborers, road networks), and (4) economic geography (e.g., spatial relationships between economic units). Most of these studies have been theoretical analyses. Empirical analyses were often conducted at the international level using cross-country data (see Henderson et al. 2001 for a review of the literature). Relatively few studies have examined the spatial variations in economic development within the United States. This is especially true for rural America. To develop effective policies to promote rural development, it is essential to understand the causes of the spatial variations in economic development in the rural United States.

This chapter presents an empirical study that evaluates the effect of natural amenities, accumulated human and physical capital, and economic geography on migration and the growth of employment and income in the Pacific Northwest. This region offers a good laboratory for studying the issue because many of its remote and rural counties are rich in natural amenities but poor in economic performance. Table 7-1 profiles the economy of the Pacific Northwest states—Idaho, Oregon, and Washington. The regional economy supported approximately 6.4 million jobs and was home to 10 million people in 2003. This region accounts for more than $200 billion in annual economic output (if ranked as a nation-state, it would be the tenth-largest economy in the world). Less than 4 percent of people in the Pacific Northwest work in natural resource–based industries.

The next section reviews recent work on migration, employment growth, and income growth, focusing on the roles of natural amenities, human capital, and economic geography as drivers of economic growth. Next, an empirical model of net migration, employment growth, and income growth is specified to estimate the effect of natural amenities, human capital, and economic geography on income growth, migration, and employment growth in the Pacific Northwest. The data, estimation method, and empirical results are then discussed. The last section summarizes results and considers future research needs.

Table 7-1. *Economic Profile of Pacific Northwest*

Economic indicators	Idaho	Oregon	Washington
Total population, 2004	1,393,262	3,594,586	6,203,788
Total population change, 2003–2004	2%	1%	1%
Poverty rate, 2002	12%	11%	10%
Number of jobs, 2003	809,640	2,094,696	3,562,494
Annual average wage per job, 2003	$28,288	$33,873	$39,181
Median household income, 2002	$38,242	$41,796	$46,399
Unemployment rate, August 2005	3%	6%	6%
Percentage of population >25 with college degree	21.7	25.1	27.7

The Literature

This section provides a brief review of the literature to inform the specification of our empirical model, which represents the interrelationships among three measures of economic growth: the net migration rate, percentage change in employment, and percentage change in median household income. The review focuses on the determinants of these measures of economic growth, particularly the role of amenities as a driver of economic growth.

Factors Affecting Employment Growth

Much research has focused on the role of the quality of life as a driver of migration and economic growth. Johnson and Beale (1994) suggest that natural amenities and other nonmarket attributes contribute to the overall quality of life and are a driving force of economic growth in rural areas. They found that rural areas classified as "recreational" had consistently higher rates of population growth than other nonmetropolitan areas. Rural areas with lower levels of amenities tend to lose economic opportunities to nearby growing urban centers (Henry et al. 1997). English et al. (2000) found that recreational counties had higher employment rates and higher income and population growth rates than the nonrecreational counties. Bukenya et al. (2003) found that economic performance has a strong positive relationship with the population's health status, education, employment, and income levels as well as social amenities. In Chapter 6 of this volume, Irwin, Randall, and Chen examined the role of environmental amenities as a driver of regional growth. They explored the conditions under which a core-periphery pattern of development emerges and considered the potential for rural environmental amenities to offset urban agglomeration benefits and "pull" a share of economic activity and population to the rural region.

The level of accumulated human capital has been identified as another major driver of economic growth. Rauch (1993) and Glaeser et al. (1995) found that the initial level of human capital in an area has a strong effect on the employment growth in that area. Acs and Armington (2004) suggest that differences in regional employment growth rates were a function of the regional levels of entrepreneurial activity, agglomeration effects, and human capital. They found many cases where the employment growth rate was not closely related to the population growth rate.

Employment growth rates were significantly higher in smaller regions than larger regions even after controlling for population growth. Simon and Nardinelli (2002) measure the level of human capital using two variables: the share of adults (defined as persons 25 years or older) with at least a high school degree and the share of adults who are college graduates. They find that both measures have a positive impact on regional growth.

Factors Affecting Migration

There is strong empirical evidence that the level of natural amenities is a major determinant of migration patterns. McGranahan (1999) found that rural areas located near coasts, lakes, or mountains tend to have higher population growth rates than areas with lower levels of natural amenities. Marcouiller et al. (1996) found that demand for amenities is strongly related to income and that the number of seasonal homes has increased in areas with high amenities. In-migration rates in the counties that depend on recreation activities were twice as high as in other nonmetropolitan counties during the 1970s and continued to have higher in-migration rates during the 1990s (Green 2001). McGranahan and Beale (2002) found that low population density, location away from metro areas, and a low levels of natural amenities are three major factors in the loss of population from rural counties during the 1990s. The decline of traditional rural industries also leads to population loss in rural communities (Albrecht 1993). Rural areas also tend to have lower-wage jobs than urban areas, and thus distance from the city affects employment opportunities and population growth (Gibbs and Cromartie 2000). Greenwood et al. (1986) estimate the linkages between employment changes and migration. They find that in an average year, two extra jobs attract about one additional net migrant, and one additional net migrant has a direct effect on area employment of almost 1.4 jobs. Population density may also affect migration because it affects the types of services and jobs available to residents. McGranahan and Beale (2002) found that counties with fewer people are more likely to lose their population, and such counties tend to be adjacent to each other.

Factors Affecting Income Growth

Several theoretical studies have analyzed spatial variations in economic development. Henderson et al. (2001) reviewed these studies and suggested that the spatial inequalities in economic development have to do partly with spatial variations in institutions and natural endowment, and partly with geography—the spatial relationship between economic units. However, relatively few studies have empirically examined the effect of these factors on economic development, particularly in the context of rural development in the United States. Roback (1982) develops an equilibrium model of firm and household location decisions to examine the role of wages and rents in allocating workers to locations with different levels of amenities. She applies the model to explain wage differences in major U.S. cities and finds that amenities have a significant effect on wages and rents. Extending Roback's work, Blomquist et al. (1988) develop a quality of life index that incorporates the effects of amenities on wages and housing prices for 253 urban counties in the United States. Partridge et al. (2007) assess whether agglomeration economies in the major Canadian metropolitan areas lead to population growth in or near these cities and find that disparities such as the concentration of Canadians along its southern border may explain migration patterns. Rappaport and Sachs (2003) analyzed the effect of coastal proximity on the concentration of economic activity in the United States and found that the coastal concentration derives primarily from a productivity effect but also, increasingly, from a quality-of-life effect. Levernier et al. (2000) use U.S. county-level data to explore potential explanations for the observed regional variation in the rates of poverty. Factors considered include those that relate to both area economic performance and demographic composition. Deller et al. (2001) estimated a structural model of regional economic growth to determine the role of amenity and quality-of-life attributes in regional economic growth. They found predictable relationships between amenities, quality of life, and local economic performance. Several other studies suggest that quality of life plays an increasingly important role in community economic growth (e.g., Dissart and Deller 2000; Halstead and Deller 1997; Rudzitis 1999; Gottlieb 1994).

Recently, Wu and Gopinath (2007) developed empirical models to evaluate the relative contributions of natural amenities, accumulated human and physical capital, and economic geography to the spatial variations in economic development across counties in the United States. They found that for a given level of human capital and local infrastructure, amenities have a negative effect on income because households are willing to substitute amenities for wages. However, because amenities attract human capital, which in turn attracts firms, locations with superior natural amenities tend to have a higher demand for labor and thus higher wage rates. In addition, locations with superior amenities also have higher housing prices and larger percentages of developed land because of households' preferences for high-amenity locations. Firms also prefer locations with higher amenities because of potential savings in labor costs. In contrast to Wu and Gopinath (2007), who focus on the spatial variations in the level of economic development, this study focuses on the pace of economic growth.

Historically, poverty rates in rural (nonmetropolitan) areas in the United States have been higher than poverty rates in metropolitan areas. For example, in 1987 there were 13 percent more employed workers whose earnings were below the poverty line in the rural areas than in the metropolitan areas (Gorham 1992). Ohman (1999) studied the effect of amenities and urban adjacency on economic growth and income inequality in the nonmetropolitan Pacific Northwest and found that amenity or urban-adjacent counties show the most growth, in both population and employment, but also have the greatest income inequality.

Empirical Model

Based on the literature review, a simultaneous equation system is specified to represent the interdependency among migration, employment growth, and income growth. The explanatory variables for the simultaneous system include natural and social amenities, accumulated human and physical capital, and economic geography. Specifically, the system is designed to examine how the initial conditions in 1990, including natural endowments, accumulated human and physical capital, and economic geography, affect net migration rates and percentage changes in employment and median household income between 1990 and 2000:

$$EG_{i90\text{-}00} = \alpha_1 + \alpha_2\, NM_{i90\text{-}00} + \alpha_3\, IG_{i90\text{-}00} + \alpha_4\, Income_{i,90} + \alpha_5\, EmpDen_{i,90}$$
$$+ \alpha_6\, Unemp_{i,90} + \alpha_7\, Amenity_{i,90} + \alpha_8\, Crime_{i,90} + \alpha_9 College_{i,90} + \alpha_{10}\, Road_{i,90}$$
$$+ \alpha_{11}\, Urban_{i,90} + \alpha_{12}\, NRDep_{i,90} + \alpha_{13}\, EdExp_{i,90} + \alpha_{14}\, HealthExp_{i,90}$$
$$+ \alpha_{15}\, HomeOwn_{i,90} + \alpha_{16}\, Idaho + \alpha_{17}\, Washington + \varepsilon_i$$

$$NM_{i90\text{-}00} = \beta_1 + _{,2}\, EG_{i90\text{-}00} + \beta_3\, IG_{i90\text{-}00} + \beta_4\, Income_{i,90} + \beta_5\, PopDen_{i,90}$$
$$+ \beta_6\, Unemp_{i,90} + \beta_7\, Amenity_{i,90} + \beta_8\, Crime_{i,90} + \beta_9\, College_{i,90} + \beta_{10}\, Road_{i,90}$$
$$+ \beta_{11}\, Urban_{i,90} + \beta_{12}\, NRDep_{i,90} + \beta_{13}\, EdExp_{i,90} + \beta_{14}\, HealthExp_{i,90}$$
$$+ \beta_{15}\, HomeOwn_{i,90} + \beta_{16}\, Idaho + \beta_{17}\, Washington + \mu_i$$

$$IG_{i90\text{-}00} = \gamma_1 + \gamma_2\, EG_{i90\text{-}00} + \gamma_3\, NM_{i90\text{-}00} + \gamma_4\, Income_{i,90} + \gamma_5\, Unemp_{i,90}$$
$$+ \gamma_6\, Amenity_{i,90} + \gamma_7\, Crime_{i,90} + \gamma_8\, College_{i,90} + \gamma_9\, Road_{i,90} + \gamma_{10}\, Urban_{i,90}$$
$$+ \gamma_{11}\, NRDep_{i,90} + \gamma_{12}\, EdExp_{i,90} + \gamma_{13}\, HealthExp_{i,90} + \gamma_{14}\, HomeOwn_{i,90}$$
$$+ \gamma_{15}\, Idaho + \gamma_{16}\, Washington + \nu_i$$

where the three endogenous variables, $EG_{i90\text{-}00}$, $NM_{i90\text{-}00}$, and $IG_{i90\text{-}00}$ are, respectively, the percentage change in total employment, the net migration rate, and the percentage change in median household income from 1990 to 2000 in county i. The net migration rate is defined as the percentage change in population net of natural changes due to births and deaths between 1990 and 2000. $EmpDen_{i,90}$ and $PopDen_{i,90}$ are the employment and population densities per square mile in 1990; $Income_{i,90}$ is the median household income in 1990; $Amenity_{i,90}$, $Crime_{i,90}$, $Urban_{i,90}$, $Road_{i,90}$, $EdExp_{i,90}$, $HealthExp_{i,90}$, $NRDep_{i,90}$, and $HomeOwn_{i,90}$ measure, respectively, natural amenities, crime rate, urban influence, road density, expenditure on education, expenditure on health, natural resource dependence, and homeownership in 1990; and ε_i, μ_i, and ν_i are error terms. A detailed description of the variables and the data sources can be found in the data section.

Each of the three equations in the equation system is specified as a spatial error model (Anselin 2002) to deal explicitly with the spatial dependency between error terms for neighboring counties. Formally, the error terms in the three equations are specified as

$$\varepsilon_i = \lambda_1 \sum_j w_{ij}\, \varepsilon_j + \varphi_i$$
$$\mu_i = \lambda_2 \sum_j w_{ij}\, \mu_j + \eta_i$$
$$\nu_i = \lambda_3 \sum_j w_{ij}\, \nu_j + \psi_i$$

where λ_1, λ_2, and λ_3 are the spatial autoregressive parameters, w_{ij} is the elements in the i-th row and the j-th column of a spatial weights matrix W, and φ_i, η_i, and ψ_i are the remaining disturbances and are assumed to be i.i.d. standard normal. W is constructed using GeoData Analysis software, which uses common boundaries to define neighbors; $w_{ij} = 1$ if counties i and j are adjacent and 0 otherwise. This implies that the random error in each county is a function of the random errors in all the adjacent counties. A set of state dummies for Idaho and Washington are added in the employment, migration, and income growth equations to control for possible differences in government policies and other factors specific to individual states. Oregon is the reference state.

Estimation Methods

The simultaneous equation system is estimated using generalized spatial three-stage least squares (GS3SLS) developed by Kelejian and Prucha (2004). The GS3SLS estimator takes into account potential spatial autocorrelation as well as the cross-equation correlation of the error terms. Ordinary least squares separately applied to each structural equation would result in biased and inefficient estimators when spatial autocorrelation, contemporaneous correlation, and endogeneity problems are present.

The GS3SLS estimator contains three stages. In the first stage, the model parameters are estimated using two-stage least squares (2SLS) and instrumental variable techniques. In this study, all exogenous variables are chosen as instrumental variables. The residuals from the 2SLS estimates are used to test for spatial autocorrelation using Moran's I statistic. The Moran's I statistic ranges from -1 to $+1$, with -1 indicating strong negative autocorrelation, $+1$ strong positive autocorrelation, and a value of 0 no spatial autocorrelation. The test results show that spatial autocorrelation exists in each of the three equations. Thus, in the second stage the residuals from the 2SLS are used to estimate the spatial autoregressive parameters λ utilizing the generalized moment estimator (Kelejian and Prucha 2004). After the spatial autoregressive parameters λ are estimated, data are transformed using the matrix, $\hat{P}_i = I - \hat{\lambda}_i W$ where I is an N by N identity matrix. Since the system is estimated using the cross-sectional data, heteroscedasticity may be a problem. White's (1980) test was used to test for a null hypothesis of homoscedasticity against the alternative of heteroscedasticity of the error terms. The null hypothesis cannot be rejected at the 5 percent level of significance. After the endogeneity and spatial autocorrelation are corrected in the first two steps, the simultaneous equation system is estimated using seemingly unrelated regression estimators in the third stage.

Data

The simultaneous equation system is estimated using the county-level data from Oregon, Washington, and Idaho. Of the 119 counties, 36 are in Oregon, 44 are in Idaho, and 39 are in Washington. Data used in this study are drawn from several sources. The data for median household incomes in 1990 and 2000, unemployment rates in 1990, average crime rates in 1990, and net migration rates between 1990 and 2000 were obtained from the U.S. Census Bureau (2000). The data on road density come from the U.S. Department of Transportation (2000).

The level of natural amenities in a county is measured using the natural amenity index developed by the Economic Research Service (2004a). The index is based on six factors: warm winter (average January temperature), winter sun (average number of sunny days in January), temperate summer (low winter-summer temperature gap), summer humidity (low average July humidity), topographic variation (topography scale), and water area (water area as a proportion of total county area).

Economic geography in a county is described using the urban influence code developed by the Economic Research Service (2004b). This agency divides counties into 12 groups based on urban influence. Metro counties are divided into two groups by the size of the metro area—those in large areas with at least one million residents, and those in areas with fewer than one million residents. Nonmetro, micropolitan counties are divided into three groups by their adjacency to metro areas—adjacent to a large metro area, adjacent to a small metro area, and not adjacent to a metro area. Nonmetro, noncore counties are divided into seven groups by their adjacency to metro or micro areas and whether they have their own town of at least 2,500 residents.

The natural resource dependence index was estimated by calculating the ratio of income from farming, fishing, and forestry to total personal income in the county in 1990. The percentages of government expenditures on health and on education in each county in 1990 were calculated by dividing these expenditures by the total government expenditures in the county.

Human capital represents embodied knowledge and skills and is a measure of the accumulated effect of activities such as formal education. In this study, human capital is measured using the percentage of county residents 25 or older having a college degree. It represents the quality of labor force in the county. The unemployment rate in 1990 measures the general labor market conditions at the beginning of the study period, 1990 to 2000. Table 7-2 defines the variables used in the empirical analysis and the data sources.

Estimation Results

The estimation results are presented in Table 7-3. Overall, the model performs well, with most of the estimated coefficients having signs consistent with economic theory. The estimated equations explain 34 percent of the variations of net migration and employment growth, and 32 percent of the variation of income growth. The coefficients on the lambda λ are significantly different from zero at the 5 percent level in each equation, indicating that error terms in all three equations are spatially autocorrelated. The factors affecting net migration rates and percentage changes in employment and median household income are discussed below.

Five variables (natural amenity, educational expenditure, homeownership, college degree, and λ_1) in the net migration rate equation are found to be statistically significant at the 10 percent level or better. These results suggest that high natural

Table 7-2. *Variable Definitions and Data Sources*

Variable	Description	Data source
EG	Percentage change in employment, 1990–2000	U.S. counties
NM	Net migration rate, 1990-2000	U.S. counties
IG	Percentage change in median household income, 1990–2000	City and county data book
EmpDen	Employment per square mile, 1990	City and county data book
PopDes	Population per square mile, 1990	City and county data book
College	Percentage of people > 25 with college degrees, 1990	U.S. counties
Unemp	Unemployment rate, 1990	U.S. counties
Income	Median household income, 1990 (thousand dollars)	U.S. counties
HomeOwn	Percentage of people who own their own homes, 1990	U.S. counties
Crime	Average crime rate in county, 1990	U.S. counties
Amenity	Natural amenity index for county, 1990	USDA Economic Research Service
Urban	Urban influence code for county, 1990	USDA Economic Research Service
HealthExp	Percentage of government health and hospital spending, 1990	U.S. counties
EdExp	Percentage of government education spending, 1990	U.S. counties
NRDep	Natural resource dependence index for county, 1990	U.S. counties calculated
Road	Road density, 1990	U.S. Department of Transportation

amenities, large government spending on education, and a higher proportion of homeownership all attract in-migration. Large government spending on education and a high proportion of homeownership may indicate high-quality schools and better social amenities. Together, these results suggest that both social and natural amenities attract migration. Human capital, as measured by the percentage of adults with a college degree, is also highly significant in the migration equation. This suggests that counties with more human capital in 1990 experienced more rapid population increase from 1990 to 2000—a result consistent with Wu and Gopinath (2007), who find that counties with more human capital attract firms, which provide more employment opportunities. The state dummies for Idaho and Washington are not significantly different from zero, indicating that there is no systematical difference in migration rates across the three states in the Pacific Northwest other than those explained by the independent variables.

In the employment growth equation, five variables (employment density, population density, college degree, natural resource dependence, and λ_2) are found to be statistically significant at the 10 percent level or better. Counties with more human capital, as measured by the percentage of adults with a college degree, had larger percentage increases in total employment, but counties with higher employment densities had smaller percentage increases in total employment, reflecting perhaps a crowding effect. This latter result is consistent with Acs and Armington (2004), who found that employment growth is significantly higher in regions with lower density of employment even after controlling for population growth. The negative coefficient on the natural resource dependence index suggests that counties that were more dependent on natural resources in 1990 had smaller percentage increases in employment between 1990 and 2000. However, counties with higher popula-

Table 7-3. *Coefficient Estimates for Equations of Net Migration Rate and Percentage Changes in Employment and Median Household Income*

	Net migration		Employment growth		Income growth	
	Coefficient	t-stat	Coefficient	t-stat	Coefficient	t-stat
Intercept	-28.622***	-2.42	-11.335**	-2.18	88.252**	1.64
$EG_{90\text{-}00}$	-0.113	-0.15			-2.845	-0.52
$NM_{90\text{-}00}$			0.017	0.20	0.461	0.44
$IG_{90\text{-}00}$	0.023	0.29	0.050	1.37		
$EmpDen_{90}$			-0.034**	-2.31	0.230	1.25
$PopDes_{90}$	-0.007	-0.57	0.022***	2.54	-0.131	-1.15
$Income_{90}$	0.000	-0.52	0.0002	1.55	-0.002***	-2.84
$College_{90}$	0.374***	3.12	0.097***	2.63	-0.138	-0.18
$UnEmp_{90}$			0.143	1.36		
$Urban_{90}$	-0.217	-0.98	0.138	1.36	-1.502*	-1.75
$HomeOwn_{90}$	0.220***	3.58			-0.218	-0.73
$Crime_{90}$	-0.0001	-0.52				
$Amenity_{90}$	2.332***	2.59	0.217	0.64	3.709	0.76
$HealthExp_{90}$	0.024	-0.42	-0.019	-0.92	0.192	0.73
$EdExp_{90}$	0.130*	1.73	-0.004	-0.17	0.470	1.23
$NRDep_{90}$	-0.942	-1.40	-0.393**	-2.00	-0.548	-0.16
$Road_{90}$	0.039	0.42	0.028	0.69	-0.310	-0.61
Idaho	-0.623	-0.42	0.429	0.93	2.782	0.44
Washington	0.791	0.51	-0.615	-0.89	10.379*	1.87
Lambda ($\lambda 1$)	0.645**	2.67				
Lambda ($\lambda 2$)			0.711***	2.45		
Lambda ($\lambda 3$)					1.231***	1.94
Moran's I statistic	0.166		0.114		0.151	
R- square	0.429		0.429		0.421	
Adjusted R-square (II stage)	0.340		0.340		0.323	
System weighted R-square	0.415					
F value	4.810		4.810		4.320	
Prob > F	0.0001		0.0001		0.0001	
White p value	0.456		0.448		0.683	
Breusch-Pagan p value	0.363		0.527		0.415	
Number of observations	119		119		119	

* Significant at the 10% level. ** Significant at the 5% level. *** Significant at the 1% level.

tion densities in 1990 (urban areas) had larger percentage increases in employment between 1990 and 2000.

In the income growth equation, four variables (median household income in 1990, urban influence, natural resource dependence, and λ_3) are found to be significant statistically at the 10 percent level or better. The negative coefficient on 1990 median household income indicates that counties with higher median household income at the beginning of the period (1990) experienced slower income growth from 1990 to 2000. One possible explanation for this result is that labor costs in those counties were already high compared with other places and firms were reluctant to locate to those counties. Counties located in more remote areas (i.e., counties with a large urban influence code) also had low income growth rates. This result is consistent with Wu and Gopinath (2007), who found that remoteness is a primary cause of spatial inequalities in economic development in the United States, and low income growth rates in those remote counties can be attributed to low demand for labor. Firms prefer locations close to the input and output markets to save transportation costs. A location with many firms will have a high demand for intermediate goods, which makes it an attractive location for intermediate producers. This in turn makes it an attractive location for firms that use intermediate goods. Such cluster or agglomeration effects do not exist in rural areas, which puts them in a disadvantaged position for attracting firms. The coefficient on the state dummy for Washington is positive and statistically significant at the 10 percent level, indicating that Washington had a higher rate of income growth than Oregon and Idaho from 1990 to 2000.

The interdependence among migration, employment growth, and income growth affects the spatial distribution of economic activity. Because amenities, accumulated human and physical capital, and economic geography appear in all three equations, they affect net migration rates and percentage changes in employment and median household income, both directly and indirectly. Their net effects on the economic indicators can be evaluated using reduced-form equations derived from the structural equations. The reduced-form equations of the net migration rate and percent changes in employment and median household income are reported in Table 7-4. The results show that almost all of the coefficients on the exogenous variables have the same signs as in the structural equations, although their magnitudes are different. Thus, all the qualitative results discussed above remained unchanged after considering the indirect effects. The only exception is the coefficient on the natural resource dependence variable, which is negative in the structural equation of income growth but positive in the reduced-form equation. However, both coefficients were statistically insignificant.

Conclusion

This chapter has examined factors that affect the spatial variations in net migration rate, percentage change in employment, and percentage change in median household income across 119 counties in the Pacific Northwest. Results show that the spatial distribution of human capital is a major factor affecting migration patterns and employment growth. Locations with more accumulated human capital attract firms and tend to have higher rates of growth in employment. Higher employment growth rates and better job prospects attract migration, which in turn leads to increased economic activities.

Natural and social amenities also play a significant role in shaping the spatial patterns of migration and economic growth. Counties with superior natural amenities, larger shares of government expenditure on education, and higher homeownership

Table 7-4. *Comparison of Structural and Reduced-Form Equations of Net Migration, Employment Growth, and Income Growth*

	Net migration		Employment growth		Income growth	
	Structural equation	Reduced form	Structural equation	Reduced form	Structural equation	Reduced form
Intercept	−28.622	−25.480	−11.335	−6.907	88.252	96.161
EmpDen$_{90}$		0.009	−0.034	−0.019		0.290
PopDes$_{90}$	−0.007	−0.013	0.022	0.013	−0.131	−0.176
College$_{90}$	0.374	0.356	0.097	0.091	−0.138	−0.235
UnEmp$_{90}$		−0.025		0.124		−0.365
Urban$_{90}$	−0.217	−0.263	0.138	0.044	−1.502	−1.751
Income$_{90}$	−0.0001	−0.0002	0.0002	−0.000	−0.002	−0.002
HomeOwn$_{90}$	0.220	0.218		−0.001		−0.112
Crime$_{90}$	−0.0001	−0.0001		−0.000		0.0005
Amenity$_{90}$	2.332	2.355	0.217	0.439	3.709	3.543
HealthExp$_{90}$	−0.025	−0.019	−0.019	−0.009	0.192	0.211
EdExp$_{90}$	0.130	0.138	0.004	0.021	0.470	0.473
NRDep$_{90}$	−0.942	−0.884	−0.393	−0.399	−0.548	0.181
Road$_{90}$	0.039	0.030	0.028	0.012	−0.310	−0.331
Idaho	−0.623	−0.661	0.429	0.474	2.782	1.127
Washington	0.791	1.050	−0.615	−0.039	10.379	10.977
Lambdaλ1	0.645	0.648		0.023		0.232
Lambdaλ2		−0.124	0.711	0.617		−1.814
Lambdaλ3		0.017		0.055	1.231	1.082

rates attract migration. However, employment growth rates tend to be low in counties that are dependent on natural resources. This suggests that the traditional industries that exploit natural resources—agriculture, fishing, timber, and mining—have become less important to the local economies as a means of job creation. Rural counties tend to have lower income growth rates and higher out-migration rates than metropolitan counties. These findings add to the increasing volume of empirical evidence that natural amenities and human capital are major drivers of migration and economic growth.

These results have implications for rural development policies. Most rural counties have lower levels of accumulated human and physical capital than do urban counties. However, many of them have higher levels of natural amenities. Public investments in infrastructure and human capital development would contribute to economic development in any place but will likely be more effective in rural areas with high natural amenities, especially when such investments enhance or improve access to natural amenities. For rural communities competing for jobs, this strategy may not be a zero-sum game, since it attracts human capital and firms from urban areas. Agglomeration effects, scale economies, knowledge spillovers, and labor market pooling will augment returns to both public investments and private human capital accumulation, which will drive endogenous economic growth in rural communities. Coordinated local and regional policies for economic development would be especially effective if the potential agglomeration effects could be fully realized.

Migration and economic growth appear to be affected by social, economic, environmental, and geographic factors. Further research is needed to examine how these factors interact with each other and what policy options are available to promote economic growth in rural communities. Although previous studies have identified natural endowments, accumulated human and physical capital, and economic geography as major causes of spatial inequalities in economic development, few studies have provided empirical estimates of the relative contribution of these factors to economic development in the context of rural America. It is of interest to examine and compare the patterns of migration and economic growth between the rural and urban areas and to ascertain how the patterns in rural and urban areas are related to each other. Further research is also needed to evaluate how firm and household location decisions respond to public policies. Such research is important because it is the responses of firms and households that ultimately determine how effective public policy can be in promoting economic development.

References

Acs, Z., and C. Armington. 2004. The Impact of Geographic Differences in Human Capital on Service Firm Formation Rates. *Journal of Urban Economics* 56: 244–78.

Albrecht, D.E. 1993. The Renewal of Population Loss in the Nonmetropolitan Great Plains. *Rural Sociology* 58(20): 233–46.

Anselin, L. 2002. Under the Hood. Issues in the Specification and Interpretation of Spatial Regression Models. *Agricultural Economics* 27(3): 247–67.

Beale, C.L., and K.M. Johnson. 1998. The Identification of Recreational Counties in Nonmetropolitan Areas of the USA. *Population Research and Policy Review* 17(1): 37–53.

Blomquist, G., M. Berger, and J. Hoehn. 1988. New Estimates of Quality of Life in Urban Areas. *American Economic Review* 78: 89–107.

Bukenya, J.O., T.G. Gebremedhin, and P.V. Schaeffer. 2003. Analysis of Quality of Life Satisfaction and Rural Development: A Spatial Approach. *Economic Development Quarterly* 17(3): 280–93.

Deller, C.D., S. Tsai, D.W. Marcouiller, and B.K.D. English. 2001. The Role of Amenities and Quality of Life in Rural Economic Growth. *American Journal of Agricultural Economics* 83(2): 352–65.

Dissart, J.C., and S.C. Deller. 2000. Quality of Life in the Planning Literature. *Journal of Planning Literature* 15(1): 315.

Economic Research Service. 2006a. Briefing Rooms: Rural Income, Poverty, and Welfare: Rural Income. Washington, DC: U.S. Department of Agriculture. http://www.ers.usda.gov/Briefing/incomepovertywelfare/RuralIncome/ (accessed May 22, 2006).

———. 2006b. Profiles of America: Demographic Data and Graphic Builder. Washington, DC: U.S. Department of Agriculture. http://maps.ers.usda.gov/Profiles/index.aspx#graphic_area (accessed May 22, 2006).

———. 2004a. Natural Amenities Scale. Washington, DC: U.S. Department of Agriculture. http://www.ers.usda.gov/Data/NaturalAmenities/ (accessed 2004).

———. 2004b. Measuring Rurality: Urban Influence Codes. Washington, DC: U.S. Department of Agriculture. http://www.ers.usda.gov/briefing/Rurality/UrbanInf/ (accessed 2004).

English, D.B.K., D.W. Marcouiller, and H.K Cordell. 2000. Linking Local Amenities with Rural Tourism Incidence: Estimates and Effects. *Social Natural Resource* 13(3): 185–202.

Gibbs, R., and J.B. Cromartie. 2000. Low-Wage Counties Face Locational Disadvantages. *Nonmetro Conditions and Trends* 11(2): 18–26.

Glaeser, E.L., J. Scheinkman, and A. Shleifer. 1995. Economic Growth in a Cross-Section of Cities. *Journal of Monetary Economics* 36: 117–43.

Gorham, L. 1992. The Growing Problem of Low Earnings in Rural Areas. In *Rural Poverty in America*, edited by Cynthia M. Duncan. New York: Auburn House.

Gottlieb, P.D. 1994. Amenities as an Economic Development Tool: Is There Enough Evidence? *Economic Development Quarterly* 8: 270–85.

Green, G.P. 2001. Amenities and Community Economic Development: Strategies for Sustainability. *The Journal of Regional Analysis & Policy* 31(2): 61–75.

Greenwood, M., G. Hunt, and G. McDowell. 1986. Migration and Employment Change: Empirical Evidence on the Spatial and Temporal Dimensions of the Linkage. *Journal of Regional Science* 26: 223–34.

Halstead, J.M., and S.C. Deller. 1997. Public Infrastructure in Economic Development and Growth: Evidence from Rural Manufacturers. *Journal of Community Development Society* 28: 149–69.

Henderson, J.V., Z. Shalizi, and A.J. Venables. 2001. *Journal of Economic Geography* 1: 81–105.

Henry, M.S., D.L. Barkley, and S. Bao. 1997. The Hinterland's Stake in Metropolitan Growth: Evidence from Selected Southern Regions. *Journal of Regional Science* 37(3): 479–501.

Johnson, K.M., and C.L. Beale. 1994. The Recent Revival of Widespread Population Growth in Nonmetropolitan Areas of the United States. *Rural Sociology* 4: 655–67.

Kelejian, H.K., and I.R. Prucha. 2004. Estimation of Simultaneous Systems of Spatially Interrelated Cross Sectional Equations. *Journal of Econometrics* 118: 27–50.

Levernier, W., M.D. Partridge, D.S. Rickman. 2000. The Causes of Regional Variations in U.S. Poverty: A Cross-Country Analysis. *Journal of Regional Science* 40: 473–97.

Marcouiller, D.W., G.P. Green, S.C. Deller, N.R. Sumathi, and D. Erkkila. 1996. *Recreational Homes and Regional Development: A Case Study from the Upper Great Lakes States.* University of Wisconsin Extension, Report No. G3651.

McGranahan, D.A. 1999. *Natural Amenities Drive Rural Population Change.* Food and Rural Economics Division, Economic Research Service, Agricultural Economic Report No. 781. Washington, DC: U.S. Department of Agriculture.

McGranahan, D.A., and C.L. Beale. 2002. Understanding Rural Population Loss. Paper presented at the Rural Sociology Society Annual Meeting, Chicago, August.

Ohman, D. 1999. Restructuring and Well-being in the Nonmetropolitan Pacific Northwest. *Growth and Change* 30: 161–83.

Partridge, M.D., O.M. Rose, and A. Alessandro. 2007. Canadian Cities as Regional Engines of Growth: Agglomeration and Amenities. *Canadian Journal of Economics* 40: 39–68.

Rappaport, J., and J.D. Sachs. 2003. The United States as a Coastal Nation. *Journal of Economic Growth* 8(1): 5–46.

Rauch, J.E. 1993. *Does History Matter Only When It Matters Little? The Case of City-Industry Location.* National Bureau of Economic Research Working Paper 4312, Cambridge, MA.

Roback, J. 1982. Wages, Rents, and the Quality of Life. *Journal of Political Economy* 90(6): 1257–78.

Rudzitis, G. 1999. Amenities Increasingly Drew People to the Rural West. *Rural Development Perspectives* 14: 23–28.

Simon, C., and C. Nardinelli. 2002. Human Capital and the Rise of American Cities, 1900-1990. *Regional Science and Urban Economics* 32: 59–96.

U.S. Census Bureau. 2000. County and City Data Book: 2000. http://www.census.gov/prod/www/ccdb.html (accessed 2005).

U.S. Department of Transportation. 2000. Highway Statistics 2000: Public Road Length. http://www.fhwa.dot.gov/ohim/hs00/hm20.htm (accessed 2005).

White, H. 1980. A Heteroscedasticity-Consistent Covariance Matrix Estimator and a Direct Test for Heteroscedasticity. *Econometrica* 48: 817–38.

Wu, J., and M. Gopinath. 2007. What Causes Spatial Inequalities in Economic Development in the United States? *American Journal of Agricultural Economics*, forthcoming.

Part III

POLICIES AND PROGRAMS FOR PEOPLE AND PLACES

CHAPTER 8

People and Places
at the Ragged Edge
Place-Based Policy for
Reducing Rural Poverty

Bruce A. Weber

PROSPERITY IS NOT EVENLY distributed across the American landscape.
Poverty, especially persistent poverty, is highly concentrated, with the highest
county poverty rates found in remote rural[1] counties. Counties with a strong historical dependence on natural resource industries are frequently places with high
and persistent poverty. In rural areas, the interdependencies that are the focus of
this volume—between humans and the environment, and between rural and urban
markets—have not worked to the benefit of the local residents.

Most current antipoverty policy in the United States, however, is essentially
place-blind. This chapter argues for more attention to "place"—the importance of
local context—in national and state antipoverty policy and in the research that
informs this policy. The chapter advances the rural economics literature in several
ways: (1) it outlines a multidisciplinary framework for exploring poverty, policy,
and place—the complex interactions between local economic and social context[2]
and household economic choices that lead to poverty; (2) it uses this framework
to summarize recent research on how local economic and social context affects
poverty and policy impacts and suggest needed research directions; and (3) it revis-
its, evaluates, and extends arguments for place-specific policies to reduce poverty.
The chapter calls attention to the distributional dimensions of rural and resource
economics, and to how rural-urban and human-ecosystem interdependencies affect
income distribution. It demonstrates that rural and resource economics can make
an important contribution in analyzing how policy alternatives might address concerns about increasing concentrations of rural poverty.

The first section of the paper introduces the geography of poverty in the
United States. The second reviews recent research that seeks to understand how
place-specific context and local economic growth affect rural poverty and policy
impacts. It also offers reasons why place-based policies may have become more

important in reducing poverty, particularly in rural areas. The next section discusses whether there is a rationale for public place-based intervention in reducing poverty, ultimately arguing that at least some necessary conditions (if the sufficient conditions) exist for government place-specific policy directed to reducing rural poverty, while recognizing its limits. The concluding section argues that we do not have an adequate understanding of how antipoverty policies work in different local contexts. This stems from a lack of understanding of the social processes underlying social capital and the functioning of intermediary institutions. Research that improved our understanding of such processes would be helpful in the design of place-specific policies to reduce rural poverty.

Poverty and Place: A Geography of Poverty

The complex geography of county-level poverty can be summarized in four stylized facts.[3] First, county poverty rates are lowest in large metropolitan areas and highest in remote rural areas.[4] The Department of Agriculture's Economic Research Service has created a classification system of "urban influence codes" that puts counties into nine categories based on metropolitan status, population size, and adjacency to metro areas. If this system is collapsed into five categories (large metro, small metro, nonmetro adjacent to large metro, nonmetro adjacent to small metro, and nonmetro nonadjacent), poverty rates increase as counties become more rural and remote. The poverty rate for large metro counties is less than 12 percent, but for remote rural (nonmetro nonadjacent) counties exceeds 16 percent (Miller and Weber 2003).

Second, poverty is geographically linked with natural resource dependence. Elo and Beale (1985) reported that poverty rates averaged 2 percentage points higher (17 percent versus 14.9 percent) in "natural-resource-dominated counties" than in all nonmetropolitan counties. Weber (1995) found that poverty rates in 1989 were higher for those counties that were historically dependent on natural resource extraction (more than 20 percent of labor and proprietor income was in agriculture, forestry, energy, mining, or fishing and related processing) than for all counties.

Third, persistent poverty is a largely rural phenomenon. Persistent-poverty counties (whose poverty rates have been 20 percent or higher for the past half-century)[5] are overwhelmingly and disproportionately rural. Fully 95 percent of persistent-poverty counties are rural and constitute 16 percent of all nonmetro counties (versus 2 percent of all metro counties). And persistent poverty increases as counties become more distant from metro areas and more rural: only 7 percent of nonmetro counties adjacent to large metro areas are persistent-poverty counties, compared with 18 percent of completely rural counties not adjacent to metro areas. Persistent-poverty counties are also geographically concentrated—in the Mississippi Delta, Appalachia, the Rio Grande, and Indian reservations of the West.

Finally, persistent poverty is increasingly a problem of remote rural areas. Between 1990 and 2000, one-third of the 1990 persistent-poverty counties saw their poverty rates drop below 20 percent and thus leave persistent-poverty status.

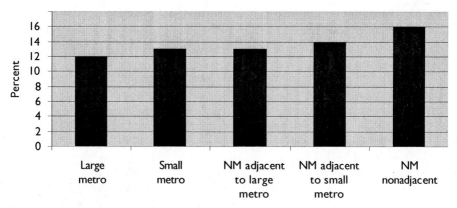

Figure 8-1. *Poverty Rates by Urban Influence Code, 1999*

Note: NM = nonmetro.

Nonmetro nonadjacent counties were less likely to exit persistent-poverty status than metro counties and adjacent nonmetro counties.

The county-level geography of poverty in this country shows economic distress increasing with rurality and remoteness. Poverty is more prevalent in the most isolated rural places and in counties dependent on natural resource extraction. Persistent poverty tends to concentrate geographically in rural regions and has become more concentrated there in recent years.

How Local Community Context Affects Poverty: Recent Research[6]

Household poverty status at any given time is determined in part by choices adults make about migration, work, asset accumulation, marriage, childbearing, and welfare program participation. These choices are conditioned by individual personal characteristics outside the control of the individual (gender, age, race, and ethnicity) as well as by previous choices about education and work, assets, family formation, and program participation.

These choices are also conditioned by the characteristics of the place where one lives. Rebecca Blank identifies five "attributes" of a place that affect local poverty and opportunity: "its natural environment, its economic structure, its public and community institutions, its existing social norms and cultural environment, and the demographic characteristics of its population" (Blank 2005, *442*). Economic structure, for example, affects the availability of jobs and services and the probable employment outcomes for the household. Formal institutions (including local governments and schools, civic organizations, churches, financial intermediaries, and for-profit and nonprofit providers of child care, health care, and job training services) affect the ability of residents to get or keep jobs. As Blank observes, however, "formal modeling of the role of 'place' is extremely difficult. Empirically measuring the impact of changes in one of these variables independent of the others also is hard because of the simultaneous causality between them" (*442*).

Macroeconomic forces (national economic growth, global economic trends) and federal and state policies (minimum wage, workforce investment act programs, earned-income tax credits, temporary assistance for needy families) have different effects on the choices people make and on their poverty status because of differences in community context.

The rurality of a place has an important influence on the community attributes identified by Blank. Rural areas are characterized by small and sparse population settlements and by distance from urban centers. Lack of scale economies in places with a small population base and lack of agglomeration economies in sparsely settled places affect both economic opportunities and services. Isolation from large urban settlements also affects economic opportunities and services in rural places in a complex and likely nonlinear way as transportation costs are traded off against scale economies in the production of nonbasic goods and services. Sparse populations and isolation from large population centers also lead to different intermediary institutions (civic organizations and faith communities) and different norms as well.

Some Evidence from Recent Research

During the past several decades, much has been learned about how place affects poverty and about the impact of federal and state policies on employment and poverty. Recent research has focused both on factors affecting poverty that are not very sensitive to policy (proximity to cities, natural resource dependence, and rurality) and those that are amenable to policy influence (local economic conditions and social capital).

- *Proximity to cities.* There appear to be spatial externalities at a regional scale. Poverty rates in rural counties not adjacent to metropolitan areas declined at a significantly slower rate in the 1990s than rates in rural counties adjacent to metro areas, other things equal (Swaminathan and Findeis 2004; Rupasingha and Goetz 2003).

- *Proximity to high-poverty tracts.* There appear to be small-scale spatial externalities (i.e., neighborhood spillover effects) in addition to the larger regional externalities: reducing poverty in one tract has spillover effects, reducing poverty in neighboring tracts (Crandall and Weber 2004).

- *Natural resource dependence.* Many studies have explored the relationship between natural resource extraction and rural poverty. Machlis et al. (1990) and Peluso et al. (1994), for example, have found strong links and identified economic and social processes unique to natural resource-dependent areas that lead to impoverishment of these places. Others, like Nord and Luloff (1993) and Fisher (2001), are not able to conclude that resource extraction per se leads to poverty, but conclude that the relationship between extraction and poverty is unique to sector and location. Even though their paper was written prior to much of the literature on this topic, Elo and Beale (1985, 5-2 and 5-13) provide what may be the best summary of this literature: "there is no major overall direct causal relationship between natural-resource activity and rural poverty.... Natural resource and poverty relationships are regionally specific and associated with particular segments of the nation's population." They identify several groups for whom there are natural resource and poverty links: farm workers, people in coal mining and agriculture in the southern Appalachians, rural blacks in the southern Coastal Plain and Mississippi Delta (for whom the "natural-resource link has been substantially broken, but whose persistent poverty is partly the legacy of the sharecropping era"), and Indian communities in the West and Great Plains (Elo and Beale 1985, 5-3).

• *Rurality.* Almost all studies of poverty and rurality have concluded that a household's odds of being poor in a metropolitan area are lower than the odds in non-metropolitan areas, controlling for demographic characteristics and local economic structure and conditions (Weber et al. 2005). Furthermore, living in a rural area moderated the effect of certain household or individual demographic characteristics. Having an education, for example, appears to have less poverty-reducing effect in rural areas. Lichter et al. (1994) found that those with more than a high school education were more at risk of poverty in rural areas than their urban counterparts. Haynie and Gorman (1999) found that "individual-level attributes and credentials" have less poverty-reducing effect for rural women than for urban women.

Few of these studies considered the possibility that living in a rural area and being poor are endogenous—that is, that poor people are more likely to choose to live in rural areas. Fisher's (2005) findings from such a study suggest that some of the observed rural-urban difference in poverty risk may be due to the residential choices of the poor as well as to local opportunities.

• *Local economic conditions.* Local job growth appears to have poverty-reducing effects, particularly in high-poverty census tracts (Crandall and Weber 2004), high-poverty rural counties (Partridge and Rickman 2005), and persistent-poverty counties (Partridge and Rickman 2007). Having a job, however, appears to reduce poverty risk less in rural areas (Brown and Hirschl 1995). Working more hours is not as effective in moving people out of poverty in rural areas as it is in urban areas (Lichter et al. 1994). And higher unemployment rates increase poverty risk more for rural women than for urban women (Haynie and Gorman 1999). Cotter (2002) found that labor market conditions account for half the difference in poverty odds between rural and urban places.

• *Community social capital.* Communities with higher social capital (greater civic participation and organizational membership) saw greater poverty reduction in the 1990s (Rupasingha and Goetz 2003). Increased social capital reduces poverty most in high-poverty tracts (Crandall and Weber 2004).

These studies lend some support to factors identified by Blank (2005) as important in reducing poverty. Blank's paper also focuses attention on critical contextual factors that have been neglected in most previous work. Most of the studies referenced above did not take community capacity or institutions into account and thus may be missing important contextual information about causes and consequences of poverty, and about what can be done to improve outcomes of public and private actions to reduce poverty. Indeed, it is likely that some of the unmeasured differences that lead to higher poverty rates in rural areas may be due to rural-urban differences in community capacity and local institutions.

Implications for Poverty Reduction Policy

The current policy environment for poverty reduction emphasizes strategies that invest in people and provide incentives for people to work, and neglects strategies that attempt to improve the local context by investing in places. The important changes in social policy in the 1990s (the expansion of federal and state earned-income tax credits, welfare reform, minimum wage increase, and the expansion of Medicaid and child care subsidies) all focus on making the worker more productive and making work pay. Although there is some evidence that the social policy changes of the 1990s do not work as well in reducing poverty in rural areas (Weber et al. 2004), almost no attention has been paid to investing in place-specific infrastructure that would increase the demand for workers or to making investments in community institutions that could increase the effectiveness of policy.

There are, however, at least three reasons why policies to improve local community context and institutions may be more important in poverty reduction now than in the past.

First, state and local governments are playing a stronger role in social policy. In the 1996 welfare reform law, the federal government gave states much more discretion in lowering barriers to work (e.g., discretion to disregard higher income in calculating benefits) and increasing asset limits for eligibility (Gais and Weaver 2002). States have also taken initiative in increasing state earned-income tax credits. Local human service systems, furthermore, have streamlined program entry and worked to ensure continuity of coverage in food stamps and Medicaid for those leaving welfare (Fossett et al. 2002). The ability of localities to use this discretion in policy formulation and implementation makes a greater difference for poverty reduction than in the past.

Second, nongovernmental (often locally based) organizations have been given new roles in delivery of welfare and workforce services. Nathan and Gais (1999) have noted the increased use of regional nonprofit organizations in providing melded welfare and workforce services. And welfare reform's charitable choice provisions gave added attention to the roles of faith-based organizations in the delivery of social services (Bartkowski and Regis 2002).

Finally, and perhaps most importantly, antipoverty policy is increasingly work-related. The success of work-related policy depends to a greater extent on local opportunities and the effectiveness of local intermediaries and social networks. The

1996 redesign of the nation's major welfare program—creating the Temporary Assistance to Needy Families program—provided incentives for working and sanctions for not working (Moffitt 2003b). Most public spending on means-tested transfer programs (eligibility for which is conditioned on having low income) goes to in-kind medical and food security programs, work-related tax credits, and work-related support services (child care subsidies, job training), not cash welfare payments (Moffit 2003a, 7).[7] Several studies have shown the importance of local context for the work outcomes of low-income adults[8] (Davis et al. 2003; Davis and Weber 2002).

The confluence of these trends—that the design and implementation of antipoverty policy have been placed increasingly in the hands of local governments and nongovernmental intermediaries, and that antipoverty policy has become more work-oriented and context-dependent—strengthens the case for place-based policies for reducing poverty—policies that increase local job opportunities, strengthen local institutions in poverty reduction efforts, and enhance the effectiveness of local work-support services and self-sufficiency strategies.

Can Place-Based Policy for Reducing Poverty Be Justified?

The intense geographic concentrations of poor people in central cities and remote rural places, combined with the evidence that policies can affect the factors causing poverty, might seem to provide prima facie evidence of a need for place-based antipoverty policies. The fact that capital and labor can move in and out of poor places, however, directs attention to the limitations of a place-based approach to poverty reduction. It may not be appropriate, some argue, to tailor policies to places because such policies may introduce inefficiencies and rigidities into factor and product markets and discourage people and capital from migrating to areas with better market-related opportunities.

This enduring discussion has engaged the attention of policymakers and academics for many decades. The central issue is captured in the felicitous title of Louis Winnick's 1966 paper "Place Prosperity v. People Prosperity," which made arguments about the role of the national government in assisting individuals and places that are economically depressed. Bolton (1992, *187*) has summarized the "place versus people prosperity" debate this way:

> The phrase suggests a conflict between two ideals or possible goals of policy. The conflict is between the ideal of improving the welfare of deserving people as individuals, *regardless of where they live,* and the ideal of improving the welfare of *groups* of deserving people defined by their spatial proximity in places. . . . The context of the debate is a 'declining' or 'depressed' place, not a prosperous and growing one; 'place prosperity vs. people prosperity' is almost never raised as an issue in designing policies to deal with rapidly growing places.
>
> The conflict in ideals implies a corresponding conflict of practical government policies. To put it simply, the opposition is between these two clusters

of policies: on the one hand, direct transfer payments to individuals or subsidies to encourage them to move out of declining regions; on the other hand, expenditures to increase infrastructure and private capital in particular places, such as grants to local governments and business, and education and worker training that are oriented toward a place's existing comparative advantage.[9]

The arguments against investing in particular places to stimulate their economies and help their low-income populations are summarized by Kraybill and Kilkenny (2003, 8–9):

> The pitfalls and shortcomings of place-based policies include that the policies may (i) generate nothing but rents for the property owners in targeted places, (ii) attract or retain (trap) poor people in poor areas, (iii) distort business as well as human migration decisions, (iv) enable the postponement of necessary adjustments, (v) create dependencies, and are (vi) subject to abuse by place-based politicians.

Their summary indictment of place-based policies argues that

> Providing subsidies to people and businesses to remain in their small rural towns may address a short-run symptom such as rural poverty. At best it may postpone a cure, at worst it actually hastens a town's ultimate demise by substituting dependency for self-improvement. Towns are dispersed across the countryside because land and natural resources are dispersed, and the businesses and people who value those resources benefit by being closer to them. If the resources of a place are no longer valuable, there is no good reason for people or business to be there. The provision of subsidies to induce people to stay in that place delays the inevitable. At worst, such subsidies actually retain the kinds of people who are least able to adjust, ultimately, to market forces.
>
> It does no good to retain (or attract) people in places that are too costly for most businesses, which cannot sustain economic activity. That turns the place into a poverty trap. It does no good to provide income transfers to people contingent on having a residence in a poorer place. That sets up perverse incentives to perpetuate place-poverty to remain eligible for larger subsidies. For the same reasons, providing higher payoffs to business owners in poorer places undermines local business incentives to grow the local economy. Place-based policies may keep poor people in poor places, support absentee wealthy, and provide perverse incentives. (Kraybill and Kilkenny 2003, 9–10)

On the other hand are arguments that place-based policies for small towns are welfare enhancing. Kraybill and Kilkenny (2003, 5) provide a compact and lucid exposition of the neoclassical economic "market failure" rationale for place-based policy as they define it:[10]

> When the assumptions necessary for competitive markets do not hold, markets fail to generate efficient outcomes. Market failure can occur due to fac-

tor immobility, monopoly, barriers to entry, externalities, and imperfect information.

Since each of the neoclassical assumptions is likely to be violated due to frictions and economies of space, market failure provides a relevant rationale for rural development policy interventions in economic systems where markets play a role in the allocation of resources. A market failure approach to policymaking would attempt to provide goods and services that private markets are not able to deliver. Policies would then be deemed efficient if the nonmarket benefits of policies and programs exceeded the costs of implementing them.

They provide four arguments for place-based policy. The first is that investments in places that emphasize and develop the uniqueness of these places can make them more attractive places to live, work, and invest. This appears to be an argument that, by creating a differentiated product in particular places, overall welfare is enhanced *and* localities benefit from the market power conferred and from the potential increasing returns generated in the process. The second argument is that there are neighborhood effects (what they call "positive spatial externalities): "the possibility of positive feedback from group to individual outcomes." This would be the case, for example, when "an individual's level of knowledge attainment is related to the knowledge level of his or her neighborhood." A third argument is that there are knowledge spillovers across firms. Policy that generated clusters of firms would increase the possibility that such spillovers would generate increasing returns.[11] Their final argument is a national efficiency argument: that national efficiency could be enhanced by policies that attract capital to regions with unemployed immobile labor.[12]

Two other "market failure" justifications for rural policy are based on a "sense of place" (public goods) and on interregional equity:

- Bolton (1992) has argued that the "sense of place" that results from personal investments that people make in particular locales has public good characteristics. It appears that rural people are willing to make these investments and that the "sense of place" in rural areas has a public good character.

- Many who discuss market failure as a rationale for public policy intervention include as an aspect of market failure an "equity" argument: that the workings of the market yield an unacceptable size distribution of income.

Can the equity criterion be extended to argue for equity in the geographic distribution of income? It is not clear, of course, that our society values, or should seek, equal opportunity across places. Even if markets functioned perfectly and wages and prices were flexible, the existence of increasing returns to scale and of agglomeration economies generates growth in cities that cannot be matched in (otherwise equally endowed) remote and sparsely settled places. That is, even perfectly functioning markets could generate unequal opportunities across places. To the extent, however, that there should be equal opportunity for all, there is a rationale for place-specific (and rural-specific) public interventions.[13]

Beyond market failure arguments, Castle has argued more generally that place-based policies are justified because groups of people in a place have independent "standing" and deserve to have their particular concerns considered in policymaking: "it is appropriate rural people have, and exercise, a degree of autonomy in addressing their common concerns and in seeking fulfillment of their aspirations" (Castle 1998, *622*). Castle and Weber (2006) use this justification to argue that even if there were no market failure, places have a uniqueness that is inherently valuable:

> ... place-based policies need to recognize and respect the uniqueness of particular places and the proper scope of local autonomy. ... The national government role in place-based policy is to set boundary conditions that address the national interest ... and to provide both the resources that local government can direct to building various forms of capital and information that is useful to localities in exercising local autonomy. (2006, *13–14*)

Ultimately, of course, investments to reduce poverty must be made in both people *and* places, and the public policy decisions are about how much to invest in people relative to places. Both urban and rural places have conditions where market failure makes place-based investments appropriate, and their uniqueness and autonomy should be fostered regardless.[14] In an era when much of the policy discussion appears to focus on the efficacy of human capital investments and individual incentive structures, it is useful to revisit arguments about the need for a public investment strategy that balances people and place considerations and to establish a rationale for such a strategy for poverty reduction. It is also useful to recognize the limits of place-based strategies deriving from perverse incentives that the policies may create, from the interdependence of rural and urban places due to trade and the mobility of labor and capital, and from the weaknesses inherent in some markets and institutions in sparsely settled places.

Place-Based Policy and Rural Poverty: Some Research Directions

Economists have been important contributors to the understanding of poverty and antipoverty policy, and economists have much to contribute to the understanding of local context. Most economic models of the extent of poverty are based on a theoretical foundation of individual and firm behavior that assumes a reasonable functioning of labor markets and capital markets and attempts to control for the effects of natural resources and amenities, differences in human capital, and migration. This theoretical foundation has also been helpful in outlining the conditions under which markets fail to produce efficient or socially acceptable outcomes and in providing a rationale for public action to correct these outcomes.

Place-based policy involves investments in places and people in particular places. Much is known about returns to public investments in physical capital and human capital in particular places (Bartik 1991; Hite 1999; Goetz and Rupasingha

2005; Barkely et al. 2005). It would be helpful for policy purposes to summarize what is known about the returns in rural places implied by this research and to develop estimates of elasticities of substitution between physical and human capital for rural and urban areas.[15] It would also be important to learn more about the migration of low-income adults and their families in response to these various public investments.

Blank (2005) suggests that an understanding of social networks and institutions is critical for understanding poverty and antipoverty policy impacts. Place-based policy could also involve investments in place-specific social networks and institutions. Another needed line of research goes beyond economic models and would seek to understand both the social underpinnings of the processes leading to poverty and the institutional context within which the social and economic processes take place.[16] This would allow for estimates of social returns to investments in social capital and institutional development, and for estimating the elasticities of substitution between physical, human, social, and institutional capital.

There is evidence that social institutions are different in urban and rural areas. Roscigno and Crowley (2001), for example, found that rural adolescents are institutionally disadvantaged with respect to some school investments and resources that affect both educational attainment and student achievement. Rural and urban areas also have different forms and patterns of social capital. Hofferth and Iceland (1998) found rural-urban differences in social capital as measured by social exchanges. This suggests the need for research on these issues in both rural and urban contexts.

The argument in this paper is that local context does indeed (and increasingly) matter for poverty reduction, and that policy can affect the local context. There is solid evidence that a household's poverty status is affected by the characteristics and economic conditions of the place of residence and that the effect of policy depends on the local context. Social scientists, however, do not have a good understanding of *how* place affects income and poverty. The design of place-based policy requires a better understanding of how the underlying social processes and institutional arrangements in communities and neighborhoods actually work. It requires answers to two fundamental questions:[17]

- *What are the individual processes and community or neighborhood processes and institutional mechanisms that generate and maintain poverty?* For example, how do "neighborhood effects" work to change individual decisions and outcomes?

- *How does antipoverty policy interact with these community-level processes to affect poverty?* For example, how do national workforce investment policies affect workers in particular local contexts?

Answering those questions would require both qualitative and quantitative research about social and institutional processes and structures, with the involvement of multiple disciplines. There are two cross-disciplinary constructs that seem particularly important in answering the two questions and in developing strategies for reducing poverty: social capital and intermediate decisionmaking.

Social Capital

Social capital has been defined as "those group arrangements that make individual actions more productive than they would be in its absence"[18] (Castle 1998, *623*). Social capital is frequently measured at the national, state, regional, or community level from aggregate measures of structural characteristics (population size, density of associations, percentage of population that is native-born, of various races or ethnicities, or living in a rural area). These community measures can be used to predict either individual outcomes (Guiso et al. 2002) or community outcomes (Rupasingha et al. 2000). Rupasingha et al. (2006) use information from a variety of secondary sources to construct a county-level measure of social capital. They use this variable to explain variations in county growth rates (Rupasingha et al. 2000) and changes in poverty (Rupasingha and Goetz 2003). This research on the relationship between social capital and poverty suggests that levels of community social capital do help explain community poverty rates, but it is based on a relatively crude measure of social capital and does not provide insight into the workings of social capital.[19]

Perhaps the most rigorous economic critique of a particular conception of social capital is in Durlauf and Fafchamps (2005). Criticizing both the theoretical and the empirical work in economics on social capital, Durlauf and Fafchamps (2005, *1692*) write,

> In terms of conceptual and theoretical studies of social capital, there is a considerable amount of ambiguity and confusion as to what social capital means. . . .
>
> With respect to empirical work in general, social capital research has led to the development of a number of interesting data sets as well as the development of a number of provocative hypotheses; much of the empirical literature is at best suggestive and at worst easy to discount. So while one can point to no end of studies in which a variable that is asserted to proxy for social capital has some effect on individuals or groups, it is usually very difficult to treat the finding as establishing a causal role for social capital. . . . The defects of the empirical social literature are unfortunate, since the work on social capital is an active front along which the "undersocialized conception of man" for which economics has been criticized (Granovetter 1985) is being addressed.

There are two attempts to articulate important aspects of social capital that seem to me to hold promise in understanding the social capital mechanisms through which localities can affect local poverty rates: collective efficacy and community social networks.

Collective efficacy. Sampson et al. (1997, *918*) define collective efficacy as "social cohesion among neighbors combined with their willingness to intervene on behalf of the common good." They work from the premise that "social and organizational characteristics of neighborhoods explain variations in crime rates that are not solely attributable to the aggregated demographic characteristics of individuals. We propose that the differential ability of neighborhoods to realize the common values of residents and maintain effective social controls is a major source of neighborhood variation in violence" (Sampson et al. 1997, *918*). They measure collective efficacy from answers to two questions in a household survey in Chicago neighborhoods. A five-point Likert scale was used on questions characterizing "informal social control" and "social cohesion" at the neighborhood level. Since answers to these questions were highly correlated, they combined the two scales into a single measure of "collective efficacy." Although this research has focused primarily on explaining neighborhood criminal activity, it could also be used to explain variations in economic viability and poverty.

Community social networks. Maureen Kilkenny (2005) builds on the social community network framework of Wasserman and Faust (1994) to suggest an analysis of the relationship of social capital and community outcomes that addresses the concerns of Durlauf and Fafchamps outlined above. She suggests how the graph-theory social network analytical approach developed in Kilkenny and Nalbarte (2000) can measure the "network based processes that generate beneficial outcomes through norms and trust," considered by Durlauf and Fafchamps to be the critical element of social capital (Kilkenny 2005, *11*). Her current research, involving a national team of collaborators, is exploring how these important social and economic linkages in 60 small communities in four states affect such community outcomes as employment growth, taxes, and poverty (Kilkenny 2005).

Intermediate Decisionmaking

In standard economic analysis, market and nonmarket outcomes are explained within a theory based on decisions in micro (firm, individual) and macro (national government) units. Castle (Chapter 12, this volume) argues that another, intermediate level of decisionmaking is required to address the concerns of rural people and places and that understanding intermediate decisionmaking and institutions requires a new theoretical base that draws on other disciplines. If one agrees that people in places should have autonomy, and given that groups exercise their autonomy through intermediary institutions (local governments, voluntary associations), the study of intermediate decisionmaking becomes a critical—and as yet underdeveloped—focus of any analysis that would take rural concerns seriously.

During the past decade, there has been a major change in the autonomy given to state and local government in the design and administration of antipoverty policy. Though how much this change has resulted in clearer articulation of local interests in crafting federal policy remains unclear, it has allowed policy to be tailored to the unique circumstances of individual places. Two of the important changes in the social safety net growing out of the 1996 reform of the welfare system were the provision of public assistance block grants to states and the granting of more flexibility to states in designing and implementing welfare programs. States responded in different ways to the devolution of responsibility. Some designed programs in which the state kept legal responsibility, provided funds, and set policy goals and administrative rules. Several created programs that shifted power and legal responsibility for the programs to the county level. Nathan and

Gais (1999, Chapter 7) provide an example of the insight that can be gained by looking at the redistribution of power under welfare reform:

> Although devolution to the states is widely discussed in describing the welfare reforms…, the real federalism story is *local*. Even in what are defined as state-administered welfare systems, there are major developments to devolve welfare and related social program responsibilities to local entities. This includes more than just counties: in many states, new or relatively new regional entities are now responsible for melding welfare and workforce responsibilities—responsibilities that are often privatized, or using a term that deserves more recognition, non-profitized. This movement is what we call *second-order devolution*.

Although local administrators were often energized by the new autonomy, welfare recipients in rural areas often did not fare as well. In a study of welfare reform in Appalachian Ohio (a state that granted authority to counties to tailor programs to local needs), welfare recipients found themselves confused by the new regulations and frustrated by what they perceived to be "capricious and irrational obstacles" (Tickamyer et al. 2002, *251*). Castle and Weber (2006, *19–20*) summarized the impact of devolution in welfare reform this way:

> The exercise of local autonomy in this federal program allows local needs and conditions to be considered explicitly in program implementation, and allows putting federal resources to use in ways that appear most beneficial to those most directly affected. The new welfare policy, however, does not work as well in places with higher barriers and fewer opportunities. It also opens the possibility of arbitrary and inconsistent exercise of authority across neighboring jurisdictions, and of outcomes that are inconsistent with the national interest. For example, local decisions about welfare receipt in the presence of a weak local economy may induce migration from poor rural to poor urban areas and exacerbate urban problems.

An analysis of intermediate decisionmaking will require moving outside the traditional boundaries of economic analysis (Castle, Chapter 12, this volume). Some insights from political science for how this analysis might proceed are suggested by Oakerson (1998, and Chapter 11, this volume).

Conclusion

Is there a role for place-based policy in reducing poverty in rural America? Both the evidence from research and the facts about poverty and policy in this country point to an affirmative answer. Furthermore, there is a rationale supporting place-specific policy strategy.

The evidence from the economics and sociology literature cited above about the effects of local community conditions on poverty and policy impacts suggests that changing local conditions could have an impact on poverty and could enhance the effectiveness of policy. The evidence from workforce development evaluations

(Hamilton 2002) suggests that local program norms (e.g., the willingness of Portland, Oregon, to let welfare recipients hold out for better jobs) and institutional collaborations (e.g., participation of business and community colleges in workforce investment initiatives) can improve employment outcomes for low-income workers. The lessons from the case studies of low-income workers in Appelbaum et al. (2003) point to the importance of local intermediary institutions and government in creating the conditions that enhance their incomes.

Even more compellingly, the realities of poverty (that most poor adults work) and policy (that antipoverty policy is becoming more work-oriented, community context–dependent, and tailored to community needs by local governments and nongovernmental intermediaries) make strengthening community capacity and local institutions increasingly important in poverty reduction efforts. The higher incidence of the working poor in rural America and the evidence that current antipoverty policies are less effective in rural areas give added urgency to the task of crafting community-based policies and investments that strengthen local capacity and institutions, increase labor demand, and enhance worker productivity in rural places.

Although economists have much to say about investments that increase labor demand and worker productivity, economics as a discipline provides an incomplete framework for understanding the intermediary institutions through which people exercise their autonomy. And economic research has not been very insightful about the social processes that underlie social networks and contribute to poverty reduction. A better understanding of these institutions and processes, drawing on insights from multiple disciplines, would provide new and useful knowledge about the links among poverty, policy, and place and inform both local collective action and national policy.

References

Appelbaum, E., A. Bernhardt, and R.J. Murnane. 2003. Low-Wage America: An Overview. In *Low-Wage America: How Employers Are Reshaping Opportunity in the Workplace*, edited by E. Appelbaum, A. Bernhardt, and R. J. Murnane. New York: Russell Sage Foundation, 1–29.

Barkley, D.L., and M.S. Henry. 1997. Rural Industrial Development: To Cluster or Not to Cluster? *Review of Agricultural Economics* 19(2): 308–25.

Barkley, D., M. Henry, and H. Li. 2005. Does Human Capital Affect Rural Economic Growth? Evidence from the South. In *The Role of Education: Promoting the Economic and Social Vitality of Rural America,* edited by L. Beaulieu and R. Gibbs. Starkville, MS: Southern Rural Development Center.

Bartik, T.J. 1991. *Who Benefits from State and Local Economic Development Policies?* Kalamazoo, MI: W.E. Upjohn Institute for Employment Research.

Bartkowski, J.P., and H.A. Regis. 2002. The Promise and Peril of Charitable Choice: Religion, Poverty Relief, and Welfare Reform in the Rural South. *Southern Rural Sociology* 18(1): 222–58.

Blank, R.M. 1997. *It Takes a Nation.* New York: Russell Sage Foundation.

———. 2005. Poverty, Policy and Place: How Poverty and Policies to Alleviate Poverty Are Shaped by Local Characteristics. *International Regional Science Review* 28(4): 441–64.

Bolton, R. 1992. Place Prosperity vs. People Prosperity Revisited: An Old Issue with a New Angle. *Urban Studies* 29(2): 185–203.

Brehm, J., and W.M. Rahn. 1997. Individual-Level Evidence for the Causes and Consequences of Social Capital. *American Journal of Political Science* 41(3): 999–1024.

Brown, D.L., and T.A. Hirschl. 1995. Household Poverty in Rural and Metropolitan-Core Areas of the United States. *Rural Sociology* 60(1): 44–66.

Castle, E.N. 1998. A Conceptual Framework for the Study of Rural Places. *American Journal of Agricultural Economics* 80(3): 621–31.

———. 2002. Social Capital: An Interdisciplinary Concept. *Rural Sociology* 67(3): 331–49.

———. 2005. An Intellectual Journey: Transgressions of a Neoclassical Economist. Working Paper AREc 05-102, Department of Agricultural and Resource Economics, Oregon State University, Corvallis.

———. 2007. Frontiers in Resource and Rural Economics: A Methodological Perspective (Chapter 12, this volume).

Castle, E.N., and B.A. Weber. 2006. Policy and Place: Requirements of a Successful Place-Based Policy. A paper written for the Rural Policy Research Institute for its tenth anniversary conference, October 16–18, 2002, Nebraska City, NB. Working Paper 06-01, Oregon State University Rural Studies Program, Corvallis, OR.

Coleman, J.S. 1990. *Foundations of Social Theory.* Cambridge, MA: Harvard University Press.

Cotter, D.A. 2002. Poor People in Poor Places: Local Opportunity Structures and Household Poverty. *Rural Sociology* 67(4): 534–55.

Crandall, M.S., and B.A. Weber. 2004. Local Social and Economic Conditions, Spatial Concentrations of Poverty, and Poverty Dynamics. *American Journal of Agricultural Economics* 86(5): 1276–81.

Davis, E.E., and B.A. Weber. 2002. How Much Does Local Job Growth Improve Employment Outcomes of the Rural Working Poor? *Review of Regional Studies* 32(2): 255–74.

Davis, E.E., L.S. Connolly, and B.A. Weber. 2003. Local Labor Market Conditions and the Jobless Poor: How Much Does Local Job Growth Help in Rural Areas? *Journal of Agricultural and Resource Economics* 28(3): 503–18.

Durlauf, S.N., and M. Fafchamps. 2005. Social Capital. In *Handbook of Economic Growth*, edited by P. Aghion and S.N. Durlauf. Amsterdam: Elsevier North-Holland. Vol. 1B: 1639–99.

Elo, I.T., and C.L. Beale. 1985. *Natural Resources and Rural Poverty: An Overview.* Washington, DC: Resources for the Future.

Fisher, D.R. 2001. Resource Dependency and Rural Poverty: Rural Areas in the United States and Japan. *Rural Sociology* 66(2): 181–202.

Fisher, M.G. 2005. On the Empirical Finding of a Higher Risk of Poverty in Rural Areas: Is Rural Residence Endogenous to Poverty? *Journal of Agricultural and Resource Economics* 30: 185–99.

Fisman, R., and T. Khanna. 1999. Is Trust a Historical Residue? Information Flows and Trust Levels. *Journal of Economic Behavior and Organization* 38(1): 79–92.

Fossett, J., T. Gais, and F. Thompson. 2002. New Systems of Social Programs? First Impressions from Field Research on Local Implementation of Health Care, Food Stamps, and TANF. Albany: Rockefeller Institute of Government.

Gais, T., and R.P. Nathan. 2001. Is Devolution Working? Federal and State Roles in Welfare. *The Brookings Review* 19(3): 25–29.

Gais, T., and K. Weaver. 2002. State Programs. In *Welfare Reform and Beyond: The Future of the Safety Net*, edited by R. Haskins, A. Kane, I.V. Sawhill, and R.K. Weaver. Washington, DC: Brookings Institution Press.

Glaeser, E.L., D.I. Laibson, and B.I. Sacerdote. 2002. An Economic Approach to Social Capital. *Economic Journal* 112(483): 437–58.

Goetz, S., and A. Rupasingha. 2005. How the Returns to Education in Rural Areas Vary across the Nation. In *The Role of Education: Promoting the Economic and Social Vitality of Rural America*, edited by L. Beaulieu and R. Gibbs. Starkville, MS: Southern Rural Development Center.

Granovetter, M. 1985. Economic Action and Social Structure: The Problem of Embeddedness. *American Journal of Sociology* 91(3): 481–510.

Guiso, L., P. Sapienza, and L. Zingales. 2002. The Role of Social Capital in Financial Development. George J. Stigler Center for the Study of the Economy and the State. Working Paper No. 173.

Hamilton, G. 2002. *Moving People from Welfare to Work: Lessons from the National Evaluation of Welfare-to-Work Strategies.* http://aspe.hhs.gov/hsp/NEWWS/synthesis02/index.htm (accessed March 13, 2007).

Haynie, D.L., and B.K. Gorman. 1999. A Gendered Context of Opportunity: Determinants of Poverty across Urban and Rural Labor Markets. *The Sociological Quarterly* 40(2): 177–97.

Hite, J. 1999. Rural Development, the Thünen Paradigm and the Death of Distance: Does Space Still Matter? In *Conceptual Foundations of Economic Research in Rural Studies: A Proceedings,* a publication of the National Rural Studies Committee. Corvallis, OR: Western Rural Development Center.

Hofferth, S.L., and J. Iceland. 1998. Social Capital in Rural and Urban Communities. *Rural Sociology* 63(4): 575–98.

Jensen, L., D. McLaughlin, and T. Slack. 2003. Rural Poverty: The Persisting Challenge. In *Challenges for Rural America in the Twenty-first Century,* edited by D.L. Brown and L.E. Swanson. University Park, PA: Pennsylvania State University Press.

Karlan, D.S. 2005. Using Experimental Economics to Measure Social Capital and Predict Financial Decisions. *The American Economic Review* 95(5): 1688–99.

Kilkenny, M. 2005. Network Analysis for Communities. Paper presented at the annual meeting of the Western Regional Science Association, San Diego, February.

Kilkenny, M., and L. Nalbarte. 2000. Keystone Sector Identification: A Graph Theory–Social Network Analysis Approach. In *The Web Book of Regional Science Regional Research,* West Virginia University: Morgantown, WV. http://www.rri.wvu.edu/WebBook/kilkenny/editedkeystone.htm (accessed April 11, 2007).

Knack, S., and P. Keefer. 1997. Does Social Capital Have Economic Payoff? A Cross-Country Investigation. *Quarterly Journal of Economics* 112(4): 1251–88.

Kraybill, D., and M. Kilkenny. 2003. Economic Rationales For and Against Place-Based Policy, paper presented at the Organized Symposium on Rural Development, Place-based Policy: Sociologists Critique Economists, at the annual meeting of AAEA-RSS, July 27–30, Montreal. http://ideas.repec.org/p/isu/genres/11730.html (accessed April 11, 2007).

Lichter, D.T., G.M. Johnston, and D.K. McLaughlin. 1994. Changing Linkages between Work and Poverty in Rural America. *Rural Sociology* 59(3): 395–415.

Littman, M. 1989. Reasons for Not Working: Poor and Nonpoor Householders. *Monthly Labor Review* August: 16–21.

Machlis, G.E., J. Force, and R.G. Balice. 1990. Timber, Minerals and Social Change: An Exploratory Test of Two Resource-Dependent Communities. *Rural Sociology* 55(3): 411–24.

Miller, K.K., and B.A. Weber. 2003. How do Persistent Poverty Dynamics and Demographics Vary across the Rural-Urban Continuum? *Measuring Rural Diversity.* 1(1). Southern Rural Development Center, November.

Moffitt, R.A. 2003a. Introduction. In *Means-Tested Transfer Programs in the United States,* edited by R.A. Moffitt. Chicago: University of Chicago Press.

———. 2003b. The Temporary Assistance for Needy Families Program. In *Means-Tested Transfer Programs in the United States,* edited by R.A. Moffitt. Chicago: University of Chicago Press.

Nathan, R.P., and T.L. Gais. 1999. *Implementing the Personal Responsibility Act of 1996: A First Look.* Albany: Rockefeller Institute Press.

Nord, M., and A.E. Luloff. 1993. Socioeconomic Heterogeneity of Mining-Dependent Counties. *Rural Sociology* 58(3): 492–500.

Oakerson, R.J. 1998. Politics, Culture, and the Rural Academy: A Response to Castle. *American Journal of Agricultural Economics* 80(3): 632–34.

———. 2007. The Politics of Place: Linking Rural and Environmental Governance. (Chapter 11, this volume).

Partridge, M.D., and D.S. Rickman. 2005. High-Poverty Nonmetropolitan Counties in America: Can Economic Development Help? *International Regional Science Review* 28(4): 415–40.

————. 2007. Persistent Pockets of Extreme American Poverty and Job Growth: Is There a Place-Based Policy Role? *Journal of Agricultural and Resource Economics* 32(1): 201–24.

Peluso, N.L., C.R. Humphrey, and L.P. Fortmann. 1994. The Rock, the Beach, and the Tidal Pool: People and Poverty in Natural Resource-dependent Areas. *Society and Natural Resources* 7: 23–38.

Putnam, R.D. 2002. Bowling Together. *The American Prospect* 13(3).

Roscigno, V.J., and M.L. Crowley. 2001. Rurality, Institutional Disadvantage, and Achievement/Attainment. *Rural Sociology* 66(2): 268–92.

Rupasingha, A., and S.J. Goetz. 2003. *The Causes of Enduring Poverty: An Expanded Spatial Analysis of the Structural Determinants of Poverty in the US.* Northeast Regional Center for Rural Development, University Park, PA, Rural Development Paper No. 22.

Rupasingha, A., S.J. Goetz, and D. Freshwater. 2000. Social Capital and Economic Growth: A County-Level Analysis. *Journal of Agricultural and Applied Economics* 32(2): 565–72.

————. 2006. The Production of Social Capital in US Counties. *The Journal of Socio-Economics.* 35(2006):83–101.

Sampson, R.J., S.W. Raudenbush, and F. Earls. 1997. Neighborhoods and Violent Crime: A Multilevel Study of Collective Efficacy. *Science* 277(5328).

Shideler, D. 2004. Determinants of Individual Social Capital Investment. Paper presented at the annual meeting of the American Agricultural Economics Association, Denver, August 1–5.

Swaminathan, H., and J. Findeis. 2004. Policy Intervention and Poverty in Rural America. *American Journal of Agricultural Economics* 86(5): 1289–96.

Tickamyer, A., J. White, B. Tadlock, and D. Henderson. 2002. Where All the Counties Are Above Average: Human Service Agency Directors' Perspectives on Welfare Reform. In *Rural Dimensions of Welfare Reform,* edited by B.A. Weber, G.J. Duncan, and L. A. Whitener. Kalamazoo, MI: W.E. Upjohn Institute for Employment Research, Part 2: 231–56.

Wasserman, S., and K. Faust. 1994. *Social Network Analysis.* Cambridge: Cambridge University Press.

Weber, B.A. 1995. Extractive Industries and Rural-Urban Economic Interdependence. In *The American Countryside: Rural People and Places,* edited by E.N. Castle. Lawrence, KS: University Press of Kansas, 159–79.

————. 2007. Rural Poverty: Why Should States Care and What Can State Policy Do? *Journal of Regional Analysis and Policy* 37(1): 48–52.

Weber, B., M. Edwards, and G. Duncan. 2004. Single Mother Work and Poverty under Welfare Reform: Are Policy Impacts Different in Rural Areas? *Eastern Economic Journal* 30(1): 31–51.

Weber, B., L. Jensen, K. Miller, J. Mosley, and M. Fisher. 2005. A Critical Review of Rural Poverty Literature: Is There Truly a Rural Effect? *International Regional Science Review* 28(4): 381–414.

Winnick, L. 1966. Place Prosperity vs. People Prosperity: Welfare Considerations in the Geographic Redistribution of Economic Activity. In *Essays in Urban Land Economics in Honor of the Sixty-fifth Birthday of Leo Grebler.* Real Estate Research Program, University of California at Los Angeles, 273–83.

Acknowledgments

Many of the ideas in this paper germinated, and were fertilized, in stimulating conversations with Emery Castle over several decades, and the paper bears his firm imprint. Intellectual debts to Rebecca Blank, Roger Bolton, Paul Barkley, Maureen Kilkenny, and David Kraybill will also be obvious. The paper builds on conversations over many years with members of the National Rural Studies Committee and colleagues in the Community Economics Network and at the Rural Policy Research Institute. I am grateful to Paul Barkley and Emery Castle for careful and insightful reading of multiple drafts of this paper, and to Tom Gallagher, Priscilla Salant, and JunJie Wu for comments on an earlier draft; and to Julia Appt for valuable stylistic suggestions and formatting the paper.

Notes

1. I follow the common practice of using the terms "rural" and "nonmetropolitan" ("non-metro") interchangeably, being fully aware of the difficulties in doing so. Similarly, I use "urban" and "metropolitan" ("metro") interchangeably. The Office of Management and Budget has classified each county as metropolitan or nonmetropolitan based on the presence of a city with more than 50,000 people and/or commuting patterns that indicate interdependence with the "core" city. The U.S. Census Bureau designates, on a much finer level, each area as rural or urban, using a definition of 2,500 people as the cutoff for urban populations. Urban populations are defined as those living in a place of 2,500 or more, and rural populations live in places with less than 2,500 people or in open country. Both of these classifications leave much to be desired in terms of poverty research. The metro-nonmetro classification uses a county geography that is often too coarse, classifying as metropolitan many residents who are rural under the Census definition but live in metropolitan counties. The rural-urban classification, using a simple cutoff of population, fails to capture geographic proximity to the opportunities afforded those rural residents who live on the fringes of large urban centers.

2. This includes such factors as location on the rural-urban continuum, natural resource dependence, presence of intermediary institutions, and levels of social capital.

3. Stylized facts 1, 3, and 4 are taken from Miller and Weber (2003).

4. If one looks at census tracts rather than counties, poverty rates are highest at both ends of the population density spectrum—in urban cores and in remote rural areas. High poverty tracts (defined as those with poverty rates of 30 percent or more in 1990) are found disproportionally in the cores of large and medium cities, and in rural counties that have been identified as "persistent poverty" counties.

5. Persistent-poverty counties—as defined in this paper—are counties that have had poverty rates of 20 percent or more in every decennial census since 1960 (i.e., in 1959, 1969, 1979, 1989, and 1999). The Economic Research Service defines persistent-poverty counties as those with poverty rates of 20 percent or more in 1969, 1979, 1989, and 1999.

6. The review of rural poverty literature and policy implications discussed in this section draws on Weber (2007).

7. It is noteworthy that, as means-tested programs become more targeted to low-income workers, work support benefits—such as child care assistance, earned-income tax credits, and transportation services—increasingly go to working families whose incomes may exceed the poverty threshold (Gais and Nathan 2001).

8. Most poor households have at least one worker. Littman (1989) found that more than half of all poor householders worked in 1986. More recent studies have found increased work behavior of poor households. In data from the early 1990s, Blank (1997) reports that most (63 percent) of poor households had at least one worker, and single mothers worked somewhat more than they had 20 years previously. Working poverty is more prevalent in rural than urban areas. The working poor constitute a higher share of poor householders in nonmetro counties than in metro counties (Lichter et al. 1994).

9. It is interesting to note that Bolton was writing in the early 1990s as national economic policy was moving toward emphasizing the supply side in national and regional development and antipoverty policy. He was summarizing and responding to a literature developed during the 1960s, when demand-oriented theory and policy were in ascendancy in regional economics, and begins his article by acknowledging a debt to Chinitz for calling attention to supply in regional models. The current paper, written during an era in which regional models incorporate supply considerations and regional development and antipoverty policies and practically ignore the demand side, is a call for more attention to the role of demand, particularly local demand for labor, in reducing poverty. It is also a call for attention to the supply of certain factors, particularly community factors not supplied directly by either individuals or firms, that are not easily incorporated into regional economic analysis.

10. Apparently unlike Bolton (1992), Kraybill and Kilkenny define "place-based policies" as "those where the location of the beneficiary is a key criterion for eligibility" (2003, 2). They do

not restrict place-based policies to those that benefit or affect "*groups* of deserving people defined by their spatial proximity in places" as Bolton does (1992, 187); they consider as "place-based policies" only those that benefit individuals or firms in a particular place—allowing individuals the option to remain part of the "group of people" in that place, or not. In addition to outlining the standard neoclassical arguments for public intervention, Kraybill and Kilkenny also discuss the impact of insights from endogenous growth theory and the new economic geography for place-based policies.

11. They note that Barkely and Henry (1997) found that nonmetro labor markets were more specialized than metro labor markets, and that rural clusters occurred more in manufacturing than in services.

12. They summarize the arguments for place-based policies in their Research Papers in Economics (RePEc) abstract as follows: "Most economists understand that 'place-based' policies are justified by (i) place uniqueness (spatial heterogeneity), (ii) undesirable spatial consequences of economic growth and change, (iii) inefficiencies due to jurisdictional fragmentation, (iv) significant spatial interdependencies between metro and non-metro places, and (v) the potential to generate greater nationwide welfare gains using place-based rather than other policies." (http://ideas.repec.org/p/isu/genres/11730.html)

13. Equal opportunity arguments apply with most force to characteristics over which individuals arguably have no control, such as race, age, and gender. Since adults can sometimes choose to move to reduce this disadvantage if they are unsatisfied with the returns to their efforts and assets in rural places, this argument is most properly applied to providing equal opportunity for children, who do not have much choice about where they live. Because children depend on adults for their economic well-being, implementing an equal geographic opportunity goal would require providing equal opportunities for the adults who support them (unless we believe that children should suffer for the bad choices of their parents).

14. The above arguments for place-specific policies apply to any place. Do rural places have characteristics that would justify place-based policies? Do the low population densities and isolation from urban centers characteristic of rural areas result in market failures that warrant rural strategies? Higher levels of unemployment and lower wages characteristic of rural areas suggest that labor markets might not work as well in rural areas, and the evidence that asset fixity increases with remoteness (Hite 1999) could indicate imperfections in capital markets. These market failures could justify public policies for rural places.

15. Paul Barkley suggested this in a review of an early version of this paper.

16. As noted in the introduction to this paper, and as often noted by sociologists (Jensen et al. 2003), models based on individual decisionmaking and well-functioning markets fail to explain persistent poverty and long-lasting interregional differences in income. As Castle has argued, understanding complex social and economic phenomena such as persistent poverty will require moving outside the boundaries of neoclassical economic theory and taking cross-disciplinary and collaborative approaches: "all systems are partial" and "the domain of economic theory [that] is defined by causal factors provided for by assumptions underlying neoclassical economic theory . . . may not include people, or circumstances, of economic significance because of the incomplete nature of causal assumptions" (Castle 2005, 57).

17. There are certainly other questions that are important in understanding the relationship of poverty and place, and other questions and dimensions of a rural poverty research agenda can be found in Weber et al. (2005).

18. Castle (2002, *332*) argues that "[t]he social capital concept provides a means of bringing communities and other small groups into economic analysis [in a way] consistent with social theory."

19. Social capital has been viewed by economists both as an individual asset (Glaeser et al. 2002; Shideler 2004; Karlan 2005) and—following Coleman (1990) and Putnam (2002)—as a community asset (Rupasingha et al. 2006). At the individual level, social capital has been measured with answers to a set of questions designed to elicit values and attitudes. Data sets commonly used to determine social capital include the General Social Survey (GSS), the Panel Study of Income Dynamics, and other household surveys. The GSS, for example, has questions related

to "trust," "fairness," and "helping" that have been used to measure social capital. Social capital measures derived from these questions have been found to be related statistically to economic growth (Knack and Keefer 1997), civic involvement (Brehm and Rahn 1997), and communication infrastructure (Fisman and Khanna 1999) in cross-country studies. Economists also attempt to assess individuals' trust levels with the "trust game" (Karlan 2005). Sometimes the survey results are used to predict individual outcomes (academic performance, use of credit, criminal behavior). At other times, individual data are aggregated to develop a collective (average) measure of social capital for a nation or region (as in Knack and Keefer 1997) and then used to predict national or regional outcomes.

CHAPTER 9

Rural Human Capital Development

Maureen Kilkenny and Monica Haddad

*H*OW CAN RURAL AREAS and small towns compete in the high-tech, global economy when the majority of the world's talented innovators as well as their customers reside in metropolitan areas? How can young people who grow up in remote, low-density places that specialize in natural resource industries (Castle 1991) learn how to invent the next new thing? This paper is about how we learn, and how learning in a place can depend on population size, variety, or culture.

A widely held view is that productivity is lower in rural areas either because people with high-value human capital migrate to cities, where they can earn a better return, or because people in low-density areas cannot benefit from the spillovers that occur with proximity or high population density. Because society has not found a way to measure the rate of learning or innovativeness in a place, we use data on student performance and school buildings instead.

A preoccupation in the recent literature has been that city people are more productive and innovative because productivity depends positively on population density (Ciccone and Hall 1996). Does that mean rural areas are doomed to lag? Not necessarily. A much more compelling explanation for the higher productivity observed in cities has recently been provided by Syverson (2004). The essence of the Syverson argument is that heightened competition in denser markets makes it harder for inefficient producers to operate profitably. This truncates the lower end of the productivity distribution, such that the measured average is higher and measured variance is lower. Syverson's careful empirical work using data on the concrete-mixing industry provides robust statistical support for his hypothesis.

Syverson maintains that if all else is equal, people in rural areas are just as productive as people in cities. The difference arises solely because competition is stiffer in cities. But there is no particular reason why a remote, low-density place cannot be an innovative place. Similarly, to understand the role of density in accumulating human capital in small and remote places, we will look at data on student "productivity" in schools of various sizes and configurations as well as locations.

We call our alternative hypothesis the "horizon effect" because we believe that just as competitors in the marketplace raise the bar, cohorts and upperclassmen can do the same with respect to learning. We will present statistical evidence that, according to one measure, the more grades there are in a school building, the better is student performance. The finding reminds us of the quintessentially rural "one-room schoolhouse" model of human capital accumulation. Our study both confirms some old ideas and offers new ones about how to enhance human capital development in small-town America.

Why should rural development specialists care about how people in rural places can get to the cutting edge? Because to prosper, a place must be innovative, with innovation defined as the application of an existing invention to a new purpose. Unfortunately, most data on innovative economic activity indicate that rural towns are not generally hotbeds of innovation.

Why must a place have innovators to prosper? Because the way to accumulate capital in a competitive market is to be a first mover and operate in the early stage of the product cycle (Vernon 1966; Duranton and Puga 2001), when there are still monopoly rents to be earned. As a product line matures, increasing local and then global competition drives prices down to marginal costs. Salaries and wages are driven down to opportunity costs, or plants close and move to lower-cost locations. A relevant insight of the product cycle is the maxim that you can say where a product is being produced even if all you know is its age. Firms producing mature products tend to locate in rural towns because rural areas have an abundance of low-cost labor and space that are used intensively by firms in the mature stage of a product cycle. Hosting firms in the final stage in the product cycle before they either die or relocate to developing countries where people still buy the product is not an enduring way to achieve rural development.

In contrast, an innovative firm employs relatively high-skilled and creative labor. That type of workforce is relatively abundant mainly in cities (Jacobs 1984; Duranton and Puga 2001). Jane Jacobs argued that cities were more innovative because their size supports variety, and variety provides more opportunity for cross-fertilization. Is there any way that a small, remote, rural community can locally grow a relative abundance of innovators?

More than one century ago, Alfred Marshall published the insight that labor with industry-specific skills is attracted to locations that are relatively dense in those industries. His theory of labor market "pooling" rationalizes to some extent why both people and firms benefit by concentrating in a location rather than spreading out and avoiding competition. Firms benefit from a larger local pool of specialized labor, which enables less costly adjustment to fluctuating demand for their products. Workers benefit from the wider local array of alternative employers, which provides more opportunities for advancement and reduces the risk of unemployment.

Rural development specialists need to know how small places can mimic the breadth, variety, innovativeness, and flexibility of cities, or at least to obtain those benefits. That is the question addressed by our research about the dependence of learning on various measures of school size. We look at schools because they vary in size, configuration, location (among many other things) and because data on student performance are widely available. We focus on two measures of size: cross-sectional and longitudinal. By "cross-sectional" we mean population at any point in time. In a school, cross-sectional size is the average number of students per grade cohort in the building. This corresponds to population density or depth in a place. By "longitudinal" we mean the number of students in one place over time. The longitudinal size of a school is the number of grades in the same building. It is a kind of size that both a one-room schoolhouse and a small town can have. We empirically investigate whether either type or size of one's learning environment matters. Our answer to that question may shed light on ways that rural people can enhance their learning environments and achieve greater global competitiveness.

Briefly, the horizon effect hypothesis assumes that the average performance of learners depends on how much effort each learner exerts and how much their teachers expect of them and challenge them in the classroom. We hypothesize that student effort and teacher expectations depend positively on the number of top performances actually observed by students and teachers. A large number of top performances in a large group induces more effort, so ultimately, larger groups should display higher average measures of achievement. If outcomes depend on effort, and if the effort of members in a group depends positively on the frequency of observations of high performance in that group (their view of the "horizon"), given the statistical fact that larger samples contain more observations of high performance, the average performance of larger groups would be higher.

Our spatial econometric analysis of building-level data from Ohio shows that there are robust positive and significant effects of the number of grades in a school. The positive effect of the longitudinal measure of size indicates that the presence of upperclassmen and predecessors contributes more positively to learning than having a large number of peers. When we also control for local demographics and spatial autocorrelation, we find that our hypotheses about horizon effects are robust, and that previously undetected class size effects are apparent. And, like most of the modern analyses of student educational outcomes, we show that it is difficult to identify any effect of spending (higher teacher salaries, for example) on learner outcomes. The most significant predictors of learning performance are neighborhood demographics, parents' education (positive), size of the school (negative), and number of grades in the school (positive).

After a brief review of the economics literature on class and school size and peer effects in school outcomes, we develop our new horizon effect hypothesis. Then we describe the data, our analytical procedures, and our findings. We conclude with a discussion of the implications for rural communities.

Relevant Literature

Class size, or pupil-teacher ratios, and peer effects have been well studied for their influence on students' performance, and yet the association with learning remains ambiguous, in part because there are many possible confounding variables.

Class Size

Class size is one of many potentially relevant measures of the inputs into learning outcomes. Quoting Hanushek (2002, *2073*):

> Studies of educational performance include a variety of different measures of resources devoted to schools. Commonly employed measures include 1) the real resources of the classroom (teacher education, teacher experience, and class size or teacher–pupil ratios); 2) financial aggregates of resources (expenditure per student and teacher salary); and 3) measures of other resources in schools (specific teacher characteristics, administrative inputs, and facilities).
>
> The real resource category receives the bulk of analytical attention. First, these best summarize variations in resources at the classroom level. Teacher education and teacher experience are the primary determinants of teacher salaries. When combined with teachers per pupil, these variables describe the most significant variations in the instructional resources across classrooms. Second, these measures are readily available and well-measured. Third, they relate to the largest changes in schools over the past three decades . . . with pupil–teacher ratios falling steadily, teacher experience increasing, and the percent of teachers with a masters' degree actually doubling between 1960 and 1990.

When the outcomes of individuals in a group—in a workplace, neighborhood, town, school, or anywhere—are better the larger the size of the group, the individuals may be benefiting from external increasing returns to scale. The urban economics literature is crammed with research on the external increasing returns to scale phenomena called agglomeration economies of scale. Much less attention has been paid to the negative aspects of size or congestion effects. Activities in which bigger is not unambiguously better are primary and secondary education.

Class size is typically measured as the number of students per teacher during a period of instruction, which is the typical teacher's pupil load, or the pupil-teacher ratio. Average class sizes across the United States range from a low of 19 in Wyoming and Vermont to a high of 30 in Utah. Small classes may allow students to receive more personal attention from their teachers. Large classes, however, can be less expensive and do not necessarily hinder instruction. Depending on teaching style, student behavior, and other factors to be discussed, large classes may be just as effective as small classes.

Indeed, the empirical evidence about the effect of class size on student performance is at best mixed. Almost three-quarters (72 percent) of 376 statistical analyses cannot reject the null hypothesis that student outcomes are unrelated to the teacher-pupil ratio in schools (Hanushek 2002). Hanushek's summary of these studies is reproduced in Table 9-1. That table documents the preponderance of null findings as well as the disparate findings about optimal class size and other public education expenditure issues. Note that there is no consensus that smaller class sizes support better student performance. The strongest evidence against the null is for teacher test scores and teacher experience. Student performance appears to depend

Table 9-1. *Percentage Distribution of Estimated Effect of Key Resources on Student Performance, Based on 376 Studies*

Resources	Number of estimates	Statistically significant (%)		Statistically insignificant (%)
		Positive	Negative	
Real classroom resources				
Teacher-pupil ratio	276	14	14	72
Teacher education	170	9	5	86
Teacher experience	206	29	5	66
Financial aggregates				
Teacher salary	118	20	7	73
Expenditure per pupil	163	27	7	66
Other				
Facilities	91	9	5	86
Administration	75	12	5	83
Teacher test scores	41	37	10	53

Source: Hanushek (2002, Table 6).

positively on teacher performance and experience (but not, apparently, on the education of the teacher).

As Hanushek points out, even strong evidence against the null must be interpreted carefully. The true direction of causality is not clear. School spending (input use) is determined through complicated political and behavioral choices by schools and parents. In many states, spending is systematically allocated in a compensatory manner. Extra resources are spent on low-achieving students to provide for more personalized attention, remedial instruction, and additional technology. It is not clear that either achievement or spending can be assumed exogenous. The identification problem results in an observed relationship that is often *negative:* high spending is often systematically correlated with low achievement. By the same token, class sizes could be small in those schools where policymakers have noticed that students need more help. Hanushek suggests that one way to overcome these limitations is to conduct controlled experiments.

Highly influential research concluding that students appear to do better in smaller classes came from a large experimental study by the state of Tennessee. "Project STAR" was a class-size reduction experiment conducted in Tennessee's elementary schools in the 1980s. Classes were composed of varying fractions of students who had been exposed to a "small-class treatment," creating groups of students with varying experimentally induced quality. Project STAR's conclusion that students in smaller classes do better has motivated major education policy changes in other states. On the basis of the STAR results, in 1996 California enacted a policy to provide significant additional funds to all schools to lower class sizes in primary grades. The demand for additional teachers to staff all the new classrooms outpaced supply. The outcome was a dramatic reduction in student performance, most likely due to the assignment of unqualified or inexperienced teachers to the new classrooms (Stecher and Bohrnstedt 1999). One implication is that it is not easy to raise student performance by reducing class size because this requires raising pupil–teacher ratios, and in the short run that entails sacrificing teacher quality. And as the findings in Table 9-1 document, teacher quality is even more important than the pupil–teacher ratio.

Another interesting approach to the question of class size was applied by Angrist and Lavy (1999). They used a Talmudic rule that has been used to determine the division of enrollment cohorts into classes in Israeli public schools to study the effects of class size on the scholastic achievement of Israeli grammar school pupils. The rule, which caps the pupil–teacher ratio at 40 to 1, is an exogenous source of variation that can be used to construct instrumental variables estimates of class–size effects using a regression-discontinuity design approach. The data display an overall positive correlation between scores and the number of students per grade, which turns out to be attributable to the fact that larger schools in Israel are more likely to be located in relatively prosperous big cities. After controlling for this positive association between test scores and urbanization, they find a significantly negative association between class size (as instrumented) and student performance.

It is also possible, however, that students can do better in larger classes or among larger cohorts because of the wider array or variety of students. As Jesse Levin (2001, abstract) writes,

> Controlling for a large number of observable characteristics and potential endogeneity in the class size variable, an educational production function is estimated using a quantile regression technique. The "conventional wisdom" that class size reduction is a viable means to increase scholastic achievement is discounted. Rather, the results point towards a far stronger *peer effect* through which class size reduction may play an important role. Due to heterogeneity in the newly identified peer effect, class size reduction is shown to be a potentially regressive policy measure.

In order for students to be able to learn from each other, there must be some dispersion among the abilities in the group. This leads to our interest in peer effects.

Peer Effects

If the performance of a group—in a workplace, a town, a school, or anywhere—depends on the composition of the group, the individuals in the group may be experiencing a type of club good externality known as a peer effect. These effects have been studied in many contexts, most notably in schools, workplaces, among teenagers, and in neighborhoods (e.g., Plotnick and Hoffman 1999; Evans et al. 1992). Research on peer effects in schools appears to have been first published by urban-regional economists Richard Arnott and John Rowse. Their 1987 paper focused on the influence of a student's classmates on his educational attainment. Their finding—that the better a student's classmates do, the better a student does—called into question the efficacy of tracking students by ability and suggested that mixing students of different abilities might be preferable.

More recent research by Hanushek et al. (2003) points out that the analyses of peer effects on student achievement can be plagued by the difficulties of separating peer effects from other confounding influences. Hanushek controls for the most important determinants of achievement, such as observable family and school characteristics, which have been shown to confound estimates of peer effects. He still finds that peer achievement has a positive effect on achievement growth and that students throughout the school test-score distribution appear to benefit from the presence of higher-achieving schoolmates.

It is also important to note that peer effects appear to be asymmetric or heterogeneous (Levin 2001). Positive effects result from increases in the numbers of high performers in a group, but there are no discernible negative effects from increases in the numbers of low-performing peers in a group. For example, Angrist and Lang (2002) studied Boston's Metco integration program, which sends mostly poor black students out of the Boston public school district to attend schools in more affluent suburban districts. The transfer doubled the proportion of students with substantially lower test scores in some schools. Although clearly this resulted in an overall decline in scores in the receiving schools, the authors found that the decline was not a peer effect but a composition effect. They found no impact on the average scores in the sample of all nontransfer students. On the other hand, they did find that some of the transfer students mildly benefited. In sum, the existing evidence suggests that low performers enjoy a positive benefit from mixing with better students, but there is no discernible negative impact on better students when low performers are added to the school.

The Horizon Effect Hypothesis

We now formalize a hypothesis that learners with more potential role models perform better:

Horizon Effect Hypothesis: If the performance of a group depends on the frequency of observations of maximum performances in the group, because the frequency of maximum observations is higher the larger the sample, then larger size groups will ultimately display higher overall performance.

The horizon hypothesis rests on two assertions: one is asymmetric peer group effects; the other is a statistical fact. The larger the sample drawn from a given distribution, the more often the maximum is observed in the sample. The more competitors in a location, the higher the minimum productivity. The more students in a building, the more often one can observe high performance. When top performances are more frequent, everyone in the school, teachers as well as students, can have higher expectations. The horizon is higher. This may inspire everyone to exert more effort or challenge. If the effort is effective, the consequence of the asymmetric peer group effect is that larger groups display higher averages.

Formally, we assume that individual performance y_{is} is a positive function of individual effort E_i of the ith student at school s, and of the level of the material (M_s) presented by teachers, among other things:

$$y_{is} = e_{is}(E_{is}, M_s, \ldots) \tag{1}$$

Let each performance be drawn independently from a distribution or probability density function (pdf) $f(y)$, with a cumulative density function (cdf) $F(y)$. Let t

$= \max\{y_{is}\}C$ i be the maximum observation of y (e.g., t for "top score," like 100 percent) in a sample of size C.

The pdf or distribution of t, $g(t)$, is

$$g(t) = C[F(t)^{C-1}]f(t) \tag{2}$$

where $F(t) = F(y)$ evaluated at t, etc. (Poirier 1995, 144).

Given that the frequency of the maximum observation t is positively related to the size of the sample, C, $g(t)$ is a function of C. (It is also true that the minimum observations are more frequent the larger is the sample size, but we assume that peer effects are asymmetric, so that is irrelevant.)

Figure 9-1 illustrates how the height of the horizon rises with the size of a group. This figure was generated using the sample statistics for math scores on the Scholastic Aptitude Test (SAT) assuming a normal distribution. The average SAT math score was 520, the maximum is 800, and the standard deviation was 115 (College Board 2006). Figure 9-1 shows the size of the group in which at least one person is expected to earn the indicated score. For example, if there is only one student, the expected score is 520. The larger the group, the higher the horizon. The group has to number at least 135 for there to be at least one perfect score of 800.

In itself, a higher number of observed maximum performances in a group does not imply a higher average. We assume that the means and variances are the same across all size samples. But the essence of the horizon effect hypothesis is that positive feedback shifts the average performances over time. An asymmetric peer effect may result from students' increasing their effort as the level of attainable achievement

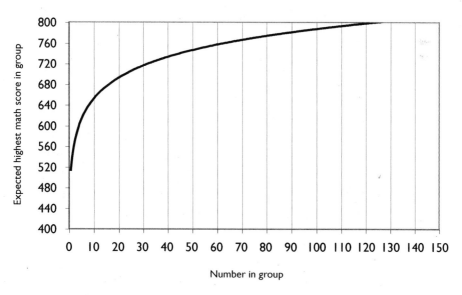

Figure 9-1. *The Horizon Effect*

Note: High performance appears to be a logarithmic function of the size of the group.

they perceive rises. Alternatively, teachers may raise the rigor of their lesson plans the more aware they are of high-achieving students in their school.

A critical assumption is that individual learner effort (and/or treatment by teachers) depends positively on the actual observation of high performances in the school, which (as noted above) is directly proportional to the size of the relevant group in the school, C_s:

$$e_{is}(E_{is}(g(t)), M_s(g(t)),\dots) = z_{is}(C_s) \tag{3}$$

which motivates us to instrument or proxy the unobserved number of high performers in a group by the observed size of the group.

But which group or which measure of size is relevant? If the cross-section (same-grade cohort) is the only relevant group, rural students and teachers may not be able to benefit from the horizon effect because there are fewer students per grade in smaller rural schools. If the longitudinal measure (number of grades per school) is the relevant group, however, rural learners can benefit from a horizon effect, since another way to see what is possible in a place is to observe one's predecessors over time. In the same way that a larger cross-sectional sample includes more observations of a maximum, a time-series or panel sample also contains more observations of high performers than any one cross-section of that panel does. Culture, tradition, or policy can make a longitudinal cohort relevant.

The cross-section measure of the horizon (X) is the number of students in a whole school building (S) divided by the number of grades (G) in the school. Clearly, $G \cdot X = S$; which means that a school size is likely to be correlated with horizon (Table 9-2).

The longitudinal "horizon" is measured by the count of all grades and ages in the school. If a horizon effect exists, the number of grades in the school would have a positive influence on the average performance of its students. We measure the number of grades in a school (G) by subtracting the lowest grade in the school from the highest grade (plus 1) and call this a longitudinal instrument for the horizon.

Confounding our ability to identify a horizon effect, there may also be internal increasing returns or size-related externalities with respect to school size. Internal increasing returns could be due to, for example, the fixed costs of school buildings. Other benefits internal to the school but external to the individual student arising from school size may also be positive. There may be "spatial spillovers," or returns to variety, arising from interactions with other students or teachers. Conversely, there may be scale diseconomies or congestion effects. In particular, because people tend to do good things unilaterally (to internalize the rewards) but do bad things in groups (to defuse responsibility or disperse the punishment), it is possible that student disciplinary problems may get worse once a critical mass of miscreants exists in a school. There should also be a larger number of minimum performances in larger samples. Thus the likelihood of reaching a critical mass of miscreants also increases with the size of a school. Average proficiency rates may therefore be negatively related to the size of a school. These are just a few of the identification problems plaguing the investigation presented here.

Empirical Estimates

We formalize a school performance function that includes both cross-section and longitudinal measures of the height of the horizon: the number of students per grade ($X=S/G$) and the number of grades (G) per school, as well as class size (R) measured by the pupil-teacher ratio, and school size instrumented by the amount spent on the building (B)[1]:

$$y = y(X, G, R, B, F, T, D; \beta) + \varepsilon \qquad (4)$$

controlling for:

    F = measures of financial resources devoted to instruction, staff support, etc.;

    T = indicators of teacher quality (experience, etc.); and

    D = student/family/neighborhood characteristics (income, education, density, etc.).

To empirically test our hypotheses, we will first estimate a learner outcome function (4) summarized as

$$Y_s = \beta X_s + e_s$$

where Y_s is the dependent variable vector, the percentage of students in school s who are proficient in a subject; and X_s is a vector of explanatory variables related to school s, including both ways to measure the height of the horizon. The horizon is measured both by the number of students in the same grade (X) and by the number of grades (G) in each building. We control for class size, measured as the ratio of students to teachers; and school size is instrumented by spending on the building. We estimated various functional forms to allow for nonlinear relationships.

We focus on schools rather than individuals because we have no data on individual educational outcomes. Furthermore, we focus on school buildings rather than school districts for three reasons. First, a school building is a closer analogy to a community than a school district. Districts sometimes comprise several communities and are more analogous to counties or states. Second, the federal No Child Left Behind Act of 2002 gives students' parents the choice of a school *building* within a school district. Thus, a very policy-relevant unit of analysis is the school

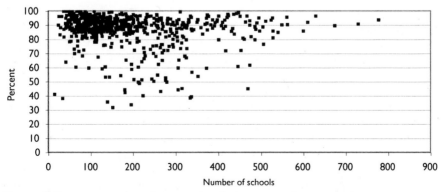

Figure 9-2. *Percent of Sophomores Proficient at Freshman Math, Ohio Schools*

building. And third, we focus on school buildings because of the aggregation problem noted by Plenzler (2004, 1, emphasis added):

> Studies that attempt to establish the relationship between economic resources and student performance are often carried out using sample data aggregated to the school district level. . . . This is primarily due to data limitations. A problem with this approach is that large urban school districts exhibit tremendous variation within the district, so using a district average student performance score and district average spending, student and teacher characteristics as well as socioeconomic population characteristics obscures this within district variation. A further problem is that smaller *rural school districts often contain only one or two elementary school buildings, so the cross-section of observations aggregated to the district level represent very different spatial scales.*

The educational outcome and school variables for school year 2001–2002 were generously shared with us by our colleague Jim LeSage and his advisee Nicole Plenzler (2004). They obtained the data from the Ohio Department of Education. We downloaded all other variables characterizing households and neighborhoods at the zip code level from the U.S. Census Bureau.

The first set of control variables concerns financial resources. We include a real average teacher salary normalized by local average housing price, per teaching full-time-equivalent expenditure on staff support, total expenditure per pupil, and the percentage of total spending on instruction. We also control for teacher quality by including the average years of teacher experience. The third set concerns student and family demographics in the zip code area where the school is located. We include the percentages of the local population who are in poverty, nonwhite, and have a master's or doctoral degree; per capita income; and population density (Table 9-2).

First we fit a nonspatial regression model using ordinary least squares (OLS):

$$y_s = \beta_0 + \beta_1 x_{1s} + \beta_2 x_{2s} + \ldots + \varepsilon_s\ s = 1, \ldots 633 \tag{5}$$

where y_s is the percentage of 10th-grade students proficient in ninth-grade math at 633 schools for the year 2001–2002; X_s are the explanatory and control variables; the elements of the vector β are the unknown parameters to be estimated; and ε is the error.

Second, we assessed the dependence of high school math proficiency on our hypothesized explanatory variables in a spatial setting. The data on the percentages of tenth-grade students who passed the math test for ninth-graders across public schools in Ohio display global and local spatial autocorrelation as well as spatial heterogeneity (Figure 9-2).

As a consequence of those findings, we chose a spatial model: (1) spatial lag; (2) spatial cross-regressive; or (3) spatial error. We anticipated that the spatial lag model would be most appropriate for the same reasons that a temporal lag or the first-differencing of time series observations can control for time-invariant unobservables to minimize missing variable bias.

We used a binary queen contiguity matrix for the spatial weights. Six spatial autocorrelation tests were computed using this spatial weight matrix: the Moran's *I* test; the Lagrange multiplier test for residual spatial autocorrelation and its

Table 9-2. *Summary Statistics*

Variable	Label	Mean	Max	Min	Stdev
Percentage of tenth-graders proficient in ninth-grade math	Y	87	100	32	11
Size (total enrollment)	S	785	2,913	56	478
Cohort size (students/grade)	X	191	728	14	124
Number of grades	G	4	6	3	0.7
Class size (students per full-time-equivalent teacher)	R	17	35	8	3.1
Building expenditures	B	$1,083,866	$5,441,190	$7,392	$762,927
Total expenditures/pupil	TEXP_P	$7,437	$14,864	$4,127	$1,584
Percentage expenditure on instruction	ISHARE	58%	83%	40%	6.2%
Average teacher experience (years)	EXPERNC	14	27	4	2.9
Spending on staff support/full-time equivalent	SS_FTE	$1,634	$8,021	$17	$1,445
Real salary (salary/house price)	SAL_H	45%	159%	16%	15%
Percentage of local population in poverty	PERPOV	9%	47%	0.9%	7%
Percentage of local population nonwhite	PERNOWHI	10%	99%	0.0%	17%
Percentage with advanced degree	PERGRA	3%	18%	0.0%	2%
Local average per capita income	INC_CAP	$20,199	$54,344	$9,739	$5,625
Local population density	POPDENSITY	1,088	10,967	17	1,737

robust version; and the Lagrange multiplier test for spatially lagged endogenous variables and its robust version (Anselin 1996). The results of these tests are in Table 9–3.

Because the statistic for the robust Lagrange multiplier (lag) test is the most significantly different from zero, we can conclude that for this data set, the spatial lag model is the recommended approach to control for the apparently positive spatial dependence. If spatial autocorrelation is ignored, the results are similar to the consequences of omitting a significant explanatory variable from the regression model—that is, the estimators are biased.

Thus, we include a function of the dependent variable in contiguous locations, called a spatial lag, as an additional covariate, following Anselin (1998). The magnitude of the spatial influence is measured by the coefficient r. The null hypothesis of no spatial autocorrelation is $H_0: r = 0$ (see below). The spatial lag model was estimated using maximum likelihood in GeoDa 0.9.5–i5 software (Anselin et al. 2004).

The spatial model of high school math proficiency rates by school is thus

$$y = \rho W y + B_0 + B_1 x_1 + B_2 x_2 + \ldots + B_{17} x_{17} + u \tag{6}$$

where y is the vector of the dependent variable, r is the spatial autoregressive parameter to be estimated, W is the queen contiguity spatial weight matrix, and Wy is the average percentage of students proficient in nearest-neighbor high schools. The B vector $(B_0, B_1, B_2, \ldots B_{17})$ includes the unknown coefficients to be estimated, X is the matrix of hypothesized explanatory and control variables, and u is the vector of error terms.

Table 9–4 presents the estimated nonspatial and spatial lag models. We can observe that the coefficient ρ on the spatial lag of the dependent variable is

Table 9-3. *Diagnostic Tests for Spatial Dependence*

Test	Statistic	p-value
Moran's I (error)	0.183	0.855
Lagrange multiplier (lag)	3.331	0.068
Robust LM (lag)	9.923	0.002
Lagrange multiplier (error)	0.006	0.938
Robust LM (error)	6.598	0.010
Lagrange multiplier (SARMA)	9.929	0.007

statistically significantly larger than zero (p-value = 0.05), indicating the presence of positive spatial dependence. And our hypothesis about horizon effects is robust (the coefficients are stable between the nonspatial and the spatial lag models).

In particular, we reject the null hypothesis that performance is independent of the longitudinal measure of the horizon. The coefficient on lnG is statistically significantly positive with 99 percent confidence. In the spatial lag model, we also reject the null that performance is independent of class size, R. The effect of class size on high school student math proficiency rates is strictly concave (Figure 9–3),

Table 9-4. *Estimation Results*

High school math proficiency model estimates (n=633)	Nonspatial model		Spatial lag model (Queen contiguity matrix)	
	OLS		Maximum likelihood	
Variable	Coefficient	SE	Coefficient	SE
Constant	84.52***	11.76	74.37***	12.59
Wy			0.10*	0.05
Cohort size (students/grade)	1.53	1.20	1.55	1.18
Number of grades	8.49***	2.76	8.45***	2.72
Class size (students per full-time-equivalent teacher, R)	1.006	0.648	1.072*	0.638
R^2	-0.026	0.016	-0.027*	0.016
Building expenditures ($10,000s)	-0.01	0.01	-0.01 *	0.01
Total expenditures/pupil	-0.000004	0.0004	0.00003	0.0003
Percentage expenditure on instruction	-31.81***	6.55	-31.73***	6.44
Average teacher experience	0.10	0.12	0.10	0.12
Spending on staff support/full-time equivalent	-0.0012***	0.0002	-0.0012***	0.0002
Real salary (salary/house price)	-5.32	3.84	-5.28	3.78
Percentage of local population in poverty	-24.15***	8.49	-21.41***	8.38
Percentage of local population nonwhite	-26.07***	2.90	-25.20***	2.90
Percentage with advanced degree	103.91***	24.81	103.41***	24.40
Local average per capita income	-0.0001	0.0001	-0.0001	0.0001
Local population density	-0.0007***	0.0003	-0.0005*	0.0003
R^2 Percentage explained	54%			
AIC Akaike criterion	4,414.9		4,413.5	
SC Schwartz criterion	4,486.2		4,489.2	

* Significant at the 10% level. ** Significant at the 5% level. *** Significant at the 1% level.

and about 20 students per teacher appears to be optimal (higher than the mean class size of 17). Finally, plain old "bigger" is not better. The effect of overall school size, instrumented using the fixed cost of buildings, is significantly negative in the spatial lag model. That negative effect is not, however, strong enough to undermine the positive effect of the longitudinal horizon (see also Figure 9-4.)

The coefficients on the spending on staff support per full-time equivalent and the share of total spending on instruction are negative and significant in both models with 99 percent confidence, consistent with the literature. As noted above, other empirical tests of the efficiency of public expenditure on schools are unable to identify whether outcomes are positively related to school spending. Note also that the coefficients on average teacher experience, real teacher salary, and total spending per pupil are insignificant.

It is also apparent that local demographics and neighborhood characteristics matter the most. The coefficients on the percentage of the area's population in poverty and the percentage of population that is nonwhite are negative and significant in both models above the 99 percent level. The coefficients on the percentage of the population with advanced degrees are positive and significant in both models with more than 99 percent confidence. And proficiency rates are significantly inversely related to population density (in contrast with Israel's case, as per Angrist and Lavy 1999). City schools do not appear to be better than rural schools.

The R^2 criterion cannot be used to compare the "fit" of nonspatial OLS and spatial models, so the Akaike Information Criterion and Schwartz Criterion are used. The best model has the lowest values of both. In our case, the difference is slight.

Implications and Discussion

The horizon effect hypothesis suggests that if the effective effort exerted by members of a group depends on the number or height of top performances in the group (the horizon), then larger groups will display higher average performances. The

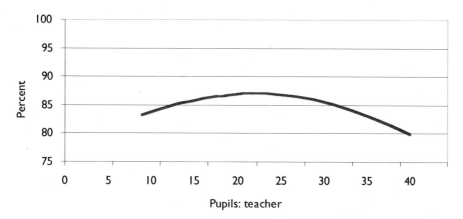

Figure 9-3. *Simulation of Estimated Effect of Class Size on Proficiency Rates*

empirical issues include how to measure the horizon (instrumented by group size), spatial bias, misspecification, and missing variable bias.

The estimated models using data on Ohio high schools, students, and neighborhood demographics all reject the null hypotheses that the percentage of high school sophomores proficient at freshman math is independent of the longitudinal measure of the horizon. In particular, proficiency rates are higher where there are more grades in one building. The net effect of increasing the number of grades (and school size, holding all else equal) is illustrated in Figure 9-4. Our spatial lag model estimates suggest that increasing the number of grades in a high school from three to six can raise the expected proficiency rate from 84 to 89 percent. The increase is, however, within the range of standard error of proficiency rates. We conclude that increasing the number of grades in a school may help, and will not hurt, sophomore performance rates in high school math.

Consider our findings in light of the reduced-form empirical evidence that productivity is higher in higher-density states (e.g., Ciccone and Hall 1996). Ciccone and Hall estimated how average labor productivity in a state depends on the distribution of employment across counties. They assumed that output was a nonlinear function $(\acute{A})$ of county workers (n_c) per acre (a_c) times the acres of land in the county, and that statewide output (Q_s) was the sum of county output:

$$Qs = \Sigma_c \left[(n_c/a_c)^\gamma \cdot a_c \right]$$

Statewide output per statewide workers $(N_s = \Sigma_c n_c)$, or statewide productivity, is thus

$$\frac{Q_s}{N_s} = \Sigma_c \frac{n_c^\lambda a_c^{1-\lambda}}{N_s}$$

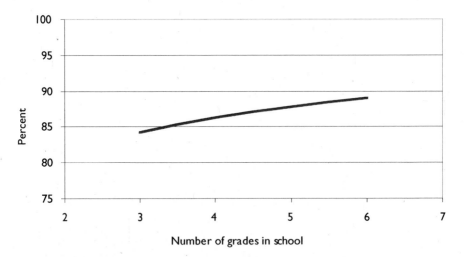

Figure 9-4. *Simulation of Net Effect of Number of Grades in School on High School Math Proficiency Rates*

Obviously, if $\gamma<1$, productivity is higher when the workforce per acre is lower. If $\gamma>1$, productivity is higher when the workforce is concentrated on a few acres. Ciccone and Hall's (1996) empirical work showed that $\gamma>1$. The average performance of the workforce appears to be higher in states where there are more workers concentrated on fewer acres.

In the Ohio school data, however, we found no statistically significant effect of student density, measured by the cross-section number of students per grade (X), on student math performance. Neither Ciccone and Hall nor most others who have found positive returns to scale or density, however, identify the process by which proximity or size affects performance. They simply assert that there is some parametric relationship through which productivity depends on size or density. They call the unidentified processes "knowledge spillovers" or "urbanization external economies of agglomeration."

We find Syverson's (2004) explanation of the higher observed average productivity in cities much more compelling. More densely populated places can support more establishments. Fixed costs and transport costs limit the size of the market that can be served by a supplier of a good or service. In a given area, the larger the number of customers in the area, the more suppliers there can be. The more suppliers there are, the tougher the competition. The observed distribution is truncated. We expect to see a higher mean and lower dispersion in higher-population places.

Like Syverson's hypothesized mechanism, the horizon effect does not rely on assumptions that students or teachers in bigger schools are intrinsically more able, nor do we assume that the "learning production function" differs across schools of different sizes. As Syverson shows, average productivity differences can arise simply because low-productivity (high-cost) firms are driven out of larger markets, where competition is stiffer. In our work, the difference in proficiency rates between longer and shorter cohorts may arise, as we hypothesize, because higher effort may be inspired in longer cohorts.

In sum, this research suggests that small towns can improve their learning environments by enhancing intergenerational communication, networking widely, and institutionalizing a "long memory." At the least, this research suggests that the old rural one-room schoolhouse may be very effective. Horizon effects could also operate among citizens, public officials, or businesses in towns.

This work also offers a hopeful policy alternative to the trend of consolidating rural schools by grade. Rural school systems that consolidate by having fewer grades with more students per grade emphasize cross-section at the expense of longitudinal horizon effects. Students in such settings do not observe much variety or depth. Teachers specialize in the few grades their schools teach and do not benefit from first-hand experience of the longer horizon. It also requires that students be bused longer distances and change school locations more often. Alternatively, schools can put more effort into publicizing and remembering students who have excelled by statewide and national standards. Although there may not be such a top-performing student in every grade in a small high school, the probability is four times higher across four grades, six times higher across six grades, and so on. The implication of this empirical investigation is that shining the lights on that horizon may pay off in terms of higher-quality rural human capital.

References

Angrist, J.D., and K. Lang. 2002. How Important Are Classroom Peer Effects? Evidence from Boston's Metco Program. *NBER Working Papers*: 9263.

Angrist, J.D., and V. Lavy. 1999. Using Maimonides' Rule to Estimate the Effect of Class Size on Scholastic Achievement. *Quarterly Journal of Economics* (May): 533–75.

Anselin, L. 1996. The Moran Scatterplot as an ESDA Tool to Assess Local Instability in Spatial Association. In *Spatial Analytical Perspectives in GIS,* edited by M. Fischer, H.J. Scholten, and D. Unwin. London: Taylor & Francis, 111–25.

———. 1998. Interactive Techniques and Exploratory Spatial Data Analysis. In *Geographical Information Systems: Principles, Techniques, Management and Applications*, edited by P.A. Longley, M.F. Goodchild., D.J. Maguire, and D.W. Wind. New York: Wiley.

Anselin, L., I. Syabri, and Y. Kho. 2004. GeoDa: An Introduction to Spatial Data Analysis. *Geographical Analysis*.

Arnott, R., and J. Rowse. 1987. Peer Group Effects and Educational Attainment. *Journal of Public Economics* 32(3): 287–305.

Castle, E. 1991. The Benefits of Space and the Cost of Distance. In *The Future of Rural America: Anticipating Policies for Constructive Change*, edited by K. Pigg. Boulder, CO: Westview Press.

Ciccone, A., and R.E. Hall. 1996. Productivity and the Density of Economic Activity. *American Economic Review* 86(1): 54–70.

College Board. 2006. *SAT Frequently Asked Questions*. http://www.collegeboard.com/highered/ra/sat/sat_scorefaq.html (accessed March 2006).

Duranton, G., and D. Puga. 2001. Nursery Cities: Urban Diversity, Process Innovation, and the Life Cycle of Products. *American Economic Review* 91(5): 1454–77.

Evans, W., W. Oates, and R. Schwab. 1992. Measuring Peer Group Effects: A Study of Teenage Behavior. *Journal of Political Economy* 100(5): 966–91.

Hanushek, E. 2002. Publicly Provided Education. In *Handbook of Public Economics* Volume 4, edited by A.J. Auerbach and M. Feldstein. Elsevier Science B.V., chapter 30.

Hanushek, E., J. Kain, J. Markman, and S. Rivkin. 2003. Does Peer Ability Affect Student Achievement? *Journal of Applied Econometrics* 18(5): 527–44.

Jacobs, J. 1984. *Cities and the Wealth of Nations: Principles of Economic Life*. New York: Random House.

Levin, J. 2001. For Whom the Reductions Count: A Quantile Regression Analysis of Class Size and Peer Effects on Scholastic Achievement. *Empirical Economics* 26(1): 221–46.

Plenzler, N. 2004. Student Performance and Educational Resources: A Spatial Econometric Examination. Master's thesis, Department of Economics, University of Toledo, May.

Plotnick, R., and S. Hoffman. 1999. The Effect of Neighborhood Characteristics on Young Adult Outcomes: Alternative Estimates. *Social Science Quarterly* LXXX: 1–18.

Poirier, D.J. 1995. *Intermediate Statistics and Econometrics: A Comparative Approach*, Cambridge, MA: MIT Press.

Stecher, B.M., and G.W. Bohrnstedt. 1999. Class Size Reduction in California: Early Evaluation Findings, 1996–98. *American Institutes for Research*, Palo Alto, CA.

Syverson, C. 2004. Market Structure and Productivity: A Concrete Example. *Journal of Political Economy* 99(5): 997–1009.

U.S. Bureau of the Census. Census 2000 Summary File 3 (SF 3)—Sample Data. http://factfinder.census.gov.

U.S. Department of Education. Fiscal Year 2001–2005 State Tables for the U.S. Department of Education. http://www.ed.gov/about/overview/budget/statetables/index.html.

Vernon, R. 1966. International Investment and International Trade in the Product Cycle. *Quarterly Journal of Economics* 80(2): 190–207.

Acknowledgments

Many thanks to Jim LeSage and Nicole Penzler for the data, and to Peter Orazem and Justin Tobias for everything else.

Note

1. B = \$21,036 + 1,352.6·S; with an R^2 of 72 percent.

CHAPTER 10

Property Taxation and the Redistribution of Rural Resource Rents

Mitch Kunce and Jason F. Shogren

*T*HE SEVERAL CHAPTERS IN THIS BOOK explore an on-and-off relationship between resource and rural economics. The tie that binds these two fields is the desire to understand how people choose to use the natural resource base to foster rural development (read: keep open the local movie theater) and transfer resource rents to urban areas (read: build schools with good athletic facilities). An inherent tension exists between capturing resource rents in rural areas and redistributing them to a broader set of people that can include those in nearby urban areas and even beyond state boundaries. Rural policymakers face the political challenge of capturing some of these rents for local development.

This chapter examines the case of Wyoming, in which rural policymakers use tax incentives to the mineral industry in the attempt to stimulate rural development. To many rural citizens, rural economic development means creating and keeping good jobs (see, e.g., Chapter 3, this volume). In many rural areas rich in natural resources, local politicians and business leaders continue to argue for tax and fiscal incentives to attract new industry and spur existing firms to boost the production of natural resources like coal, oil, and gas. Local leaders argue that rural authorities should use the tools they control—property taxation and other fiscal tools—to trigger more production, which in turn will foster economic growth and employment in their area. More production can increase employment, which increases land values and decreases the possibility that children and grandchildren will move to urban areas (also see Chapter 8, this volume).

Opinions differ as to whether these incentives actually serve to increase production from the natural resource base and add more jobs in a rural area. One view assumes that tax incentives induce a company to increase production by a significant level such that the lost tax revenues will be retrieved through the rise in local economic activity. An alternative view believes that rural development schemes do little to increase production of natural resources and increase jobs; rather, these policies simply transfer rents to a firm that often is located outside the local area. A rural resource rent of this type undercuts the standard political argument that tax breaks trigger economic development and job creation in resource-dependent rural areas. In his review of the tax incentive-development literature, Wasylenko (1997) argues that incentives have, at best, a small significant effect on where firms choose to locate. Gerking et al. (2000) also find that decreases in state-level severance tax rates for oil and gas has little impact on near- or long-term production in eight of the largest producing states. They conclude that oil production is inelastic in respect to changes in state severance taxes and income levies. The Gerking study shows that if Wyoming policymakers were to double the state severance tax, production would decrease by only 6 percent, while tax revenue would increase by more than 90 percent over a 40-year period. Their results were basically the same for eight other states, which produce about 85 percent of U.S. oil and gas production: inelastic response of production to tax incentives.

The specific question we examine in this chapter is whether a reduction in county-level property taxes will increase production in a rural economy dominated by natural resource extraction. We develop and estimate an analytical model to calculate effects of local tax changes on Powder River basin (PRB) coal production, the mine-mouth price of coal, the delivered price of coal, railroad freight charges, and local tax collections.

The PRB is located in Campbell and Converse counties. These two counties' total assessed property valuation includes the prior-year net production value of wells and mines taxable at local mill levies. In effect, this local property tax is simply an ad valorem production tax. The PRB provides an excellent case study because over the past four decades, it has become one of the largest suppliers of steam coal in the United States, producing nearly 400 million tons in 2005. The first contract for PRB coal was signed in 1956 and called for 125 million tons to be delivered over 25 years. Since then, coal producers have made substantial transaction-specific investments in capital, such as exploration, mineral leases, mining plans, mine infrastructure, and permits from regulatory agencies, as well as investments in community infrastructure (Atkinson and Kerkvliet 1989). Likewise, early coal buyers also made large transaction-specific investments in electricity generation capital and were uncertain about the performance of this new steam fuel.

Since the early 1980s, Wyoming counties have periodically granted tax incentives to the coal industry for the purpose of stimulating production, net tax collections, and job creation. For example, in Campbell County, effective industrial mill levies have decreased 22 percent since 1980. Moreover, Campbell and Converse counties have the lowest industrial mill levies in the state. To what extent have these tax breaks affected coal operations? Our results show that the local tax incentive has minimal effect on the quantities and prices of coal produced, especially when measured as percentage changes. The largest effect is about a 25 percent reduction in tax collections from coal production. Providing a property tax incentive for rural development in the PRB did not increase production or create jobs; rather, it simply transferred wealth to the industry from the local government.

Background

Our model examines how changes in county-level ad valorem production tax rates affect Powder River basin coal production. The model focuses on interrelationships among three agents in the market for PRB coal: producers, railroads, and electric utilities. Producers supply coal. The electric utilities are the main end users, burning coal to generate electricity. Railroads transport PRB coal from the producers to the utilities. We included railroads in the model because freight costs can represent up to 80 percent of delivered coal prices. Assuming coal producers operate under perfect competition, railroads exercise market power in setting transportation rates faced by utilities, and utilities have little bargaining leverage in their purchases of PRB coal.

We develop the model as a comparative-static analysis for two reasons. First, exploration is less of an issue in the case of PRB coal than it is, for example, for oil and gas. The PRB and, more generally, the United States have vast coal reserves, and their locations are known. Second, our question of *rent sharing* based on economic interactions between mines, railroads, and utilities can be better captured at a point in time than as an artifact of the optimal rate of exploitation over time.

Our characterization of industry structure differs from that used in earlier studies. Atkinson and Kerkvliet (1986, 1989), for example, suggest that sources of market power at the mine level include restrictions on federal coal leasing, long lead times required to obtain permits and to construct a mine, and economies of scale achieved by only a few mines (at the time of their studies). At the mine–power plant interface, investments in heterogeneous coal reserves and coal-specific power plants conveyed potential market power to both mines and plants. The long-term contracts designed to protect these investments limited effective competition, a situation exacerbated when these contracts contained price escalation, take-or-pay, or similar provisions. Atkinson and Kerkvliet (1989) find that power plants can gain market power by purchasing dominant shares of the production of individual mines.

Similar sources of market power were identified for railroads. Only a single railroad served each of the coal basins in Wyoming, but railroad rates were regulated prior to the passage of the Staggers Act in 1980. Also, Kolstad and Wolak (1983) examine the market power used by Wyoming and Montana to extract rents through severance taxes and find that each state can increase tax revenues by increasing rates even in the absence of collusion.

Much has changed, however, since those initial studies were conducted. For mines, the barriers to entry resulting from the 1980s moratoriums on federal coal leases have eased somewhat. Currently, there are 10 owners operating 17 mines in the PRB. Of these, 11 mines are likely to be fully exploiting scale economies with annual production of more than 10 million tons each (Lyman and Hallberg 2004). Also, transaction-specific investments associated with heterogeneous coal appear to have diminished in importance. This has reduced the potential for monopoly pricing by coal suppliers and monopsony behavior by plants.

Three points suggest that significant engineering advances have emerged to allow for a mix of coal types. First, plants now use diversified portfolios of coal and other fuels to meet their fuel requirements. Second, most PRB coal buyers purchase from more than one mine. In 2004, 80 percent of the plants for which all Wyoming coal sales could be identified purchased coal from more than one Wyoming mine. On average, plants purchased coal from 2.8 Wyoming mines. Third, evidence suggests that individual plants have learned to mix bituminous coal from other states with subbituminous coal from Wyoming (Ellerman and Montero 1998). Furthermore, long-term contracts have diminished in importance; spot market purchases and shorter-term contracts are now the norm (Kerkvliet and Shogren 1992, 2001). Current PRB coal contracts leave sellers and buyers more exposed to market forces because contracts are more likely to contain market-based reopened provisions and less likely to contain price escalation or take-or-pay provisions.

Railroad rates for PRB coal transportation rates have fallen substantially since passage of the Staggers Act in 1980 introduced deregulation. Research points to three reasons for this decline. First, railroads' costs have fallen because of technological change. Second, deregulation ended the practice of cross-subsidizing high-cost shippers through overcharging low-cost shippers. (Previously, railroads would charge high-cost shippers less than marginal cost, then make up the deficit by charging low-cost shippers rates exceeding marginal costs. This allowed railroads to concentrate more on low-cost traffic, such as unit train shipments of coal, and increase traffic densities. The cross-subsidization decreased overall rail costs, reduced union power, and ultimately lowered real wages; see MacDonald and Cavalluzzo 1996). Third, the entry of the Chicago and Northwestern Railroad into the PRB decreased rail rates more than 30 percent, with further decreases over time (Atkinson and Kerkvliet 1986). Most utilities purchasing PRB coal are served by one railroad, or at most two.

Analytical Model

Assume PRB coal producers are price takers, operate identical mines located at a single point in space, and maximize profits after taxes. Profits of a representative mine are

$$\pi^M = P^M q - G(q) - t^M P^M q \tag{1}$$

where P^M denotes the price of coal faced by all producers, q denotes the mine's output, $G(q)$ is the mine's extraction cost function, and t^M denotes the county level ad valorem production tax rate. Extraction costs rise with increases in q at an increasing rate. The first-order condition determining the mine's output decision is

$$\frac{d\pi^M}{dq} = P^M - G_q - t^M P^M = 0 \tag{2}$$

or

$$P^M = \frac{G_q}{1 - t^M} \tag{3}$$

where G_q is the marginal cost of producing another unit of coal. Subscripts denote partial derivatives. Mines produce coal until the after-tax price received equals marginal cost. The representative mine's supply curve is the portion of the marginal cost curve that lies above the average cost schedule. The industry supply curve for coal ($H(q)$) is obtained by horizontally summing the individual mine supply curves. Industry output of coal (q^*) is determined by

$$P^M = \frac{H(q)}{1 - t^M}. \tag{4}$$

A single railroad hauls coal produced by the mines along a single track to many coal-fired electric power generation plants. All power plants are located at the end of the track and thus are the same distance from the mines. They have no other sources of coal. The railroad has both monopsony power over the mines and monopoly power over the power plants. Electric power is produced for a national market, and plants receive a fixed price for each unit of power produced. Each plant has an identical inverse demand function for coal, in which the delivered price, P^D, is negatively related to the quantity of coal purchased. These individual demand functions can be horizontally summed to yield the electric power industry's aggregate inverse demand schedule for coal, $P^D = f(q)$. The railroad's per unit freight charge, P^F, equals the difference between the delivered price of coal and the mine-mouth price ($P^F = P^D - P^M$).

The railroad decides how much coal to haul to the power plants and how much to charge for its services, based on their profit function,

$$\pi^R = P^F q - C(q), \tag{5}$$

where $C(q)$ denotes the railroad's cost function. Using $P^F = P^D - P^M$, $P^D = f(q)$, and substituting equation (4) yields

$$\pi^R = qf(q) - C(q) - \frac{qH(q)}{1 - t^M}. \tag{6}$$

Equation (6) gives railroad profits in terms of utility demand for coal, railroad costs, and the industry supply of coal by the mines. The first-order condition for a profit maximum requires

$$\frac{d\pi^R}{dq} = qf_q + f(q) - C_q - \left(\frac{1}{1 - t^M}\right)\left(qH_q + H(q)\right) = 0 \tag{7}$$

and the second-order condition for a profit maximum is

$$\frac{d^2\pi^R}{dq^2} = qf_{qq} + 2f_q - C_{qq} - \left(\frac{1}{1 - t^M}\right)\left(qH_{qq} + 2H_q\right) = \Delta < 0 \tag{8}$$

Equation (7) says the railroad hauls coal until the marginal revenue from utilities equals the marginal cost of transporting the coal plus the marginal tax-inclusive expense to supply another unit of coal by the coal industry. This result reinforces the idea that the railroad acts as both a monopsonist in how much coal to haul and in its ability to set freight rates (and delivered prices) seen by the utilities. Both monopoly and monopsony power act to limit the amount of coal hauled between mines and power plants and to drive a larger wedge between P^M and P^D than would exist if transportation of coal were produced by a perfectly competitive industry. Second-order conditions are satisfied if the marginal revenue schedule cuts the aggregate marginal expense schedule (defined as the marginal coal expense schedule plus railroad marginal cost) from above. If the second-order condition is satisfied, we can rearrange equation (7) to show the effect of changes in t^M on the production of coal (q) and the three prices (P^M, P^D, P^F).

We obtain comparative static effects of changes of t^M on q by totally differentiating equation (7):

$$\frac{dq}{dt^M} = \frac{qH_q + H(q)}{\left(1 - t^M\right)^2 \Delta}$$
(9)

Assuming second-order conditions are satisfied (D < 0), if the coal supply schedule is positively sloped ($H_q > 0$), then $dq / dt^M < 0$—an increase in t^M reduces the quantity of coal produced. The magnitude of dq / dt^M depends on D; the denominator of equation (9) is reduced by the factor $(1 - t^M)^2$, which varies inversely with the level of the initial production tax, and the numerator is the mine's marginal expense of supplying an additional unit of coal before taxes. Consequently, dq / dt^M is greater (1) the smaller D, (2) the larger the initial ad valorem tax rate, and (3) the larger the marginal expense of hauling an additional unit of coal. Notice that larger values of the marginal coal expense correspond to larger values of the cost of coal production ($H(q)$) and that D does not depend on $H(q)$ (see equation (8)). These relationships imply that for given values of t^M and D, dq / dt^M increases with coal's share of aggregate marginal expense.

We can use equation (9) to compute the effects of changing the production tax on P^M, P^D, and P^F. Differentiating equation (4) and substituting equation (9) yields

$$\frac{dP^M}{dt^M} = \frac{H_q}{1 - t^M}\frac{dq}{dt^M} + \frac{H(q)}{\left(1 - t^M\right)^2}.$$
(10)

In equation (10), the first term on the right-hand side is negative (because $dq / dt^M < 0$), while the second term is positive. However, $dP^M / dt^M > 0$ if $\left[d\left(\frac{qH_q}{H(q)}\right)\bigg/ dp\right]$.[1] This derivative, which measures whether H_q grows faster or slower than $H(q) / q$ when q rises, is positive provided $H_q > 0$ and $H_{qq} \geq 0$, an outcome similar to the familiar demonstration that the slope of a marginal cost curve is greater than the slope of an average cost curve over the range of output for which marginal cost is increasing. Moreover, equation (11) shows that an increase in t^M also increases the delivered price of coal:

$$\frac{dP^D}{dt^M} = f_q\frac{dq}{dt^M} > 0.$$
(11)

Because P^M and P^D both move in the same direction when t^M changes, the sign of dP^F / dt^M is ambiguous. If we subtract equation (10) from (11), we gain more insight:

$$\frac{dP^D}{dt^M} - \frac{dP^M}{dt^M} = \frac{dP^F}{dt^M} = \left(f_q - \frac{H_q}{1 - t^M} \right) \frac{dq}{dt^M} - \frac{H(q)}{\left(1 - t^M\right)^2} \qquad (12)$$

Equation (12) shows that rail rates rise with increases in t^M provided that the utility's demand schedule for coal is more steeply sloped than the coal industry's supply function and $H(q)$ is sufficiently small. Next, we develop an analytical model, and after that, we present numerical calculations of dP^F / dt^M on the basis of econometric estimates of the model parameters.

Estimation

We use the analytical model to quantify effects of local production tax changes on output and prices of coal. The idea is to estimate the major model parameters econometrically, and then use these values to compute the comparative static results. Estimation procedures must recognize that the actual market for coal has many features disregarded in the model. For example, electric power plants can burn fuels other than coal (such as natural gas), and they are located at different distances from the mines. Railroad freight costs are related to quantity of coal hauled and to the distance it must travel. Coal produced by the mines is not homogeneous, and mine costs are not identical. Estimation methods must control for these and other important factors to obtain the desired relationships. Given our approach, we now report estimates of (1) coal supply, (2) utility demand, and (3) railroad costs.

Coal Supply

We present estimates of a net-of-tax supply schedule of coal ($H(q)$) produced in the Powder River basin of Wyoming. Estimates of the supply function make use of mine-specific cost data estimated by Lyman and Hallberg (2004). In 2000, the Wyoming Geological Survey prepared cost estimates and production information on currently operating, recently closed, and proposed new coal mines in the PRB and other coal-producing regions in Wyoming. These data were used to prepare a five-year forecast of direct mining costs per ton for each mine, assuming operation at capacity. Our analysis is based on the direct cost estimates for the period 2000–2004. Regarding cost data, capacity operation is defined as an economic limit to production and, for all mines, lies below maximum allowable annual production permitted under state air quality regulations. Direct mining costs would include anticipated wages and salaries, expenses for materials and supplies, and capital costs required to deliver coal from the mine to a railcar. These cost estimates, which exclude corporate overhead, royalties, taxes, final reclamation accruals, and depreciation, differ substantially between mines. Cost differences are due to variations in mine ratios (overburden thickness), capital intensity, mining methods, and other factors.

Our estimate of the supply function exploits the differences in direct costs between mines because no information is available on production costs at output levels below capacity. The major assumption is that direct production costs per ton vary little with output up to the point of capacity operation and then turn sharply higher. For each mine, direct cost per ton would (approximately) equal marginal cost per ton at output levels below capacity, and mines would choose to produce at capacity whenever the mine price exceeds direct cost per ton. Also, the PRB supply curve for coal can be visualized as a step function by first ordering mines from lowest to highest in direct cost and then plotting the direct cost of each mine against cumulative output. Advantages of this approach are that it identifies the mines that would be operational at a given mine price, the mines that would open (or reopen) if the price rises, and the mines that would close if the price falls.

We obtained a continuous approximation to the PRB coal supply function by regressing the natural logarithm of direct operation cost in dollars *(COST)* on cumulative output in millions of short tons *(CUMTONS)*. This functional form was chosen because the plot of the cost step function suggests an exponential relationship between cost and cumulative output. Results are

$$ln(COST)_j = 0.187 + 0.0011 \; CUMTONS_j + e_j \qquad (13)$$
$$(2.764) \quad (6.813)$$

where the subscript j indexes mines, e_j, is a measured residual, and t-statistics are shown in parentheses. This regression uses data from 22 mines, 17 in current operation, and $R^2 = 0.70$. Including observations on five relatively high-cost, nonoperating mines is warranted because they provide information about the shape of the cost curve at output levels above current production. As shown in equation (13), the coefficient of *CUMTONS* is positive and significantly different from zero at conventional levels, suggesting that incremental cost of coal production in the PRB increases at an increasing rate with output; that is, $H_q > 0$ and $H_{qq} > 0$. We defer until later our discussion on the appropriate level of output at which to evaluate these derivatives.

Utility Demand

We estimate the demand function for PRB coal by applying an adaptation of Heckman's (1979) two-step estimator to data on fuel purchases by utilities. In the first step, equations are estimated to predict whether a utility will purchase PRB coal, and in the second step, demand equations for PRB coal are estimated for utilities that purchased this fuel. The idea is to account for how coal produced in the PRB competes in a marketplace with other fuels, such as natural gas and coal produced elsewhere, since transportation costs increase with distance and often represent a large fraction of its delivered price. For example, as a utility's distance from PRB rises, the probability it will purchase PRB coal is expected to fall (other things constant). Also, as the mine-mouth price of PRB coal falls relative to prices of other fuels, the economic market area for PRB coal is expected to expand. The demand schedule must not only allow for current buyers to increase coal purchases as the mine-mouth price falls, but also for the "economic reach" of PRB coal to expand. Correspondingly, as delivered coal prices rise, the demand schedule must account both for current buyers who substitute against Wyoming coal in favor of other fuels and for the most distant utilities to discontinue buying altogether.

First-step probit equations are estimated using panel data on a total of 416 U.S. electric power plants over the period 1985–2000 and are used to predict the probability that a utility purchases PRB coal. Plants are included in the sample if they burned coal from any source in at least one year between 1985 and 2000. Nuclear and hydroelectric power stations are excluded from the sample because they were not designed to use coal. The panel is unbalanced because some coal-fired plants did not operate in each year (i.e., older plants were retired and new plants came on line during the sample period). A total of 6,238 observations are available; a sample size of 6,656 would be expected if the panel were balanced. The dependent variable is binary and equals one if coal is purchased (see below), zero otherwise.

Estimation of this equation raises two general issues. The first is how best to exploit the panel structure of the data. Random effects estimation was chosen because the probit model does not lend itself well to a fixed-effects treatment of heterogeneity among cross-sectional units (see Greene 1997). But heterogeneity among electric power plants is important to consider because they exhibit substantial differences in unobserved engineering characteristics that contribute to explaining whether low-sulfur, low-Btu PRB coal might be purchased. The second issue is how to measure the cost of PRB coal faced by utilities: the decision whether to purchase PRB coal may be determined simultaneously with its delivered price, and the delivered price is known only for utilities that actually purchased PRB coal.

To avoid both of those problems, instruments for the real delivered price were constructed using the predicted values from a regression of this variable on the straight-line distance (in miles) between each plant and Gillette, Wyoming (the community at the center of coal mining activity in the PRB). These regressions were run in a Box-Cox (see Greene 1997) framework by applying nonlinear least squares to all available observations on plants that purchased PRB coal. Predicted values of real delivered price were assigned to all plants (whether they purchased PRB coal or not) based on the distance variable. Estimates are shown in equation (14):

$$RDPRICE_{PRB}=12.24+0.056DISTANCE\text{*}+e \qquad \lambda=0.83 \qquad (14)$$
$$(6.95) \ (6.23) \qquad\qquad\qquad (16.50)$$

The regression used 1,389 observations. The t-statistics are shown in parentheses beneath coefficient estimates and l is the estimate of the transformation parameter applied to $DISTANCE$, i.e., $DISTANCE\text{*}=(DISTANCE^l - 1)/l$. Estimates show that the real delivered price of coal increases at a decreasing rate with the distance it is shipped (i.e., coefficients of $DISTANCE^*$ are positive and significant, and values of l are significantly less than unity at conventional levels).

Table 10-1 shows the sample means, definitions, and data sources for explanatory variables used in the probit regression. Explanatory variables include the pre-

Table 10-1. *Demand Data Description and Means Stage I Probit*

Variable	Description and source	Means
DISTANCE	Distance between Gillette, Wyoming, and all Wyoming coal-buying power plants, in miles "as the crow flies"	760
RDPRICEHAT	Predicted delivered price in 2000$	33.940
RGASPR	Weighted, average annual natural gas price paid by plants that burn coal, 1985–2000, in 2000$/MMBTU using GDP deflator (FERC Form 423, Annual)	3.015
GENER	Net annual electric power plant (coal) generation, 1985–2000, in billions of Kwh (Monthly Power Plant Report, EIA/DOE, Annual Summaries)	3.994
D1990	Dummy variable = 1 if year is 1990–2000, 0 otherwise	0.575

dicted delivered price of coal, the real price of natural gas (a substitute for coal in electricity generation), the size of the power plant in kilowatt hours generated, and a dummy variable indicating whether the observation was after 1990 (when federal Clean Air Act amendments limited sulfur emissions). All data in Table 10-1 are from publicly available government and industry sources.

Table 10-2 presents results from the probit regression. The dependent variable indicates whether coal is purchased from any PRB mine. The estimates of the ratio of the power plant variance component to the sum of all variance components $(r = 0.818)$ highlight the importance of accounting for cross-sectional heterogeneity. Marginal effects of explanatory variables, rather than the underlying probit coefficients, are presented because they are easier to interpret. The marginal effect of the instruments for delivered price $(RDPRICEHAT)$ is negative and highly significant, indicating that more distant power plants face higher delivered prices and are thus less likely to buy PRB coal. For example, the probability that a power plant will purchase PRB coal declines by about 1.5 percent for a $1 increase in delivered price, when evaluated at the means of all variables. Remaining results suggest that the probability a power plant will burn PRB coal is positively related to the size of the plant $(GENER)$ and the price of substitute fuels $(RGASPR)$. The positive marginal effect of $(D1990)$ indicates that demand for PRB coal expanded after passage of the 1990 Clean Air Act amendments.

The dependent variable for the second-step coal demand regression of the quantity of coal delivered to utilities in the regression is the natural logarithm of quantity of coal purchased. Table 10-3 presents definitions, sample means, and data sources for explanatory variables. Explanatory variables include the real delivered price of Wyoming coal, the real prices of two substitute fuels (natural gas and coal obtained from a state other than Wyoming), plant size measured in kilowatt hours of electricity generated annually, and the inverse Mills ratio computed from the first-stage probit regression. Results of a Hausman (1978) test indicate that a random effects specification is rejected at conventional levels of

Table 10-2. *Stage I Random Effects Probit Models*[a]

Variable	Marginal effects (t-stat)
CONSTANT	−0.396 (−0.86)
RDPRICEHAT	−0.015 (−16.40)
RGASPR	0.012 (3.12)
GENER	0.107 (8.36)
D1990	0.027 (3.78)
Summary statistics	
CHI-SQUARED (1 df)	3,044.6
PSEUDO R²	0.55
N	6,238
RHO	0.818

[a] Dependent variable is binary and equals 1 if a power plant purchased PRB coal in a given year, 0 otherwise. Unbalanced panels for 416 coal-buying power plants.

significance. F-tests indicate that cross-sectional effects are jointly significant and $R^2 = 0.83$.

Table 10-4 shows the outcome from the second-step coal demand regression of the quantity of coal delivered to utilities on various explanatory variables (including the delivered price of coal), using panel data for the period 1985–2000. This equation was estimated as an ordinary demand function rather than an inverse demand equation, as specified in the conceptual model, to facilitate calculations of effects of prices and, ultimately, taxes (see below). The sample size reflects observations limited to those utilities that actually bought coal from a PRB mine. This regression uses information from the previously discussed probit regressions (the inverse Mills ratio, [MILLS] as an explanatory variable to control for the likelihood that a utility buys coal from a PRB mine. The regression reported in Table 10-4 was estimated using one-way fixed effects. Time effects were jointly insignificant at conventional levels when added to an equation already containing cross-sectional controls. Controlling for sources of heterogeneity among power plants (such as distance from Wyoming) is important because the conceptual model assumed that all utilities were located at the same distance from the mines. Coefficient estimates

Table 10-3. *Demand Data Description and Means Stage II Ordinary Demand*

Variable	Description	Means
RDPRICE	Weighted average annual delivered price of Wyoming coal, 1985–2000, in $2,000/ST using GDP deflator (FERC Form 423, Annual)	24.14
QUANTITY	Annual Wyoming coal purchased by power plant, 1985–2000, in MMST (FERC Form 423, Annual)	1.969
RGASPR	Weighted average annual natural gas price paid by plants that burn Wyoming coal, 1985–2000, in $2,000/MMBTU using GDP deflator (FERC Form 423, Annual)	2.828
OTHERCOAL	Weighted average annual price of non-Wyoming coal in $2,000/MMBTU using GDP deflator (FERC Form 423, Annual)	1.596
GENER	Net annual electric power plant (coal) generation, 1985–2000, in billions of Kwh (Monthly Power Plant Report, EIA/DOE, Annual Summaries)	4.07
MILLS	Inverse Mills ratio (Heckman 1979)	1.447

in Table 10-4 are interpreted conditionally on the fixed effects; they show effects on coal purchases holding distance (and other fixed factors) constant.

The results suggest that the real delivered price of coal is inversely related to the quantity of coal purchased and positively related to the real natural gas price. Coefficients estimated are interpreted as percentage changes; for example, if the delivered price of PRB coal increases by $1, the quantity of coal demanded falls by about 1.4 percent. Alternatively stated, the price elasticity of demand for PRB coal evaluated at the means of delivered price ($24.14) and annual quantity purchased per year (1.97 million short tons, MMST) would be low, about −0.33. Note, however, that this price elasticity applies only to plants that are existing buyers of PRB coal and disregards the expansion or contraction of the market area when the price changes, a related aspect we consider below. Existing buyers of PRB coal do not alter their use of this fuel given price changes. Relatively fixed engineering characteristics of boilers used in the generation of electricity may be partly responsible for this outcome. The coefficient of *OTHERCOAL* is negative but not significantly different from zero at conventional levels. This outcome provides weak evidence that non-Wyoming coal and PRB coal are complements and may reflect the fact that many plants are engineered to burn a blend of coals from two or more sources. The coefficient of *GENER* is positive and significant, indicating that the quantity of coal sold to a utility is an increasing function of the amount of electricity that it generates. The coefficient of the real price of natural gas is positive and significantly different from zero as well, suggesting that natural gas is a substitute for PRB coal. Finally, the coefficient of the inverse Mill's ratio *(MILLS)* is positive and significant at conventional levels.

Table 10-4. *Ordinary Demand, One-Way Fixed-Effects Estimates*[a]

Variable	Coefficient (t-stat)
RDPRICE	−0.014 (−2.19)
RGASPR	0.234 (3.12)
OTHERCOAL	−0.163 (−0.45)
GENER	0.509 (1.70)
MILLS	0.71 (4.34)
Summary statistics	
R^2	0.83
F TEST, PLANT EFFECTS (df)	32.7 (171,1186)
F TEST, TIME EFFECTS (df)	1.1 (15,1170)
HAUSMAN	36.8
N	1,362

[a] Dependent variable is the natural log of quantity. Unbalanced panels with 172 plants.

We are interested in the coefficient estimate of *MILLS* because it suggests the importance of incorporating the coal demand function estimates into a selection model. A practical advantage of a selection model is that it allows changes in the market area for PRB coal in addition to changes in quantity demanded by existing purchasers (see Greene 1997 for further discussion, examples, and computational details). Intuitively, this point is easiest to see when estimating the second-stage equation as an ordinary, rather than as an inverse, demand function because *MILLS* is a function of the delivered price. In the estimates presented, the "market area" effect is considerably larger than the "existing purchasers" effect. For example, the "market area" effect of a change in delivered price on natural logarithm of quantity purchased is calculated by differentiating *MILLS* with respect to delivered price and multiplying by the coefficient of *MILLS* (0.71) from the regression equation. This yields a value of about −0.189, which exceeds the corresponding "existing purchasers" effect of −0.014 by a factor of more than 13.5. This calculation suggests that after combining the two effects, the price elasticity of demand (evaluated at means of delivered price and quantity) is −2.23. We discuss these two effects more below, when we calculate the effects of tax rate changes.

Railroad Costs

Data used to estimate railroad costs are taken from the 1988–2000 Carload Way-bill Sample from the Surface Transportation Board of the Interstate Commerce Commission. Data consist of a random sample of railroad shipments originating, terminating, or passing through Wyoming. For each year, the data were filtered to eliminate noncoal shipments and coal shipments consisting of fewer than 50 cars of coal. The filter was applied to eliminate intermittent coal shipments to various steam and processing plants whose associated costs are likely to be different from those for regular shipments to power plants. Each year, the filtered waybill sample captured shipments of 65 million to 141 million tons of PRB coal, representing 35 to 45 percent of total PRB coal shipments. For the shipments remaining in the sample after the filters were applied, standard point location codes were used to identify the originating PRB mine and the destination power plant. We use these resulting mine-plant pairs as the units of observation.

In the regression, 207 mine-plant pairs were identified for coal shipments between 1988 and 2000. Transactions did not occur for some of these pairs in some years, so the data form an unbalanced panel of 1,060 observations. Data were applied in a two-way fixed-effects framework to obtain an estimate of the railroad cost function for coal transportation $C(q)$. The estimates automatically control for distance (and other time-invariant mine-plant characteristics) along each transportation route—a crucial aspect of the estimation procedure, given the conceptual model.

The dependent variable is the natural logarithm of the railroad's reported variable cost of operation associated with hauling coal along a particular route in a given year. The Surface Transportation Board (2000) computes this cost measure on the basis of railroad-specific accounting and operating data using the Uniform Railroad Costing System. Excluding general and administrative expenses, the cost averages about 63 percent of the reported freight charges for all 207 routes over the 13-year sample period. Only two explanatory variables were used because available data contain few variables that vary both across transportation routes and over time. These variables measure (1) quantity of coal shipped along a route in a particular year and (2) whether the railcars used were privately owned. Table 10-5 presents sample means and more complete definitions of variables.

Table 10-6 shows the regression results. Both mine-plant pair-specific and time-specific effects jointly differ significantly from zero at conventional levels and $R^2 = 0.89$. Additionally, the coefficients of $QUANTITY$ and $CAROWN$ are positive and highly significant. Because mine-plant-specific factors are controlled by fixed-effects estimation, the coefficient of $QUANTITY$ measures the incremental effect on variable cost arising from shipping an additional million tons of coal along each route. For given values of q, we can compute values for C_q and C_{qq}. These calculations are described in the following section.

Table 10-5. *Rail Cost Data Description and Means*

Variable	Description	Means
RAILCOST	Sampled annual (coal) rail variable-cost, railhead to railhead, 1988–2000, in millions of $2,000, using GDP deflator, computed by Surface Transportation Board using Uniform Railroad Costing System (Carload Waybill Sample, Surface Transportation Board, 1988–2000)	8.246
QUANTITY	Sampled (annual) Wyoming coal delivered to power plant, 1988–2000, in MMST (Carload Waybill Sample, Surface Transportation Board)	0.950
CAROWN	= 1 if rail cars are privately owned, 0 if owned by railroad (Carload Waybill Sample, Surface Transportation Board)	0.84
RAILMILES	Rail miles between origin Wyoming railhead and destination power plant railhead (Carload Waybill Sample, Surface Transportation Board)	978

Estimating Changes in Coal Purchases and Prices

We now combine the empirical estimates with our analytical model to calculate effects of local tax changes on PRB coal production, the mine–mouth price of coal, the delivered price of coal, railroad freight charges, and local tax collections. The tax variable modeled is an *effective* rate rather than the statutory nominal rate. Counties in Wyoming grant numerous credits and exemptions against taxes levied, so nominal rates overstate amounts actually paid. The local production tax rate is computed as total local production tax collections in 2000 divided by the gross value of PRB coal production (State of Wyoming 2000).

We model a supposed 2-percentage-point reduction in the effective local production tax, from 7 to 5 percent. The method used to evaluate this tax change is straightforward, and it is helpful to clarify four aspects of procedures. First, we compute estimates of effects on PRB production using equation (9) together with estimates of utility demand for Wyoming coal (see Table 10-4), railroad costs (see Table 10-6), and the estimated mine cost function (see equation 13). Second, the mine cost function and its derivatives were evaluated at PRB's 2000 sample output level of 305 MMST. Third, because the empirical analysis of railroad costs treated mine-plant pairs as the unit of observation, derivatives of the railroad cost function were evaluated at the 2000 average quantity of coal hauled along the 207 routes considered (1.1 MMST).

Fourth, treatment of utility demand parameters requires more explanation. Recall that the effect of a delivered price change on quantity of PRB coal purchased is divided into two effects—an "existing plant" effect and a "market area" effect. The conceptual model is based on the inverse demand function for coal, whereas estimates of an ordinary demand function were presented in Table 10-4. After computing the two effects, we combined them in the estimated ordinary

Table 10-6. *Rail Cost, Two-Way Fixed-Effects Estimates[a]*

Variable	Coefficient (t-stat)
CONSTANT	-0.399 (-4.54)
QUANTITY	0.98 (21.64)
CAROWN	0.497 (5.53)
Summary statistics	
R^2	0.89
F TEST, MINE-PLANT PAIR EFFECTS (df)	9.7 (206,852)
F TEST, TIME EFFECTS (df)	4.9 (10,841)
HAUSMAN	29.2
N	1060

[a] Dependent variable is the natural log of the real rail variable cost.

demand equation and then derived an inverse demand function using the implicit function theorem. Derivatives of this inverse demand function were evaluated at the 2000 average quantity of PRB coal purchased by plants that bought this fuel in positive amounts (2.2 MMST).

Table 10-7 presents results from computing the various values needed to evaluate the comparative static results from the conceptual model. Four features of these calculations warrant further comment. First, $D = -12.64$, implying that the second-order conditions are satisfied. Second, evaluating $H(q)$ at $q = 305$ MMST gives a value for the marginal cost of coal production of $5.09, which is slightly below the average 2000 coal price of $P^M = $5.48. This outcome suggests an incentive to open additional mines, provided the marginal costs of operation at capacity are less than P^M and provided this price is expected to hold into the future. Third, Table 10-7 reveals evidence of the monopsony power of railroads. The marginal expense of supplying another unit of coal is $H(q) + qH_q$. Substituting values from Table 10-7 and using $q = 305$ MMST suggests that this value is $6.22, which exceeds marginal cost ($H(q)=$5.09) by $1.13, or about 22 percent. Fourth, railroad's monopoly power over utilities also can be illustrated using the figures in Table 10-7. Marginal revenue is given by $f(q) + qf_q = $18.47 - $5.24 = $13.23, when the utility demand function for PRB coal is evaluated at $q = 2.2$ MMST.

Table 10-8 shows the effects of reducing the effective production tax by 2 percentage points (7 to 5 percent) of the value of coal produced. Output of coal rises

Table 10-7. *Computed Values to Evaluate Comparative Statics*

Component	2000 estimates
$p^D = f(q)$	18.47
f_q	−2.38
f_{qq}	1.08
C_q	9.12
C_{qq}	10.032
$H(q)$	5.09
H_q	0.00372
H_{qq}	0.00008
t^M	0.07
p^M	5.48
	−12.64

Table 10–8. *Effects of Local Production Tax Reduction*

Effect	2000 estimates
Change in production (MMST)	1.42 (0.47 %)
Change in mine price	$−0.12 (−2.15 %)
Change in delivered price	$−0.02 (−0.12 %)
Change in freight rate	$0.10 (0.77 %)
Change in tax revenue (millions)	$−31.41 (−26.9 %)

by 1.42 MMST (0.47 percent) and the mine-mouth price of coal falls by about $0.12 from $P^M = 5.48 to $P^M = 5.36. The average delivered price of coal falls by about $0.02, a decline of about 0.12 percent. The freight rate per ton of coal hauled along a route of average length rises by about 0.77 percent from $18.47 − $5.48 = $12.99 to $18.45 − $5.36 = $13.09. The tax change has little effect on quantities of coal produced and relevant prices, especially when measured as percentage changes.

The largest effect of the tax reduction is on coal production tax collections. From values given in Table 10-7, we can separate the change in local production tax revenue into three components: (1) the loss in tax revenue from the rate reduction ($33.43 million), (2) the gain in tax revenue from the increased quantity of coal produced ($2.56 million), and (3) the loss of tax revenue from the decline in the mine-mouth price ($0.54 million). In total, the counties lose $31.41 million in tax revenue, a decline of about 26.9 percent in collections.

Conclusion

In some ways, this book is a discussion of how rural populations depend on the rents generated by natural resources. Rural people are interested in keeping more of these rents for themselves rather than sending them off to urban dwellers who might view resources as an amenity rather than a necessary factor of production (see, e.g., Chapter 6, this volume). The issue explored in this chapter is whether lower local tax rates increase production in the natural resource–based industries that underpin the development of rural economies. For a case study of coal production in the Powder River basin, Wyoming, our answer is no. The results suggest that a reduction in property taxation on coal has negligible effect on quantities of coal produced but reduces tax collections by more than 25 percent. Our findings support the view that common rural development schemes do not necessarily increase the production of natural resources; rather, lower taxes more likely represent a transfer of rents to the private sector (firm or transportation or both) from the local jurisdiction. This rural resource rent giveaway undercuts the frequently heard political argument in the rural interior West of the United States that tax breaks trigger development and create jobs in rural areas that are heavily dependent on natural resource extraction.

We conclude with a final observation on the interdependence of tax breaks and environmental standards. Along with tax breaks, local policymakers try to attract jobs and capital through lax environmental regulations. The ongoing coal-bed methane development in Campbell County, Wyoming, is a good example. The methane is natural gas found in coal seams. Extraction of this gas requires bringing large volumes of groundwater to the surface and discharging it onto the land. Officials in Campbell County (and the state) weakened standards and provided minimal monitoring of saline, sodicity, arsenic, and barium levels in the water discharged from coal-bed methane wells. About 15,000 such wells have been developed in the Powder River basin in Wyoming to date, and another 35,000 could be developed.

Have these lax standards attracted new jobs that otherwise would go to other regions? The evidence suggests the answer is "not many." For 2000–2003, the growth period of coal-bed methane development, mining sector jobs in the county increased by 206—roughly a 4 percent increase. Median wages in the county have kept up with inflation over this same four-year period. Observers fear for the future environmental integrity since high-salinity, high-sodicity water discharge is common practice in Campbell County. Few permanent jobs in exchange for less environmental quality does not appear to be a sustainable strategy to many observers.

References

Atkinson, S., and J. Kerkvliet. 1986. Measuring the Multilateral Allocation of Rents: Wyoming Low Sulfur Coal. *Rand Journal of Economics* 17: 416–30.
———. 1989. Dual Measures of Monopoly and Monopsony Power: An Application to Regulated Electric Utilities. *Review of Economics and Statistics* 71: 250–57.
Coal Outlook. Various yearly issues. Arlington, VA: Pasha Publications.
Coal Week. Various yearly issues. Columbus, OH: McGraw-Hill.
Ellerman, A.D., and J.-P. Montero. 1998. The Declining Trend in Sulfur Dioxide Emissions: Implications for Allowance Prices. *Journal of Environmental Economics and Management* 36: 26–45.
Energy Information Administration. 1977–1997. Coal Industry Annual. Federal Energy Regulatory Commission. Various years. Monthly Report of Cost and Quality of Fuels for Electric Plants.
———. 1993–1997. All months. Monthly Power Plant Data. http://www.eia.doe.gov/cneaf/electricity/page/eia759.html. EIA-759.

———. 1995. *Energy Policy Act Transportation Rate Study: Interim Report on Coal Transportation.* U.S. Department of Energy. Washington, DC, EIA b.

———. 1999. *Inventory of Electric Utility Power Plants in the United States.* U.S. Department of Energy. Washington, DC, EIA-IPP.

———. 2000. *Model Documentation Coal Market Module of the National Energy Modeling System.* U.S. Department of Energy. Washington, DC. January.

———. [date?] *The U.S. Coal Industry in the 1990's: Low Prices and Record Production.* U.S. Department of Energy. Washington, DC. September.

———. Various years. Monthly Power Plant Report, Form EIA-759.

———. Various years. Steam Electric Operation and Design Report, EIA-767.

Federal Energy Regulatory Commission. 1993–1997. Monthly Cost and Quality of Fuels for Electric Plants. http://www.eia.doe/cneaf/electricity.page/ferc423.html. Ferc-Form 423.

Gerking, S., W. Morgan, M. Kunce, and J. Kerkvliet. 2000. Mineral Tax Incentives, Mineral Production and the Wyoming Economy. *Report to the State of Wyoming,* http://w3.uwyo.edu/~mkunce/ExecSum.pdf.

Greene, W. 1997. *Econometric Analysis,* 3rd edition. Saddle River, NJ: Prentice-Hall.

Hausman, J. 1978. Specification Tests in Econometrics. *Econometrica* 46: 1251–71.

Heckman, J. 1979. Sample Selection Bias as a Specification Error. *Econometrica* 47: 153–61.

Kerkvliet, J., and J. Shogren. 1992. The Impacts of Environmental Regulation on Coal Procurement Strategies: Design Coal and Multi-Attributed Quality. *Journal of Environmental Management* 35: 83–91.

———. 2001. The Determinants of Coal Contract Duration for the Powder River Basin. *Journal of Theoretical Economics* 127: 608–22.

Kolstad, C., and F. Wolak, Jr. 1983. Competition in Interregional Taxation: The Case of Western Coal. *Journal of Political Economy* 91: 443–60.

Lyman, R., and L. Hallberg. 2004. Wyoming Coal Mines and Markets, *Wyoming State Geological Survey Annual Report 2000-2004.* Laramie, WY.

MacDonald, J., and L. Cavalluzzo. 1996. Railroad Deregulation and Employment Effects. *Industrial and Labor Relations Review* 50: 80–91.

State of Wyoming. 2000. Department of Revenue. Annual Report.

Surface Transportation Board. 1988–2000. STB Carload Waybill Sample. Washington, DC.

Wasylenko, M. 1997. Taxation and Economic Development: The State of the Economic Literature. *New England Economic Review* (March/April): 37–52.

Note

1. To demonstrate more fully that $dP^M/dt^M > 0$, recall equation (10):

$$\frac{dP^M}{dt^M} = \frac{H_q}{(1-t^M)}\frac{dq}{dt^M} + \frac{H(q)}{(1-t^M)^2}.$$

Substituting in equation (9) yields

$$\frac{dP^M}{dt^M} = \frac{q[H_q]^2 + H_q H(q) + \Delta(1-t^M) H(q)}{\Delta(1-t^M)^3}.$$

Then substituting equation (8) for Δ in the numerator yields

$$\frac{dP^M}{dt^M} = \frac{(1-t^M)[H(q)][qf_{qq} + 2f_q - C_{qq}] - [qH_{qq} H(q) + H_q H(q) - q[H_q]^2]}{(1-t^M)^3 \Delta}.$$

Thus, $dP^M / dt^M > 0$ if $\Delta < 0$ (second-order conditions are satisfied; see the text) and $d(qH_q/H(q))/dq > 0$.

CHAPTER II

The Politics of Place

Linking Rural and Environmental Governance

Ronald J. Oakerson

*B*OTH RURAL AND ENVIRONMENTAL policies have important and unique place-based effects. This is true even if the relevant place is planet Earth, and the policy concerns rightly deserve to be tagged "global." More often, the places of concern are more bounded—considered local or regional—and the effects of rural and environmental policies vary significantly from place to place. A general interest in "rural America" quickly translates into particular interests in specific areas or regions—the Mississippi Delta, perhaps, the eastern Kentucky highlands, or the Adirondack dome—each of which corresponds to a distinctive culture and way of life tied to a particular environment and resource base.[1] As Emery Castle and Dave Ervin point out in Chapter 1 of this volume, rural and environmental problems are increasingly tied together, and it is the commonality of place that binds them. Put simply, they share the same geography.[2]

Outsiders prize a rural region for its unique qualities, and so do the home folks. Economically, a region may be valued for its particular natural resource base or its strategic location. Most regions, however, are also home to communities of people that have managed to sustain themselves across several generations and therefore have developed distinct local or regional cultures. Rural cultures are associated with ways of life closely tied to patterns of resource use: consider a fishing village, a mining community, a logging community, or various sorts of farming communities. In each case the resource base blends with the culture it helps to support to sustain a unique way of life.

Place-based concerns fall into two distinct sets—with some overlap between them. One set derives from human settlement and its values—shelter, infrastructure, employment, education, recreation, environmental amenities, or more generally, the community and its way of life. The other set derives directly from the resource base—water, soil, vegetation, wildlife, minerals, climate—and its economic uses, including the production of food and fiber, extraction of raw materials, environmental amenities, recreation, and ecosystem services. As ecologists have taught us, the resource base is ultimately an integrated whole, such that if relevant use thresholds are passed, sustainability becomes the overriding concern for both community and environment.

Within the bounds of sustainability, however, conflicts occur between community-based and environmental values, as well as between the values within each set. Although community values are primarily local, environmental values are not. Among community values, trade-offs may be required between employment and environmental amenities; among resource base and environmental values, trade-offs occur between resource extraction and ecosystem services. Between the two sets of values, local concerns with employment and infrastructure are likely to conflict significantly with the environmental concerns of nonlocals. Two values—environmental amenities and recreation—are found in both sets, though even these may have distinguishing nuances for locals and nonlocals.[3]

Community and environmental concerns display a reverse pair of asymmetries: most of the economic forces affecting rural communities originate elsewhere and require local adaptation, whereas most of the global effects of environmental degradation originate locally and depend on local action to ameliorate them. International economics shapes more and more of the agenda of local politics, just as local resource extraction and use shape the global agenda of environmentalism.

At this complex nexus of community and environment lies the politics of place in rural America. A focus on place can help to overcome the long-standing practice of separating issues of environmental protection in rural areas from issues of rural community development. Driving the politics of place is the adjudication of conflict among diverse values that must share the same physical space while serving both locals and nonlocals. At the center of the conflict is a tension between aspects of community and aspects of environment—between environmental preservation and community preservation.

Place-based politics is no longer purely local, if it ever was: its distinctive mark is the process of negotiating the increasingly permeable boundary between local communities and external demands and effects. Historically, rural governance has been primarily a state and local matter (and likely should remain so), while environmental governance has been increasingly nationalized. Nonetheless, there is also a significant history of federal involvement in rural development, just as state governments have remained active in natural resource management despite the growing (and often preemptive) federal presence in environmental regulation. Both environmental and rural community concerns need to be addressed at multiple levels of government.

A more constructive politics of place depends on linking rural and environmental concerns in ways that recognize the diversity and uniqueness of rural places. To illustrate, I draw on a single example—the Adirondacks of upstate New York—throughout the discussion that follows. Although the politics of place is ubiquitous, it has seldom been as fully on display as in the Adirondack region. Here, in 1892, with the conservation movement gaining steam, the state legislature created what it chose to call the Adirondack Park, a huge expanse of forests, mountains, lakes, and streams that now, after numerous expansions of its boundaries, accounts for one-fifth of the state's land area, roughly the size of the neighboring state of Vermont. Nested within the park is a preexisting state forest preserve. Two years after the park's formation, a constitutional convention extended the protection of the state constitution to the forest preserve, now almost half the area of the park. The "Forever Wild" clause,[4] which remains very much in effect, prohibited logging in the forest preserve, thereby assigning an extraordinary legal and political weight to wilderness values. But the park is also home to some 130,000 year-round residents—and another 130,000 seasonal residents—as well as the usual array of local governments and school districts. With just over half of the park's land in private ownership, development pressures led in 1971 to the formation of the Adirondack Park Agency, essentially a regional land use control board with planning authority that extends to both privately owned and publicly owned areas.

The coexistence of wilderness and rural community within officially prescribed regional boundaries makes the Adirondacks an especially useful case for understanding the politics of place. The conflict between community and environmental values has often been acute, reaching a high point in the 1970s, when many local residents responded with outrage to the unprecedented extension of state zoning authority over a local rural area (Terrie 1997). Yet there are also sustained efforts at collaboration on the part of multiple governmental and nongovernmental groups, endeavoring to find ways to pursue diverse values jointly—wilderness preservation, recreation, and economic development (McMartin 2002). Resource economist Ross Whaley, a former president of the College of Environmental Science and Forestry (part of the State University of New York system) who until recently chaired the Adirondack Park Agency, sees the park as a potential model of sustainable development (Whaley et al. 2003). Whether or not this turns out to be so, the Adirondack Park provides an instructive window on the intersection of rural and environmental concerns.

As we explore the frontier of rural and environmental policies at the outset of the twenty-first century, the politics of place may help us map out their relationship.[5] Such a project is initially theoretical, referring to the political theory of policy and organization; this is my focus here. A theory that can make sense of current patterns of organization and diagnose existing problems may also suggest alternative possibilities. The hoped-for product is not a blueprint for policy formation but a sense of organizational possibilities and some corresponding guideposts for realizing them, offered provisionally as a set of propositions and principles subject to revision with further experience.

The Intergovernmental Context

The search for practical principles of place-based governance in the United States occurs of necessity in an intergovernmental context. The overarching story of intergovernmental relations and the environment in the twentieth century is a tale of significant but incomplete nationalization, divided into two main chapters. Early in the century, a conservation movement arose and led to the assignment of considerable responsibility for environmental stewardship to federal agencies, in particular the U.S. Forest Service (1905) and the National Park Service (1916), alongside the stewardship of similar state agencies. Both federal and state responsibilities grew incrementally over a half-century. Later, in a second chapter, the environmental movement that produced the first Earth Day in 1970 led to a series of federal laws—most notably, the National Environmental Policy Act (1969), the Clean Air Act (1970), the Clean Water Act (1972), and the Endangered Species Act (1973)— that nationalized a great deal of environmental regulation, previously the primary responsibility of states. Although important stewardship responsibilities and regulatory authority came thus to rest in the hands of federal officials, significant responsibilities for natural resource management and environmental regulation have remained with state and local governments.[6]

By the end of the century, the nationalization of environmental policy was being subjected to critical scrutiny. A renewed interest in "civic environmentalism" (John 1994), "environmental federalism" (Anderson and Hill 1997), and devolution (Scheberle 2004) arose in response to the evident difficulty of imposing a national regime of regulation on the diverse environmental circumstances of a nation that spans the North American continent—and more. Yet many environmental problems cannot be confined within political boundaries, and some of the more severe problems are clearly national in scope, if not global. Efforts to sort out functions between levels of government have met with little success, largely because of the complexity of environmental problems. Shared responsibility—with all its attendant ambiguities—is the norm across multiple functions.

The Competing Claims of Community and Environment

The intersection of rural and environmental policy is shaped by the empirical relationship among rural and environmental values; in the Adirondack Park, for example, the evolving trade-off is between preserving wilderness and providing social and recreational opportunities, such as snowmobiling. Solving the environmental problem is not a simple problem of maximizing environmental values but instead the much more complex problem of arriving at appropriate trade-offs among a host of values over time.[7] To simplify the discussion, I collapse a large number of values into two: community and environment. I assume that both are essential values, part of the bedrock of human existence, and that one does not consistently outrank the other on some grand ordinal scale. Rather, the ranking is contingent on circumstances and preferences that vary spatially as well as temporally—from place to place and time to time.

The nature of community and its value to human beings has been highlighted and clarified in recent years by the investigation of social capital (Coleman 1988). The concept of social capital can be understood from the standpoint of an individual: it is one's ability to draw on others for help. As such it is analogous to money in the bank, an account from which one can make withdrawals provided it has been maintained through deposits of generosity. The social capital model gives us useful insight into community as a process—creating and sustaining various ways to maintain goodwill and collaboration among community members while drawing on the reservoir thus created to cope with problems, both individually and collectively. As Robert Putnam (2000) has shown, higher levels of investment in social capital are empirically associated with more desirable social outcomes in education, security from crime, economic prosperity, community health, and even a general sense of happiness.

In contrast to community preservation, interest in environmental preservation has a broader constituency and has frequently originated from outside the area to be preserved. The Adirondacks provide a case in point. The major support for Adirondack preservation was urban: for much of its existence, the Association for the Protection of the Adirondacks, which over its life earned the nickname "Watchdog of the Forest Preserve," was governed from Wall Street (Terrie 1997).[8] Initially, the New York City dwellers were concerned about protection of the Hudson River watershed, on which they were dependent. Later, as "wilderness" was gradually transformed from an enemy of civilization into a highly valued environmental amenity (Nash 2001), the Adirondack wilderness took on an iconic value that seemed to transcend its value to local residents. Advocates of Adirondack preservation have consistently stressed that the Adirondack Park is a place that belongs to the people of New York State, not simply to its residents. This idea has caused considerable irritation for Adirondack residents, who are, after all, the resident citizens of the park. The unique value of a vast wilderness located in the urban Northeast has nonetheless tended to override the frequently expressed local desires in the Adirondacks for more conventional sorts of economic development. Historically, the presence of highly valued environmental resources and amenities in a strategic location gave nonlocals a decisive voice.

It seems especially tempting, intellectually, to talk about "the environment" abstractly, as if it were a separate realm, and thus implicitly neglect the community values interwoven in its fabric. This was certainly the case in the early history of the Adirondack Park: the deliberations accompanying its formation and the protection of its forests gave scant attention to the plain fact that people lived there, people who considered the forest and its waterways and wildlife theirs to use as they pleased (Terrie 1997). By the same token, local communities may be inclined to discount environmental values, such as ecosystem services, that benefit mainly others outside the immediate area. The politics of place at its best would correct for both intellectual tendencies, explicitly addressing the intersection of rural and environmental concerns at multiple levels. Perhaps it would be better if we ceased to speak of "the environment" and spoke instead only of "environments" and their communities. In the case of the Adirondack Park, policymakers inadvertently created a context in which the competing claims of community and environment would eventually be required to acknowledge one another—this because the park has always contained private land, as well as numerous towns and villages. Today, it seems impossible to pursue one set of values without explicitly taking the other into account.[9]

Like environments, rural communities are almost everywhere under assault. Once sustained by the economy of agriculture and resource extraction, many rural communities are threatened with the loss of the various sorts of capital—social as well as physical and human capital—that those economic activities brought with them. The greatest challenge facing the Adirondack Park today is not to preserve the wilderness, though this will always be problematic, but to restore and sustain local communities adjacent to wilderness. The fact that the two challenges must be faced together is what makes the Adirondacks a paradigm case.

The Multiplication of Agency Relationships

To appreciate the challenge of linking rural and environmental concerns, we must understand something of the history and theory of public policy in America. One of the basic features of environmental policy, as it has developed historically in the United States, is the multiplication of agency relationships. By *agency*, I refer to the relationship between a principal and an agent who represents the principal. Principal–agent relationships can be private (as in the relationship between lawyer and client) or public. The history and structure of environmental policy in the United States can be understood in terms of the theory of *public* agency as formulated by John Dewey (1927). In this case the principal is a public—a group affected "indirectly" (as Dewey would say) by the actions of others, with "indirect" effects referring to actions unmediated by *direct* relationships such as exchange or reciprocity.[10] "Officials," Dewey (1927, 19) wrote, "are . . . public agents . . . , doing the business of others in securing and obviating consequences that concern them." Such agents are charged with the protection of specific values of concern to their publics or constituencies.

Public agency of this sort has the character of a trust (Sax 1970). Ordinarily, we think of agents as representing persons, but in this case agents in a sense represent certain publicly shared values. In effect, agents hold certain values in trust for the public. Consider the now-classic question, "Should trees have standing?" (Stone 1974). That is, should trees be afforded legal standing in court so as to claim the legal protections afforded trees? Since trees cannot speak and act for themselves, I rephrase the question, Should trees have agents? Just as we assign an incompetent person an attorney, we can appoint agents for trees. Trees in effect have standing if there are agents with adequate authority, resources, and incentive to stand up for them—in court, if necessary. The same can be true of any human value its public deems important enough to be so represented. An important and ancient question, of course, is, who will watch the watchers? Who will hold public agents accountable? More on this below.

The multiplicity and diversity of values imply a need for *multiple agency relationships* (hereinafter, "multiple agency"). Each value is sustained in very different ways and potentially affected by widely different patterns of behavior. Environmental values tend to be represented in agency relationships in one of two ways: (1) public landownership and management and (2) public regulation of private and public behavior. Note that the two great stages of nationalization in environmental policy addressed first one, then the other. The public values at stake are often subject to trade-off. Each resource type is subject to multiple uses, implying multiple valuations and multiple publics (in Dewey's terms). Diverse values—land, water, wildlife—are frequently the responsibility of the officials who head up administrative agencies, each with substantial autonomy. The required agency relationships increase in both number and complexity as one set of concerns impinges on another.[11]

Recognition of the need for multiple agency was evident in the early development of federal and state stewardship responsibilities, leading to the establishment of multiple natural resource agencies at both levels of government. Multiple agency was largely ignored in 1970, however, when President Nixon established the Environmental Protection Agency (EPA) by executive order, consolidating several regulatory responsibilities in a single agency. Even within the consolidated EPA, however, program offices specialized by resource or medium (air, water, soil) enjoy substantial autonomy because of their separate statutory bases (Rosenbaum 2006). Moreover, much of its work is done through its 10 regional offices (Rabe 2006). Despite recurrent interest in consolidation, it is unlikely that multiple agency can be effectively eliminated in the environmental area at any level of government, not to mention across levels.

Administrative agencies multiply in number because it is difficult for a single agency to exercise responsibility for multiple values subject to trade-off.[12] Bureaucratic processes are more likely to be managed effectively when a single major value is predominant, lending clarity to the agency's mission.[13] EPA suffers in this sense from its large number of diverse responsibilities (Rosenbaum 2006). At the same time, autonomous agencies sometimes exhibit only a difference of emphasis. The differences between the U.S. Forest Service and the National Park Service present a well-known case in point. Both agencies have distinctive histories that position them as the guardians of related but distinct values: environmental preservation, resource conservation (which implies resource use), outdoor recreation, and public education. Each has had difficulty balancing these diverse value claims, and each has developed somewhat different trade-offs (Clarke and McCool 1985).[14] Across levels of government, Koontz (2002) finds that the management of state and national forests tends to reflect different agency priorities—the states emphasizing timber production, and the federal government, environmental protection.

The Adirondack Park offers a similar example. Two state agencies share responsibility for the forest preserve—the Department of Environmental Conservation (DEC) as manager and the Adirondack Park Agency (APA) as planner. If DEC leans toward use values while APA tilts toward preservation values, both sets of values gain more effective representation in public policy than if there were only a single agency with a single order of priorities.[15]

The number of government agencies thus created has often prompted complaints about the "fragmentation" of governmental authority (see V. Ostrom 1989). The complaint neglects the fact that the multiplication of agency relationships derives from the complexity of the environment itself—multiple, interrelated values subject to trade-off. Complexity in the environment arguably requires complexity in the political and administrative system that seeks to regulate it.

The conflict between values related to rural places and environments does not typically correspond to a conflict between public and private interests. More often, it is a conflict between competing public goods. For example, wilderness as a value competes with numerous other values that often find expression in various public improvements. Wilderness requires a large roadless area, but roads are usually viewed as public improvements; it requires free-flowing streams, but dams provide public goods such as flood control and electric power; it requires restrictions on the recreational uses of motorized vehicles, uses that in other contexts are viewed as public benefits; it may also require restriction on the construction of facilities such as cell towers and water towers that provide valued services to the public. If wilderness is to have an advocate and protector, that agent should not be one who is charged with the provision of competing public goods.

The Need for Local Agency

Community values, too, depend on public agency. In particular, local communities need agents to represent community values vis-à-vis those who represent other values, including environmental values. Protecting and sustaining community values—community preservation, if you will—is the primary purpose of local governments. Often this sense of purpose is articulated as the protection of local property values, reflected in real estate prices (see, e.g., Peterson 1981), but the purpose of local government is much broader, extending to the protection of social capital as well as physical capital. In sum, we can think of a local government as a corporate agency charged with the protection of the place-based values of importance to a specific local community. This is the overarching reason that communities choose to acquire corporate agency by incorporating as municipalities.

Rural community formation is often viewed as a secondary outcome of non-local decisions related to transportation infrastructure or resource extraction—settlements motivated primarily by nonsettlement considerations. Community is then a social outcome of individual choices but not a social choice (see Chapter 2, this volume). Without agency, a community is unable to act; it becomes little more than the local product of forces beyond its control.

Such forces are always at work: a factory is closed because of international competition; a school is consolidated because it cannot satisfy the requirements of a state law; an interstate highway bisects (or bypasses) a town or village; a government regulation causes local layoffs. Or more positively, market demand surges for locally made products, a national chain decides to locate in town (not always viewed as an unmixed blessing), or a local museum becomes a statewide tourist destination. In either case, the image created is one of local communities existing at the mercy, if you will, of national and international decisions that may exhibit little care for local impacts.

Although purely intentional communities are rare, the idea of community is never devoid of intentionality. Intentionality demands agency. If community is a basic value of importance to people, local people will seek to shape their community on the basis of intentionality—to mold it to serve their hopes and aspirations—and to preserve it.

Local public agency is ordinarily governmental, for governmental agency enables a local community to act collectively in the presence of free-rider and holdout problems (Olson 1965).[16] The relevant dimensions of local government authority include the police power (which allows for zoning), eminent domain, and the power to tax and spend.[17] Voluntary community association, while a critically important complement to governmental organization, cannot entirely substitute for it. Indeed, studies of urban and suburban America suggest that lower-cost access to local government authority increases the incentives for civic engagement, bringing social capital resources to bear on local public problems.[18] Of course, rural America also exhibits diverse governmental structures (Oakerson 1995), ranging from small and intensely self-governing New England towns to the more extensive counties of the South. Studies that would examine the relationship between governmental structure and civic engagement (or social capital) in rural areas have yet to be done.

An organized local community works best when its members occupy symmetrical positions.[19] For example, the residents who live around a lake are all more or less equally affected by their behavior on the lake. If they pollute the lake and the fish die, they all lose the ability to fish. If they permit motorized craft, they all pay for that decision in terms of the peace and quiet foregone. This does not mean they will all agree on the appropriate trade-offs; but the trade-offs are similar for everyone concerned. Local residents can effectively use a single corporate agency to address this problem because no one is in a position to benefit mainly at others' expense. And once a clear majority preference has established itself, remaining dissenters are free to vote with their feet, if the issue is of sufficient importance to them.

Local problems, however, do not occur at a single scale. Some are more "local" than others. Community members who occupy symmetrical positions with respect to one problem are often in asymmetrical positions vis-à-vis others outside the immediate community with respect to a different problem. For example, city neighborhoods tend to reflect the interests of pedestrians, but cities reflect the demand for traffic flow. Although nearly all residents to some extent both drive and walk, only in the context of the larger jurisdiction do residents occupy symmetrical positions as drivers.

In these terms, a strong case can be made for numerous levels of local government.[20] In fact, local government in the United States is not—and should not be construed as—a single level of government. Typically, the tasks of local governance are distributed among multiple nested jurisdictions, one nested inside the other, like Chinese boxes.[21] In upstate New York, for example, villages are nested within townships, and townships, school districts, and cities are nested within counties. But this is just the beginning. Soil conservation districts are nested within counties (their boundaries are in fact coterminous); tax districts are nested within townships; and a host of special purpose or district governments can, at local option, be nested within townships or counties or cut across other boundaries as seems appropriate, serving a variety of purposes.

The nested character of local governance provides important capabilities. One is that it permits multiple local agency, bringing with it the ability to represent diverse local values. Multiple boundaries, represented abstractly as a set of concentric circles, allow us to consider rural places in various contexts, some broader, others narrower. Nested jurisdictions increase the capacity for relevant collective action by multiplying the scales at which it can occur.[22]

The principal alternative to nested jurisdictions is a consolidated regional government. In this model there is only a single agency relationship—and a single arena of collective action. Within that arena multiple values must contend for single-agency representation. It is difficult within a single arena to privilege more localized values without threatening less localized values. The struggle of neighborhoods to be heard in great cities is a case in point. The only place represented by public agency is the larger place defined by the more inclusive boundary of the regional jurisdiction. The debate has been played out mainly in metropolitan areas (see Warren 1966): is the metropolis a single community or a community of communities? Rural regions can be expected to raise much the same question.

The need for multiple agency therefore holds for community values as well as for environmental values. Each set of values is diverse and often subject to trade-off. Moreover, local communities require agents to represent community values vis-à-vis those who represent diverse environmental values, such as trees. The need for multiple agency and the problems and tensions that flow from that multiplicity take us directly into issues of accountability in the context of interorganizational and intergovernmental relations.

Citizens as Monitors

Agents are accountable to principals, and agents who exercise public discretion are accountable to members of the public—the relevant citizenry. In a small local community, especially one that is fairly homogeneous, accountability is a relatively low-cost process. In a larger jurisdiction, such as one of the 50 states or the nation, accountability is made more problematic by the high costs of monitoring administrative behavior and the lack of incentive for individual citizens to bear those costs. Despite the incentive deficit, Joseph Sax (1970) has long argued that citizens often make the best monitors.

When endowed with appropriate statutory or constitutional authority, individual citizens are empowered to act as agents of the "public" to which they belong for the purpose of monitoring their administrative agents and calling them to account. This is especially appropriate when the agency relationship is usefully viewed as a public trust—when administrators represent values, such as trees, in which members of the public share an interest. Elsewhere I have referred to this type of citizen authority as the "anyone rule" (V. Ostrom 1987). Whereas administrative agency usually entails the assignment of authority to individuals in particular positions (administrators, attorneys-general, governors), citizen agency involves assigning authority to anyone who is a member of the relevant community. Citizen agency is frequently appropriate in situations that entail citizen coproduction of services—for example, the authority of any one person to summon police. More generally, the rule of law is strengthened when any individual person is able to invoke the protection of the law. Administrators exercise discretion only within the limits specified by law, and citizens affected by administrative actions are appropriate guardians of those legal boundaries.

The incentive deficit for individuals is usually addressed by means of voluntary organization in the context of civil society. Associations of the like-minded take on the role of monitor. A host of environmental and rural organizations exist to play such roles. What is missing is frequently not the desire to act or even the resources, but the authority.

The impact of assigning authority to citizens as monitors of administrative agents is well illustrated in the case of the Adirondack Park. Article XIV of the New York State Constitution, the Forever Wild clause, is in effect an assignment of authority to citizens. By outlawing the cutting of timber within the Adirondack forest preserve, the constitution gave citizens legal standing to challenge the administrative discretion of those charged with its stewardship. The existence of constitutional authority gave citizens ample incentive to organize for the purpose of monitoring the relevant state agency, now the Department of Environmental Conservation.[23] Several such organizations have been formed—the Association for the Protection of the Adirondacks, the Adirondack Council, and the Residents Committee to Protect the Adirondacks, to name three of the most active. As a result, DEC's (or its predecessor's) use of management discretion has been carefully monitored for more than a century and, on important occasions, challenged successfully in court.

The Variable Organization of Multiple Agency

Multiple agency presents its own set of organizational issues insofar as relationships among agents come to the fore. First, multiple agency does not just happen; it is a product of deliberate institutional design, and its maintenance may require continuing attention to institutional adaptation and reform in view of changing circumstances. Secondly, multiple agency means that good governance necessarily becomes an essentially collaborative process, although the maintenance of collaboration depends on the availability of the legal and political means to process conflict.[24]

Agency theory considers the principal–agent relationship to be problematic—mainly because the information advantages held by agents allow them to substitute their own preferences for the preferences of principals. In the case of public agency, the problem is compounded by transaction costs among individual members of a public. When agents also can exercise authority over the members of the public principal (as in the case of governmental agency), the problem is compounded still further. One might think that multiple agency relationships would make accountability even more problematic—more agents to keep track of—but that conclusion does not necessarily follow.

The American political system affords several institutional models for organizing multiple agency relationships. Federalism is fundamentally a multiple agency model. As James Madison (1788) put it in *Federalist* 46, "The federal and state governments are in fact but different agents and trustees of the people. . . ." In his conception the people of each state have two sets of agents—state and federal. The federal design of the U.S. Constitution constitutes one set of answers to the question of how to organize multiple agency relationships. State-local relations, although frequently represented in standard texts as unitary in nature, also provide a model for organizing multiple agency, one that is similar to the federalism that relates state and nation, yet different in important respects. The multijurisdictional organization of metropolitan areas provides yet another model of complex multiple agency (Oakerson 1999).

Understood in terms of agency theory, Madison's argument (1788) is that multiple agency strengthens the position of the public as principal. Referring to state and federal governments, he noted in *Federalist* 51 that "a double security arises to the rights of the people. The different governments will control each other. . . ." By drawing on the capabilities of multiple agents to hold one another accountable, citizens as principals gain significant leverage. The focus of attention shifts to the relationships among agents, who engage in deliberation and contestation with one another to the benefit of their principals. In the presence of severe information asymmetries, there is no reason to expect that singular agents would be more accountable to their constituents than multiple agents. Rather, principals gain information and influence from the competition and contestation that emerge among multiple agents.

Within large, general-purpose jurisdictions, such as those of state and federal governments, multiple agency takes the form of a number of semiautonomous administrative agencies sharing related or partially overlapping areas of responsibility. Note that multiple agency requires a high degree of autonomy among agencies at the same level of government. Multiple agency is weakened by agency consolidation and reorganization that strengthen the overall chain of command within the executive branch. Within the federal government in particular, multiple agency is sustained by the important role played by Congress and its committee structure in authorizing and giving oversight to administrative agency actions. The legislative body creates multiple agency by means of the authorizing statutes that establish and define the authority of the various administrative units. Courts participate in the agency process by construing and applying the requirements of existing statutes, overturning administrative actions that, when challenged by an appropriate party with standing, are thought to exceed the authority granted by the legislature. Accountability to Congress as principal, either directly or indirectly through the courts, actually strengthens agency autonomy vis-à-vis the executive branch and therefore supports multiple agency.

It may be argued that multiple agency at the same level of government is incoherent: why should one not expect two federal agencies (or two agencies within the same state) to exhibit consistent priorities? The quest for this sort of coherence, however, presumes that all values can be measured on a single scale, leading to a simple ordering of priorities. If this were true, politics would be a much more straightforward process. Instead, politics may be better viewed as a process of deliberation and choice among values that cannot be reduced to a single scale.[25] Multiple agency then enables the political community to make more discriminating trade-offs among many different values by giving each one a seat at the governance table. By adjusting the statutory authority of administrative agencies, legislators can manage their agency relationships in an ongoing way and reserve major decisions about value trade-offs to themselves. In the process, contestation among agencies generates information and argumentation of use to elected legislators.

Multiple agency across territorial jurisdictions, one nested inside the other, presents a different situation. In the case of federalism, multiple agency is created by the U.S. Constitution. Congress, the federal legislature, is extended only a limited grant of authority by means of enumerated powers. Included, however, is the power to regulate interstate commerce, which in the post–New Deal period became a blanket source of justification for all manner of regulation, since Congress viewed virtually all commerce as ultimately interstate in nature. Only toward the end of the twentieth century did the U.S. Supreme Court resume its practice of reviewing federal legislation with a limited conception of interstate commerce in mind.[26] The states nonetheless have always retained very broad concurrent authority to regulate economic activity unless preempted by federal law. The legal powers of the states in this regard are understood to be plenary—without limit unless explicitly limited by state or federal constitutions.

The diversity of environmental conditions is not, however, confined to interstate differences. Intrastate diversity in some cases can be as great as interstate diversity: consider northern versus southern California, for example, or western versus eastern Washington and Oregon. States are able to address the need for diversity within their borders by creating local, special-purpose governments—or, as frequently done, by providing for their creation at local discretion. The later is accomplished through general enabling legislation, which establishes the terms and conditions under which local voters or locally elected officials may act to create a new unit of local government with powers specified by state law. The relationships among those local units can then be adjusted by state legislation. This approach allows the states to fit local and regional jurisdictions to the physical contours of environmental or natural resource problems—for example, shaping a regional jurisdiction to fit the physical boundaries of a watershed or groundwater basin.

The workability of multiple agency relationships depends on how well those relationships are designed institutionally—on who decides what in relation to whom. The simple existence of multiple agency does not ensure a workable design, and environmental regulation has been fraught with difficulties. Consider, for example, the regulation of wetlands (Gaddie and Regens 2000). Operational responsibility for wetlands regulation under federal law is vested in the U.S. Army Corps of Engineers. The oversight of wetlands protection, however, is assigned to EPA, which lacks the resources to control the Corps—not so much financial resources as political resources, the Corps being one of the more autonomous, politically powerful administrative agencies in Washington. At the same time, responsibility for wetlands protection conflicts with the Corps' historic mission to promote water-based transportation and flood control. The Corps is sometimes not viewed, therefore, as a highly credible guardian of wetland values. Moreover, state agencies are allowed to assume operational responsibility if approved by EPA. While EPA looks favorably on state assumption, the Corps does not; nor, it turns out, do most states, for EPA's favorable attitude seems to be based on its greater ability to exercise effective oversight of state agencies. Yet state agencies are often critical of federal regulation for neglecting local variation in conditions. States are free to impose more stringent wetlands protection, but not to relax federal standards. Other agencies also get involved. For example, the U.S. Fish and Wildlife Service participates in regulatory decisions pertaining to wetlands that support endangered species.

The wetlands case illustrates some of the major problems with the current organization of multiple agency relationships in environmental regulation. One is the problem of unequal power among administrative agencies (Clarke and McCool 1985), as illustrated by EPA and the Corps. Another is overcentralization and standardization. Baumol and Oates (1988) concluded their classic economic analysis of environmental policy with the observation that the "attempt to impose rigid, uniform national standards for environmental quality is likely to come at a substantial cost," even while affirming that some significant role for the federal government would always remain. By the end of the century numerous voices were calling for the devolution of authority to states and localities. Yet as the wetlands case again illustrates, federal efforts to devolve or share authority have not always met with success. Partial devolution from the top down is generally more difficult to achieve than partial integration from the bottom up.[27]

The upshot is that it is difficult to find a resource type or aspect of environmental policy that does not jointly involve federal, state, and local agencies.[28] Although there may be some prospect for resorting functions between federal and state governments, shared responsibility for functions rather than functional sorting is the more likely scenario for improving environmental policy.[29] A region large enough to exhibit substantial resource diversity is bound to require the attention of multiple administrative agencies operating at more than a single level of government. The only feasible way for environmental governance to occur in this context is through contestation and collaboration.

The Possibility of Regionalism

As argued above, multiple agency can be organized in a great variety of ways, using many different institutional designs. It is the precise institutional arrangements in effect that shape the patterns of contestation and collaboration among multiple agents and lead to variable outcomes. Dissatisfaction with the prevailing patterns and their outcomes in the environmental area has led to a growing interest in the possibility of *regional* arrangements (Cortner and Moote 1999; Scheberle 2004; Lowry 2006). The interest in regionalism stems from two related sources of frustration: first, the organization of environmental law and policy mainly by resource type—water, air, forests, wildlife—often fails to take into account the strong interdependencies among resources in the context of a specific ecosystem; second, uniform national policies and regulations fail to account for place-based sources of diversity. The two concerns overlap substantially. For example, the implications of a national endangered species policy for other resources vary significantly from one region of the country to another; the trade-offs among competing values vary—often dramatically—from place to place. The need to take account of the interdependencies among resources in a specific ecological context leads to interest in a regional approach that potentially allows for better control of ecosystem effects.

Institutionally, multiple agency may become unworkable when required to operate on a scale that is too large—larger than the scale of problems being addressed. Considered on a national scale, the trade-offs among competing values become too crude, insufficiently discriminating among varied circumstances from one part of the country to another.[30] The key is to find a scale of organization that internalizes *most* of the relevant externalities—that embraces *most* of the important interdependencies among natural resources. (I emphasize "most" because insisting on complete internalization drives one to the largest scale of organization—likely to be global.) Noss and Cooperrider (1994, *11*) define an ecoregion (or bioregion) as a large landscape that "can be distinguished . . . on the basis of climate, physiography, soils, species composition patterns," or other variables. This definition is perhaps suitably ambiguous, leaving open the basis on which a particular ecoregion would be delineated—though many environmental analysts prefer the use of watersheds to define the relevant domain of regional organization (Van Dyke 2003).

For the politics of place, regionalism offers an equally potent opportunity to bring environmental policy and rural policy into a productive working relationship. The potential use of ecoregions for addressing environmental issues brings environmental concerns face to face with rural concerns focused on community values. In many cases, ecoregions will also bring to the foreground issues related to the increasingly problematic rural-urban interface. The plain fact is that significant populations of people live and work in most ecoregions, however defined, demanding that problems of environmental preservation be addressed explicitly in the context of human community and its development.

The interest in regionalism of course raises important issues of regional governance. Appropriately conceptualizing the governance of ecoregions and designing institutional arrangements that fit the politics of the particular place are critical to success. The potential design issues can only be suggested here.

The threshold issue is most likely the adoption of a boundary rule. Whereas the concept of region is somewhat open-ended, the delineation of a specific region must be clear and definitive. It is essential to know who or what is inside the region and who or what is not; otherwise, collective action will be thwarted by ambiguity about the scope of the relevant group.[31] For decades the Adirondack Park was little more than the area "inside the Blue Line," as locals call the boundary drawn by state legislators in 1892 (literally using a blue pencil in committee). Yet the Blue Line enabled policymakers to act collectively with respect to that region. In particular, it allowed for the gradual expansion of the forest preserve within the park and, thereby, an incremental growth in the forest acreage protected by the state constitution's Forever Wild clause.

The conceptualization of ecoregional governance raises important issues regarding the role of science vis-à-vis politics. Some theorists tend to view the governance of an ecoregion primarily in scientific and technical terms. The terminology generally used—ecosystem management—suggests an approach that is mainly technical in its orientation. I use the term *governance* in part to emphasize the trade-offs required among competing values, trade-offs that cannot be made on purely technical grounds. In the absence of value conflict, the main questions are technical in nature; the presence of value conflict takes us squarely into the realm of politics. The primary role of science is to make sure the political discussion is as well-informed as possible. Defining the relevant trade-offs requires both the generalizations offered by science and the time-and-place information associated with systematic knowledge of a specific region. This means, however, that the direction and scope of scientific and technical inquiries related to specific places or regions must to some extent be guided by the contours of political discussion, not simply by the theoretical imperatives of pure science.

Because value trade-offs are inherent in the governance of ecoregions, multiple agency should continue to be central to their governance. Multiple agency is certainly the most likely institutional scenario for regional governance, given existing governance patterns at federal, state, and local levels. A typical ecoregion is likely to include the following agency relationships:

- nested local governments acting as agents for local community values;

- a variety of federal and state agencies acting as landholders, representing the values associated with state and national forests, state and national parks, and other federal and state lands;

- private, commercial landholders, accountable to corporate managers and shareholders;

- not-for-profit land and easement holders; and

- various state and federal regulatory agencies charged with representing values of interest both to local residents and to nonresidents—water quality, air quality, landscape preservation, wildlife conservation, wilderness values, recreation, and broad-based ecosystem services.

Regional governance therefore ought not to be conceptualized in single-agency terms, nor should regionalism be viewed as requiring the consolidation of local governments or agencies or the creation of a dominant regional authority. Regional governance is more fruitfully viewed as a process based on collaboration, not consolidation, where collaboration is sought among numerous local, regional, state, and federal agencies, each representing different but related values.[32]

Although the experience of the Adirondack Park is highly relevant to the governance of ecoregions, its relevance has perhaps been obscured by the nomenclature, "park." In ordinary language, the Adirondack Park is hardly a park at all, or else it is a park built on a very different model. Unlike any of the national parks in the lower 48 states, the Adirondack Park encompasses what may be fairly characterized as an ecoregion. Its boundaries conform to the geologic dome that gives rise to its distinctive ecology (Jenkins 2004). By contrast, the Everglades and Yellowstone, for example, contain within their boundaries only a fraction of the land area required to sustain their distinctive ecosystems. The biodiversity found within the 2.2-million-acre Yellowstone National Park is sustained by an ecoregion "variously defined as 14–19 million acres in size" (Noss and Cooperrider 1994, 135). At 6 million acres, the Adirondack Park is sufficiently large to afford a high level of protection to its diverse biotic communities.

Of course, when "park" boundaries are extended to include the entire ecoregion, the nature of park governance is dramatically altered. In governance terms, the Adirondack Park more closely resembles a place such as the Columbia River National Scenic Area, which Cortner and Moote (1999, 121) describe as "not a national park, national forest, or wilderness area" but instead a 295,000-acre area "managed by a partnership among the USDA Forest Service, a bi-state regional planning agency (The Columbia River Gorge Commission), the states of Washington and Oregon, and the area's six counties." Similarly, the Adirondack Park is governed jointly by the Adirondack Park Agency (a regional planning and zoning agency), the Department of Environmental Conservation (which manages the forest preserve), 12 counties and 92 towns, and the state of New York. If we think of Yellowstone as the greater Yellowstone ecoregion rather than the national park, its governance becomes similar to that of the Adirondack Park, except that it is even more complex: some 28 state and federal agencies and committees share in its governance (Noss and Cooperrider 1994). What is missing from the Yellowstone region is regional institutions defined so as to enhance coordination and collaboration, permitting regional decisionmaking to occur. Like the Adirondack Park, the governance of ecoregions will typically entail multiorganizational arrangements that operate on a collaborative basis.

Polycentricity and Regional Governance

Traditionally, the theory of public administration was built on a single-agency model with subagents organized hierarchically and held accountable through a chain of command (see V. Ostrom 1989). Multiple agency obviously requires a different model. Federalism offers a special model of multiple agency, as does the separation of powers. For a more general model of multiple agency relationships, I turn to the concept of polycentricity. Initially formulated by Michael Polanyi (1951) and Vincent Ostrom and colleagues (V. Ostrom et al. 1961), polycentric theory has been applied to public administration in general (V. Ostrom 1989) and developed most fully in relation to the governance of metropolitan areas (Oakerson and Parks 1988; V. Ostrom 1991; Oakerson 1999, 2004) and the provision of infrastructure in developing countries (Ostrom et al. 1993). Its application to metropolitan areas, as multijurisdictional regions, is suggestive for the governance of ecoregions.

Polycentric governance is characterized by semiautonomous decisionmakers who interact within a common framework of rules. Two institutional conditions must be present: (1) there must be multiple independent centers of authority, and (2) their independence must not be absolute. Rather, all authority must be subject to limits, and those limits must be inherent in the authority of others. No single decisionmaker is dominant. Although each decisionmaker has substantial independence of others, their independence is limited and qualified, such that none are fully autonomous. In a democratic context the allocation of authority should include authority to be exercised by citizens—including the anyone rule.

Polycentric arrangements tend to exhibit a number of characteristics desirable in a system of regional governance. Multiple agency permits a diversity of values to be represented. Numerous sources of initiative are available, encouraging public entrepreneurship and innovation, but successful initiatives must satisfy a range of values represented by multiple agents. Ample scope exists for collaboration in problem solving that affects multiple values; at the same time, conflict among values tends to be open and public rather than hidden in the recesses of bureaucracy. Some values can be privileged as a matter of law and claimed as rights by affected citizens, in court if necessary. Others can be negotiated and compromised in order to strike a balance among competing values. In particular, regionalism can bring the values associated with both community and environment onto the table simultaneously, requiring that each take appropriate account of the other. This requires that the values of local community be represented at a regional level through multiple agents reflecting nested communities.

Importantly, polycentricity also tends to create "civic space" within which civic organizations are formed around the protection and promotion of important values. This is especially true when individual citizens are authorized to lay claim to public values in which they share an interest. Much of the initiative and discussion in a polycentric system is the work of these groups. They should be expected to make up an important part of the governance structure of an ecoregion. Collaboration among public agents (in Dewey's sense) should be conceptualized as essentially civic in character, occurring in the realm of civil society and therefore based on willing consent and inclusive of citizen agents alongside governmental agents.

The design of a regional governance arrangement requires finding a balance between legal constraint and political or administrative flexibility. Decisionmakers must be constrained to take multiple values into account; at the same time, there must be sufficient flexibility to allow for settlement of the issues that arise. Agents must not be so closely tied to the particular values they represent that they cannot negotiate with others; neither can they be permitted to give away the store. It is especially important that regional administrators for federal and state agencies have sufficient discretion to deliberate and negotiate in good faith with other agents in the region.

Regions need to have recourse to a variety of decisionmaking facilities. Included are facilities for joint deliberation. Fred Van Dyke (2003, *296*) argues that "ecosystem management requires the creation of permanent committees, boards, or working groups in which all agencies with jurisdiction or interest in the ecosystem are represented." Decisions often must be formalized in interagency agreements, state statutes, or federal legislation. Deliberation among agents occurs against the backdrop of potential legal recourse if legal limits are exceeded. This implies the availability of judicial remedies and the standing to invoke judicial proceedings. Finally, the common framework of rules within which multiple agents interact must be subject to revision in view of changing circumstances, usually the work of legislatures, state or federal.

Although polycentricity is an institutional arrangement often filled with tension and conflict, it also exhibits entrepreneurship and collaboration. The potential for tension and conflict is the price paid for arrangements that are responsive to multiple values and seek collaboration rather than dominance.

Summary and Conclusion: Governance Principles

To sum up, I sketch below a provisional set of propositions and principles for practicing the politics of place:

1. The protection of the values inherent in both community and environment depends on a multiplicity of public agency relationships (multiple agency).
2. To protect community, multiple agency should include local governments whose boundaries define self-identified communities.
3. Distinct environmental values require separate agency representation. Multiple agency should therefore also include administrative agencies defined by more inclusive jurisdictions—state and federal. Trees may indeed need their own agents.
4. Multiple agency should include citizen agency that allows any citizen to represent specific values of community and environment and authorizes them to hold administrative agents accountable to those values as trustees. The empowerment of citizens can be expected to generate a robust civil society composed of numerous nongovernmental or civic organizations focused on one or another value of interest to various publics.
5. Multiple agency relationships may work best when focused on a specific place of sufficient scale to embrace most of the interdependencies among relevant natural resources—an ecoregion. Regionalism offers the additional advantage of linking rural and environmental policy, creating a well-defined arena in which both sets of concerns can be simultaneously addressed.
6. Ecoregions require a polycentric approach to governance, an approach in which semiautonomous agents interact within a framework of rules, allowing for both contestation and collaboration among those agents.

The frontier of rural and environmental policy is likely to include continued reliance on multiple agency relationships at all levels of government. This implies that governance will necessarily consist both of contestation and collaboration, a process in which citizens as monitors of public agency are important participants. Federalism and the legal architecture of state-local relations provide the institutional ingredients needed to experiment with environmentally based regionalism, using multiple agency relationships to pursue environmental preservation and community preservation as joint projects. Just as locals need to recognize the far-reaching environmental consequences of local action, so do nonlocals need to be sensitive to place-based community concerns. A locality serves both residents and nonresidents, and residents' strong sense of community, *when tied to a sense of environmental stewardship,* may be the best protection a local environment can have. Well-constituted ecoregions can possibly provide the politics of place with the regional decisionmaking arena it needs, one that can be used to work out the complex and discriminating trade-offs that the values of community and environment require.

References

Anderson, T.L., and P.J. Hill. 1997. *Environmental Federalism.* Lanham, MD: Rowman & Littlefield Publishers.

Baumol, W.J., and W.E. Oates. 1988. *The Theory of Environmental Policy,* 2nd edition. New York: Cambridge University Press.

Clarke, J.N., and D. McCool. 1985. *Staking Out the Terrain: Power Differentials among Natural Resource Management Agencies.* Albany: State University of New York Press.

Coleman, J.S. 1988. Social Capital in the Creation of Human Capital. *American Journal of Sociology* 94: S95–S120.

Cortner, H.J., and M.A. Moote. 1999. *The Politics of Ecosystem Management.* Washington, DC: Island Press.

Dahl, R.A. 1990. *After the Revolution? Authority in a Good Society*, revised edition. New Haven and London: Yale University Press.

Dewey, J. 1927. *The Public and Its Problems.* Denver: Alan Swallow.

Downs, A. 1967. *Inside Bureaucracy.* Boston: Little, Brown & Co.

Gaddie, R.K., and J.L. Regens. 2000. *Regulating Wetlands Protection: Environmental Federalism and the States.* Albany: State University of New York Press.

Grodzins, M. 1966. *The American System: A New View of Government in the United States.* Chicago: Rand McNally & Co.

Heikkila, T., and A.J. Gerlak. 2005. The Formation of Large-scale Collaborative Resource Management Institutions: Clarifying the Roles of Stakeholders, Science, and Institutions. *Policy Studies Journal* 33(4): 583–612.

Jenkins, J., with A. Keal. 2004. *The Adirondack Atlas: A Geographic Portrait of the Adirondack Park.* Syracuse and Blue Mountain Lake: Syracuse University Press and Adirondack Museum.

John, D. 1994. *Civic Environmentalism: Alternatives to Regulation in States and Communities.* Washington, DC: CQ Press.

Koontz, T.M. 2002. *Federalism in the Forest: National versus State Natural Resource Policy.* Washington, DC: Georgetown University Press.

Lowry, W.R. 2006. A Return to Traditional Priorities in Natural Resource Policies. In *Environmental Policy: New Directions for the Twenty-First Century*, 6th edition, edited by N.J. Vig and M.E. Kraft. Washington, DC: CQ Press, 311–32.

Madison, J. 1788. *The Federalist* No. 46 and *The Federalist* No. 51. In *The Federalist,* edited by A. Hamilton, J. Madison, and J. Jay. New York: The Modern Library, 304–12, 335–41.

McMartin, B. 2002. *Perspectives on the Adirondacks: A Thirty-Year Struggle by People Protecting Their Treasure.* Syracuse: Syracuse University Press.

Nash, R.F. 2001. *Wilderness and the American Mind*, 4th edition. New Haven and London: Yale University Press, *Nota Bene.*

Noss, R.F., and A.Y. Cooperrider. 1994. *Saving Nature's Legacy: Protecting and Restoring Biodiversity.* Washington, DC: Island Press.

Oakerson, R.J. 1995. Structures and Patterns of Rural Governance. In *The Changing American Countryside: Rural People and Places*, edited by E.N. Castle. Lawrence: University Press of Kansas.

———. 1999. *Governing Local Public Economies: Creating the Civic Metropolis.* Oakland: ICS Press.

———. 2004. The Study of Metropolitan Governance. In *Metropolitan Governance: Conflict, Competition, and Cooperation*, edited by R.C. Feiock. Washington, DC: Georgetown University Press, 17–45.

Oakerson, R.J., and Roger B. Parks. 1988. Citizen Voice and Public Entrepreneurship: The Organizational Dynamic of a Complex Metropolitan County. *Publius: The Journal of Federalism* 18(4) (Fall): 91–112.

Oliver, J.E. 2001. *Democracy in Suburbia.* Princeton and Oxford: Princeton University Press.

Olson, M. 1965. *The Logic of Collective Action: Public Goods and the Theory of Groups.* Cambridge, MA: Harvard University Press.

Ostrom, E. 1990. *Governing the Commons: The Evolution of Institutions for Collective Action.* Cambridge: Cambridge University Press.

Ostrom, E., L. Schroeder, and S. Wynne. 1993. *Institutional Incentives and Sustainable Development: Infrastructure Policies in Perspective.* Boulder, CO: Westview Press.

Ostrom, V. 1987. *The Political Theory of a Compound Republic: Designing the American Experiment*, 2nd edition. Lincoln and London: University of Nebraska Press.

———. 1989. *The Intellectual Crisis in American Public Administration*, 2nd edition. Tuscaloosa and London: University of Alabama Press.

———. 1991. *The Meaning of American Federalism: Constituting a Self-Governing Society.* San Francisco: ICS Press.

Ostrom, V., C.M. Tiebout, and R. Warren. 1961. The Organization of Government in Metropolitan Areas: A Theoretical Inquiry. *American Political Science Review* 55 (December): 831–42.
Reprinted in V. Ostrom (1991).

Peterson, P. 1981. *City Limits.* Chicago: University of Chicago Press.

Polanyi, M. 1951. *The Logic of Liberty: Reflections and Rejoinders.* Chicago: University of Chicago
Press.

Putnam, R.D. 2000. *Bowling Alone: The Collapse and Revival of American Community.* New York:
Simon & Schuster, Touchstone.

Rabe, B.G. 2006. Power to the States: The Promise and Pitfalls of Decentralization. In *Environmental Policy: New Directions for the Twenty-First Century,* 6th edition, edited by N.J. Vig and
M.E. Kraft. Washington, DC: CQ Press, 34–56.

Rosenbaum, W.A. 2006. Improving Environmental Regulation at the EPA: The Challenge in Balancing Politics, Policy, and Science. In *Environmental Policy: New Directions for the Twenty-First
Century,* 6th edition, edited by N.J. Vig and M.E. Kraft. Washington, DC: CQ Press, 169–92.

Sax, J.L. 1970. *Defending the Environment: A Handbook for Citizen Action.* New York: Vintage Books.

Scheberle, D. 2004. Devolution. In *Environmental Governance Reconsidered: Challenges, Choices, and
Opportunities,* edited by R.F. Durant, D.J. Fiorino, and R. O'Leary. Cambridge, MA, and London: MIT Press, 361–92.

Stone, C.D. 1974. *Should Trees Have Standing? Toward Legal Rights for Natural Objects.* Los Altos,
CA: William Kaufmann.

Terrie, P.G. 1997. *Contested Terrain: A New History of Nature and People in the Adirondacks.* Blue
Mountain Lake and Syracuse: The Adirondack Museum and Syracuse University Press.

United States v. Lopez. 1995. 514 U.S. 549.

Van Dyke, F. 2003. *Conservation Biology: Foundations, Concepts, Applications.* Boston: McGraw-Hill.

Warren, R.O. 1966. *Government in Metropolitan Regions: A Reappraisal of Fractionated Political Organization.* Davis: Institute of Governmental Affairs, University of California–Davis.

Whaley, R., R. Curran, and S. Erman. 2003. A Research Agenda for the Adirondacks. *Adirondack
Journal of Environmental Studies* 11(2): 21–24.

Whyte, W.H. (1968). *The Last Landscape.* Philadelphia: University of Pennsylvania Press.

Wilson, J.Q. 1989. *Bureaucracy: What Government Agencies Do and Why They Do It.* New York: Basic
Books.

Notes

1. This was one of the first lessons many of my colleagues and I learned from our experience with the National Rural Studies Committee, which, under the leadership of Emery Castle, brought an interdisciplinary, multiregional perspective to bear on the study of rural America
over the span of a decade beginning in 1987.

2. The same can in a sense be said of urban and environmental problems, but the difference
is that rural areas contain much more by way of environmental resources—land, forests, lakes,
wildlife—for which rural people often effectively have stewardship. This makes for a closer tie
(or a different sort of tie) between *rural* and environmental problems than between *urban* and
environmental problems.

3. Note, however, that the contest is between values, not simply between people. This means
that the conflict often divides individual minds as well as groups. Because all of us must live *some-
place,* a principled and inclusive approach to the politics of place requires all of us to consider a
range of trade-offs, some of which make for hard choices.

4. Article XIV, New York State Constitution.

5. Environmental policy is obviously much broader than rural policy; the concern here is
with their intersection.

6. Barry G. Rabe (2006, *35–36*) summarizes the scope of state responsibility as follows:
"States . . . collectively issue more than 90 percent of all environmental permits, complete more
than 75 percent of all environmental enforcement actions, and rely on the federal government

for less than 25 percent of their total funding on environmental and natural resource concerns. Many areas of environmental policy are clearly dominated by states, including most aspects of waste management, groundwater protection, land use management, transportation, and electricity regulation. Even in policy areas that bear a firm federal imprint, such as air pollution control and pesticides regulation, states have considerable opportunity to oversee implementation and move beyond federal standards if they so choose."

7. My focus here on trade-offs does not imply that there is no complementarity among the values at stake or that policies cannot be designed to reduce the severity of trade-offs.

8. Terrie (1997, *116*) reports that of 28 trustees in 1912, 18 lived in New York City but only one inside the park.

9. This is a personal observation based on closely following the governance of the Adirondack Park over the past five years in conjunction with a semester-long undergraduate program called "Wilderness and Democracy," conducted by Houghton College at its campus on Star Lake, located within the park's boundaries.

10. In the language of economics, Dewey's "indirect effects" are externalities.

11. Clarke and McCool (1985) aptly refer to the sharing of related responsibilities for diverse natural resource values in the federal government as "staking out the terrain" in a book by the same title.

12. Anthony Downs (1967, *223–28*) remains instructive on this point. See his discussion concerning goal consensus in administrative organizations.

13. The best source on this point is James Q. Wilson (1989); see in particular pages 157–58.

14. Also Wilson (1989, *63–64*).

15. I am indebted to conversations with Ross Whaley for these insights.

16. I do not mean to exclude so-called private governments—residential community associations or subdivision associations formed by developers and governed by local residents. These are clearly corporate agencies created for the express purpose of protecting local community values, and they often do so very effectively. Their effectiveness is tied to the fact that membership is not optional (being required by deed covenant), any more than paying municipal taxes is optional if one owns property in a municipality.

17. William H. Whyte's classic, *The Last Landscape* (1968), explains how these public powers can be used in concert to protect environmental values.

18. Within metropolitan areas, small, well-defined municipalities, such as those found in most suburbs, exhibit greater civic engagement than large municipalities, such as central cities, which of necessity embrace a multitude of identifiable neighborhood communities. See Oliver (2001).

19. Economists are more inclined to use the language of reciprocal and nonreciprocal externalities. Persons who occupy what are here called symmetrical positions generate reciprocal externalities, whereas those in asymmetrical positions experience nonreciprocal externalities.

20. Of course, one should also posit some limit to the number of nested jurisdictions based on transaction costs. I discuss this issue more fully in Oakerson (1999, 2004).

21. The analogy is borrowed from Robert A. Dahl (1990).

22. This is a topic I have explored more carefully in the context of metropolitan areas. See Oakerson (1999).

23. Although not necessarily at a constitutional level, Rabe (2006, *37*) notes the widespread use of citizen referenda among the states in the enactment of environmental legislation, which he characterizes as having grown in recent years "at an exponential rate."

24. Collaborative governance is the subject of a growing literature in the environmental field. See in particular Heikkila and Gerlak (2005).

25. If each of the distinct values associated with environment and community is viewed as a moral imperative not subject to trade-off, coherent policymaking becomes impossible. It is not multiple agency relationships that threaten coherence but the effort to maximize *competing* values without recognizing the need for trade-offs. See the discussion by Vincent Ostrom (1991, *114–16*).

26. The crucial case is *United States v. Lopez* (1995), in which the U.S. Supreme Court declared unconstitutional a federal law that criminalized the possession of firearms within 1,000 feet of a school, holding that Congress had exceeded the scope of its enumerated power to regulate interstate commerce.

27. See also Rabe's (2006) discussion of difficulties with the Clinton administration's National Environmental Performance Partnership System.

28. There is nothing new about this observation. Morton Grodzins (1966), a pioneering student of intergovernmental relations, wrote extensively about such patterns of shared responsibility.

29. Although Rabe (2006) sees greater scope for functional sorting, he acknowledges the appropriateness of shared responsibility in many areas of environmental policy.

30. The devolution of environmental responsibility to the states implies the acceptability of different states making different trade-offs, arriving at different outcomes.

31. Elinor Ostrom (1990) identifies clearly defined boundaries as an important principle to follow in crafting institutions for the governance of specific common-pool resources. The same principle may perhaps be applicable to the governance of more complex multiresource ecoregions.

32. Heikkila and Gerlak (2005) describe and compare four cases of regional collaboration, each of which embraces multiple agencies addressing complex resources with multiple values at stake: the Columbia River Basin, the Chesapeake Bay program, the San Francisco Bay–Delta program, and the Comprehensive Everglades Restoration plan. All are characterized by some mixture of contestation, conflict resolution, and collaboration.

CHAPTER 12

Frontiers in Resource and Rural Economics

A Methodological Perspective

Emery N. Castle

*A*S DISCUSSED IN THE PREFACE, two interdependencies underlie research
frontiers in resource and rural economics. One pertains to differing expectations for resources and environmental systems. Farmers, foresters, and commercial fisher people have one view of natural resources; those who improve the quality
of their lives with natural resource amenities have another. Yet a common natural
environment and a single social and economic system must serve both urban and
rural people.

This chapter begins with a discussion of methodology, focusing first on change
in the structure of economics, and then on economics as a separate, inexact, and
incomplete social science. This is followed by a discussion of how a recent development in economics—new growth theory—has affected, and has been affected
by, resource and rural economics. The theory of intermediate decisionmaking and
institutions is developed and then applied to a particular local place. The application demonstrates that state and local government decisions benefited a local place
over a 45-year timespan without adverse effect on micro or macro interests. It is
concluded that frontier research in resource and rural economics will result in the
further integration of the two fields.

The Methodology of Resource and Rural Economics

The perspectives of two philosophers of science are employed here. One is that of
Thomas Kuhn (1962), as set forth in his seminal work on scientific revolutions. The
other belongs to Daniel Hausman (1992), who has provided a fundamental critique
of neoclassical economic theory. Kuhn's perspective directs attention to linkages
between resource and rural economic literature and revolutionary developments in

the parent discipline of economics. Hausman identifies the inexact and incomplete nature of economic theory and explains why economics is regarded as a separate science. These issues are of fundamental importance here. Will the basic structure of prevailing economic theory provide for investigation of frontier resource and rural economic issues? Conversely, will resource and rural economics make the best use of that which economics and other basic disciplines offer? These questions are now addressed.

Scientific Revolutions

In *The Structure of Scientific Revolutions,* Thomas Kuhn (1962) classifies scientific activity as either normal or revolutionary. According to Kuhn, normal science results from a revolutionary discovery sufficiently interesting to attract other scientists to its elaboration. The elaboration of normal science consists of (1) the development of methods of study and instrumentation necessary to exploit the discovery; (2) theoretical work called "puzzle solving"; and (3) empirical observations made interesting by the discovery. A discovery typically requires new instruments and methodologies for its elaboration. There will be "puzzles" to be solved inherent in the premises underlying the discovery. For example, both A and B may be implied by the discovery, but the relation of A to B may not be explicit. Normal science is not motivated to test, disprove, or overthrow the discovery upon which it is based. Rather, it tends to become defensive of the discovery itself.

How, then, does a "revolution" occur? Anomalies play an important role. Anomalies arise if prevailing science cannot rationalize or explain an existing condition or event. An accumulation of anomalies may cause a scientific crisis, but a revolution will not happen until a conceptual framework is advanced that rationalizes accumulated anomalies and is sufficiently interesting to attract other scientists to its elaboration. A revolutionary discovery permits comprehension of much that was not previously understood—a new way of looking at old problems. Scientific revolutions may reorient an entire discipline, create a new discipline, or establish a field within a discipline.

Kuhn used examples from physics and chemistry to illuminate his view of scientific revolutions, but his concept applies well to economics. Adam Smith (1776) and John Maynard Keynes (1936) were revolutionary economists. Economic phenomena came to be viewed differently than they were prior to the existence of their respective theories about the wealth of nations and persistent unemployment.

How are fields within a discipline, such as resource and rural economics, affected by scientific revolutions (say) in economics? Kuhn does not discuss explicitly the linkage between applied and revolutionary science. Nevertheless a relationship exists and needs to be made explicit. *Normal science proceeds from within the framework of a discovery; in contrast, problems in applied science arise in society.* Applied science contributes to revolutionary science by the discovery, description, and classification of anomalies. Scientists at the forefront of their disciplines often welcome opportunities to consider applied science anomalies because such anomalies may not be uncovered in normal science. Where do the frontiers in resource and rural economics lie? Are they well within the boundaries of normal economics at any given time? Or do they give rise to anomalies that establish a need for revolutionary economics that may well modify the boundaries of the parent discipline?

Fundamental early efforts that helped establish a theoretical base for resource and environmental economics can be traced to Arthur Pigou (1920) and Harold Hotelling (1931). The rapid development of welfare economics during and after World War II provided a theoretical framework for benefit–cost analysis. In 1952 S.V. Ciriacy-Wantrup's seminal *Resource Conservation: Economics and Policies* provided the rationale for resource economics as a field within economics. Two innovative concepts advanced by Wantrup continue to have application—contingent valuation and the safe minimum standard. The former makes use of survey information to estimate the market value of nonmarket goods; the safe minimum standard provides an economic evaluation of reversible and irreversible resource depletion.

Resources for the Future (RFF), founded in 1952, contributed greatly to the standing of resource and environmental economics as a distinct field of study. RFF was founded, and supported for many years, by prestigious individuals and organizations and would have attracted attention for that reason alone. But it did more than that: it encouraged outstanding scholars, including economists, to direct their attention to resource economics and policies. By the first Earth Day in 1970, a substantial literature in resource and environmental economics and policy existed. (See literature reviews by Fisher and Peterson 1976, Castle et al. 1981, and Castle 1999). Thereafter, public support for the field developed rapidly and greatly.

From the outset, resource economists drew upon outstanding economists for assistance with difficult applied problems. A number of Nobel Laureate economists have participated in RFF efforts. The boundaries of the field have often been expanded by viewing familiar problems with new techniques, and from different perspectives. In Chapter 2 (this volume), Bromley raises cogent questions about the current orientation of resource and environmental economics. In his view, the correct question appears to be whether the right revolutionary economists are involved in identifying new frontiers, rather than whether revolutionary economists are contributing. And economics is not the only place to look for an answer to this question.

In *Knowledge and the Wealth of Nations: A Story of Economic Discovery*, David Warsh (2006) provides an account of how a new way of looking at an old problem (the "new growth theory") came about. The new growth theory was developed during the 1980s and early in the 1990s, with the principal actors being members of elite economics departments in prestigious universities. The potential inherent in the name, "new growth theory," was of interest to rural economists. Persistent per capita income differences of trading partners between and within countries constituted an anomaly that traditional neoclassical economic theory had been unable to rationalize. The paradox had been extensively documented by such economists as Kaldor (1985) and Myrdal (1957) and by rural economists. Even so, there were few direct links between rural economists and those working to create the new growth theory. The academic journals and other printed material gave rural economists evidence that potentially revolutionary developments were underway.

Paul Romer (1990), Paul Krugman (1991), and W. Brian Arthur (1997) are generally regarded as new growth theory pioneers. Their published work did not begin to appear until late in the decade of the 1980s. Romer's *Journal of Political Economy* article "Endogenous Technological Change" appeared in October 1990. Krugman's principal output was in the late 1980s and early 1990s. Brian Arthur's publications have dates during the 1985–1995 decade.

Rural economists drew upon and advanced the new growth theory in a variety of ways. Maureen Kilkenny extended Krugman's work with articles in the *Journal of Regional Science* (1998a) and *Growth and Change* (1998b). In 1996 Bruce Weber and I arranged a three-day workshop for rural economists on the new growth theory and the "new institutional economics." Paul Krugman served as one of the workshop leaders. Forty-seven rural economists from across the United States participated. In a survey taken a year later, a strong majority reported that the workshop had had a positive impact on their programs. James Hite's 1997 article in the *Review of Agricultural Economics* entitled "The Thünen Model and the New Economic Geography as a Paradigm for Rural Development Policy" embellished central place theory with insights provided by the new growth theory.

The experience described above provides evidence that both resource and rural economics have ties to, and benefit from, revolutionary economists and economics. If the frontiers of resource and rural economics are to be advanced, resource and rural economists need to continue to invest in maintaining and strengthening such linkages. The genuine interest in the anomalies and paradoxes arising in resource and rural economics displayed by seminal thinkers Tjalling Koopmans, Theodore Schultz, and Kenneth Arrow is indeed impressive.

Economic Theory: An Inexact, Incomplete, and Separate Science

Both resource and rural economists have a vested interest in knowing about the methodological characteristics of the theory they employ. Classical and neoclassical economic thought has provided the dominant theoretical base for economic research in the western world for more than two centuries. It is an adaptable and ever-changing paradigm that continues to be explored. In 1776, Adam Smith coined the phrase "the invisible hand," perhaps the most famous in all economic literature. An abbreviated context follows:

> ... *every* individual necessarily labours to render the annual revenue of society as great as he can. He *generally* neither intends to promote the public interest, nor knows how much he is promoting it ... he intends his own gain and ... is led by **an invisible hand** to promote an end that was not part of his intention ... By pursuing his own interest he *frequently* promotes that of society more effectually than when he really intends to promote it. (*423*, italics and bold added)

The first word in the above quotation, "every," is an inclusive term. It is followed and qualified by the words "generally" and "frequently." From 1776 onward, classical and neoclassical economists have sought general application, but then, implicitly or explicitly, they have qualified, excepted, and modified. Resource and rural economics are similarly affected. Generality is important, yet preciseness in particular circumstances is desirable as well.

The philosopher Daniel Hausman (1992) characterizes economics as an inexact and separate science. To appreciate why he does so, consider the following possible premise in an economic model of a market: "The acquisition of wealth is the primary motivation of all producers." Imagine, however, that in fact, all producers are motivated to acquire wealth, but it is not the primary motivation of some. All producers are accounted for by the premise, but some are not described accurately. The model provides an inexact account of its economic domain.

Although not discussed by Hausman, premises may also fail to provide a complete accounting of all items within an economic domain. Consider the following: "All goods are homogeneous." If, in fact, 10 percent of the commodities in a market are heterogeneous, the premise provides an incomplete accounting even though 90 percent of the items in a class are described accurately. Deductions from models with *inexact* premises may provide for all items in a class, but not necessarily with accuracy. Deductions from models with *incomplete* premises may fail to account for all items in a class, even though those that are accounted for are described with precision.

Economic theory, then, may be inexact or incomplete depending on the assumptions employed. Whether these theory characteristics are important at the frontiers of resource and rural economics is an empirical question, a subject addressed below.

Hausman (1992) labels economics a separate science because economists have maintained their separateness even when evidence from other disciplines conflicts with economic assumptions about human behavior. The appeal of economics as a separate science is that it provides a consistent frame of reference for a wide range of economic phenomena. Because it is separate, economics has the capacity to account for, and relate, components of its entire domain. This creates information that cannot be obtained in any other way and provides justification for economics as a distinctive body of thought.

Oakerson (political science, Chapter 11, this volume) and Brown (demography and sociology, Chapter 14, this volume) discuss economic phenomena from perspectives not likely to be employed by economists. Differing perspectives are of potential value in science both across and within disciplines. Differing perspectives may be reinforcing (e.g., Oakerson's discussion of place, and the definition of place, below, in this chapter), each adding strength to the conclusions of the other. The absence of agreement, or inconsistencies, may also be valuable, calling as it does for explanations of discrepancies (anomalies). Both resource economics and rural economics have benefited from knowledge provided by surrounding disciplines. All disciplinary knowledge is partial; it should not be surprising that more than one discipline may contribute to understanding of particular phenomena. As noted in Chapter 1, resource and rural economics have developed differently. Resource economics arguably has become more separate than it was early in its history. Much rural economics work is considered part of the multidisciplinary field of rural studies (Castle 1995). The five frontier areas identified in Chapter 1 for resource and rural economics all call for contributions from disciplines in addition to economics.

Application of Theoretical Models

We now turn to examples of how resource and rural economic frontiers are affected by the methodological issues discussed above. The following example pertains to how the new growth theory contributes a different way for resource and rural economists to view familiar problems. The second example demonstrates the incompleteness of economic theory by its neglect of intermediate decisionmaking.

Places and People in the Countryside: Does the New Growth Theory Make a Difference?

Central place theory, admittedly abstract and unrealistic, has long been used to account for distance and space in economic analysis (Thünen 1951). It postulates a "central place," the fountainhead of economic activity, surrounded by a "featureless plane." This highly simplified model provides insight for the location of economic activity, land use, and land values. Yet inexact and incomplete premises have resulted in the neglect of certain realities. Distance and space are not the only attributes of land that matter (Hite 1997). Consider first the way land is used near cities and densely populated places. If proximity to the central city is the sole significant attribute of land, minimizing the cost of distance becomes the only economic objective that matters. "Skip distances" and urban "sprawl" will be undesirable. However, if the plane surrounding populous places is not featureless but diverse, skip distances and sprawl may be seen in a different light. Natural amenities and hazards, assumed away by the featureless plane, are of economic significance (Wu 2001).

Irwin, Randall, and Chen (Chapter 6, this volume) and Wu and Mishra (Chapter 7, this volume) attribute economic importance to natural amenities. Natural amenities, of course, may be enhanced or diminished by humans. And human-created as well as natural amenities are significant economically. Schools, cultural attractions, and recreational facilities provide examples. However, natural resource economics, standing alone, does not give explicit attention to human-enhanced amenities. The possible positive interaction of natural and social amenities in location decisions qualify as frontier subjects in both resource and rural economics (see Bruegmann 2005 for a historical view of the spatial expansion of cities).

As noted earlier, unequal but enduring economic prosperity among areas within an economy, as well as among economies that trade, is a paradox that has puzzled economists for decades. Traditional neoclassical economic theory leads to the conclusion that returns within and across economies should converge over time as a result of specialization, migration, and trade. Nevertheless, underemployment, unemployment, and low rural income have, at one time or another, been serious recurring problems in most developing countries around the globe, and underline rural-urban interdependence. As useful as it is for certain purposes, central place theory is unable to resolve this paradox.

After World War II and well into the 1980s, economic theory became increasingly preoccupied with equilibrium issues. Much equilibrium modeling was aided by specific, limiting assumptions. Two such assumptions—constant returns to scale, and homogeneous goods or commodities—are convenient premises when equilibrium systems are modeled; conversely, increasing returns and differentiated goods are not. By 1980, when the new growth theory began to emerge, it was difficult to find mention, much less discussion, in many intermediate textbooks of either monopolistic competition (differentiated goods) or increasing returns.

The paradox of enduring differences in the economic welfare of regions within and among economies provided stimulus for the new growth theory. Its rudiments began to emerge in the 1980s, with greater specificity appearing in the 1990s (Warsh 2006). The theory directed attention to incomplete premises in traditional neoclassical economic growth theory. The traditional theory considers the growth of knowledge and the development and use of technology to be exogenous variables in economic systems. The new growth theory set forth a hypothesis of how knowledge and technology arise from, and are used within, an economic system. Two venerable but recently neglected concepts in economic theory—increasing returns and monopolistic competition—were resurrected and incorporated in the new growth theory (Buchanan and Yoon; Chamberlin 1950).

Differentiated products, the essence of monopolistic competition, provide incentive for knowledge creation. Increasing returns (or decreasing costs per unit of output) arise as industry output expands and specialization increases. Improved productivity, in turn, results in rising incomes. Rising incomes and population growth increase the extent of the market and provide powerful incentive for the development and application of new knowledge. Public policies pertaining to intellectual property rights emerge as being of critical importance. Can a discovery and the resulting technology be treated as an excludable public (nonrival) good? If so, financial incentive may be provided for its discovery and use.

Serious scholars know about and make allowance for obvious inexact and incomplete premises, such as featureless planes, wealth accumulation being the primary motivation of all producers, homogeneous goods, and constant returns to scale. Yet intellectual systems like central place theory and competitive market theory combine such premises with an exogenous technology assumption. The resulting theoretical economic system moves to a deduced equilibrium end point in a linear fashion. The new growth theory would have us think differently. And if we think differently, we can imagine different explanations for observable events. We can imagine farm firms buying inputs from, and selling commodities to, very large metropolitan firms that operate in increasing return industries. Goods and services coming from other farm firms move into niche markets. And niche markets flourish if that which is traded can be differentiated by location, processing, marketing, or advertising. By taking advantage of natural and human-created amenities, many rural nonfarm enterprises cater to numerous affluent urban consumers.

Kilkenny (Chapter 5, this volume) discusses both central place and new growth theory in terms of empirical realities in the countryside. Two implications are striking.

First, excess capacity often exists in rural service industries, and as a consequence, increased population and economic activity become exceedingly attractive. It may well be logical, from a national perspective, to treat output from government investment across the nation as subject to constant returns to scale. Yet from within a locality, additional investment may yield increasing returns. By the same token, rural wages may be regarded differently depending on perspective. Lower relative rural wages may encourage migration to higher-paying urban employment, a desirable outcome from the perspective of traditional theory. The new growth theory may cause rural wages to be viewed differently. Even though higher relative rural wages may discourage migration or even attract more rural workers, their rural presence may take advantage of excess capacity in such places.

Stubborn economic phenomena also exist that cannot be rationalized by either central place or new growth theory. Consider the highly significant research of Mills, who established that the percentage of the rural U.S. nonfarm labor force has been remarkably stable for many decades. Such stability has existed in other countries as well, even though the rural percentage is higher in the United States. Why is this the case? The economies of rural places have been revolutionized as economic development has occurred. This is especially true for agriculture, where labor per unit of output has declined drastically. Economic analysts often implicitly assume that rural economic activity affected by economic reorganizations in the countryside will mainly affect the agricultural industry. This is a manifestation of the myth that rural and agricultural are synonymous. Neither theory provides a ready explanation of the Mills findings, although they are more plausible in light of the new growth theory because it better accommodates diverse rural economic activities than would be expected on a featureless plane. Furthermore, decreasing costs in the provision of rural services may at least partially offset increasing returns in urban places. Theories can be flawed, and the way they are used can be flawed as well.

The new growth theory emphasizes organic growth processes, feedback, path dependence, and trajectories. It is concerned with the relative impact of population growth and rising incomes in both rural and urban places. Krugman (1991), Hite (1997), and Kilkenny (1998a, 1998b) demonstrate how the new growth theory enriches economic geography and illustrate Kuhn's observation that scientific discoveries typically are add-ons rather than replacements.

Numerous unfinished tasks remain on the rural economics research agenda. First, an improved theoretical basis needs to be established for the empirical findings of Mills concerning rural nonfarm workers. Second, realistic empirical conditions should be reflected in rural-urban economic models. There has long been a tendency to assume that increasing returns apply mainly to urban places (see Krugman 1991, *103*). Third, increased attention needs to be paid to the support provided by nonmarket social institutions for many rural residents. Young, healthy, and well-educated rural people have migrated in large numbers for several decades to places of greater economic opportunity. Those remaining in rural places are disproportionally older, less healthy, and more economically disadvantaged. Such people typically rely heavily on a range of nonmarket social support systems. These systems occur under varying conditions of geographic space and distance as well as population density. They need to be understood in that context (see Chapter 8, this volume). Fourth, the endogenous technology assumption of the new growth theory fails to reflect the role of government in the creation, development, and application of technology (Ruttan 2001,

2006). Ruttan would not deny that imaginative, well-educated people and secure intellectual property rights provide stimuli for economic growth, but he calls attention to the importance of public and private sector relations in the creation and adoption of innovations.

Intermediate Decisionmaking

Intermediate decisionmaking is an important economic activity neglected by an incomplete economic theory. Its normative base rests on the possibility that local people can better realize their aspirations if some degree of autonomy exists. Such autonomy, however, must rest on the assumption that economic interests inherent in the economic theory of micro and macro decisionmaking are respected and preserved. Intermediate decisions occur at the intersection of geographic space, common interests, and identifiable jurisdictional unit.

The principal purpose of benefit–cost analysis is to measure the effect on net national product of prospective, macrolevel government decisions. Benefit–cost typically neglects the intermediate, or regional, costs or benefits of macrolevel public investments. The rationale for doing so is that regional gains or losses in one location will be offset by opposite effects in another. This rationale is appropriate under assumptions of a fully employed economy and constant returns to scale. Intermediate decision theory does not require modification of traditional benefit–cost procedures. Nevertheless, individual (micro) and aggregate (macro) choices may be affected if appropriate attention is given intermediate decisions. For example, Kneese (1962) advanced a regional, or basin-wide, firm concept to deal with pollution externalities. Accordingly, an economic activity resulting in an environmental externality would be justified by national benefit–cost analysis only if a region-wide polluting firm were willing to pay compensation for damages caused by the externality. The implicit assumption here is that there is only one allocation of resources that will satisfy these conditions. Nevertheless, if it is empirically possible for a locality to use its assets in more than one way to meet national efficiency conditions, a case for intermediate decisions has been established. *Intermediate decisionmaking is justified if it is not at the expense of economic efficiency of individuals or firms at the micro level, or of established interests at the macro level. The scope of intermediate decisions will be in proportion to the number of ways local decision units can use their autonomy to satisfy micro and macro conditions.* In other words, intermediate decisions are concerned with economic surpluses in the economy not accounted for by, and intermediate to, micro and macro decisions. These surpluses, arising from local comparative advantage, provide local flexibility to accommodate environmental and community interests described by Oakerson (Chapter 11, this volume).

Both state and local government actions are included in intermediate decisions. Explicit provision is made in the U.S. Constitution for state government. Local government may be established by states but is not mandatory. The following illustrations and examples pertain mainly to local government or local communities, although state and local relations are treated explicitly in some instances. Intermediate decisions arise in at least three contexts.

Category 1: Administrative efficiency. Both federal and state government may delegate duties and responsibilities to local government. One reason for doing so is to take variation in local conditions into account. It is often noted the United States has not emphasized place-based public policies. Nevertheless, it does have numerous public policies that apply regardless of location. Local administration of such policies is a way to accommodate differences in population density and geographic distance. Over a 25-year period I served on natural resource and environmental policy boards and commissions in Oregon. I cannot recall a single controversial resource or environmental public policy decision that was not illuminated by local public testimony or information. This did not necessarily reflect poorly on the competence of state or federal program personnel, but typically, local people had knowledge of unique local circumstances.

Category 2: Supply-demand imbalances for local resources or services. Competition is often viewed as a healthy condition in both the private and the public sectors of an economy. However, competition may be counterproductive in some circumstances. Consider a situation in which several local areas have relatively homogeneous inducements for the attraction of footloose industries. Assume further there are many more communities attempting to attract industry than there are industries seeking such locations. As noted, rural places often have considerable excess capacity, and declining unit costs, of service-related activities. Under such circumstances, political pressure is likely to arise to provide tax breaks or sacrifice environmental quality to attract external investments. Kunce and Shogren (Chapter 10, this volume) analyze a specific example of this general case.

Such conditions direct attention to the appropriate level of the intermediate decisionmaking unit to deal with particular problems. For example, if supply exceeds demand for local services provided by numerous local units, decisionmaking at a different level (regional, state, federal) may be needed to curtail destructive competition among local governments. Unless such circumstances are addressed, intermediate decisions may adversely affect individual or aggregate interests identified above. Where intermediate group decisions are made, as well as whether certain decisions should even be at the intermediate level, are appropriate subjects for both economic and political science study.

Category 3: Economically unique local places. This category includes those places that have an economic advantage in the provision of certain goods or services. This economic superiority provides options for a local place so long as established individual (micro) and aggregate (macro) choices are respected.

Intermediate decisionmaking is crucial to an understanding of local economies. Otherwise, there is little justification for separate fields of either rural or urban economics. Superficially, this does not appear to be a debatable topic. There surely must be reasons local people devote time, energy, and treasure to making myriad group decisions. Nevertheless, a theoretical base for intermediate decisions supported by empirical findings does not exist. A possible reason is an assumption that such decisions result only for reasons of convenience (category 1 above). State and federal agencies may find the countryside sufficiently heterogeneous or so inaccessible that geographic delegation makes pragmatic sense. If this is all that is involved, local decision units need have little autonomy. Yet, in fact, in most states' local units of government have significant autonomy to deal with a range of issues.

Intermediate choices arise, then, because of the possibility that cooperative local group action may be a more effective way of realizing individual aspirations than independent individual action. Numerous state and local groups may arise as a result. Central place theory, collective choice theory, and public finance are of obvious relevance. (Thünen 1951; Olson 1965; Tiebout 1965a, 1965b).

The theoretical model. The intermediate decisionmaking model set forth here pertains to a place, when *place* is defined as the intersection of a specified geographic space, a community of humans, and some type of jurisdictional unit (Oakerson, Chapter 11, this volume; Castle and Weber 2006). Geography pertains to how the natural characteristics of a place—topography, flora, and fauna—interact with political and sociological attributes. For example, rivers often become boundaries for places. Communities are groups of humans that share interests, goals, or values. These shared holdings may stem either from similar ethnic or cultural backgrounds, or from recently discovered commonalities, such as living in the same floodplain or other geographic space. A jurisdictional unit is a politically recognized organization authorized to make decisions that obligate individuals within a group (Clark 1984). Jurisdictional units may be imposed externally, as, for example, a local unit of government created by state government, or may arise from mutual agreement of people from within a place.

As noted, the normative base for intermediate decisions is that local people enjoy sufficient autonomy to address common concerns and seek fulfillment of aspirations (Castle 1998). Such autonomy requires the existence of an entity with responsibility for relating concerns and aspirations to means of accomplishment. A coordination role is required comparable to that assumed for the firm in production economics, or the individual or family in consumption economics.

The intermediate decision model presented next was influenced by sociologist Coleman and new growth theorists Arthur, Romer and Krugman.[1] Coleman (1990) describes social capital arrangements as consisting of an expectation of reciprocity, a means of enforcing obligations, and the existence of trust. Oakerson (Chapter 11, this volume) describes social capital as a process of creating and sustaining goodwill among community members as they accommodate the needs of environment and community. The need here is for a decision unit capable of making choices for a local group. Such units may include local units of government as well as nongovernmental organizations.[2]

The selection of an acceptable outcome, from multiple possible outcomes, is the principal responsibility of intermediate decisionmaking institutions. Following Arthur (1997), the term trajectory is used here to describe such an outcome. *Trajectory* is especially appropriate because the public assets involved typically have value in more than one time period. The selection and management of trajectories is a major responsibility of local decisionmaking units, although the model presented here can be modified if a different choice indicator is more appropriate.

Using capitalization to identify items that are suitable variables in a formal decision model, we can say that the selection of a trajectory is assumed to be affected by public goods and public assets for which the decision unit has responsibility, and by information and knowledge as well as expectations. Possible decisions are affected by boundary conditions, assumed here to include (1) the external economy, (2) natural resources and natural environment, and (3) institutions. Boundary conditions may act as constraints, but they may also be sources of greater future flexibility and opportunity than have existed historically.

The rudimentary theoretical model described above was applied to a place that permitted past trajectory decisions to be described and evaluated. Fortunately a study existed, made approximately 45 years ago, of a place that faced a major trajectory decision (Stoevener et al. 1972). The study made use of then-state-of-the-art techniques in assigning market values to outdoor recreation and water quality (pioneering resource economic techniques). The study results permitted a rigorous empirical test of whether the conditions required to justify intermediate decisionmaking could actually occur. The trajectory decision required was whether a pulp and paper mill should be permitted to locate in an estuary, and if so, how the effluent would be managed. The place was the Yaquina Bay estuary in Oregon, an economically unique (category 3) place.

The estuary touches Toledo, Oregon, at one end, and Newport, Oregon, on the ocean side. In 1960 the Georgia-Pacific Corporation wished to locate a pulp and paper mill on the estuary in Toledo. Had Georgia-Pacific given minimal treatment to the effluent and then discharged it in the estuary, the direct and indirect economic recreation benefits and other ecosystem services would have been diminished drastically and perhaps irreversibly. The Clean Water Act and the Environmental Protection Act were not in existence at that time. State and local authorities prevailed on Georgia-Pacific, at its considerable expense, to bypass the estuary and pump the effluent overland to the ocean. This did little for the water quality of the ocean near Newport. Even so, it protected the water quality of the estuary and the aquatic resources. The 1960 Yaquina Bay realities were isolated and are described below to match variables in the theoretical model set forth above.

Trajectories. There was a relatively narrow band of trajectories available to the community in the late 1960s and early 1970s. Even so, there were at least three principal possible trajectories that could have been chosen. One would have given high priority to the pulp and paper mill, perhaps at the expense of the environmental quality of the estuary. A different trajectory would have protected environmental quality, carrying the risk that the pulp and paper mill would locate elsewhere. The trajectory chosen was an attempt to protect environmental quality and accommodate the industry as well.

Public goods and assets under local public jurisdiction. The Yaquina Bay estuary provided significant public goods. The magnificent bridge that spans the space where the estuary becomes the ocean was even then a significant tourist attraction (Edmonston 1999). Precise claims to estuary use did not exist. The Sanitary Authority for Oregon was active in working with local places to protect environmental quality.

Current information and knowledge. The economy surrounding Yaquina Bay was characterized by high seasonal unemployment. The indirect benefits of the proposed pulp and paper mill consisted, in large part, from increased employment.

Expectations. It was anticipated that outdoor recreation would increase in importance, especially in the Yaquina Bay area, if the environmental quality of the estuary

204 • Emery N. Castle

could be preserved. The recreational fishery was expected to increase relative to the commercial fishery.

Boundaries conditions imposed by the external economy. In 1960 economic opportunities in Toledo and Newport were limited mainly to those associated with the natural resource base—specifically forestry, outdoor recreation, and some commercial fishing. (Boundaries conditions may reflect constraints, but they may also constitute opportunities.)

Natural resource and environmental boundaries. In 1960 there remained considerable uncut timber in the nearby costal mountain range. Prime timberland was decreasing, but there was reason to believe fiber suitable for pulp and paper would continue to be available. The water quality of the estuary could not accommodate both outdoor recreation and the effluent from the pulp and paper mill.

Institutional boundaries. Much of today's environmental legislation and related institutions did not exist in 1960. The state Sanitary Authority and its successor agency, the Oregon Environmental Quality Commission, were the principal state environmental agencies.

The study results identified six possible bargaining situations that conceivably could have arisen (Stoevener et al. 1972). The actual bargaining situation, however, permitted state and local government to impose a waste disposal method that was 5.4 times more costly than minimal treatment plus the cost of all externalities that would have been associated with minimal treatment. Had the basin-wide firm criteria been used, the trajectory actually chosen would never have been considered. Clearly, the estuary economy was unique and permitted micro and macro decisions to be accommodated in more than one way. No estimate of the economic value of the estuary location to Georgia-Pacific was published in the research study, and if Georgia-Pacific made such an estimate, it was treated as proprietary.

Input-output models of the estuary economy for 1970 and for 2000 were constructed and compared for the purpose of evaluating the trajectory chosen decades earlier. The pulp and paper mill continues to operate. Manufacturing, including pulp and paper production, constituted about 18 percent of employment in 1970 but declined to approximately 7 percent by 2000. On the other hand, services accounted for about 20 percent of employment in 1970 but increased to nearly 30 percent by 2000. A great deal of the service employment has been made possible by preservation of the estuary ecosystem. The Hatfield Marine Science Center is located there, as is the Oregon Coast Aquarium. The trajectory chosen by local and state interests in the 1960s has served this place well.

Intermediate decisionmaking enriches the content of both resource and rural economics. The tools of resource economics, as well as its subject matter, are needed to estimate the consequences of possible decisions. Rural economics is enriched because a precise definition of *place* is required consisting of the conceptual integration of geographic space, human communities, and jurisdictional units.

Economic models that evaluate micro and macro economic efficiency may appropriately neglect intermediate choices. *The converse does not hold.* If the welfare of local people can be improved, both micro and macro interests will be benefited indirectly. Intermediate decisionmaking clearly has a place at the frontiers of resource and rural economics.

Summary

An empirical investigation of intermediate decisionmaking in a place over time permits a precise view of the role of intermediate decisionmaking in economic theory. The investigation demonstrates that more than one possible intermediate decision can satisfy micro and macro economic decision criteria. When such conditions exist in a place, autonomy in the pursuit of local aspirations will not necessarily diminish individual choice or economy-wide objectives.

A variety of circumstances give rise to intermediate decisions. The empirical example was based on an economic surplus resulting from comparative advantage. A different situation arises if spatial variation makes it efficient for central units of government to delegate certain administrative responsibilities and tasks.

Decentralization of decisionmaking is not always desirable. Kunce and Shogren (Chapter 10, this volume) describe the consequences when localities compete for extraction industries by forgiving taxes. Excess capacity and declining costs in local places often cause increased population and economic activity to be highly attractive. Success in doing so may be at the expense of particular groups within the local community. It may also result in the exploitation of resources that will diminish the longer-run comparative advantage of a place. If so, evidence exists suggesting certain intermediate decisions are inappropriately located.

Finally, the selection of the choice indicator or criterion used to guide intermediate decisions is of fundamental importance. A trajectory choice criterion was used in the empirical example. Other decisions will be of a different nature, and appropriate choice indicators will be affected accordingly. Choice criteria actually used by intermediate decision units, as well as those that could possibly be used, are appropriate subjects for investigation.

Conclusion

A methodological perspective of frontiers in resource and rural economics permits the following conclusions to be drawn:

1. The history of resource and rural economics reveals that both have been receptive to discoveries and seminal contributions in the parent discipline of economics. Generally, both have behaved in accord with Kuhn's description of scientific revolutions. Both contribute to their parent discipline by the preservation and description of paradoxes and anomalies arising from application of accepted theories. Issues continually arise in resource and rural economics that were not uncovered when economic theory was developed.

2. The frontiers of resource and rural economics will be dependent on the separate science of economics. Yet the integration of complex systems affecting the natural environment and human communities is beyond the analytical capacity of any particular discipline; the involvement of multiple disciplines in the future will be essential.

3. The new growth theory considers technical change to be endogenous in economic systems and thereby addresses inexactness in traditional economic theory. Because technical change has transformed rural America, the new growth theory

is of obvious relevance to rural economics. Rising incomes, population growth, and changes in the location of economic activity affect the relative demand for both natural and human resources. This different way of looking at familiar problems holds the prospect of providing a better understanding of rural–urban interdependence—a subject of interest in both resource and rural economics.

4. Intermediate decisionmaking is of obvious relevance to both resource and rural economics, but traditional micro and macro economic theory is incomplete in this respect. Intermediate decisions arise in different contexts. One includes decisions delegated by a higher authority for reasons of convenience. Another stems from the comparative advantage of places that makes it possible to meet micro and macro economic objectives in more than one way. Others may arise from supply-demand imbalances for rural resources and services.

Consideration of fundamental problems in both resource and rural economics will require further integration of the two fields. The integration of urban and rural economies will direct attention to urban demands for ecosystem services. Neither traditional nor new growth theory provides a complete model for the study of rural and urban economic interdependence. The quest for such understanding remains at the frontiers of both resource and rural economics.

References

Arthur, W.B. 1997. *Increasing Returns and Path Dependence in the Economy.* Ann Arbor: University of Michigan Press.

Bruegmann, R. 2005. *Sprawl, A Compact History.* Chicago: University of Chicago Press.

Buchanan, J. M. and Y. J. Yoon, 1994. *The Return to Increasing Returns.* Ann Arbor: The University of Michigan Press.

Castle, E.N. (ed). 1995. *The Changing American Countryside: Rural People and Places.* Lawrence: University Press of Kansas.

Castle, E.N. 1998. A Conceptual Framework for the Study of Rural Places. *American Journal of Agricultural Economics* 80(3): 621–31.

Castle, Emery N. 1999. Natural Resource and Environmental Economics: A Retrospective View. *Review of Agricultural Economics* 21(2): 288-304.

Castle, E.N., and B.A. Weber. 2006. Policy and Place: Requirements of a Successful Place-Based Policy. Working Paper #06-01, Department of Agricultural Economics and Rural Studies Program. Corvallis: Oregon State University.

Castle, E.N., M.M. Kelso, J.B. Stevens, and H.H. Stoevener. 1981. Natural Resource Economics, 1946–75. In *A Survey of Agricultural Economics Literature,* vol. 3, edited by Lee R. Martin. Minneapolis: University of Minnesota Press, 391–500.

Chamberlin E. H. 1950. *The Theory of Monopolistic Competition: A Re-orientation of the Theory of Value,* 6th ed. Cambridge: Harvard University Press.

Ciriacy-Wantrup, S.V. 1952. *Resource Conservation: Economics and Policies.* Berkeley: University of California Press.

Clark, G.L. 1984. A Theory of Local Autonomy. *Annals of the Association of American Geographers* 74(2): 195–201.

Coleman, J. 1988. Social Capital in the Creation of Human Capital. *American Journal of Sociology* 94: S95 –S120.

———. 1990. *Foundations of Social Theory.* Cambridge, MA, and London: Belknap Press of Harvard University Press.

Edmonston, G.P., Jr. 1999. Coastal Jewels. *Oregon Stater* 84(4): 20–29.

Fisher, A.C., and F.M. Peterson. 1976. The Environment in Economics: A Survey. *Journal of Economic Literature* 14: 1–33.

Hausman, D.L. 1992. *The Inexact and Separate Science of Economics.* Cambridge: Cambridge University Press.

Hite, J.C. 1997. The Thünen Model and the New Economic Geography as a Paradigm for Rural Development Policy. *Review of Agricultural Economics* 19(2): 130–240.

Hotelling, H. 1931. The Economics of Exhaustible Resources. *Journal of Political Economy* 39: 37–75.

Kaldor, N. 1985. *Economics without Equilibrium.* New York: M.E. Sharpe.

Keynes, J.M. 1936. *The General Theory of Employment, Interest and Money.* London: Macmillan.

Kilkenny, M. 1998a. Transport Costs and Rural Development. *Journal of Regional Science* 38(2): 293–312.

———. 1998b. Transport Costs, the New Economic Geography and Rural Development. *Growth and Change* 29(3): 259-80.

Kneese, A.V. 1962. *Water Pollution: Economic Aspects and Research Needs.* Washington, DC: Resources for the Future.

Krugman, P. 1991. History versus Expectations. *Quarterly Journal of Economics* 106(2): 651-67.

Kuhn, Thomas S. 1962, 1970, 1996 editions. *The Structure of Scientific Revolutions.* Chicago and London: University of Chicago Press.

Myrdal, G. 1957. *Economic Theory and Underdeveloped Regions.* London: Duckworth.

Olson, M. 1965. *The Logic of Collective Action: Public Goods and the Theory of Groups.* Cambridge, MA: Harvard University Press.

Pigou, A.C. 1920. *The Economics of Welfare.* London: Macmillan.

Romer, P. 1990. Endogenous Technical Change. *Journal of Political Economy* 98(5): S71–102.

Ruttan V.W. 2001. *Technology, Growth, and Development: An Induced Innovation Perspective.* New York: Oxford University Press.

———. 2006. *Is War Necessary for Economic Growth?* New York: Oxford University Press.

Smith, A. 1937 (1776). *The Wealth of Nations,* with an introduction by Max Learner. New York: Random House.

Stoevener, H.H., J.B. Stevens, H.F. Horton, A. Sokoloski, L.P. Parrish, and E.N. Castle, Project Leader. 1972. Multi-Disciplinary Study of Water Quality Relationships: A Case Study of Yaquina Bay, Oregon. Corvallis: Oregon Agricultural Experiment Station (cited by the American and Western Agricultural Economics Associations for quality of research).

Thünen, J.H. von. 1951. English translation. Edited by Peter Hall, translated by Carla M. Wartenberg. Oxford: Pergamon Press.

Tiebout, C.M. 1965a. A Pure Theory of Public Expenditures. *Journal of Political Economy* 64: 416-24.

———. 1965b. Exports and Regional Economic Growth. *Journal of Political Economy* 64: 160–64.

Warsh, D. 2006. *Knowledge and the Wealth of Nations: A Story of Economic Discovery.* New York: W.W. Norton.

Wu, J.J. 2001. Environmental Amenities and the Spatial Pattern of Urban Sprawl. *American Journal of Agricultural Economics* 83(5): 691–97.

Acknowledgments

Bruce Weber brought great insight to his reading of an earlier version of this chapter. Special appreciation is due JunJie Wu for his contribution to its organization and structure. Thanks are also expressed to Paul Barkley, Joel Darmstadter, George McDowell, and Thomas Johnson.

Notes

1. James Coleman's social capital concept was employed here. Krugman's QJE article on history and expectations was useful in putting path dependence and expectations in perspective.

Writings by Brian Arthur caused me to consider the significance of multiple equilibrium and path dependence.

2. The frontiers of resource and rural economics identified in this book do not provide an explicit and separate treatment of social capital or economic institutions, perhaps because such problems are fundamental to all of economics.

It is helpful to consider social capital distinct from institutions. In one case the principal focus is on group actions and decisions. In the other, attention is directed to rules and procedures. Group action or consensus often is necessary before rules or procedures can be formulated. Coleman noted social capital typically is required before human capital formation occurs (Coleman 1988). Practical politicians know that trust must be established within groups before institutions or legislation can be created. Much democratic government activity is an attempt to build trust across groups as a basis for consensus.

Part IV

THE NEXT 25 YEARS

CHAPTER 13

Resources and Rural Communities

Looking Ahead

Kathleen Segerson

ALTHOUGH BOTH RELATE FUNDAMENTALLY to the concept of land, the fields of resource economics[1] and rural economics have developed fairly independently over the past decades. Resource economists have historically focused much of their attention on the role of pollution externalities, the design of policies to induce efficient pollution control, the measurement of the costs and benefits of changes in environmental quality, and the optimal extraction or use of renewable and nonrenewable resources.[2] In contrast, research by rural economists has focused primarily on migration and the generation of income and jobs in rural communities and the potential for economic growth in these areas (Barkley, Chapter 3, this volume).

A basic premise of this volume is that despite the independence of their historical development, resource economics and rural economics are, in fact, inextricably linked in many ways. Production activities in rural communities tend to be resource based (e.g., farming, forestry, and mining). In addition, the industrialization and development that lead to environmental externalities can often affect rural communities, as can policies designed to correct these externalities (e.g., to improve water quality or restore wetlands).[3] Rural areas also provide open space and other environmental amenities.

Given the link between resource economics and rural economics highlighted in the previous chapters in this volume, it seems natural in looking ahead to ask whether any emerging issues in the field of resource economics have implications for rural economies and suggest opportunities where more concerted integration of the two fields might prove fruitful. This chapter identifies two such issues. The first is the fundamental and bidirectional link between human systems and ecosystems, and the crucial role of ecosystem services in supporting human systems. The second is the role of sustainability as a normative goal in environmental policy design. Both issues are gaining increased visibility and attention not only in the academic literature but also in policy arenas. In addition, both suggest the need for a broadening, or possibly even a rethinking, of the standard efficiency approach to environmental and resource-based externalities that has been the focus of resource economics to date. Both also can have implications for rural communities.

In the sections that follow, we first discuss these two issues in general, drawing from the existing and emerging literature within resource economics. We then turn to a discussion of the role they might play in a future strategy aimed at preserving rural communities. We conclude with some thoughts on future research that could contribute to the evaluation and possible development of such a strategy.

Human-Ecosystem Interactions: The Importance of Ecosystem Services

There has been a growing recognition that ecosystems provide numerous and varied services to human populations through a wide range of ecological functions and processes (see, e.g., Daily 1997). A typology developed by the Millennium Ecosystem Assessment (MA), a large international effort undertaken by the United Nations, identified the following types of ecosystem services (see MA 2005b):[4] (1) provisioning services (e.g., food, fuelwood, fiber, biochemicals, genetic resources, and fresh water); (2) regulating services (e.g., flood protection, human disease regulation, water purification, air quality maintenance, pollination, pest control, and climate control); (3) cultural services (e.g., cultural, spiritual, and aesthetic values and a sense of place); and (4) supporting services (e.g., soil formation, primary productivity, biogeochemistry, and provisioning of habitat).

The growing interest in the provision of ecosystem services stems from the increasing recognition that human systems and ecosystems (and their associated functions, processes, and services) are inextricably linked. Numerous examples illustrate the importance of this link. They include not only traditional air and water pollution (such as sulfur dioxide emissions, ground-level ozone, and eutrophication) but also land conversions that lead to deforestation or loss of wetlands and biodiversity; global warming; changes in the nitrogen cycle; invasive species; and aquifer depletion.

A fundamental characteristic of the linkage between human systems and ecosystems is that it is bidirectional—that is, not only do human activities affect the environment, and more specifically the ecosystems within it, but also these ecosystems have a direct impact on human activities.[5] The publicity surrounding the study by Costanza et al. (1997), which put a dollar value of $33 trillion—nearly twice the value of the world gross domestic product—on global ecosystem services, raised public awareness about the dependence of human systems on ecosystems. Similarly, the Millennium Assessment (2005a) raised awareness about the impact of human systems on ecosystems. In particular, it found that (1) human activities have had a substantial and in some cases irreversible impact on ecosystems; (2) these changes have generated benefits (e.g., food, water, timber, fuel) but at growing costs in terms of lost ecosystem services for both current and future generations; (3) the degradation could be significantly worse over the next decades; and (4) reversing ecosystem degradation is possible but requires a change in policies, institutions, and practices.

Economists have historically analyzed the link between human systems and the environment using traditional externality theory based on damage functions (see, e.g., Baumol and Oates 1988). However, the growing environmental concerns about wide-ranging ecosystem-human links suggest that the externality created by human actions is much more fundamental than implied by the traditional approach. As a result, a new paradigm is emerging within environmental economics, in which "natural capital," or more specifically the flow of ecosystem services, plays a central role (Barbier and Heal 2006). This paradigm recognizes that addressing many current environmental concerns will be more challenging than controlling traditional pollution externalities. In particular, the ecological effects of human activities of concern over the coming decades are likely to be

- larger in magnitude (i.e., nonmarginal);

- longer lasting;

- broader in their geographical scope (often global);

- more uncertain; and

- possibly more susceptible to instability and threshold effects.

As a result, these effects will be more difficult to predict, measure or quantify, and value.

Demand, Supply, and Markets for Ecosystem Services

As with other goods and services, an economic approach to understanding and evaluating the provision of ecosystem services draws on the distinction between the demand for these services and their supply. In addition, it asks whether markets can be used to bring demanders and suppliers together to ensure that these services are provided (e.g., Heal 2001). In this sense, it treats ecosystem services as simply another commodity. In many ways ecosystem services resemble other economic goods or services, but they have some characteristics that distinguish them from standard commodities as well. Some of those similarities and differences are described briefly here.

The Demand Side

According to economic theory, the demand for goods and services, including ecosystem services, is derived from the value that individuals ascribe to them. This value can include both anthropocentric values—that is, contributions to human welfare or utility—and nonanthropocentric or intrinsic values. The anthropocentric value of ecosystems services stems not only from their direct provision of commodities, such as timber and fish, but also from their indirect contributions (as intermediate products or processes) to the production of final products valued by individuals, such as recreation, suitable climate, clean water, and clean air. These products constitute sources of use value. Ecosystem services can also generate anthropocentric nonuse value, such as existence or bequest value (e.g., Turpie 2003; Spring and Kennedy 2005). For example, individuals may value the existence of a particular species or type of habitat for themselves or for future generations. In addition, individuals may value certain ecosystems or their components for nonanthropocentric reasons, such as moral, religious, or cultural reasons (e.g., Azqueta and Delacamara 2006; Hoffman and Sandelands 2005).

Conceptually, the anthropocentric value of environmental and other natural resources can be captured simply by including variables reflecting the associated stock or flows in the utility functions of individuals. For example, ecosystem services can affect human well-being or utility through their effect on economic variables that ultimately affect consumption flows. In addition, the stock of environmental or biological resources can directly affect utility. For example, if individuals directly value species, open space, or other natural amenities, the associated stocks will enter an individual's utility function directly. If the relevant ecological or environmental variables are included in the utility function, as final or intermediate products and as stocks or flows, then in principle the anthropocentric demand for the associated ecosystem services can be derived using standard principles from economic theory. In addition, the benefits from changes in those services can be estimated using economic valuation methods (either market or nonmarket).

Although in principle the demand for ecosystem services and the benefits associated with changes in services are similar to those for other goods and services, in practice they can be much more difficult to determine, for several reasons. The first relates to the difficulty of predicting and quantifying or characterizing ecological effects. In most applications, information about the benefits resulting from a specific action (such as a proposed regulation) is needed. To specify the change that is to be valued, it is necessary to predict the impacts of the action not only on the ecosystem and its components, but also on the flow of ecosystem services it provides. However, our ability to predict these impacts, particularly in terms of changes in services, in limited. Ecosystems are complex, nonlinear, dynamic systems that vary considerably from site to site. As a result, predicting the specific biophysical changes in the ecosystem itself, and then predicting the resulting change in the stream of ecosystem services over time and space, poses major challenges to estimating the value of, and hence demand for, ecosystem services.

Second, even if changes in the flow of services can be predicted, the values or benefits associated with those changes can be very difficult to ascertain. Individuals may be familiar with some ecosystem goods and services, such as timber and recreation, but will likely have much less familiarity with or awareness of the contributions of other types of services, such as biodiversity. Lack of understanding or awareness will be of particular concern when valuing intermediate ecological goods or processes (such as habitat or microbial processes) or when the change will affect not only current but future utility as well. In this latter case, value estimates would have to be predicated on assumptions or predictions about demographic and other future conditions that would be expected to affect the benefits associated with a given change.

Finally, conventional economic valuation methods cannot capture nonanthropocentric values or the values of future generations, except to the extent that they are reflected in bequest values. For example, contingent valuation is not likely to capture the moral value that many people place on protection and preservation of environmental assets (Stevens et al. 1991). For this reason, some have advocated the use of deliberative processes that both provide information about ecosystem services and allow for expression of values that reflect considerations other than those embodied in the neoclassical concept of willingness to pay (e.g., Gregory and Slovic 1997; Wilson and Howarth 2002).

The challenges associated with valuing ecosystem services have led to several recent studies aimed at improving ecosystem valuation. For example, the National Research Council (NRC 2005) recently published a report focused on expanded use of economic valuation methods for estimating the benefits of aquatic ecosystem services. Similarly, the U.S. Environmental Protection Agency (EPA) has recently undertaken activities relating to ecological valuation. EPA recently completed a strategic plan for improving the agency's ability to estimate the ecological benefits resulting from its own actions (U.S. EPA 2006), and its Science Advisory Board convened a multidisciplinary committee to advise the agency on ways to improve ecological valuation within the agency. The committee's draft report calls for an expanded approach to ecological valuation that draws on multiple methods (in addition to economic valuation) for characterizing the value of ecosystems and the services they provide (U.S. EPA 2007). Efforts of this type should lay a foundation for developing and applying improved methods for understanding and quantifying or characterizing the myriad contributions of natural capital to human well-being.

The Supply Side

Understanding the human-ecosystem link necessitates not only understanding the contributions of ecosystems to human well-being but also the human behaviors that cause ecosystem degradation or preservation and the factors that affect that behavior. This includes the study of practices that could reverse the degradation of ecosystems, as well as the policies, institutions, and incentives embodied in our current economic and social systems that influence resource use. All of these factors will affect the provision or "supply" of ecosystem services now and in the future.

The provision of ecosystem services is complicated by several factors. One is the interrelationship among services, which implies a form of joint production. In some cases, services will be complementary—that is, increasing the provision of one will simultaneously increase the provision of another (e.g., Heal and Small 2002; Batie 2003; Feng and Kling 2005). For example, open space can provide both aesthetic services as well as habitat for valued wildlife, implying that more open space yields both types of benefits. In other cases, services will be competing—that is, increasing one service will lead to a decrease in another service, implying that a trade-off exists (MA 2005a). For example, converting land from forest to cropland would increase one ecosystem service (food) but potentially decrease others (biodiversity, habitat, timber). Similarly, use of surface water to meet water demands can negatively affect in-stream habitats and the fish and other species that depend on streams and the services they provide. These interrelationships imply that in general, ecosystem services cannot be considered individually; instead, we need to think in terms of the portfolio of services that is produced.

A second complication stems from the relationship between the provision of ecosystem services and the spatial configuration of land use. This relationship has at least two related dimensions. One derives from the relationship between natural capital and development patterns. Because individuals value open space and other environmental amenities, heterogeneity in the spatial location of these amenities can contribute to "leapfrog" development and sprawl (Wu and Plantinga 2003; Wu 2006). The resulting development patterns have important implications for the demand for ecosystem services, including water, open space, recreational services, and waste assimilation. The second dimension relates to fragmentation. For some land uses, the benefits of that use depend not only on the total number of acres devoted to it but also on how those acres are spatially configured and whether the acreage is fragmented (Bockstael 1996). A prime example is habitat for species (Parkhurst et al. 2002), but spatial configuration may also be important in the provision of other ecological services, such as flood control and pollination.

Conventional economic analysis has not adequately considered the spatial externalities associated with the provision of ecosystem services. Although spatial models have long been used within urban economics, the urban models do not typically consider the role of environmental and natural resources (other than land) and the potential externalities (both short- and long-run) created by different development patterns. Resource economists interested in land use patterns have begun incorporating spatial externalities in both theoretical and empirical work (e.g., Irwin and Bockstael 2002, 2004; Wu and Plantinga 2003; Wu 2006; Irwin et al., Chapter 6, this volume), but there is much left to be done. Tools such as spatial econometrics and geographic information systems allow explicit consideration of spatial issues, not just for displaying or representing spatial information but also as an input into land use modeling and as a means of incorporating spatial considerations into economic models of decisionmaking. However, when spatial patterns affect the provision of a public rather than a private good (as is often likely to be the case), private landowners and the private market have no incentive to consider them when making land purchase and use decisions. Historically, spatial externalities have been addressed by local communities through zoning and related land use regulations. However, although land use regulation can prevent the contiguous location of incompatible land uses, in general it cannot adequately address many of the spatial externalities associated with the demand for or supply of ecosystem services. This suggests the need for alternative policy approaches specifically designed to internalize these spatial externalities.[6]

Markets

A fundamental principle of economics is that markets can play a critical role in ensuring the provision of goods and services for which there is sufficient demand. In this spirit, interest is growing in promoting the creation of markets to provide ecosystem services (e.g., Chichilnisky and Heal 1998; Heal 2000, 2001; Daily and Ellison 2002; Murtough et al. 2002; Kumar 2005). In this context, *market* is used broadly to include both private markets and public payments linked to the provision of ecosystem services.[7] Examples of successful markets include ecotourism in Africa and Central and South America based on the conservation of endangered species (Heal 2001), leases or concessions and other direct payments to conserve biodiversity in Africa and Central and South America (Ferraro and Kiss 2002), payments to U.S. farmers to retire land or adopt conservation practices related to improved water quality, wildlife habitat management, or wetlands protection (NRCS 2002), establishment of tradable permit markets for control of nutrient pollution (Breetz et al. 2004), and the use of ecolabels to promote purchases of environmentally friendly products (e.g., Teisl et al. 2002; Bjørner et al. 2004).

Although the use of market-based incentives appears promising for some types of ecosystem services, reliance on markets in this context faces some significant challenges. The first relates to the implication for the distribution of property rights. Establishing a market in which suppliers of ecosystem services are paid for their production implicitly assigns full property rights to the landowner, under which the landowner is free to use his property as he wants and need not protect or conserve ecological functions or processes (or, correspondingly, provide ecosystem services) unless he chooses to do so. This approach constitutes a departure from the traditional approach to controlling environmental externalities, which is generally based on the "polluter pays" principle, under which externalities are internalized through mandatory regulation or taxation, implying that society rather than the polluter holds property rights (see, e.g., Baumol and Oates 1988).[8] Thus, increased reliance on markets to ensure provision of ecosystem services requires an acceptance of this fundamental shift in how property rights and the associated responsibilities are viewed. In particular, it will require acceptance of the notion of paying for conservation rather than requiring it. In principle a change in the framing of the problem implied by a shift in property rights should have no effect on outcomes, but experimental evidence suggests that in practice it will (e.g., Sonnemans et al. 1998).

Second, even with a clear assignment of property rights to landowners or others engaged in activities that affect the flow of ecosystem services, in many cases it will be difficult to establish a well-functioning market for these services. An effective market[9] requires three components: demanders, suppliers, and an exchange or payment vehicle for "buying" the good or service. Though straightforward in the context of standard commodities (e.g., an apple or chair or even a ton of sulfur dioxide emissions), these three components become more complicated in the context of ecosystem services.

An obvious complication stems from the public good characteristics of many ecosystem services. Although some ecosystem services are private goods, many of these services generate benefits that are nonexcludable—that is, they are enjoyed by all, including those who do not buy them, and hence a classic free-rider problem arises (e.g., Heal 2001). To surmount this problem, the demander or purchaser of the service often has to be a representative government body or other collective organization, such as a nonprofit environmental organization acting on behalf of others.

With regard to the payment vehicle, different approaches exist for purchasing ecosystem services—that is, rewarding suppliers for supplying these services. Examples include paying price premiums for goods produced by processes that also produce ecosystem services (e.g., sustainable forest products), subsidizing inputs used in ecofriendly production activities, and making direct conservation payments to landowners who engage in land uses that, for example, protect biodiversity and habitat or directly provide ecosystem services like carbon sequestration. Several studies have explored (and in some cases compared) these alternative payment vehicles.[10] However, the exact amount of services being purchased with these payments is not always clear. Although some ecosystem services (such as timber or fish) are readily quantified in standardized units, others (such as biodiversity, nutrient cycling, or climate regulation) are not.[11] As a result, the exchanges often involve goods or services or even activities that are linked to (or proxies for) ecosystem services rather than the ecosystem services themselves.

The above discussion suggests that in principle market-type mechanisms have the potential to increase the provision of ecosystem services, although realizing that potential in practice will often be difficult. Nonetheless, the increased recognition of the importance of these services and the factors that affect their demand and supply, both now and in the future, is paving the way for efforts to increase the use of markets in this context.

Sustainability

We turn next to a second major issue that is gaining more attention in resource economics and is likely to be the focus of considerable interest in the future—namely, sustainability. To date, most economic analysis has used economic efficiency as an evaluative benchmark or normative goal.[12] Although information about benefits and costs is useful in evaluating alternatives, many people, including both economists and noneconomists, have raised serious objections to using efficiency as the primary goal for evaluating policy options, on ethical and other grounds.[13] A common criticism is that efficiency does not adequately consider the distribution of resources across groups within the economy and over time. In addition to the ethical and conceptual concerns, in the context of the human–ecosystem interactions discussed above, practical implementation of efficiency analysis is particularly difficult for at least three reasons: (1) the difficulty of estimating or measuring the benefits and costs of these types of environmental changes (due to uncertainty about the underlying science or the associated values); (2) the limitations of standard partial equilibrium, marginal analysis in this context (due, for example, to the inability to capture adequately potential threshold effects); and (3) the potential for significant intergenerational impacts (due to the long-term nature of the ecological effects) and concerns about whether simple discounting adequately protects the interests of future generations.

There is a growing interest among noneconomists, and some economists, in incorporating concern for sustainability into normative analysis. This is reflected in statements by prominent policymakers espousing sustainability (e.g., U.S. EPA

2005). To many, it provides a preferable alternative to normative analysis based on economic efficiency. Although this concept means different things to different people, the notion of promoting good outcomes that can be sustained over time has intuitive appeal, particularly to those concerned about future generations.

A fundamental question then is how economic analysis based on efficiency as traditionally defined compares with economic analysis based on sustainability. In particular, would evaluating policy options based on sustainability rather than efficiency change fundamental policy prescriptions? This question is particularly important given the dependence of human systems on natural ecosystems and the potential for large-scale, long-term environmental impacts from human actions. If efficiency and sustainability criteria yield identical policy prescriptions, then economic results or prescriptions based on efficiency would also promote sustainability. If or when the two yield different prescriptions, then basing prescriptions on efficiency would imply the adoption of policies that are in some sense not sustainable. In this case, we must address the issue of "what comes next" if society proceeds down a path that is not sustainable. For example, if development in an urban area exceeds the level that can be supported on a sustainable basis by the current water supply in the area, what is likely to happen in the long run and how is the demand for water by the urban population going to affect surrounding areas?

Although there has been some work in economics on sustainability (e.g., Batie 1989; Heal 1998; Pezzey and Toman 2002a; Arrow et al. 2004), it has not received much attention in mainstream resource economics, which continues to focus on efficiency. A focus on sustainability instead would imply a different mindset, but one that is perhaps more conducive to discussions across disciplines and with policymakers, especially regarding issues with long-term ecological or environmental consequences (Batie 1989).

One challenge that arises in adopting sustainability as a normative goal is the lack of a commonly agreed-upon definition (comparable to the definition of efficiency). Alternative definitions of sustainability currently exist (Pezzey and Toman 2002a, 2002b). For example, EPA (n.d.) has defined sustainability as "the ability to achieve continuing economic prosperity while protecting the natural systems of the planet and providing a high quality of life for its people." This definition suggests that sustainability is defined, at least partially, in biophysical terms. Alternatively, drawing from the World Commission on Environment and Development, Pezzey and Toman (2002b, 165) define sustainability as "the problem of ensuring that future generations are no worse off than today's." This definition essentially invokes a Rawlsian notion of intergenerational social welfare and defines sustainability in terms of maintaining utility rather than biophysical stocks. Pezzey and Toman then relax this somewhat when defining the *economics* of sustainability to include any work with the following characteristics (Pezzey and Toman 2002b, 166–67):

- some concern for intergenerational equity or fairness in the decisionmaking of a whole society over many generations;

- some recognition of the role of finite environmental resources; and

- some recognizable, if perhaps unconventional, use of economic concepts such as cost, production, momentary (instantaneous) utility, or some kind of aggregating of utility over time into (intertemporal) welfare.

In one sense, sustainability concerns can be considered by simply adding an intergenerational equity constraint (of the type suggested by Pezzey and Toman's definition) to a standard efficiency problem (Pezzey 1997). Under this approach, sustainability can be viewed as maximizing the present discounted value of the flow of utility from consumption subject to a constraint that sets a lower boundary for the utility at any given time or a constraint that requires that utility not decrease over time. Whether adding such a constraint involves a trade-off—that is, implies a reduction in efficiency—depends on whether the constraint is binding, which in turn depends on several factors, including the specific form of the sustainability constraint, the degree of substitutability between natural and human or manufactured capital (and hence the nature of the interaction between economic and biological or environmental variables), the extent of technological progress, and the magnitude and nature of the utility discount rate (Pezzey 1997; Arrow et al. 2004). If a trade-off does exist, it implies that in general, efficient policies as advocated by many economists do not yield sustainability. Nonetheless, some policies designed to promote efficiency, such as those designed to correct the underpricing of natural resources, might contribute to both efficiency and sustainability goals (Arrow et al. 2004).

Of course, the potential trade-off between sustainability and efficiency assumes that the instantaneous preferences used to define efficiency depend only on current consumption and that a concern for sustainability enters as a constraint. An alternative and in many ways more appealing approach, used by Heal (1998), is to derive sustainability as an optimal outcome driven from first principles rather than imposed as a constraint. He postulates two axioms as the underlying basis of sustainability (Heal 1998, 8):[14]

- a symmetric treatment of the present and of the long-term future, which places a positive value on the very long run, together with

- explicit recognition of the intrinsic value of environmental assets.

Interestingly, simply including the environmental stocks in the utility function can yield a solution to an otherwise standard model of the efficient use of an exhaustible resource under which a positive level of the stock is permanently conserved (Krautkraemer 1985), implying a form of sustainability. This is a potentially fruitful approach to reconciling efficiency and sustainability, which shows that under certain preference structures efficient paths are also sustainable paths. Heal (1998, 9) notes that

> if we value the long-run adequately, and recognize the intrinsic value of environmental assets, then everything else that is associated with sustainability in the areas of climate change, biodiversity, nuclear waste disposal, etc., is logically implied. Valuing the long-run, and valuing the environment as more than an input to human activity, will lead to selection of what one thinks of intu-

itively as "sustainable" policy options when considering policies toward global warming, species preservation, and the management of nuclear waste. . . . So although valuing the long-run and valuing environmental assets do not themselves prescribe precise sustainable policies on issues such as climate change and biodiversity, they are necessary conditions for the systematic and consistent selection of such policies as "optimal."

A crucial question is then whether the preference structures under which sustainability could be an implication of efficiency rather than a constraint on it are, in fact, representative of actual preferences over stocks and flows of economic and environmental variables. To answer this, we need information about the intrinsic value of environmental resources or the utility derived directly from the stocks of environmental assets, and the corresponding "demand" for preserving or protecting these stocks and the associated ecosystem functions and processes that support them. However, it is not clear that accurate information about intrinsic values can be obtained from standard economic valuation methods, such as contingent valuation, given the implicit assumptions underlying these methods and their focus on marginal changes (see discussion above). Nonetheless, this information is a critical input in understanding the concerns about sustainability and how a normative goal of sustainability relates to an economic efficiency goal.

Implications for Rural Communities

The above sections discuss two emerging issues that are likely to be prominent in discussions of natural resource use and environmental protection in the coming years: the bidirectional link between human systems and ecosystems, and sustainability. We turn next to the implications of this for rural communities. The main message of the following discussion is twofold. First, there is an opportunity for rural communities to be important contributors both to the supply side of markets for ecosystem goods and services and to broad sustainability goals. Second, by taking advantage of these opportunities, rural communities can also contribute to their own long-run sustainability.

As people increasingly recognize the importance of ecological services, particularly those services linked in some way to land, they will demand that more land be dedicated or protected to provide these services, and much of the land providing these services will be located in rural areas. A well-known example is the role of the Catskill Mountains watershed in providing high-quality drinking water to the residents of New York City (NRC 2005). Similarly, agricultural land in rural areas can be the source of numerous external benefits or services, which are often referred to as "rural amenities" stemming from the "multifunctionality" of agricultural and rural land uses (e.g., Heal and Small 2002; Batie 2003; Nickerson and Hellerstein 2006). These include the provision of scenic views, wildlife habitat, or open space; protection of groundwater and surface water quality; increased self-sufficiency through growing *local* food supplies; and preservation of an agrarian cultural heritage and the family farm.[15]

On the other hand, population and income growth will lead to increased demand for use of land for other purposes, such as development. This will lead to increased competition for land for alternative uses and as a result increased pressure for land conversion, especially at the urban-rural fringe. This conversion in turn reduces the supply of ecosystem services from this land (Heimlich and Anderson 2001). To the extent that migration is driven by a demand for greater access to natural amenities, conversion pressures will actually be greater in areas where amenity endowments are greater.[16]

A basic economic principle is that the decision to convert or sell land depends on the relative magnitudes of the private returns to the land in its current use (e.g., farming) and the private returns in an alternative use (e.g., development). Whereas the development returns are primarily private (and hence reflected in the price a prospective buyer is willing to pay for the land), many of the returns from agricultural or other rural uses of land, including the returns from the rural amenities it provides, are primarily external—that is, realized by people other than the landowner. Thus, in many cases, the private returns to keeping the land in its current use are much smaller than the public returns, creating an inefficient amount of conversion.

A second basic principle is that an inefficiency of the type described above can be reduced or eliminated by internalizing the external benefits generated by a given activity. This is precisely what a market in ecosystem services is designed to do. Such a market would allow agricultural and other rural landowners to capture some of the ecosystem services their land generates in its current use. This would increase the returns from its current use and reduce the likelihood that the land will be converted to development.

The idea of government payments to agricultural and rural landowners in exchange for conservation-related activities is not new. For example, the Conservation Reserve Program, originally designed to reduce soil erosion, has been used to promote production of ecosystem services relating to biodiversity and wildlife habitat (Szentandrasi et al. 1995), salmon restoration (Wu and Skelton-Groth 2002), and erosion and water quality (Babcock et al. 1996). Other, similar programs designed to pay farmers for directly or indirectly supplying ecosystem services include the Environmental Quality Incentives Program, the Wetlands Reserve Program, and the Wildlife Habitat Incentives Program. Likewise, private nongovernmental organizations such as The Nature Conservancy, as well as states and regional authorities, have used direct payments to landowners for conservation purposes (e.g., Ferraro and Kiss 2002; Ferraro 2006). These can be broadly interpreted as creating "markets" for these services, where the purchaser is the government acting on behalf of its citizens or the nongovernmental organization acting on behalf of its contributors and funders.

Although direct government payments to farmers can in principle both promote conservation and keep some land at the urban-rural fringe from being sold for development, the potential for this to simultaneously generate ecosystem services and preserve and enhance rural communities is limited, for four reasons. First, even though direct payments may benefit landowners, to the extent that these programs retire working agricultural land, they can negatively affect sectors of the rural economy dependent on agriculture production (Hyberg et al. 1991). Second, payment schemes targeted toward individual parcels do not account for spatial externalities, such as the benefits from agglomeration (Irwin et al. 2006), or adequately address the demands of nonfarm rural residents (Feinerman and Komen 2003). Third, if the aim of these programs is to maximize conservation benefits given available funds, *ceteris paribus*, they will target land with a lower opportunity cost, since the payment necessary to induce owners of this land to join the program will be lower. As a result, land near the urban-rural fringe, which is subject to the greatest conversion pressure, will be less likely to be enrolled (Parks and Schorr 1997). Finally, the use of these markets is clearly limited by the availability of public conservation funds.

Although government payments constitute a form of "public market" for some ecosystem services, it is also possible to establish private markets in which private individuals purchase ecosystem services directly from agricultural or rural landowners. Of course, these markets can develop only in contexts where these services can be made excludable. The most notable examples are services related to recreation, such as hiking, hunting, and fishing. Farmers and rural landowners have the potential to market these services to generate additional revenue from farm-related or rural environments. This revenue in turn can raise the value of land in an undeveloped state (see, e.g., Henderson and Moore 2006) and thereby reduce the likelihood of conversion for development. Unlike the public markets, these markets would most likely affect landowners on the urban-rural fringe, where demand for these services by urban residents is likely to be higher. In addition, landowners have an incentive to consider spatial externalities that affect the flow of services, since improvements in services should directly affect the revenue generated by the land. Many of these services can be provided without retiring highly productive land, thereby avoiding the negative impacts on the local economy associated with reduced agricultural production. In fact, attracting recreationists can increase the demand for complementary services that can be provided by other local businesses. Finally, the size of the potential market is not constrained by the availability of public funds.

The multifunctionality of agriculture, and more generally the ability of rural land to supply multiple ecosystem services, could provide a strategy for sustaining rural communities. Such a strategy underlies the European Union's new rural development policy (Feinerman and Komen 2003). Through public and private markets for ecosystem services, rural communities can generate additional income from activities that are consistent with maintaining the agrarian character of these communities.

A rural development strategy based on markets for ecosystem services would also be consistent with sustainability goals. This includes not only sustainability of these communities themselves, but also sustainability of the type discussed in the previous section. If environmental stocks are valued, for either their service potential or their intrinsic worth, then promoting their protection through ecosystem markets would contribute to sustainability defined in either biophysical or utility terms.

Conclusion

This chapter has discussed two emerging issues in resource economics that have been increasingly recognized and are likely to receive considerable attention in the coming years: the fundamental interaction between human systems and ecosystems (and the importance of ecosystem services), and the use of sustainability as a normative policy goal. These issues are of importance for rural communities since these communities can both supply ecosystem services and contribute to sustainability goals. Their role can also be the foundation for a strategy to preserve rural communities through the development of public or private markets for ecosystem services. Such a strategy would be built on explicit recognition of the multi-functionality of agricultural and other rural land and the value of providing the associated natural amenities and other ecosystem services that are increasingly demanded.

A rural development strategy based on this premise would benefit from additional economic research related to the following topics:

- the value of different ecosystem services and ecological changes, including not only the magnitude but also both the source of this value (e.g., intrinsic versus utilitarian, stock versus flow) and the important characteristics underlying it;

- the demographic and other trends that are likely to affect those values, and hence the demand for ecosystem services, both over time and over space;

- the profitability of joint production of ecosystem services, as well as the implications of both complementarity and substitutability of different services;

- the potential for rural communities in different locations to meet the demand for ecosystem services in the coming years;

- the effectiveness and efficiency of alternative policies designed to promote the provision of ecosystem services through public or private markets, particularly in rural areas;

- the extent to which alternative policies encourage landowners to consider spatial externalities related to the provision of ecosystem services when making land use decisions; and

- the link between the multifunctionality of agricultural and other rural land uses and sustainability in its various forms.

Future research in these and related areas could provide a basis for simultaneously promoting sustainability, conserving essential ecosystems that contribute to human well-being, and preserving rural communities.

References

Abraham, R., G. Chichilnisky, and R. Record. 1998. North-South Trade and the Dynamics of the Environment. In *Sustainability: Dynamics and Uncertainty*, edited by G. Chichilnisky, G. Heal, and A. Vercelli. Dordrecht: Kluwer Academic Publishers, 77–107.

Arrow, K., P. Dasgupta, L. Goulder, G. Daily, P. Ehrlich, G. Heal, S. Levin, K.-G. Mäler, S. Schneider, D. Starrett, and B. Walker. 2004. Are We Consuming Too Much? *Journal of Economic Perspectives* 18(3): 147–72.

Azqueta, D., and G. Delacamara. 2006. Ethics, Economics, and Environmental Management. *Ecological Economics* 56(4): 524–33.

Babcock, B.A., P.G. Lakshminarayan, J. Wu, and D. Zilberman. 1996. The Economics of a Public Fund for Environmental Amenities: A Study of CRP Contracts. *American Journal of Agricultural Economics* 78(4): 961–71.

Barbier, E.B., and G.M. Heal. 2006. Valuing Ecosystem Services. *Economists' Voice* 3(3): 1–6.

Batie, S.S. 1989. Sustainable Development: Challenges to the Agricultural Economics Profession. *American Journal of Agricultural Economics* 71(5): 1083–1101.

———. 2003. The Multifunctional Attributes of Northeastern Agriculture: A Research Agenda. *Agricultural and Resource Economics Review* 32(1): 1–8.

Baumol, W.J., and W.E. Oates. 1988. *The Theory of Environmental Policy.* Cambridge: Cambridge University Press.

Bjørner, T.B., L.G. Hansen, and C.S. Russell. 2004. Environmental Labeling and Consumers' Choice—An Empirical Analysis of the Effect of the Nordic Swan. *Journal of Environmental Economics and Management* 47(3): 411–34.

Bockstael, N.E. 1996. Modeling Ecosystems and Ecology: The Importance of a Spatial Perspective. *American Journal of Agricultural Economics* 78: 1168–80.

Boyd, J., and S. Banzhaf. 2006. What Are Ecosystem Services? The Need for Standardized Environmental Accounting Units. Discussion Paper 06–02, January. Washington, DC: Resources for the Future.

Breetz, H.L., K. Fisher-Vanden, L. Garzon, H. Jacobs, K. Kroetz, and R. Terry. 2004. *Water Quality Trading and Offset Initiatives in the U.S.: A Comprehensive Survey.* Rockefeller Center, Dartmouth College, Hanover, NH.

Bromley, D.W. 1990. The Ideology of Efficiency: Searching for a Theory of Policy Analysis. *Journal of Environmental Economics and Management* 19(1): 86–107.

Castle, E.N. 1999. Natural Resource and Environmental Economics: A Retrospective View. *Review of Agricultural Economics* 21(2): 288–304.

Chichilnisky, G., and G.M. Heal. 1998. Economic Returns from the Biosphere. *Nature* 391: 629–30.

Chichilnisky, G., G. Heal, and A. Vercelli. 1998. Introduction. In *Sustainability: Dynamics and Uncertainty*, edited by G. Chichilnisky, G. Heal, and A. Vercelli. Dordrecht: Kluwer Academic Publishers, vii–xiv.

Costanza, R., R. d'Arge, R. de Groot, S. Farber, M. Grasso, B. Hannon, K. Limburg, S. Naeem, R.V. O'Neill, J. Paruelo, R.G. Raskin, P. Sutton, and M. van den Belt. 1997. The Value of the World's Ecosystem Services and Natural Capital. *Nature* 387: 253–60.

Cropper, M.L., and W.E. Oates. 1992. Environmental Economics: A Survey. *Journal of Economic Literature* 30(2): 675–740.

Daily, G.C., ed. 1997. *Nature's Services: Societal Dependence on Natural Ecosystems.* Washington, DC: Island Press.

Daily, G.C., and K. Ellison. 2002. *The New Economy of Nature: The Quest to Make Conservation Profitable.* Washington, DC: Island Press, Shearwater Books.

Deacon, R.T., D.S. Brookshire, A.C. Fisher, A.V. Kneese, C.D. Kolstad, D. Scrogin, V.K. Smith, M. Ward, and J. Wilen. 1998. Research Trends and Opportunities in Environmental and Natural Resource Economics. *Environmental and Resource Economics* 11(3-4): 383–97.

Feinerman, E., and M.H.C. Komen. 2003. Agri-environmental Instruments for an Integrated Rural Policy: An Economic Analysis. *Journal of Agricultural Economics* 54(1): 1–20.

Feng, H., and C.L. Kling. 2005. The Consequences of Cobenefits for the Efficient Design of Carbon Sequestration Programs. *Canadian Journal of Agricultural Economics* 53(4): 461–76.

Ferraro, P.J. 2006. Integrating Biophysical and Economic Information to Guide Land Conservation Investments. In *Economics and Contemporary Land Use Policy: Development and Conservation at the Rural-Urban Fringe,* edited by Robert J. Johnston and Stephen K. Swallow. Washington, DC: Resources for the Future.

Ferraro, P.J., and A. Kiss. 2002. Direct Payments to Conserve Biodiversity. *Science* 298: 1718–19.

Ferraro, P.J., and R.D. Simpson. 2002. The Cost Effectiveness of Conservation Payments. *Land Economics* 78(3): 339–53.

Ferraro, P.J., T. Uchida, and J.M. Conrad. 2005. Price Premiums for Eco-Friendly Commodities: Are 'Green' Markets the Best Way to Protect Endangered Ecosystems? *Environmental and Resource Economics* 32(3): 419–38.

Gregory, R., and P. Slovic. 1997. A Constructive Approach to Environmental Valuation. *Ecological Economics* 21: 175–81.

Heal, G. 1998. Interpreting Sustainability. In *Sustainability: Dynamics and Uncertainty*, edited by G. Chichilnisky, G. Heal, and A. Vercelli. Dordrecht: Kluwer Academic Publishers, 3–22.

———. 2000. *Nature and the Marketplace: Capturing the Value of Ecosystem Services*. Washington, DC: Island Press.

———. 2001. Biodiversity as a Commodity. *Encyclopedia of Biodiversity*, Volume 1. Academic Press.

Heal, G.M. and A.A. Small. 2002. Agriculture and Ecosystem Services. In *Handbook of Agricultural Economics*, Volume 2, Part 1, edited by B.L. Gardner and G.C. Rausser. Elsevier.

Heimlich, R.E., and W.D. Anderson. 2001. *Development at the Urban Fringe and Beyond: Impacts on Agriculture and Rural Land*. Agricultural Economic Report No. 803. Washington, DC: Economic Research Service, U.S. Department of Agriculture.

Henderson, J., and S. Moore. 2006. The Capitalization of Wildlife Recreation Income into Farmland Values. *Journal of Agricultural and Applied Economics* 38(3): 597–610.

Hoffman, A.J., and L.E. Sandelands. 2005. Getting Right with Nature: Anthropocentrism, Ecocentrism, and Theocentrism. *Organization and Environment* 18(2): 141–62.

Hyberg, B.T., M.R. Dicks, and T. Hebert. 1991. Economic Impacts of the Conservation Reserve Program on Rural Economies. *Review of Regional Studies* 21(1): 91–105.

Irwin, E.G., and N.E. Bockstael. 2002. Interacting Agents, Spatial Externalities, and the Endogenous Evolution of Residential Land Use Patterns. *Journal of Economic Geography* 2(1): 31–54.

———. 2004. Land Use Externalities, Growth Management Policies, and Urban Sprawl. *Regional Science and Urban Economics* 34(6): 705–25.

Irwin, E. G., K.P. Bell, and J. Geoghegan. 2006. Forecasting Residential Land Use Change. In *Economics and Contemporary Land Use Policy: Development and Conservation at the Rural-Urban Fringe*, edited by R.J. Johnston and S.K. Swallow. Washington, DC: Resources for the Future.

Johnston, R.J., and S.K. Swallow. 2006. *Economics and Contemporary Land Use Policy: Development and Conservation at the Rural-Urban Fringe*. Washington, DC: Resources for the Future.

Krautkraemer, J. 1985. Optimal Growth, Resource Amenities, and the Preservation of Natural Environments. *Review of Economic Studies* 52(1): 153–70.

Kumar, P. 2005. Markets for Ecosystem Services. Winnipeg, Manitoba: International Institute for Sustainable Development.

Millennium Ecosystem Assessment (MA). 2005a. *Ecosystems and Human Well-being: Synthesis*. Washington, DC: Island Press.

———. 2005b. *Ecosystems and Human Well-being: A Framework for Assessment*. Washington, DC: Island Press.

Murtough, G., B. Aretino, and A. Matysek. 2002. Creating Markets for Ecosystem Services. Staff Research Paper Series. Melbourne: Australian Productivity Commission.

National Research Council (NRC). 2005. *Valuing Ecosystem Services: Toward Better Environmental Decision-Making*. Washington, DC: National Academy Press.

Natural Resources Conservation Service (NRCS). 2002. Farm Bill 2002: Summary of NRCS Conservation Programs. Washington, DC: U.S. Department of Agriculture, July.

Nickerson, C.J., and D.M. Hellerstein. 2006. Farmland Preservation Programs and the Importance of Rural Amenities. In *Economics and Contemporary Land Use Policy: Development and Conservation at the Rural-Urban Fringe*, edited by R.J. Johnston and S.K. Swallow. Washington, DC: Resources for the Future.

Parkhurst, G.M., J.F. Shogren, C. Bastian, P. Kivi, J. Donner, and R.B.W. Smith. 2002. Agglomeration Bonus: An Incentive Mechanism to Reunite Fragmented Habitat for Biodiversity Conservation. *Ecological Economics* 41(2): 305–28.

Parks, P.J., and J.P. Schorr. 1997. Sustaining Open Space Benefits in the Northeast: An Evaluation of the Conservation Reserve Program. *Journal of Environmental Economics and Management* 32(1): 85–94.

Pezzey, J.C.V. 1997. Sustainability Constraints versus 'Optimality' versus Intertemporal Concern,
and Axioms versus Data. *Land Economics* 73: 448–66.

Pezzey, J.C.V., and M.A. Toman, eds. 2002a. *The Economics of Sustainability.* Alershot, UK: Dart-
mouth/Ashgate Publishing Company.

———. 2002b. Progress and Problems in the Economics of Sustainability. In *The International
Yearbook of Environmental and Resource Economics 2002/2003*, edited by Tom Tietenberg and
Henk Folmer. Cheltenham, U.K.: Edward Elgar, 165–232.

Ribaudo, M.O. 1998. Lessons Learned about the Performance of USDA Agricultural Nonpoint
Source Pollution Programs. *Journal of Soil and Water Conservation* 53: 4–10.

Sonnemans, J., A. Schram, and T. Offerman. 1998. Public Good Provision and Public Bad Pre-
vention: The Effect of Framing. *Journal of Economic Behavior and Organization* 34: 143–61.

Spring, D.A., and J.O.S. Kennedy. 2005. Existence Value and Optimal Timber-Wildlife Management in a Flammable Multistand Forest. *Ecological Economics* 55(3): 365–79.

Stavins, R.N. (ed.) 2000. *Economics of the Environment: Selected Readings,* 4th edition. New York
and London: Norton.

Stevens, T.H., J. Echeverria, R.J. Glass, T. Hager, and T.A. More. 1991. Measuring the Existence
Value of Wildlife: What Do CVM Estimates Really Show? *Land Economics* 67(4): 390–400.

Szentandrasi, S., S. Polasky, R. Berrens, and J. Leonard. 1995. Conserving Biological Diversity and
the Conservation Reserve Program. *Growth and Change* 26(3): 383–404.

Teisl, M.F., B. Roe, and R.L. Hicks. 2002. Can Eco-labels Tune a Market? Evidence from Dol-
phin-Safe Labeling. *Journal of Environmental Economics and Management* 43(3): 339–59.

Turpie, J.K. 2003. The Existence Value of Biodiversity in South Africa: How Interest, Experience,
Knowledge, Income and Perceived Level of Threat Influence Local Willingness to Pay. *Ecological Economics* 46(2): 199–216.

U. S. Environmental Protection Agency (EPA). 2005. We have a responsibility to sustain—if not
enhance—our nation's environment for future generations. Speech by EPA Administrator Steve
Johnson, June 27.

———. 2006. Ecological Benefits Assessment Strategic Plan. EPA-240-R-06-001. Washington, DC.

———. 2007. Draft C-VPESS Report, Toward an Integrated and Expanded Approach for Ecological Valuation. http://www.epa.gov/sab/pdf/c-vpess_draft_03-09-07.pdf. (accessed
March 15, 2007).

———. n.d. Sustainability Home Page. http://www.epa.gov/sustainability (accessed May 1, 2006).

Wilson, M.A., and R.B. Howarth. 2002. Discourse-Based Valuation of Ecosystem Services: Establishing Fair Outcomes through Group Deliberation. *Ecological Economics* 41(3): 431–43.

Wu, J. 2006. Environmental Amenities, Urban Sprawl and Community Characteristics. *Journal of
Environmental Economics and Management* 52: 527–47.

Wu, J., and A.J. Plantinga. 2003. The Influence of Public Open Space on Urban Spatial Structure. *Journal of Environmental Economics and Management* 46(2): 288–309.

Wu, J., and K. Skelton-Groth. 2002. Targeting Conservation Efforts in the Presence of Threshold Effects and Ecosystem Linkages. *Ecological Economics* 42(1–2): 313–31.

Notes

1. *Resource economics* is used broadly here to refer to the field that encompasses both environmental economics and natural resource economics.

2. For surveys of the field, see Cropper and Oates (1992), Deacon et al. (1998), and Castle
(1999), as well as Bromley (Chapter 2, this volume).

3. See the recent papers in Johnston and Swallow (2006) for discussions of development and
conservation in rural areas.

4. This typology reflects a broad view of the concept of ecosystem services that highlights
the many ways in which ecosystems support human systems. An alternative approach, advocated

by Boyd and Banzhaf (2006), defines ecological services more narrowly as "components of nature, directly enjoyed, consumed, or used to yield human well-being." This narrower definition distinguishes between intermediate and end products of nature and includes only the latter as ecosystem services. Boyd and Banzhaf argue that this narrower definition is more useful because it is more consistent with economic and standard accounting principles and avoids double-counting of the contributions of nature. For example, they argue that nutrient recycling is an ecological function but not an ecological service itself, since it is not an end product. In addition, they exclude from their definition goods such as recreation, which are produced by combining ecological inputs with other inputs (such as time).

5. In terms of standard economic parlance, the human-ecosystem interaction implies a coevolution of economic variables (e_t) and biological or environmental/ecological variables (b_t) over time that can be represented by the following system of dynamic equations (Chichilnisky et al. 1998; Abraham et al. 1998):

$$\frac{de_t}{dt} = f(e_t, b_t), \frac{db_t}{dt} = g(e_t, b_t).$$

6. An example of such a policy is the agglomeration bonus (see Parkhurst et al. 2002). Under this policy, landowners who retire land that is contiguous to other retired land would receive a bonus reflecting the greater habitat benefit associated with retiring such an acre relative to retiring an acre without the agglomeration benefit.

7. Direct or indirect payments by governments to promote conservation or provision of ecosystem services are, of course, a form of subsidy. Nonetheless, they are typically included in discussions of market-based approaches to encourage production of ecosystem services.

8. This traditional view applies primarily to industrial polluters. To reduce agricultural pollution, federal policymakers in the United States have typically relied on voluntary programs, which implicitly assign property rights to farmers. See Ribaudo (1998) for a discussion of these programs.

9. The term here simply refers to a market that is successful in generating production and sale of a good or service. Clearly, an effective market is not necessarily an efficient market.

10. There is a growing literature examining these approaches. See, for example, Heal (2000), Daily and Ellison (2002), Ferraro and Simpson (2002), and Ferraro et al. (2005).

11. See Boyd and Banzhaf (2006) for a discussion of measuring ecosystem services in standardized units.

12. For related reviews that focus on the field of natural resource and environmental economics, see Castle (1999) and Bromley (Chapter 2, this volume).

13. Efficiency analysis is typically implemented through benefit–cost analysis. There is an extensive literature criticizing the use of benefit–cost analysis. See, for example, Bromley (1990, Chapter 2, this volume) and the debate in Stavins (2000).

14. These axioms can be formalized in a dynamic economic model by including not only consumption (c_t) but also the stocks of environmental assets (b_t) as an explicit argument in the utility function, i.e., writing utility as $u(c_t, b_t)$ rather than simply $u(c_t)$, and by placing some weight in the objective function on the long run. Note, however, that this only captures an anthropocentric notion of the intrinsic value of the environmental assets.

15. Of course, agricultural production is also a demander of ecosystem services and can be a source of significant ecosystem degradation. See Heal and Small (2002) for an overview of agriculture as both a demander and supplier of ecosystem services.

16. There is support in both the theoretical and the empirical literature for the link between natural amenities and economic growth and migration. Wu and Mishra (Chapter 7, this volume) summarize this literature and provide additional empirical evidence regarding this link. Irwin et al. (Chapter 6, this volume) develop a theoretical model that examines the conditions under which natural amenities can drive economic growth in rural areas through migration.

CHAPTER 14

The Future of Rural America Through a Social-Demographic Lens

David L. Brown

HE TERM *RURAL AMERICA* evokes an image of stability, a repository of unchanging structures and institutions, a buffer against rapid social and economic change. Although rural norms and values are more resistant to change than those in urban areas (Beale 1995), rural institutions and economic structures have been transformed along with those elsewhere in society. Accordingly, structural *change,* not structural *stability,* is the typical situation in rural America. As Fuguitt and his colleagues concluded in their comprehensive analysis of rural and small town demography, "These changes have been pervasive, affecting people in rural and small town settings as well as those who live in more highly urbanized and densely settled locales" (1989, *425*).

This chapter examines rural change through a social-demographic lens. This perspective contends that population dynamics affect and are affected by changes in social institutions, the natural environment, economic transformations, culture, and public policy (Brown and Kandel 2006). For example, although urbanization can be considered a strictly demographic process of population redistribution (Tisdale 1942), social demographers broaden the inquiry by examining how population concentration affects people's life chances, health, and social norms, for instance, and how these changes in turn affect rates of natural increase occurring in various types of areas, and the direction of migration flows.

Below, I examine major dimensions of rural demographic and socioeconomic change during the last quarter-century, the nature and magnitude of these changes, and their implications for the future of rural America as a place to live and work. My benchmark for discussing these changes is 1970, the year I entered the Ph.D. program at the University of Wisconsin and became a professional social scientist.

I will confine my analysis of social-demographic changes to four general themes that have been shown to characterize rural population dynamics during the recent past:[1]

- the rural population's changing size and increasing demographic diversity;

- changing rural livelihoods;

- the incorporation of rural people and communities into expanding metropolitan regions; and

- winners and losers: new opportunities for some areas and persisting disadvantage for others.

It is important to recognize that many of the changes affecting rural people and communities are a continuation of long-term transformations and hence would have been predictable in 1970. Other changes, in contrast, are distinct breaks with the past and would have been inconceivable at that time. The lesson I draw from this is that we social scientists must be humble about our ability to forecast the future. These reservations aside, and with all modesty, my goal in this chapter is to identify social-demographic changes that will affect rural opportunities and the quality of life over the next generation.

Demographic Changes

Population size. The nonmetropolitan population[2] has been relatively stable, at 54 million to 56 million, since 1970. However, while the absolute size of the non-metro population has remained about the same, its share of the total U.S. population has declined substantially, from 27.2 percent in 1970 to 19.9 percent in 2000 (Table 14-1).[3] Two main reasons account for the metropolitan category's increasing share since 1970. First, international migration became an increasingly important component of national population growth during this time, and although some migrants move directly to nonmetro areas, most settle in metropolitan gateways (Zuniga and Hernandez-Leon 2005). The second reason for the declining non-metro share is that rapidly growing nonmetropolitan counties are continuously creamed off into the metropolitan category as a result of the reclassification process that follows each decennial census. Hence, reclassification not only shifts counties from the nonmetropolitan to the metropolitan category but also results in a slower-growing nonmetropolitan residual population.

Given the nonmetro sector's declining share of the U.S. population over the past quarter-century, can internal migration reverse the trend? Much has been written about the increased importance of internal migration as a component of the relative rates of population change between metropolitan and nonmetropolitan areas. However, as demonstrated by the rural population turnaround of the 1970s, its reversal during the 1980s, and the nonmetro rebound of the first part of the 1990s, the direction of net migration has become variable, and increases in one decade have tended to counterbalance losses in others (Johnson and Cromartie 2006). Hence, it is difficult to envision this component of change reversing the nonmetro sector's long-term decline.

Social demographers have studied the shifting balance of net internal migration between metropolitan and nonmetropolitan counties for more than 50 years, and

Table 14-1. *Population Size and Composition of Nonmetropolitan U.S. Counties, 1970 and 2000*

	1970[a]	2000
Population (million)	54,388.0	56,078.0
Percentage of U.S. total	27.2	19.9
Median age	28.1	37.0
Percentage 65+	11.1	14.6
Percentage younger than 18	35.8	28.2
Percentage African American	9.4	8.5
Percentage Hispanic[b]	2.6	5.7
Regional distribution (total)		
Northeast	13.3	9.8
Midwest	31.6	30.2
West	12.5	15.5
South	42.6	44.5
Regional distribution (African American)		
Northeast	1.7	1.2
Midwest	4.8	6.0
West	1.5	1.6
South	92.2	90.2
Regional distribution (Hispanic)		
Northeast	2.7	3.1
Midwest	15.9	12.9
West	60.6	37.6
South	21.1	46.3

Sources: U.S. Census of Population 2000; 1970 data from Current Population Report, P-23, No. 35.

[a] 1970 nonmetro counties do not include those reclassified as metro in 1973.

[b] Spanish origin in 1970.

many have concluded that social and economic restructuring, improved transportation and communication infrastructure, and other aspects of rural modernization have resulted in a process of rural-urban convergence that when combined with a notable preference for smaller places facilitates both suburban expansion and rural population deconcentration (Brown et al. 1997). Although I am in substantial agreement with these assessments, I disagree with scholars who predict continuous metro-to-nonmetro net migration and rural-urban population deconcentration in the future. My own assessment is that migration-led population deconcentration is contingent on favorable economic conditions in rural communities and labor markets. In other words, I expect the direction of net migration to be toward nonmetropolitan areas when relative economic conditions are favorable there, but not when metro areas are economically better off. Over the long term, then, I expect internal migration gains in nonmetro counties during economically successful decades to be cancelled out by net losses in times of nonmetro economic weakness. Hence, I do not expect metro-to-nonmetro migration to reverse the nonmetro category's diminishing share of the U.S. population over the next several decades. Moreover, since metro areas capture the lion's share of international migration, positive net internal migration from metro to nonmetro areas will serve only to slow the nonmetro category's declining share of the nation's population. This prediction of a declining rural share of the nation's population could have been made in 1970 only if one expected continuous net out-migration from nonmetro to metro areas, since international migration's growing contribution to metro population growth was not anticipated at the time. In fact, many scholars in the 1970s predicted an "end of international migration" (Livi Bacci 1974).

Population composition. The people of rural America look dramatically different today than in 1970, especially with respect to age and race and ethnic composition (Kirschner et al. 2006). For example, the median age of the nonmetro population increased by 9 years between 1970 and 2000, from 28.1 years to 37 years (Table 14-1). This unprecedented increase in population aging is the result of substantial declines in younger persons combined with increases in persons age 65 and older. Although dramatic, this aging trend would have been predictable in 1970 because the demographic processes accounting for it had already begun at that time. The baby boom had been replaced by historically low rates of fertility in both urban and rural areas (Fuguitt et al. 1989). Although rural fertility still exceeded that in urban areas in 1970, childbearing rates in both residence categories had declined significantly from the baby boom highs experienced during the 1950s and 1960s. Persons aged 65 and older had also begun to increase as a percentage of the nonmetro population by the 1970s. As Fuguitt and his colleagues showed in their 1989 book, the increased proportion of rural persons age 65 and older was mostly a result of aging in place (i.e., younger persons surviving to age 65), but in-migration of older persons to rural retirement destinations had also began by the late 1960s and accelerated in the 1970s. In other words, rural aging was a result of both "natural increase" and net in-migration, although the relative importance of these two processes differed in different regions.

Today the primary determinants of the continued aging of the nonmetro population are not much different than in the 1970s, except that these processes appear to be stronger. Fertility remains low by historical standards, and nonmetro fertility dropped below metro fertility for the first time in American history during the 1990s (Johnson and Cromartie 2006; Long and Nucci 1998). As a result, the number of counties experiencing natural decrease—more deaths than births—almost doubled, from around 500 in 1990 to almost 1,000 in 2000, and the vast majority of these counties are rural (Johnson 2004). Moreover, retirement migration to rural destinations also accelerated. The number of U.S. counties with 15 percent or higher immigration at ages 60-plus increased from 190 in 1990 to 277 in 2000. This number will probably increase even more dramatically in the near future as the baby boom cohorts age into their retirement years. To the extent that these aging baby boomers are geographically mobile, a disproportionate number can be expected to find their way to nonmetropolitan retirement destinations (Glasgow and Brown 2006).[4]

Rural America is also much more ethnically diverse today than in 1970. At that time 9.4 percent of nonmetro persons were African American and only 2.6 percent were Hispanic.[5] Moreover, 92 percent of nonmetro African Americans lived in the South, which was 20 percent African American at the time, and almost two-thirds of nonmetro Hispanics lived in the West. Today, African Americans still account for about the same proportion of the nonmetro population (8.5 percent) and are still overwhelmingly located in the South (Table 14-1). In contrast, Hispanics have more than doubled, to 5.7 percent of the nonmetro population, and they are much less highly concentrated in the West. In fact, according to the 2000 census, a higher proportion of nonmetro Hispanics live in the South than in the West. The dramatic growth and redistribution of the Hispanic population would not have been predicted in 1970. It represents one of the most important population changes in contemporary rural America. I expect this trend to intensify in the future as a result of continued immigration from Mexico and other parts of Latin America, and labor deficits in low-wage rural industries such as food processing and tourism where domestic workers are reluctant to obtain jobs (Kandel and Parrado 2006).

Douglas Massey and his associates have written eloquently about the United States–Mexico migration system. As Durand et al. (2005, *18*) have observed, "In a few short years Mexican immigration has been transformed from a narrowly focused process affecting just three states into a nationwide movement." These authors are mostly referring to the spread of Mexican migration from traditional gateways to a broad range of cities and regions, but nonmetropolitan destinations have also received their share. Some of this nonmetro-destined migration involves farmworkers, but the majority does not. Direct migration from Mexico to nonmetro communities is strongly motivated by economic factors and involves jobs in a variety of food-processing activities, other manufacturing, construction, and personal services. In addition to Hispanic in-migrants, most of whom are from Mexico, nonmetro communities have also begun to receive new residents from a wide variety of Asian nations. Some of these persons are highly educated and fill professional and entrepreneurial niches; others work alongside Mexicans in meat processing, construction, and low-paid service jobs in the tourism industry.

Changing Rural Livelihoods

Economic restructuring. The notion of a rural economy that is heavily dependent on resource-based activities has been anachronistic for several decades. Even in 1970, less than 20 percent of nonmetro workers held jobs in farming, forestry, mining, and other extractive pursuits (Table 14-2). By 2000 this figure had declined to 9.6 percent. Although dependence on extractive jobs was notably higher in some regions than in others, even in these places economic restructuring had already begun to delink farming and other traditional resource-based industries from rural life. The now-familiar story is that the rural economy has gone through two long-term transformations—from heavy dependence on extractive industries to greater reliance on manufacturing and goods production, and then, along with the rest of the U.S. economy, to much greater dependence on services. In 1970, service jobs (including public administration) already accounted for one-third of nonmetro employment, and this number has increased to 4 of every 10 nonmetro jobs at the present time. Manufacturing, in contrast, declined from about 20 percent of nonmetro jobs in 1970 to

15 percent in 2000 (Table 14-2).[6] Even though manufacturing has held on to its share of nonmetro jobs better than in metro areas, the trend is still toward less reliance on goods production than was true a generation ago (Vias and Nelson 2006).

The significant increase in services shown in Table 14-2 is important not simply because of the increased number of service jobs, but also because of the changing composition of income generated by these occupations. U.S. Bureau of Economic Analysis data on earnings by industry (not shown here) permit one to disaggregate earnings from services by type of job. These data show that while the share of all employment attributable to all kinds of services increased by 55 percent during 1970–2000, the share of earnings from professional services in specific areas increased by more than 85 percent, to 13.2 percent of all nonmetro earnings. Accordingly, professional services have become a much more important source of nonmetro income than was true a generation ago.

Although the future sectoral composition of the rural economy is not entirely clear, it seems likely that professional services will continue to increase as a source of nonmetro income. Some of this increase will be associated with the rising demand for health care associated with the aging of the baby boomers and the migration of relatively well off retirees to particular rural communities. It is not clear, however, whether an increase in producer services is also to be expected. Regardless, increases in professional services occupations can be expected to enhance rural income and well-being in the future.

In contrast to the optimistic scenario for professional services, the situation for manufacturing is less rosy. The deregulated global economy with its neoliberal trade policies is likely to wring several more percentage points from manufacturing's share of rural economic activity. However, by 2030, I expect this decline to stabilize, with manufacturing's share of nonmetro jobs settling somewhere between 10 and 12 percent. Unfortunately, this relative stability will likely be accomplished by par-

Table 14-2. *Selected Characteristics of Nonmetropolitan Economies and Workers, 1970 and 2000*

	1970	2000
Percentage who cross county line for work	19.0	27.0
Percentage of women in labor force	38.4	54.3
Industry of employment		
Extraction (agriculture, forestry, fishing, mining)	17.3	9.6
Construction	4.4	5.8
Manufacturing	20.1	15.4
Transport, communication, utilities	4.2	4.1
Wholesale trade	2.4	3.1
Retail trade	14.6	16.8
Finance, insurance, real estate	2.4	3.1
Services	15.4	23.9
Public administration	17.3	16.1

Sources: 1970 demographic data from Current Population Report, P-23, No. 35; employment data from Bureau of Economic Analysis. 2000 demographic data from 2000 Census; employment data from Bureau of Economic Analysis.

ticipating in the "race to the bottom," by competition for low-wage, peripheral-sector jobs; by continuing to resist organized labor's efforts to improve wages and benefits; and by providing employers with subsidies that diminish the benefits of locating a plant in one's community. Current data show that nonmetro manufacturing firms already pay their workers markedly lower wages than is true in metro areas, and this relative wage has diminished over the past generation. As Vias and Nelson (2006) have shown, the ratio of metro to nonmetro manufacturing wages declined from 78 percent in 1970 to only 70 percent in 2000. Some of this difference reflects the greater prevalence of durable manufacturing in metro areas, but some of it reflects lower pay for similar jobs in similar firms. Moreover, the loss of U.S. manufacturing jobs can be expected to slow in the future if ethnic minority workers continue to arrive in such large numbers that an attractive low-wage domestic labor supply in both metro and nonmetro labor markets is assured. In other words, rather than off-shoring jobs to less developed countries, manufacturers now have the option of importing low-wage workers for domestic production.

Commuting. Another important dimension of rural economic change concerns the increasing separation of workplace from place of residence. In 1970, 19 percent of nonmetro workers traveled to another county for work, compared with 27 percent in 2000 (Tigges and Fuguitt 2003), and by 1990 more than 40 percent of employed persons were intercounty commuters in 20 percent of nonmetro counties (ERS 2002).[7] This process has led to increasing interdependence among nonmetro areas and between them and their metro neighbors. In addition, recent research in England shows that long-distance rural commuting is intensified by in-migration to rural areas. Champion et al. (2007) showed that rural in-migrants were 1.6 times as likely as nonmigrants with similar characteristics to commute 20 km or more to work.

Increased commuting indicates that nonmetro areas are taking on an essentially residential function and leaving the employment and commercial functions to their more highly urbanized neighbors. Researchers have not carefully considered the social and economic implications of this process of separation. How does increased commuting affect gasoline usage and carbon emissions? Where do commuters shop and obtain professional services (Green 2001)? Does heightened commuting indicate that income needed to support residential services is leaking from rural communities? Does time spent commuting diminish residents' availability to participate in local society (Putnam 2000)? Researchers need to examine these questions to determine whether predominately residential rural communities will be able to maintain a reasonable quality of life.

Amenity-based development. Many analysts have pointed to the increasing rural dependence on amenity-based jobs—those in recreation, tourism, and retirement. U.S. Bureau of Economic Analysis data (not shown here) indicate that entertainment, recreation, and tourism increased from 1.1 to 1.8 percent of nonmetro earnings between 1970 and 2000. Although this is a high rate of increase, it is still a small share of all income from nonmetro jobs. Still, with the aging of the baby boomers and the likely migration of many more retirees to nonmetro destinations, recreation- and retirement-related jobs will undoubtedly increase in the future.

As with commuting, it is not immediately obvious whether increased dependence on recreation and retirement bodes well or ill for nonmetro communities, and although there is some overlap, retirement migration destinations should probably be considered separately from tourism areas. Because retirees have relatively high incomes and can effectively demand a wide variety of goods and services, this trend is probably beneficial for destination communities (Glasgow and Reeder 1990; Stallman et al. 1999). Moreover, recent research indicates that retirement migration brings social as well as economic benefits, since retiree in-migrants quickly establish ties in their new communities and participate in a wide range of social and voluntary organizations (Brown and Glasgow 2008).

Increased dependence on recreation and tourism may also benefit rural America. A recent study by the U.S. Department of Agriculture's Economic Research Service found that median household income was more than $3,000 higher in the 311 counties identified by that agency as having a high dependency on recreation and tourism compared with other nonmetropolitan counties. Even though many tourism-related jobs are low-wage, seasonal positions with little possibility for career advancement, it appears that increased dependence on these sectors has an overall positive effect on rural economic development. Future research, however, should also consider whether and how dependence on recreation and tourism adversely affects income distribution (Reeder and Brown 2005).

In summary, rural America's economic future is uncertain, and despite some cause for optimism, not all current trends suggest that tomorrow's rural economy will be distinctly better than the current situation. Rural communities are likely to take on an increasingly residential function in the future, with most jobs and service and commercial establishments located elsewhere. To the extent that rural economies are able to retain their manufacturing base, these jobs are likely to be in firms producing nondurable products and offering low wages and skimpy benefits. Tourism and recreation are likely to become a larger part of rural economic activity in the future, and this appears to have beneficial effects on income and other measures of economic well-being. However, since many of the jobs in this industry are low paying, seasonal, and offer little career advancement, increased dependence on recreation and tourism may have deleterious effects on income distribution. Retirement destination communities are also likely to proliferate in the future in response to the aging of the baby boomers, and this trend may offer opportunities in well-paying professional and service industries such as health care, and other benefits such as organizational leadership and technical expertise.

Expanding Metropolises

America's metropolitan areas have been expanding outward since at least the 1920s. Writing in 1959, Leo Schnore showed that almost one-third of metropolitan areas with 100,000 population in 1950 had begun to decentralize by the 1920s, and almost two-thirds were growing more rapidly at their peripheries than in their centers a decade later. As Hawley observed in 1956, "Suburbanization is old stuff" (89). Relatively high rates of population growth in selected nonmetropolitan areas that are located adjacent to existing metropolitan statistical areas plus the Office of Management and Budget's adoption of the more permissive[8] core-based system for delineating metropolitan areas resulted in the reclassification of 298 counties from nonmetropolitan to metropolitan between 1990 and 2000. Four-fifths of these new metropolitan counties (236 of 298) were peripheral additions to existing metropolitan areas.

Given the fundamental structure of metropolitan areas and the manner in which they grow and expand, scholarship necessarily focuses on both the establishment of new centers and changing patterns of social and economic integration between the center (or centers) and outlying areas. Many scholars have observed that metropolitan regions are characterized by functional interdependence between core and periphery areas, but these relationships are not egalitarian: the center dominates and organizes its hinterland (Tilly 1974). Accordingly, much urban scholarship tends to focus on the center. In this view, the periphery lacks agency and is passively absorbed by the more highly organized urban "growth machine" (Logan and Molotch 1988). This coalition of growth advocates commodifies rural land and overcomes more diffuse rural interests that prize land for its use value (Molotch 1976; Logan and Crowder 2002). In other words, metropolitan expansion is seen as an unstoppable process with its own political-economic dynamic.

John Cromartie (2006) has described a four-stage developmental framework for understanding the demographic processes that result in enhanced rural integration within the metropolitan sphere. In stage 1, rural areas experience little or no metro influence, but in stage 4, these same areas are fully incorporated into the metro economy and community. In between these two end states, rural areas become increasingly integrated through heightened commuting and population deconcentration from the center. These demographic processes are accompanied by the development of transportation infrastructure, new residential subdivisions and commercial centers, and changing land use and landscape patterns. This is not necessarily a continuous or linear process, and each of the four stages has its own set of challenges. Nonetheless, for better or for worse, the trend for many of America's rural communities is closer integration within expanding metropolitan regions.

Metropolitan expansion raises concerns about unplanned rural land use change (Daniels 1999). Rural interests in particular are concerned that metropolitan expansion into previously rural territory will result in dramatic increases in the rate of conversion of rural land to urban and built-up uses. Research by Pfeffer et al. (2006) shows that when farmland is sold in metropolitan counties, it tends to be converted to nonfarm uses, but that farmland sales in nonmetropolitan areas contribute to further consolidation and concentration within agriculture. In other words, conversion of farmland to urban and built-up uses is contingent on where it is located.

Although Department of Agriculture research shows a continuous pattern of rural to urban land use conversion during the past 50 years, the rate of conversion has been relatively low; it has declined from 3.5 percent per year in the 1960s and 1970s, to 1.8 percent per year in the 1980s, to 1.4 percent annually in the 1990s (ERS 2005).[9] In 1997, The U.S. Department of Agriculture's Natural Resource Inventory estimated that 73 million acres of U.S. land were in urban use (Census calculated 61 million acres). The inventory shows that urban land use has been stable at around 3 percent of the nation's land base since 1945, and cropland has been stable at about 20 percent. During this same time, the proportion of land in forest use has increased, and the proportion used for grazing has declined. So although metropolitan expansion does result in the conversion of rural to urban land, the magnitude of the change is not large. Moreover, given the relatively low rate of change in the number of U.S. households, there is little reason to fear that demographic pressures will result in large-scale losses of farmland in the foreseeable future (Brown et al. 1982). This is not to deny that farmland conversion might not be a significant problem in particular regions or specific locales, but such losses will not undermine the nation's ability to raise a sufficient amount of food and fiber to satisfy both domestic needs and international demand.

Winners and Losers

Rural America's overall socioeconomic condition has improved markedly from 1970 to 2000. As shown in Table 14-3, average income increased, the poverty rate declined, and educational attainment improved. However, not all areas have benefited from these improving conditions. Rural America is extremely diverse, and during the past several decades, successful areas have become bifurcated from areas left behind in persistent disadvantage.

As indicated in the previous section on rural livelihoods, some rural areas are finding new economic vitality because they are within commuting range of nearby metropolitan centers, because their natural amenities support tourism and recreational development, or because retirees have chosen to move there. In each instance, these new economic bases appear to have attracted younger, wealthier, healthier, and better-educated populations than the longer-term residents they join. For example, although retirement destinations are defined by their higher-than-average immigration rate among retirement-age persons, they also attract working-age migrants to fill service jobs generated by the growing presence of a relatively large number of well-off older residents. Even though many of these jobs are in low-paid service industries, some are in health care, financial services, and

Table 14-3. *Socioeconomic Characteristics of Nonmetropolitan Population, 1970 and 2000*

	1970	2000
Median family income	9,314	34,600
Percentage in poverty	19.1	11.3
Percentage less than high school graduates	54.2	23.2
Percentage college graduates	7.6	15.5

Sources: U.S. Census of Population 2000; 1970 data from Current Population Report, P-23, No. 35.

other well-paying professions (Brown and Glasgow 2008). Similarly, although many recreation and tourism jobs are seasonal and low paying, recreation development appears to elevate median household incomes in such areas, even after adjusting for higher housing prices and increases in the overall cost of living (Reeder and Brown 2005). Finally, commuters may procure goods and services where they work, leaking income from the community, but commuters also buy houses or rent apartments where they live, pay real estate taxes, patronize local stores, join religious congregations, and participate in clubs, the PTA, and other local service organizations. So although having a large proportion of the population living in one place and working in another may not be optimal for community and economic development, it is preferable to the wholesale abandonment of rural places in favor of residences that are closer to work. Everything considered, then, recreation-, retirement-, and commuting-dependent areas appear to be today's rural winners.

In contrast, the overall rural situation is less optimistic. Nonmetro median household income lagged metro income by more than $10,000 in 2003 ($35,112 versus $46,060), and more than 14 percent of nonmetro residents (7.5 million persons) were poor compared with 12 percent of their metropolitan counterparts. Moreover, rural poverty is not evenly spread among demographic groups or regions (see Figure 14-1). A third or more of nonmetro African Americans and Native Americans were poor in 2002, and the poverty rate among Hispanics was 26.7 percent. In contrast, only 11 percent of nonmetro non-Hispanic whites were poor at this time (ERS 2004).

Nonmetro poverty also has a distinctive geographic pattern, and some rural areas have been continuously mired in deep disadvantage throughout the past generation. According to the 2000 census, about 12 percent of persons who live in highly urbanized nonmetro counties within commuting range of a nearby metro center were poor, but this rate increases regularly as one descends the urban hierarchy.

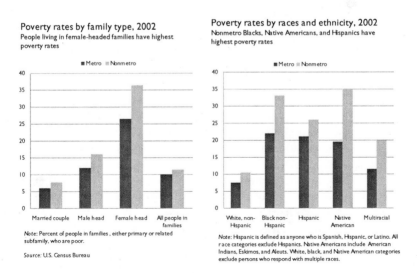

Poverty rates by family type, 2002
People living in female-headed families have highest poverty rates

Note: Percent of people in families, either primary or related subfamily, who are poor.

Source: U.S. Census Bureau

Poverty rates by races and ethnicity, 2002
Nonmetro Blacks, Native Americans, and Hispanics have highest poverty rates

Note: Hispanic is defined as anyone who is Spanish, Hispanic, or Latino. All race categories exclude Hispanics. Native Americans include American Indians, Eskimos, and Aleuts. White, black, and Native American categories exclude persons who respond with multiple races.

Figure 14-1. *Poverty Rates for Selected Groups*

More than 17 percent of persons living in completely rural counties that are not adjacent to a metro area were poor at the time of the last census.

Nonmetro poverty also has a regional pattern, being highest in the South and West and lowest in the Northeast. Within the South and West, deep economic depression is concentrated in particular areas. The Economic Research Service has identified 386 counties that have had poverty rates of at least 20 percent in each census since 1970. The vast majority of these persistent-poverty areas (340 out of 386) are nonmetropolitan, and they are clustered in Appalachia, across the mid-South, in the Mississippi Delta, the Rio Grande Valley, and in Indian country. Almost one-quarter of the South's nonmetropolitan population lives in these chronically depressed areas (ERS 2004).

Persistent rural poverty in the United States has become self-perpetuating. It is a function of past legacies of discrimination, racism, rigid stratification, and patronage systems that regulate access to education, jobs, and other opportunities (Duncan 1999; Billings and Blee 2000; Harris and Worthen 2003). Moreover, the fact that 340 nonmetro counties have had 20 percent or higher poverty rates continuously since 1970 indicates that the substantial public investments in regional economic development and poverty alleviation have not accomplished their goals of ameliorating deprivation in areas of concentrated disadvantage. Short of a public works program of unprecedented proportions targeted to persistently poor rural areas, there is no reason to expect these depressed areas to improve their social and economic security and overall well-being in the foreseeable future. Historical legacies and contemporary structures associated with class and race constrain pathways to a better future. It is likely that the majority of these persistently poor rural areas will remain in this disadvantaged situation for decades to come.

The Future of Rural America

The demographic trends and changes discussed in this chapter and the predictions I make about these issues are summarized in Table 14-3. In brief, I predict that the rural population will continue to decline as a percentage of the nation's total population even as it remains about the same absolute size. Population gains in one decade will likely be counterbalanced by declines in the next to yield little population growth over a significant time horizon. Urban populations will grow more rapidly because the vast majority of immigrants, the major source of contemporary population growth in the United States, will continue to concentrate here. In addition, continued natural decrease in the Plains states and retirement in-migration elsewhere will continue to age the rural population. Rural areas will also become more ethnically diverse as a result of immigration. In particular, it seems likely that Hispanics will continue to grow as a component of the rural population, and their presence will continue to spread from their original regional location in the Southwest.

With respect to the restructuring of economic activities, I expect manufacturing and other forms of goods production to stabilize at about 10 to 12 percent of rural jobs. Most new manufacturing establishments are not being created in the United States or in other developed nations, and there is no reason to expect that rural or

Table 14-3. *Rural Futures over the Next Generation*

Issues, trends since 1970	Predictable in 1970?	Forecast over next generation
Changing demographics		
1. Declining rural (nonmetro) share of total population	No	Continued decline in rural (nonmetro) share
2. Aging of rural population	Yes	Continued aging
3. Increased racial, ethnic diversity, and regional redistribution	No	Continued Hispanic increase in South and Midwest
Changing rural livelihoods		
4. Slowed pace of restructuring from goods production to services; growth in professional services	Yes and no	Leveling off of decline in goods production; low pay for many new manufacturing jobs; continued growth in professional services, especially in health sector, but not necessarily in producer services sector
5. Increased rural-to-urban commuting	Yes	Increasingly residential function for rural areas
6. Increased dependence on amenity-based industries	Yes	Dependence on amenity-based industries, with possibility of increased income inequality
Rural incorporation into metro areas		
7. Greater social and economic integration of rural into metro sphere	Yes	Continued growth of metro dominance
8. Slow but steady conversion of farmland to urban and built-up uses	Yes	Continued slow, gradual land conversion to urban uses
Winners and losers		
9. Winners: recreation, retirement, commuting	Yes	Continued higher than average growth, but equity implications uncertain
10. Losers: persistent underdevelopment and chronic poverty in parts of South and Southwest and among minorities	Yes	Continued disadvantage in these areas and population subgroups

urban America will experience a surge in manufacturing employment. However, rural economies, especially in the South, should be better able to compete for manufacturing employment than their urban counterparts because of their lower wage structures, fewer regulations, relative lack of unionization, and lower taxes (McGranahan 2001; ERS 2006). As is true in the rest of the nation, net job growth in rural economies will be concentrated in the service sector. However, rural service growth is likely to be rather specialized, especially in niches associated with amenity-related industries and residential functions. It is unclear whether economies concentrated on such specialized bases will produce a high proportion of well-paying jobs or heighten income inequality and social separation between the owners of capital and the low-skill workers who provide personal and consumer services. The share of nonmetro earnings from professional services has increased dramatically during the past 30 years, and it is likely to continue to do so in the future. Health services, in particular, will likely expand in rural areas, but it is uncertain whether rural economies can expect an increase in well-paying producer services as well.

Many rural communities are assuming an increasingly residential function as more working-age persons commute to jobs in nearby (and not so nearby) metropolitan areas. It is unclear how this increased separation between place of residence and place of work will affect rural communities in the future. Many observers are concerned that commuters will spend most of their income where they work; other observers see the division between place of residence and place of work as a potentially beneficial partnership through which both localities are able to prosper.

Metropolitan areas expanded outward during the twentieth century, incorporating rural population and territory, and it is likely that this process will continue, with implications for local social organization, the location of economic activities, and protection of the natural environment. However, as for the increase in rural-to-urban commuting, it is not clear whether further urban expansion will positively or negatively affect the rural social or natural environment. For example, research by Heimlich and Anderson (2001) shows that farming is quite profitable in the city's "shadow," and the pace of urban land conversion, while steady, has not accelerated during the past half-century (Lubowski et al. 2006). Rural incorporation in the metropolitan economy, more rural-to-urban commuting, amenity-oriented rural development, retirement migration, and stable or slowly growing population size may all provide opportunities for rural development in the future, but these opportunities present themselves at the same time that poor and underdeveloped rural communities persist and are largely invisible on the policy agenda. Moreover, the increase in the rural Hispanic population and its redistribution into the South and Midwest raise concerns of spreading rural inequality and disadvantage.

Implications of the Trends and Changes

The trends and changes portrayed in this paper identify opportunities as well as challenges for rural people and communities. Sociodemographic transformations induce changes in other aspects of community, but the effects of population change on local society are not automatic. They are mediated by local social structure and by the larger structural and policy environments in which localities are embedded. To assume that a unit change in population size or composition automatically and mechanistically results in a similar magnitude of change in economic activity, poverty reduction, farmland conversion, or public service utilization is to deny the agency of actors and the instrumentality of community institutions. The demographic changes described in this chapter could result in smaller, older, and poorer rural populations; declining communities; and increasing domination by external forces. But an alternative future might be innovative communities taking advantage of niche opportunities, creatively turning national and global processes to their own advantage, effectively incorporating ethnically diverse citizens into community institutions, and maintaining valued ways of life. The translation of these sociodemographic changes into enhanced or diminished rural well-being is contingent on how individual communities position themselves with respect to external forces and whether, during this era of devolution and privatization, federal and state governments are able and willing to develop strategies and policies that facilitate meaningful social and economic life in the nation's geographic periphery.

Although global and national forces have the potential to undermine localities, communities with strong social structures are better able to mediate these forces and negotiate effectively with external actors. Much has been written about the type of local social organization that succeeds best in the global environment (Flora and Flora 2003; Luloff and Bridger 2003; Lyson and Tolbert 2003). Community development scholars disagree on the exact nature of local social structures that contribute most to community viability, but they do agree that strong and responsive social organization is needed for rural America to avoid being overwhelmed by globalization.

What is not understood, however, is why effective community social organization is more likely to emerge in some populations than in others. The answer to this question cannot be obtained by simply comparing contemporary situations. Researchers need to examine the historical and political roots of contemporary inequality and be cognizant of the constraints that these legacies place on the capacity of communities to democratically determine their future development paths[10] (Schafft and Brown 2003). Rural developers cannot simply travel the countryside admonishing rural people to develop stronger communities. Social exclusion and other detrimental characteristics that weaken community have developed over time, and hierarchical power relations will not be easily flattened

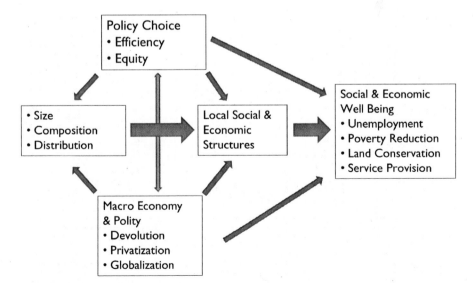

Figure 14-2. *Localities Are Embedded in Macro Structural and Policy Environments*

regardless of the promise of enhanced community-wide benefit (Duncan 1999). A community that excluded African Americans or coal miners in the past is not likely to include new Hispanic residents who work in the nearby chicken plant today. Research on community power shows that communities with a high degree of concentrated power and social exclusion are not sustainable (Tolbert et al. 2002; Flora et al. 1992). A small number of well-off residents or absentee owners may reap short-term rewards, but over the long term, such places will do poorly. Accordingly, strong local communities are a key to rural America's future in the globalized world, and development of such communities is contingent on a free, open, and inclusive contestation between ideas and interests. Social science research can contribute to strengthening communities by providing evidence-based information about the manner in which different configurations of power shape the capacity for community self-determination.

The research agenda that is shaped and motivated by this and the other questions raised in this chapter requires creative multidisciplinary conceptualizations, research designs, and analytical strategies. No single discipline has a corner on this area of research. Economists, sociologists, geographers, demographers, and political scientists can all contribute to the systematic analysis of rural economy and society.

The demographic transformations discussed in this chapter have distinct implications for rural America's social and economic well-being. These implications are at least partly contingent on whether state and federal governments promote and facilitate rural development, or whether they conclude that rural places are inefficient and do not merit public support. As Drabenstott et al. (1987) observed 20 years ago, the rural policy choice is between state actions to encourage population and economic retention in rural areas, or a deregulated market-driven policy that encourages capital and labor to move from underperforming rural economies to more efficient sites of production (see also Brown 1998).

Strong social structure and effective government policies go hand in hand. Moreover, policy prescriptions must be attentive and responsive to the historical and political roots of contemporary inequality in wealth, power, and opportunity between and within places. Subsidizing private business or public service provision in weak communities may produce a short-term respite, but for sustainable development to occur, localities have to produce equitable and accessible institutions that spread the benefits of growth widely, and they must promote accountable community institutions that accomplish long-run communal goals.

The demographic trends and changes described in this chapter could propel rural people and communities on either an upward or a downward trajectory, depending on the future rural development choices we make at the local, state, and national levels. The future of rural America depends on this difficult policy choice. Challenges will not become opportunities without an informed public debate, and a well-articulated strategy that maps out clear options for public and private actions and investments. Social scientists have a role in informing this policy choice. Rigorous research into the determinants and consequences of rural development and underdevelopment will increase the likelihood that rural people and communities will have options and opportunities in the future.

References

Beale, C. 1995. The Non-Economic Value of Rural America. Paper presented at USDA experts workshop on the value of rural America, Washington, DC.

Billings, D., and K. Blee. 2000. *The Road to Poverty: The Making of Wealth and Hardship in Appalachia*. New York: Cambridge University Press.

Brown, D.L. 1998. Enhancing the Spatial Policy Choice with Ecological Analysis. In *Continuities in Sociological Human Ecology*, edited by M. Micklin and D. Poston. New York: Plenum, 195–213.

D.L. Brown, and Glasgow, N.. 2007. *Rural Retirement Migration*. Dordrecht: Springer.

Brown, D.L., and W. Kandel. 2006. Rural America through a Demographic Lens. In *Population Change and Rural Society*, edited by W. Kandel and D.L. Brown. Dordrecht: Springer, 3–23.

Brown, D.L., and L. Swanson (eds.). 2003. *Challenges for Rural America in the 21st Century*. University Park: Penn State University Press.

Brown, D.L., M. Brewer, R. Boxley, and C. Beale. 1982. Assessing Prospects for the Adequacy of Agricultural Land. *International Regional Science Review* 7(3): 273–85.

Brown, D.L., G.V. Fuguitt, T. Heaton, and S. Waseem. 1997. Continuities in Size of Place Preferences in the United States. *Rural Sociology* 62(4): 408–28.

Champion, T., M. Coombes, D.L. Brown. 2007. In-commuting and Longer Distance Commuting in England, 2001. Paper presented to annual meeting of the Population Association of America, New York, March 31.

Cromartie, J. 2006. Metro Expansion and Nonmetro Change in the South. In *Population Change and Rural Society*, edited by W. Kandel and D.L. Brown. Dordrecht: Springer, 233–53.

Daniels, T. 1999. *When City and Country Collide*. Washington, DC: Island Press.

Drabenstott, M., M. Henry, and L. Gibson. 1987. The Rural Economic Policy Choice. *Economic Review* 72: 41–58.

Duncan, C. 1999. *Worlds Apart: Why Poverty Persists in Rural America*. New Haven: Yale University Press.

Durand, J., D. Massey, and C. Capoferro. 2005. The New Geography of Mexican Migration. In *New Destinations: Mexican Immigration in the United States,* edited by V. Zuniga and R. Hernandez-Leon. New York: Russell Sage Foundation, 1–20.

Economic Research Service (ERS). 2002. Measuring Rurality: County Typology Codes. Washington, DC: U.S. Department of Agriculture.

———. 2004. Rural Poverty at a Glance. RDRR No. 100. Washington, DC: U.S. Department of Agriculture.

———. 2005. Land Use, Value and Management: Urbanization and Agricultural Land Briefing Room. www.ers.usda.gov/briefing/landuse/urbanchapter/htm.

———. 2006. Rural Income, Poverty, and Welfare: Non-farm Earnings. www.ers.usda.gov/briefing/incomepovertywelfare/nonfarmearnings/htm. Washington, DC: U.S. Department of Agriculture.

Flora, C., and J. Flora. 2003. Social Capital. In *Challenges for Rural America in the 21st Century*, edited by D.L. Brown and L. Swanson. University Park: Penn State University Press, 214–27.

Flora, C., J. Flora, J. Spears, L. Swanson, M. Lapping, and M. Weinberg. 1992. *Rural Communities: Legacy and Change*. Boulder: Westview Press.

Fuguitt, G., D.L. Brown, and C. Beale. 1989. *Rural and Small Town America*. New York: Russell Sage Foundation.

Fuguitt. G., T. Heaton, and D. Lichter. 1988. Monitoring the Metropolitanization Process. *Demography* 25(1): 115–28.

Glasgow, N., and D.L. Brown. 2006. Social Integration among Older Inmigrants. In *Population Change and Rural Society*, edited by W. Kandel and D.L. Brown. Dordrecht: Springer, 177–96.

Glasgow, N., and R. Reeder. 1990. Economic and Fiscal Implications of Nonmetropolitan Retirement Migration. *Journal of Applied Gerontology* 9(4): 433–51.

Green, G. 2001. *Kenosha County Consumer Study. Report, Kenosha County Economic Development Corporation*. Madison: University of Wisconsin Press.

Harris, R., and D. Worthen. 2003. African Americans in Rural America. *Challenges for Rural America in the Twenty-First Century*, edited by D.L. Brown and L. Swanson. University Park: Penn State University Press.

Hawley, A. 1956. *The Changing Shape of Metropolitan America*. Glencoe: Free Press.

Heimlich, R., and W. Anderson. 2001. Development at the Urban Fringe and Beyond. Agriculture Economic Report No. 803, Washington, DC: U.S. Department of Agriculture.

Johnson, K. 2004. The Rising Increase in the Incidence of Natural Decrease in Rural American Counties. Paper presented at the annual meeting of the Rural Sociological Society, Sacramento, August.

Johnson, K., and J. Cromartie. 2006. The Rural Rebound and Its Aftermath: Changing Demographic Dynamics and Regional Contrasts. In *Population Change and Rural Society*, edited by W. Kandel and D.L. Brown. Dordrecht: Springer, 25–49.

Kandel, W., and D.L. Brown (eds.) 2006. *Population Change and Rural Society*. Dordrecht: Springer.

Kandel, W., and E. Parrado. 2006. Rural Hispanic Population Growth: Public Policy Impacts in Nonmetro Counties. In *Population Change and Rural Society*, edited by W. Kandel and D.L. Brown. Dordrecht: Springer, 155–76.

Kirschner, A., E. Berry, and N. Glasgow. 2006. The Changing Faces of Rural America. In *Population Change and Rural Society*, edited by W. Kandel and D.L. Brown. Dordrecht: Springer, 53–74.

Livi Bacci, M. 1974. Final Report in *International Migration: Proceedings of a Seminar on Demographic Research on International Migration*. Buenos Aires, Paris: CICRED.

Logan, J., and K. Crowder. 2002. Political Regimes and Suburban Growth. *City and Community*. 1(1): 113–35.

Logan, J., and H. Molotch. 1988. *Urban Fortunes: The Political Economy of Place*. Berkeley: University of California Press.

Long, L., and A. Nucci. 1998. Accounting for Population Turnarounds in Nonmetropolitan America. *Research in Rural Sociology and Development* 7: 47–70.

Lubowski, R., M. Vesterby, S. Bucholtz, A. Baez, and M. Roberts. 2006. Major Uses of Land in the United States: 2002. Economic Information Bulletin No. 14. Washington, DC: U.S. Department of Agriculture.

Luloff, A., and J. Bridger. 2003. Community Agency and Local Development. In *Challenges for Rural America in the 21st Century*, edited by D.L. Brown and L. Swanson. University Park: Penn State University Press, 203–13.

Lyson, T., and C. Tolbert. 2003. Civil Society, Civic Communities, and Rural Development. In *Challenges for Rural America in the 21st Century*, edited by D.L. Brown and L. Swanson. University Park: Penn State University Press, 228–40.

McGranahan, D. 2001. New Economy Manufacturing Meets Old Economy Education Policies in the Rural South. *Rural America* 15(4): 19–27.

Molotch, H. 1976. The City as a Growth Machine: Toward a Political Economy of Place. *American Journal of Sociology* 82(2): 309–32.

Pfeffer, M., J. Francis, and Z. Ross. 2006. Fifty Years of Farmland Change. In *Population Change and Rural Society*, edited by W. Kandel and D. L. Brown. Dordrecht: Springer, 103–29.

Putnam, R. 2000. *Bowling Alone*. New York: Simon and Schuster.

Reeder, R., and D. Brown. 2005. Recreation, Tourism and Rural Well-Being. ERR-7, Economic Research Service, August. Washington, DC: U.S. Department of Agriculture.

Schafft, K., and D.L. Brown. 2003. Social Capital, Social Networks and Social Power. *Social Epistemology* 17(4): 329–42.

Schnore, L. 1959. The Timing of Metropolitan Decentralization: A Contribution to the Debate. *Journal of the American Institute of Planners* (November): 200–206.

Stallman, J., S. Deller, and M. Shields. 1999. The Economic and Fiscal Impact of Aging Retirees on a Small Rural Region. *The Gerontologist* 39(5): 599–610.

Tigges, L., and G. Fuguitt. 2003. Commuting: A Good Job Nearby? In *Challenges for Rural America in the Twenty-First Century*, edited by D.L. Brown and L. Swanson. University Park: Penn State University Press, 166–76.

Tilly, C. 1974. *Urban World*. Boston: Little Brown.

Tisdale, H. 1942. The Process of Urbanization. *Social Forces* 20: 311–16.

Tolbert, C., M. Irwin, T. Lyson, and A. Nucci. 2002. Civic Community in Small-Town America: How Civic Welfare Is Influenced by Local Capitalism and Civic Engagement. *Rural Sociology* 67(1): 90–113.

Vias, A., and P. Nelson. 2006. Changing Livelihoods in Rural America. In *Population Change and Rural Society*, edited by W. Kandel and D.L. Brown. Dordrecht: Springer, 75–102.

Zuniga, V., and R. Hernandez-Leon. (eds.) 2005. *New Destinations: Mexican Immigration in the United States.* New York: Russell Sage Foundation.

Acknowledgment

I acknowledge Kai Schafft's thoughtful comments and suggestions, especially in the paper's implications section.

Notes

1. These four themes emerged in two recent volumes on rural America that I coedited: *Challenges for Rural America in the 21st Century* (Brown and Swanson 2003) and *Population Change and Rural Society* (Kandel and Brown 2006).

2. In this chapter I use the terms *rural* and *nonmetropolitan (nonmetro)* interchangeably, although they are conceptually and technically different.

3. The nonmetropolitan delineation used in the 1970 data presented in Tables 1–3 is the official delineation of that time as used in the Current Population Survey. In contrast, the 2000 data presented in these tables are the nonmetropolitan numbers as determined by the 2000 census. This obviously introduces measurement error into the statistical comparison, but as Fuguitt et al. (1988) demonstrated, this is an appropriate analytic strategy if one's objective is to examine the impact of metropolitanization across time.

4. It should be noted, however, that nonmetro retirement destinations also attract younger persons to fill the service jobs generated by a growing elderly population. Hence, retirement immigration does not contribute to aging as much as might be expected.

5. *Hispanic* is defined as being of Spanish origin in 1970. Hence 1970–2000 comparisons of the size and location of the Hispanic population are not strictly comparable.

6. The industry of employment data in Table 14-2 are from the Regional Economic Information System produced by the U.S. Bureau of Economic Analysis and show full- and part-time employees by industry and by place of work. I am indebted to Nick Beleiciks for producing the 1970–2000 comparable employment and earnings data.

7. This indicates the importance of distinguishing between place of residence and place of work in employment data. The latter concept is used in Bureau of Economic Analysis data and shows the economic activity present in localities. The former is used in the census and shows the economic activities of resident workers regardless of where their jobs are located.

8. The new system relaxes the standards for aggregating 50,000 persons within an urbanized area, the main criterion for becoming a metropolitan area. However, the rules for including peripheral counties through commuting have probably become a bit more restrictive.

9. These conversion rates vary depending on whether one uses census data on rural land or data from the Natural Resource Inventory, in which lower density utilization is counted as urban. In other words, more rapid urban conversion is indicated in the inventory because large-lot residential uses are more likely to be counted as urban.

10. I am indebted to Kai Schafft for this insight and this language.

Index

Adirondack region, 170–175, 177, 179, 183–185
agency relationships, 174–176, 179–182, 184
amenities, 88–92
amenity-based development, 235–236
anthropocentric values, 214
antipoverty policy. *see* poverty
Arrow, Kenneth, 15
Ayres-Kneese framework, 47

Bailey, Liberty Hyde, 30
Bangladesh, 23
benefit-cost analysis
  inspiration for, 14–16
  and intermediate decisionmaking, 200
  Porter Hypothesis, 19
  and social welfare, 21–24
bioregions, 183–185
Brock, William A., 20–21

capital
  land as, 34–36
  in rural areas, 33
  social, 122, 130–131n, 135–138, *136, 146,* 172–173
Carver, Thomas Nixon, 34, 40n
Castle, Emery
  contributions of, 24–25, 43–46
  on rural areas, 63
central place theory, 197
CES (constant elasticity of substitution) functions, 50–51
CGE (computable general equilibrium) models, 50–53
circular flow model (CFM), 46–49

citizen authority, 178–179
class size, 135–137, *136, 146*
  See also human capital development factors
coal production, tax incentives, 151–167, *159, 160, 161, 162, 164, 165, 166*
Colander, David, 20–21
collective efficacy, 122–123
Columbia Basin Irrigation Project, 35
Commission on Country Life, 30–31, 40n
commoditization of nature, 13–14
community social networks, 123
commuting, 235
complexity theory, 20–21
computable general equilibrium (CGE) models, 50–53
concentration-response model, 53–59, *55, 56*
constant elasticity of substitution (CES) functions, 50–51
core regions, 85–87

decisionmaking, intermediate, 200–205
demographic changes in rural areas, 230–233, *231, 241*

Ecological Economics, 16–17
economic base employment multipliers, 65–67, *66, 67*
economic growth
  and natural amenities, 82–92
  spatial variations, 94–95
economic theory, described, 195–196
economic urban geography influence code, 101
ecoregions, 183–185

ecosystem services, 213–218
employment growth
    factors, 96–97
    spatial variations, 94–106, *96, 102, 103, 105*
environmental regulations, 12–13, 181–182
ethnic diversity in rural populations,
    232–233
Executive Order 12291, 18–19

federalism, 179–180
Flood Control Act (1936), 18
"Forever Wild" clause, 171
    See also Adirondack region
Friedman, Milton, 15
frontier subjects, 7–8

Ganges River, 22–23
Grange, 30
GS3SLS estimator, 100

Hausman, Daniel, 196
high priority frontier subjects, 7–8
horizon effect hypothesis, 133–134,
    138–148, *139, 141, 143, 144, 145, 146*
human capital development factors
    class size, 135–137, *136, 146*
    peer effects, 137–138
human ecosystem interactions, 212–213

income growth
    factors, 97–98
    spatial variations, 94–106, *96, 102, 103, 105*
intergovernmental context, 171–172
intermediate decisionmaking, 200–205
intrastate diversity, 181
"the invisible hand", 195

Journal of Economic Perspectives, 19

Kelley, Oliver Hudson, 30, 39 n3, 39 n4
Kneese, Allen, 45, 47
Krugman, Paul, 63–64
Kuhn, Thomas, 192–193

land as capital, 34–36
local agency, 176–178
    See also public agency relationships
localization economies of scale, 70–72,
    78–79
logical positivism, 15–16

macro theory, 37
Madison, James, 179–180
markets, and social choices, 15
Marshall, Alfred, 133
metropolitan expansion, 236–238, 242

micro theory, 36–37
migration
    effects of, 34
    factors, 97
    policies affecting, 36
    spatial variations, 94–106, *96, 102, 103, 105*
    See also population size
Millenium Ecosystem Assessment (MA),
    212–213
moving costs, 67–72, *69, 70,* 78, 88
multiple agency relationships, 174–176, 184
    organizational issues, 179–182
multiplier models, 65–67, *66, 67*

National Grange, 30
natural amenities
    and economic growth, 82–92
    index, 101
natural resource economics. *see* resource
    economics
nature, commoditization of, 13–14
nested CES functions, 50–51
nested jurisdictions, 177–178, 180–181
New Delhi, 22–23
new economic geography models, 63–64,
    72–75
new growth theory, 197–200
nonmarket goods, and CGE models, 50–53
numerical model, 53–59, *55, 56*

Ohio school profile, 142–148
outmigration. *see* migration

Pacific Northwest region
    Columbia Basin Irrigation Project, 35
    economic profile, 95–106, *96, 102, 103,
    105*
    Yaquina Bay, 203–204
People's Party, 30
place-based policy, 117–125, 169–187
polycentricity, and regional governance,
    185–186
population size
    demographic changes, 230–233, *231, 241*
    growth rates, 82
    See also migration
Populists, 30
Porter Hypothesis, 19
positive economics, 15–16
poverty
    geography, 112–113, *113*
    persistent-poverty counties, 129 n5
    policy issues, 111, 116–125
    recent research, 113–117
    rural areas, 111–125, *113, 238,* 238–240,
    239

working poor, 129 n8
Powder River Basin (PRB), effects of tax changes, 151–167, *159, 160, 161, 162, 164, 165, 166*
Project STAR, 136–137
property taxation
  analytical model, 153–164, *159, 160, 161, 162, 164*
  incentives, 150–151
public agency relationships, 174–176, 179–182
  See also local agency
public finance, 12, 88–89

Reagan, Ronald, 18
reciprocal model, 53–59, *55, 56*
regionalism
  and polycentricity, 185–186
  possibility of, 182–185
regions
  Adirondack region, 170–175, 177, 179, 183–185
  core regions, 85–87
  ecoregions, 183–185
  Pacific Northwest region, 35, 95–106, *96, 102, 103, 105,* 203–204
  Yellowstone region, 184–185
regulations, environmental, 12–13
"regulatory relief" act, 18–19
rent sharing, 156–164, *159, 160, 161, 162, 164*
resource economics
  conceptual approach of, 20–24
  emergence of, 11–17
  future challenges, 14–24
  intellectual tradition of, 1
Resources for the Future (RFF), 194
Robbins, Lionel, 15–16
Roosevelt, Theodore, 30
Rural America. *see* rural change
rural areas
  capital in, 33
  Castle on, 63
  definition, 30, 40 n5, 129 n1
  demographic changes, 230–233, *231, 241*
  economic characteristics, 233–235, *234, 241*
  persistent-poverty counties, 129 n5
  See also poverty
rural change
  amenity-based development, 235–236
  commuting, 235
  demographic changes, 230–233, *231, 241*
  economic characteristics, 233–235, *234*
  future of, 240–244, *243*
  metropolitan expansion, 236–238, 242

socioeconomic characteristics, *238,* 238–240, *239*
rural depopulation. *see* migration
rural development, 150–151, 224, 235–236
rural economics
  emergence of, 29
  intellectual tradition of, 1
  potential contributions of, 37–38
rural multipliers, *66,* 66–67, *67*
rural populations
  demographic changes, 230–233, *231, 241*
  ethnic diversity, 232–233
  future of, 240–244, *241, 243*
  implications for, 221–224
  socioeconomic characteristics, *238,* 238–240, *239*
  trends, 75–79, *76*

Santa Fe Institute, 20
school size, 135–137, *136*
scientific revolutions, 193–195
shipping goods, 71
simultaneous equation system, 98–106, *102, 103, 105*
Smith, Adam, 195
social capital, 122, 130–131n, 135–138, *136, 146,* 172–173
social choices, 15
social welfare, 21–24
sociology
  emergence of, 29
  potential contributions of, 37–38
spatial variations in economic growth, 94–95
sustainability, 218–221

tax incentives, 150–151
tax revenues, 88–89
Thatcher, Margaret, 18
transportation costs, 67–72, *69, 70,* 78, 88

virtual income, 49–50

welfare economics, 14–16, 21–24, 49–50
West Virginia, 34
wetlands regulation, 181–182
Wisconsin, 34–35
working poor. *see* poverty
Wyoming
  tax incentives, 151–167, *159, 160, 161, 162, 164, 165, 166*
  Yellowstone region, 184–185

Yaquina Bay, 203–204
Yellowstone region, 184–185